FOR REFERENCE

RFART
I

T5-BSH-657

OCT 1 2 2010

The Rauch Market
Research Guide
to the
U.S. Paint Industry

RFART

<u>Sixth Edition</u>

The Rauch Market Research Guide to the U.S. Paint Industry

Grey House Publishing

4919 Route 22
PO Box 56
Amenia, NY 12501-0056

PUBLISHER	Leslie Mackenzie
EDITOR	Richard Gottlieb
EDITORIAL DIRECTOR	Laura Mars
PRODUCTION MANAGER	Kristen Thatcher
WRITER/RESEARCHER	Melissa Doak
MARKETING DIRECTOR	Jessica Moody

Grey House Publishing, Inc.
4919 Route 22
Amenia, NY 12501
518.789.8700
FAX 845.373.6390
www.greyhouse.com
e-mail: books@greyhouse.com

While every effort has been made to ensure the reliability of the information presented in this publication, Grey House Publishing neither guarantees the accuracy of the data contained herein nor assumes any responsibility for errors, omissions or discrepancies. Grey House accepts no payment for listing; inclusion in the publication of any organization, agency, institution, publication, service or individual does not imply endorsement of the editors or publisher.

Errors brought to the attention of the publisher and verified to the satisfaction of the publisher will be corrected in future editions.

Except by express prior written permission of the Copyright Proprietor no part of this work may be copied by any means of publication or communication now known or developed hereafter including, but not limited to, use in any directory or compilation or other print publication, in any information storage and retrieval system, in any other electronic device, or in any visual or audio-visual device or product.

This publication is an original and creative work, copyrighted by Grey House Publishing, Inc. and is fully protected by all applicable copyright laws, as well as by laws covering misappropriation, trade secrets and unfair competition.

Grey House has added value to the underlying factual material through one or more of the following efforts: unique and original selection; expression; arrangement; coordination; and classification.

Grey House Publishing, Inc. will defend its rights in this publication.

Copyright © 2010 Grey House Publishing, Inc.
All rights reserved
Printed in the USA

The Rauch market research guide to the U.S. paint industry.

Biennial
Spine title: U.S. paint industry
ISSN: 8755-0261

1. Paint industry and trade—United States—Periodicals. 2. Paint industry and trade—United States—Directories.   II. Title: Rauch market research guide to the United States paint industry   III. Title: Rauch market research guide to the US paint industry IV. Title: US paint industry   V. Title: U.S. paint industry

HD9660.P253 U665

338.4/76676/0973   85-641071

ISBN   978-1-59237-428-1 softcover

TABLE OF CONTENTS

SECTION 3

SECTION 4

SECTION 5

INTRODUCTION

This is the Sixth Edition of *The Rauch Market Research Guide to the U.S. Paint Industry*. Offering comprehensive data on this $18.9 billion industry, this Guide covers the economics, materials, manufacturing, products, markets and sales of the more than 500 leading U.S. paint producers. It includes significant discussion on allied products and services, from farm equipment to personal electronics, as well as detailed listings of valuable industry resources.

Sections 1, 2 and 3 comprise the "handbook" of this edition, filled with detailed industry data – economic forecasts, government and industry regulations, domestic and foreign markets, raw materials and end products. You will find precise figures on pricing, wages, volume, material availability and performance both historically and in light of the global economic recession that began in 2008.

In addition to the accessible language of these sections, 64 figures, tables, charts and graphs highlight and support the text. A list of these – title and page number – follows this Introduction.

Following the technical information, **Section 4** provides industry sources in three major categories: Associations and Societies; Trade and Technical Publications; and Events and Trade Shows.

Section 5 lists 500 leading paint producers, with current contact and company details, including product lines, annual sales, and key personnel.

This edition of *The Rauch Market Research Guide to the U.S. Paint Industry* ends with an index of key personnel in the industry, with nearly 1,000 executives and their company.

Not only does this *Guide* offer valuable data to help you make decisions crucial to the success of your business – decisions made more difficult due to the uncertainty created by an economy in recovery – but also provides the most relevant paint industry information, saving valuable time searching a variety of widely scattered sources.

LIST OF TABLES AND FIGURES

INTRODUCTION

The U.S. paint industry, with total sales of $21.2 billion in 2007 and more than $18.9 billion in 2008, includes companies engaged primarily in the manufacture of paints in paste and ready-mixed form, varnishes, lacquers, enamels, and powder coatings. It is associated with such allied products as fillers and sealers, thinners and paint removers, and other miscellaneous products. Paints are a part of the chemical and allied products industry (NAICS 325, SIC 28) which had shipments of $738.3 billion in 2007, the fourth largest U.S. manufacturing industry. While its products touch every sector of the U.S. economy, paint industry shipments, regardless of how measured, represent only 0.13% of GDP in 2008, down from 0.16% in 2003 and 0.24% in 1990.

Figure 1-1 shows the estimated quantity and value of paint products 2004-2008. Figure 1-2 shows the structure of the paint industry. It provides a picture of the flow from raw material derivation through manufacturing and packaging to end-use. As shown, the raw materials used in paint manufacturing are derived mainly from fossil fuels, but also from minerals and agricultural-based materials.

Shipment data in units and dollars for paint, varnish and lacquer are available from the U.S. Census Bureau in *Current Industrial Report M325F* (formerly *M28F*), published quarterly and annually. Industry economic data are also reported as Paints and Allied Products (NAICS code 325510) and in the Annual Survey of Manufactures (ASM) or every fifth year in the Economic Census, Manufacturing—Industry Series Sector 31. Companies who report to the U.S. Census Bureau are classified in the industry that they mainly serve. They also report detailed information on all products as classified in the Standard Industrial Classification system,

ECONOMICS

HIGHLIGHTS

Introduction

■

Industry Shipments

■

Company Performance

■

Industry Profitability

■

Prices

■

Containers

■

Operations/Productivity

■

Employment/Productivity

■

Regional Patterns/Distribution

■

Goverment Regulations

■

Outlook

■

Forecast

■

Foreign Trade

■

World Production and Markets

Figure 1-1 Estimated quantity and value of shipments of paint and allied products, 2004-08

Product class code	Product description	Year	Quantity	Value
3255101	Architectural coatings	2008 a/	682.0 a/	8,669.0
		2007	776.7	9,065.2
		2006	767.6	9,003.1
		2005	759.3	8,485.8
		2004	803.6	8,623.3
3255104	Product coatings OEM	2008	344.1 b/	5,662.5
		2007	369.7	5,960.0
		2006	381.7	6,090.4
		2005	410.1	6,032.0
		2004	404.2	5,867.3
3255107	Special purpose coatings	2008 c/	196.3 c/	4,604.8
		2007 a/	206.9	4,597.2
		2006	210.4	4,298.0
		2005	211.1	4,020.1
		2004	154.5	3,525.8
325510B	Miscellaneous allied paint products	2008	(S)	(S)
		2007	177.2 a/	1,535.2
		2006	189.9	1,478.6
		2005	189.8	1,407.2
		2004	171.9	1,216.7

Source: "Table 1. Summary of Estimated United States Quantity and Value of Shipments of Paint and Allied Products: 2004-2008," in Paint and Allied Products - 2008, MA325F(08)-1, U.S. Census Bureau, July 2009, http://www.census.gov/manufacturing/cir/historical_data/mq325f/index.html (accessed December 20, 2009)

Note: Data for 2004 through 2008 are estimates of the total U.S. value of shipments of paint, varnish, and lacquer. These estimates were developed by increasing the product class totals shown in Table 2 by adjustment factors. These factors are: 1.012 for "Architectural coatings", 1.002 for "Product coatings OEM", 1.013 for "Special purpose coatings", and 1.024 for "Miscellaneous paint products." These factors are used because the annual survey panel was selected to measure approximately 95 percent of the total shipments in the paint industry (NAICS 325510 former SIC 2851). The adjustment factors (based on the 2007 Economic Census - Manufacturing relationships) bring each product class value up to 100 percent. Quarterly data for 2008 and 2007 reflect the adjusted totals in Table 1 and are shown in Table 3 along with the quarterly data originally published in the Current Industrial Reports quarterly series MQ325F (MQ28F), Paint, Varnish, and Lacquer.

Estimation symbols - Percent of estimation for each item is indicated as follows:
a/ - 10 to 19 percent of this item has been estimated.
b/ - 20 to 29 percent of this item has been estimated.
c/ - 30 to 49 percent of this item has been estimated.
(S) - Withheld because estimates did not meet publication standards

Figure 1-2 Structure of the Paint Industry

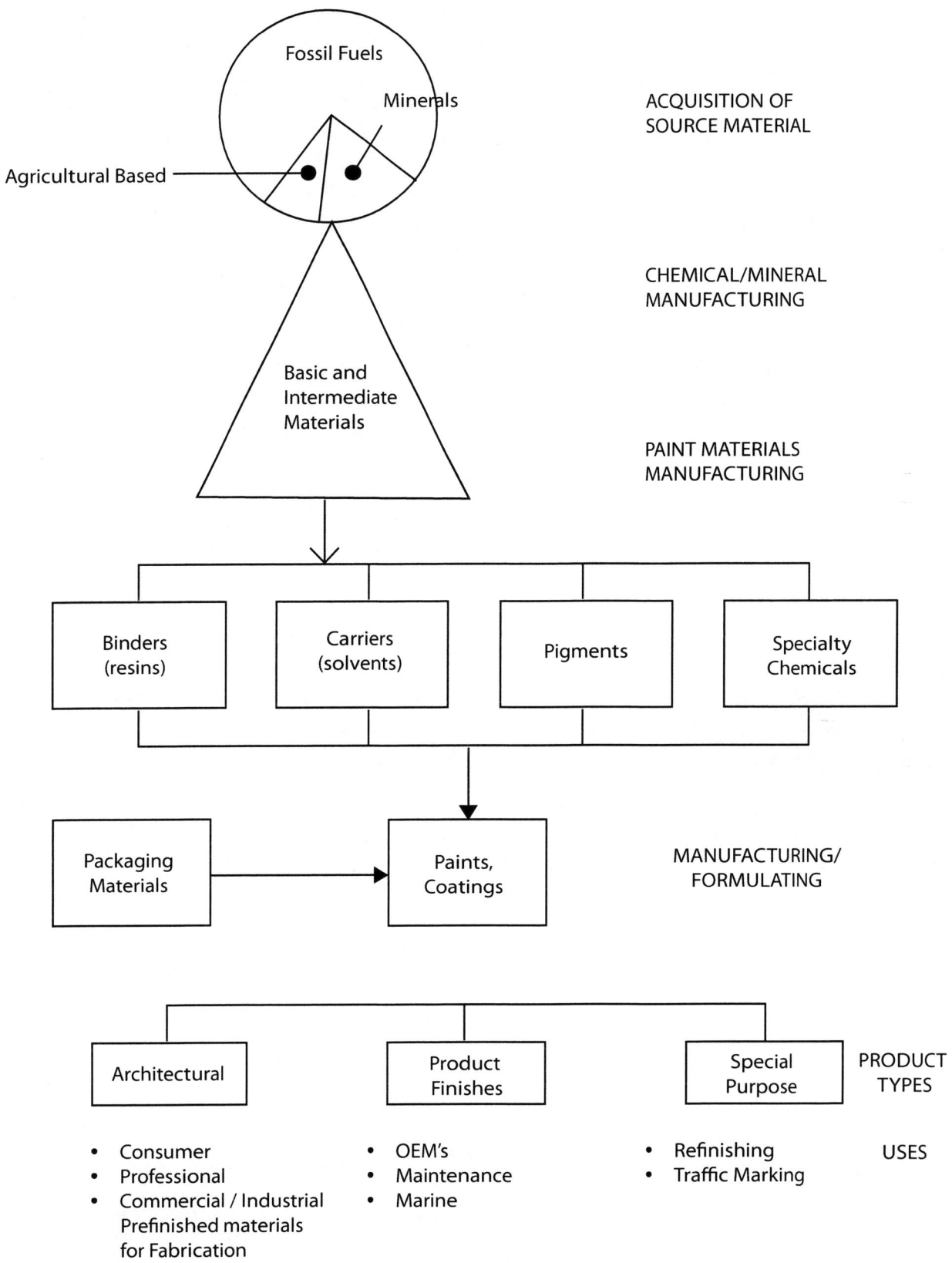

which after 1997 was reclassified as the North American Industry Classification System. As a result, the value of industry shipments includes data on secondary products also made by manufacturers classified in the paint industry. Due to reclassification of some types of products, and the time required to convert some of the reports to the new system, some data may not be directly comparable to previous years or to each other.

Figure 1-3 shows shipments of primary products and re-sales totaled $22,839.4 million in 2007. Paint was sometimes made as a secondary product in other industries; there were $513.4 million in shipments from other industries in 2007, making up only 2.3% of total paint shipments. The paint industry shipped $254.4 million in secondary products in 2007.

U.S. paint companies operated 1,369 plants in 2007. Of those plants, 905, or 66.1%, employed fewer than twenty workers ("Sector 31: EC073I1: Manufacturing: Industry Series: Detailed Statistics by Industry for the United States: 2007," 2007 Economic Census, U.S. Census Bureau, 2009, http://factfinder. census.gov/servlet/IBQTable?_bm=y&-geo_id=01000US&-ds_name=EC073I1&-

NAICS2007=325510&-_lang=en). In 2009, however, nine companies operating in the United States had sales of one billion dollars or more, suggesting the high degree of consolidation in the industry. The leading U.S. paint producer, PPG Industries, Inc., had approximately $10.1 billion in coatings sales in 2009 according to the industry trade journal, *Paint & Coatings World* (Karen Parker, "PCI 25 Reflects Industry Consolidation," July 2009, http://www.pcimag. com/Articles/Feature_Article/BNP_GUID_9-5-2006_A_10000000000000618036).Nevertheless, while a number of companies sell paint nationwide, the paint industry remains a regional business because of high shipping expenses, difficulties in maintaining prompt deliveries to distant locations, and other distribution problems.

There is also a high degree of product and market specialization among major producers. For example, PPG Industries is the largest producer in coatings for wood-flooring and also specializes in supplying paints for electronics. DuPont Coatings & Color Technologies Group, the second largest U.S. producer, is the largest producer of titanium dioxide (a pigment used in paint) in the world, and also specializes in automotive

Figure 1-3 Paint Production by Class of Manufacturer, 2007

	Product Shipments of Paint Industry (Millions of Dollars)	Product shipments of Paint and Allied Products, Other Industries (Millions of Dollars)	Shipments of Paint Products, All Industries (Millions of Dollars)
Total Value of Shipments			
Primary Products	$21,622.5	$513.40	$22,135.90
Secondary Products	$660.5		
Misc. Receipts			
Resales	$1,216.9		
Other (a)	$53.0		
Subtotal Professional	$1,269.6		
TOTAL	$23,575.0		

Source: Adapted from "Sector 31: EC073I1: Manufacturing: Industry Series: Detailed Statistics by Industry for the United States: 2007," 2007 Economic Census, U.S. Census Bureau, 2009, http://factfinder.census.gov/servlet/IBQTable?_bm=y&-geo_id=01000US&-ds_name=EC073I1&-NAICS2007=325510&-_lang=en (accessed November 30, 2009)

and industrial coatings. Sherwin-Williams, the third largest coatings producer in the United States, was the largest supplier to the Do-It-Yourself (DIY) and contractor market segments, the leader in private-label business, and also the largest retailer through company-owned shores. Valspar, the fourth largest U.S. paint company, is the leading supplier of coil coatings. PPG, DuPont, and BASF are leaders in OEM (original equipment manufacturer) automotive finishes.

Paints and coatings are used to decorate walls and other surfaces, provide a pleasing, but long-lasting finish on durable products, and protect and maintain most surfaces and goods produced. Some 45% of paint shipments are used on existing surfaces and equipment. For the most part, paints in liquid form are applied as a thin film by a variety of methods. Products are grouped as architectural coatings, OEM (original equipment manufacturer) product coatings, and special purpose coatings. Architectural coatings are applied to interior or exterior surfaces of residential, commercial, institutional, or industrial buildings. OEM product coatings are applied to products in the factory (for example, on automobiles, wood furniture, appliance finishes, and coatings on metals). Special purpose coatings include marine paints, traffic and highway paints, aerosol paints, and other coatings where durability is the most important factor.

The paint industry is a mature business that is highly fragmented in types of paints, end uses and technology, and can be characterized by change in practically all segments. Many grades of paint have become commodity-type products—meaning that there is very little difference between brands, and consumers shop primarily based on price. However, due to emission and hazardous waste regulations, considerable effort continues to be spent on developing new high performance water-based coatings, high-solids

and solvent-free liquid finishes, powder coatings and radiation curable materials.

The industry is very competitive and concentrated. There have been constant acquisitions and consolidation as illustrated by the reduction of the number of companies in the industry. There were 1,131 U.S. paint companies operating in 2007, down from 1,200 in 2003. The number of factories operating also dropped from 1,560 in 2003 to 1,369 in 2007 ("Sector 31: EC073111: Manufacturing: Industry Series: Detailed Statistics by Industry for the United States: 2007," 2007 Economic Census, U.S. Census Bureau, 2009, http://factfinder.census.gov/servlet/IBQTable?_bm=y&-geo_id=01000US&-ds_name=EC073111&-NAICS2007=325510&-_lang=en). The industry also faces competition from alternate materials for interior and exterior surfaces. Vinyl wall coverings compete with interior paints, vinyl siding competes with exterior paints, and plastics compete with automotive OEM coatings. Corrosion-resistant metals or polymers have niches in markets where coatings might otherwise be used.

The paint business continues to endure many challenges such as shifting technologies, intermittent raw material shortages, varying costs, increased imports of finished goods, changing consumer living patterns, and slowing population growth. The housing and credit crises that began in the fourth quarter of 2008 also severely challenged the industry, erasing growth in 2008 and causing the industry to contract in 2009. All this is occurring in an environment of increasing regulation by federal and state authorities, including regulations on air pollution, hazardous waste, worker and consumer safety, labeling, packaging and transportation. Customer needs, such as ease of application, VOC and HAP levels, and aesthetics also increasingly influence product development.

INDUSTRY SHIPMENTS

As shown in Figure 1-4, the value of shipments for paints, coatings, varnishes, lacquers and miscellaneous allied products (solvents, thinners, paint removers, pigment dispersions, putty, caulks and glazing compounds, and ink vehicles) totaled $21,157.6 in 2007, up only 0.1% compared to 2006. Although preliminary total figures were not yet in for 2008, the value of shipments of architectural coatings and OEM product finishes had both decreased in 2008, reflecting the global economic recession that began in that year. The slowing growth reflected a long-term trend. Growth from 1990 to 2000 averaged 3.5% a year, down from 6.1% annually between 1980 and 1990. Average growth from 2000 to 2005 had risen slightly to 3.7% per year, but dropped to 3% per year from 2005 to 2007. By 2008, total sales were decreasing.

As shown in Figure 1-5, unit volume increased steadily between 1980 and 2000 before beginning to drop in 2005. Industry shipments were particularly weak from 2005 through 2008. However, growth varied among the several product types. Architectural coatings grew by 1.5% a year in the 1990s, down

from 2.4% a year in the 1980s. Between 2000 and 2007 growth in unit volume rebounded to 2.6% on average per year, before contracting by 12.2% in 2008. OEM product finishes increased at 3% a year in the 1990s, up from 0.7% in the 1980s. Thereafter, unit volume of OEM product finishes actually contracted by an average of 2.7% per year. Special purpose coatings grew by 3.8% in the 1980s, but decreased slightly by 0.7% annually in the 1990s. Special purpose coatings rebounded somewhat between 2000 and 2005, growing at an annual rate of 3%, before contracting again between 2005 and 2008 at an annual rate of 2.3%. Growth of architectural coatings from 2005 to 2007 was offset by declines in shipments of OEM product finishes and special purpose coatings. All industry segments decreased gallons shipped in 2008.

In 2008, architectural coatings represented the majority of gallons shipped; 56% of gallons of coatings shipped were architectural coatings, 28% were OEM product finishes, and 16% were special purpose coatings. However, architectural coatings represented a smaller segment of total sales (46%), while special purpose coatings accounted for 24% of total sales and OEM project finishes

Figure 1-4   U.S. Shipments of Paint, Varnish and Lacquer in Millions of Dollars, Selected Years, 1980-2008

Year	Architectural Coatings	OEM Product Finishes	Special Purpose Coatings	Total (including allied paint products)
1980	$2,812.5	$2,445.5	$1,249.4	$6,497.4
1985	$3,830.8	$3,486.4	$1,962.2	$9,279.4
1990	$4,913.6	$4,032.6	$2,781.5	$11,727.7
1995	$6,057.1	$5,279.9	$3,076.7	$14,413.7
2000	$6,461.4	$6,110.4	$3,837.0	$16,601.3
2005	$8,485.8	$6,032.0	$4,020.1	$19,945.1
2006	$9,003.1	$6,090.4	$4,298.0	$20,870.1
2007	$9,065.2	$5,960.0	$4,597.2	$21,157.6
2008	$8,669.0	$5,662.5	$4,604.8	---

Source: Adapted from "Table 1. Summary of Estimated United States Quantity and Value of Shipments of Paint and Allied Products: 2004-2008," Current Industrial Reports M325F, U.S. Census Bureau, http://www.census.gov/manufacturing/cir/historical_data/ma325f/index.html (accessed November 30, 2009).

Industry Shipments by Segment, Percentage of Volume, 2008

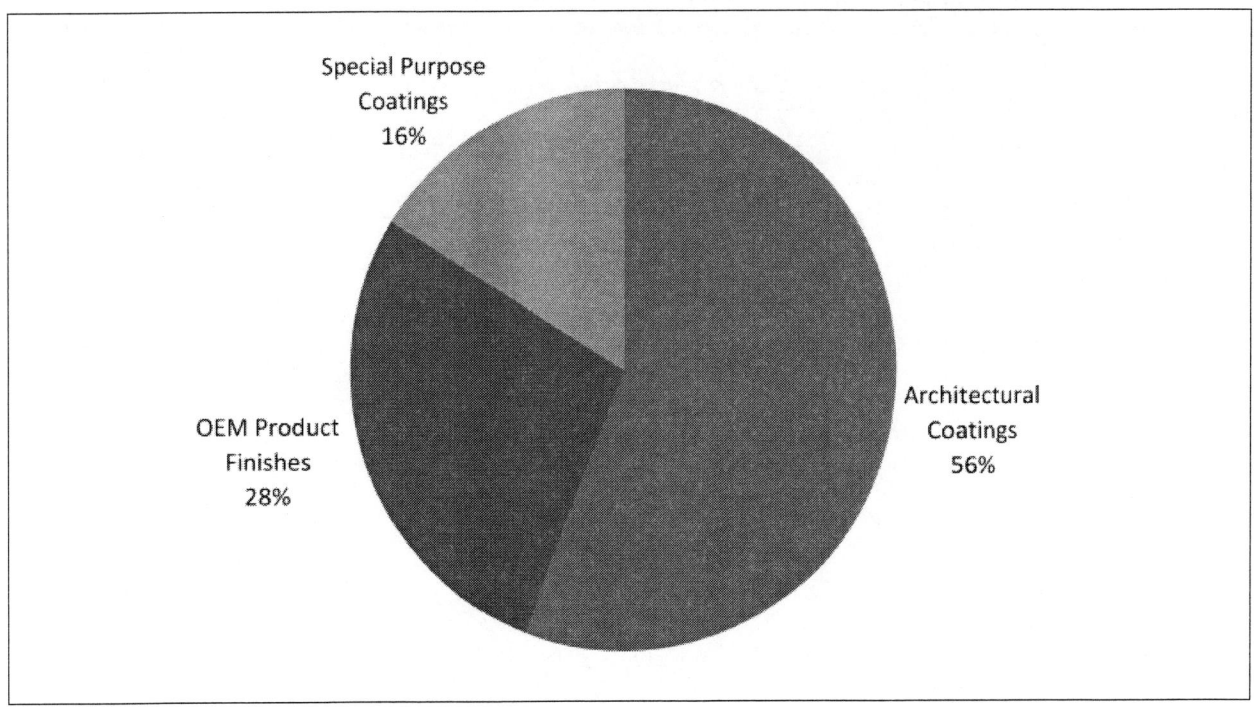

Industry Shipments by Segment, Percentage of Dollars, 2008

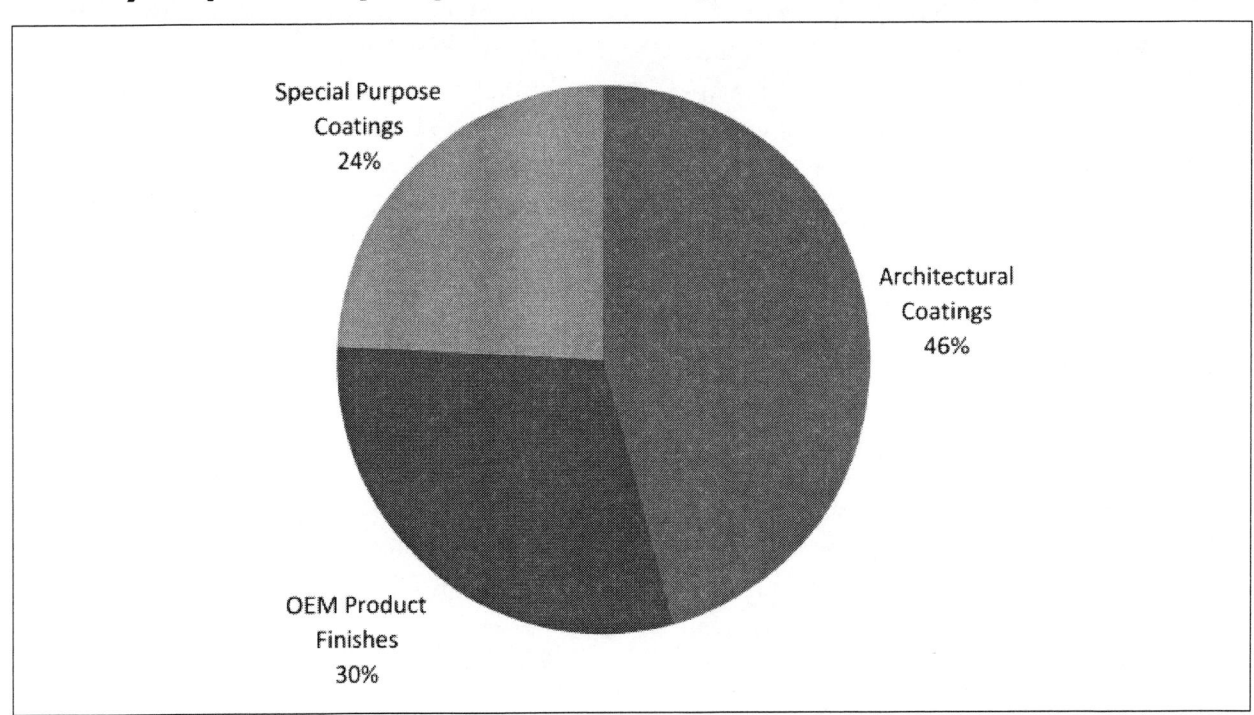

Figure 1-5   U.S. Shipments of Paint, Varnish and Lacquer in Millions of Gallons, Selected Years, 1980-2008

	Architectural Coatings	OEM Product Finishes	Special Purpose Coatings	Total (including allied paint products)
1980	438.9	315.9	134.7	889.5
1985	477.9	352.4	145.4	975.7
1990	558.4	338.6	195.6	1,092.6
1995	621.1	376.2	195.1	1,192.4
2000	650.6	453.4	182.4	1,286.4
2005	759.3	410.1	211.1	1,380.5
2006	767.6	381.7	210.4	1,359.7
2007	776.7	369.7	206.9	1,353.3
2008	682.0	344.1	196.3	1,222.4

Sources: Adapted from "Table 1. Summary of Estimated United States Quantity and Value of Shipments of Paint and Allied Products: 2004-2008," Current Industrial Reports M325F, U.S. Census Bureau, http://www.census.gov/manufacturing/cir/historical_data/ma325f/index.html (accessed November 30, 2009).

represented 30%. A detailed discussion of types of paints in each product class is given in Section 3—Products and Markets.

Seasonality is a fact of life in the paint industry that reflects variable patterns of consumption based on weather conditions and OEM activity. Use of architectural coatings, and to some degree special purpose coatings, follows an annual pattern of peaking in the good weather months and ebbing in the fall and winter. Special purpose coatings include industrial maintenance products, whose application also often depends on weather conditions. The range of monthly consumption for OEM finishes is narrower, due partly to controls used during application and cure. Usage ebbs in the summer and winter and also during periods of plant shutdowns and reduced product demand.

COMPANY PERFORMANCE

The paint industry continues to consolidate, with higher concentration among the leading suppliers. According to the annual list of the top companies in North America, in 2008, only 27 companies had sales of more than $50 million, down from 43 companies

in 2003 (Karen Parker, "PCI Reflects Industry Consolidation," *Paint & Coatings Industry*, July 2009). The increasing level of concentration is illustrated by share of sales of the leading suppliers. In 2008, PPG Industries Inc. ranked first with coatings sales of $10.1 billion worldwide, with 44.9% of sales, or $7.1 billion, in the United States. This represented nearly one third (32.1%) of all paint and coatings sales in the United States. Another measure of the increasing concentration is provided by the *Economic Census*, as shown in Figure 1-6. The data illustrate the growing control by the larger suppliers.

As noted above, there have been many major acquisitions in the past ten years. Two of the top ten paint and coating manufacturers in the world were acquired in 2008. The British company ICI Paints was acquired by AkzoNobel, the world's largest paint and coatings manufacturer based in the Netherlands; and the Dutch company SigmaKalon Group BV was acquired by PPG, the world's second largest paint and coatings manufacturer based in Pittsburgh ("PCI Reflects Industry Consolidation," *Paint & Coatings Industry*, July 1, 2009).

Although there have been several major mergers and acquisitions over the past 10 years, the total number of acquisitions has actually declined as fewer smaller and middle-sized companies have been acquired. In the 1980s to the mid-1990s, some 20 to 30 acquisitions occurred annually, but by 1998 the number had shrunk to 14. In the 2008 to 2010 period, mergers and acquisitions dropped off markedly during the recession (Sean Milmo, "Acquisitions and Divestments... Or the Lack of Them," *Coatings World*, March 2010, pp. 30-31).

INDUSTRY PROFITABILITY

It is difficult to measure profitability since many large paint companies are part of larger organizations, and fewer specialized paint companies exist due to the many mergers and acquisitions in recent years. In addition, most paint companies are privately held and do not divulge financial data. However, the Census Bureau collects some information on expenses in the Economic Census. Because of extensive advertising for consumer paints and heavy promotion for industrial products, the selling, general, and administrative expenses of these companies are high; paint companies spent $29.4 million on advertising and promotions in 2007, $18.4 million on communication services, and $77.9 million on professional and technical services. Paint companies also have a heavy investment in land, buildings, and equipment. In 2007, paint companies spent $332.9 million on capital expenditures. Annual payroll totaled $2.2 billion, fringe benefits totaled $642.2 million, materials cost $12 billion, fuels cost $70.5 million, and electricity cost $109.5 million.

Figure 1-6 Concentration of U.S. Producers of Paints and Coatings, Selected Years, 1967-2007

Year	Number of Companies	Product Shipments, in Millions of Dollars
1967	1,459	2,703.8
1972	1,318	3,505.8
1977	1,288	6,629.7
1982	1,170	9,162.1
1987	1,121	12,762.4
1992	1,129	14,490.1
1997	1,205	14,911.6
2003	1,200	16,124.7
2007	1,131	22,135.9

Source: Economic Censuses, U.S. Census Bureau, http://factfinder. census.gov/servlet/DatasetMainPageServlet?_program=ECN&_ tabId=ECN1&_submenuId=datasets_4&_lang=en.

PRICES

Average prices for paints and coatings of all types have shown gradual but steady increases over the past two decades. The trend for both paint raw materials and prepared paints during the period from 1994 to 2009 is given in Figure 1-7. As shown, prices for raw materials rose sharply after 2000. Manufacturer's prices for all prepared paints just barely kept pace until 2008, when the price of prepared paint rose sharply.

Figure 1-8 gives the average price for each paint classification for selected years since 1980. The average price for architectural coatings at the manufacturers' level increased at an average annual rate of 3.2% a year during the 1980s but dropped significantly to only at 1.2% annually during the 1990s. By the first decade of the twenty-first century, prices for architectural coatings were rising again by an average of 3.1% per year. Compared to other segments of the paint industry, architectural paints are relatively mature and very price-competitive with strong national competition as well as with a large number of regional

Figure 1-7 Price Indexes of Paint and Paint Raw Materials, 1994-2003

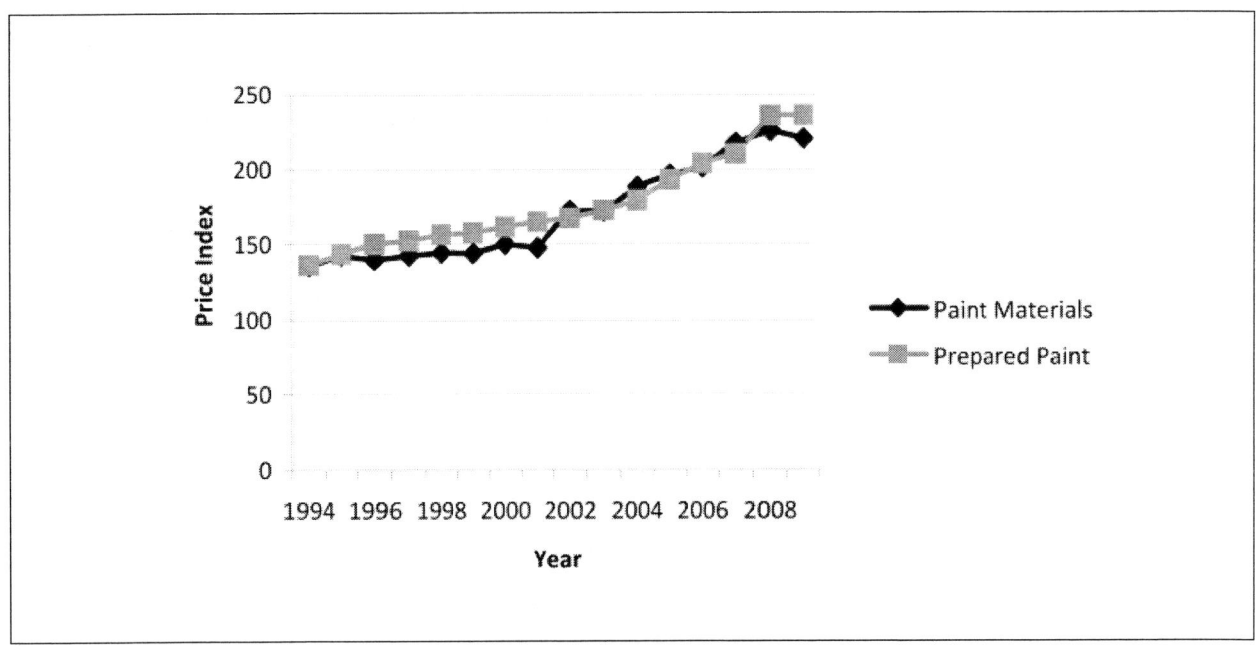

Figure 1-8 Average Manufacturers' Prices for Paints, Selected Years, 1980-2008

Average Price, Dollars /Gallon			
Year	Architectural Coatings	Product Finishes-OEM	Special Purpose Coatings
1980	$6.41	$6.57	$9.20
1985	$8.02	$9.89	$13.49
1990	$8.79	$11.91	$14.22
1995	$9.73	$13.70	$15.70
2000	$9.92	$13.57	$19.77
2001	$10.55	$13.69	$21.14
2002	$9.91	$13.46	$18.32
2003	$9.76	$13.69	$18.69
2004	$10.73	$14.52	$22.82
2005	$11.18	$14.71	$19.04
2006	$11.73	$15.96	$20.43
2007	$11.67	$16.12	$22.22
2008	$12.71	$16.46	$23.46

Source: Created by Melissa Doak for Grey House Publishing from "Table 1. Summary of Estimated United States Quantity and Value of Shipments of Paint and Allied Products: 2004-2008," Current Industrial Reports: MQ325F-Paint, Varnish, Lacquer, U.S. Census Bureau, http://www.census.gov/manufacturing/cir/historical_data/mq325f/index.html (accessed December 30, 2009) and previous Current Industrial Reports.

and local producers. Product quality varies also, in terms of resin content, pigment loading and filler content. Both interior and exterior paints now have a large water-based segment, so average prices are not influenced as greatly by the normal volatility in crude oil prices. Prices per gallon for waterborne products range $2.00 to $4.00 lower at the manufacturer's level than those for solvent-based products. Thus the average price for architectural paints has not risen as rapidly as inflation. Producers of architectural coatings face toughening environmental regulations in many parts of North America and Europe that limit the volatile organic compounds (VOC) in paint and other coatings. As 2010 approached, Tim Wright of *Coatings World* reported in "Exterior Architectural Coatings Market" (October 2007) that these tightening regulations were the most immediate issue facing paint and coatings companies.

For the most part, prices for OEM finishes are based on negotiations between supplier and manufacturer, and the products specially formulated for each manufacturer's production operation. In such selected markets as transportation, appliance, container coatings and furniture coatings, prices are usually extremely competitive. Major national producers supply these markets, leaving little room for regional or local producers. Additionally, production batches for many products are measured in thousands of gallons and shipments for these products are made in tank wagons, drums and tote bins. The average price for OEM coatings grew by a healthy average of 6.1% a year during the 1980s but growth dropped to an average of 1.3% annually during the 1990s before increasing slightly to an average of 2.4% between 2000 and 2008. (See Figure 1-8.)

The OEM sector is the most technically sophisticated and product development and innovations are an important characteristic. Innovations in resins, high-solids coatings,

water-based coatings, and powder coatings have helped increase the value of OEM coatings over the past several decades. Kerry Pionforte of *Coatings World* reported in "OEM and Industrial Coatings Market," (June 2005) that research and development in the first decade of the twenty-first century focused on developing environmentally-compliant and water-based products, products that require less energy to use (for example "cool" coatings that do not require heat to cure), and better colors to help manufacturers set their products apart from the competition. In many cases, the necessity for product innovations is prompted by the need of OEM manufacturers to reduce application costs and to comply with solvent emissions and waste disposal regulations.

Special purpose coatings are one of the most expensive categories of the paints and coatings industry. Prices increased by an average 4.5% a year during the 1980s, by 3.4% a year on average during the 1990s, but at only 2.2% a year between 2000 and 2008. (See Figure 1-8.) Some categories in this segment of the industry are highly specialized, including automotive and machinery refinishes and marine coatings, and have a limited number of producers. High technical content and the necessity to maintain extensive inventories characterize this industry segment. Some other categories, such as industrial maintenance coatings, are more competitive with both national and regional producers. For such product lines as heavy marine coatings and some industrial maintenance applications, on-site technical supervision by paint company representatives is essential. Product liability can be a requirement on some painting jobs. Increasing requirements for more environmentally-acceptable coatings also has an influence on pricing. HAP emission limits have been issued for auto refinish paints that will eventually impact prices. Higher solids coatings, with their greater coverage rates per gallon, will yield a higher price per unit.

Figure 1-9 gives the Producer Price Indexes of select product categories for 1999 through 2009, as reported by the Bureau of Labor Statistics. As illustrated, prices for special purpose coatings have risen to the highest level during this period, with the largest increases for automotive finishes. Prices for architectural coatings also grew, especially after 2004, whereas prices for OEM finishes showed only a modest increase, due primarily to lower prices for automobile finishes in a very competitive industry and slow growth in most other product categories.

CONTAINERS

The *2007 Economic Census* reports that primary producers of paints spent $827.2 million on containers in that year ("Sector 31: EC073113: Manufacturing: Industry Series: Materials Consumed by Kind for the United States: 2007," U.S. Census Bureau, 2009). The majority of the money was spent on metal containers ($459.3 million), while

$184.8 million was spent on plastic containers and $183.1 million was spent on all other containers.

Until recently, one-gallon cans were made almost exclusively from metal, but plastics are gaining in use ("Rethinking the Paint Can," *Home Channel News*, April 14, 2003, pp. 11-12). In 2009, a clear plastic container that opened like a traditional metal can was introduced ("PET Paint Containers," *Packaging Digest*, February 2009, p. 16). One-quart and smaller cans and drums are generally made from metal, although plastic was making inroads here as well ("Plastic Paint Containers," *Do-It-Yourself-Retailing*, January 2004, p. 17).

On the other hand, about 40% of five-gallon pails and practically all two-gallon containers are now produced from plastics. High density polyehthylene (HDPE) containers have gained a share of paint packaging over the past decade. While stacking strength is limited, the 25% reduction in container weight is a significant factor in the packaging and shipping of paints. Plastic containers have also successfully penetrated the packaging

Figure 1-9 Producer Price Indexes for Paint, 1999-2009

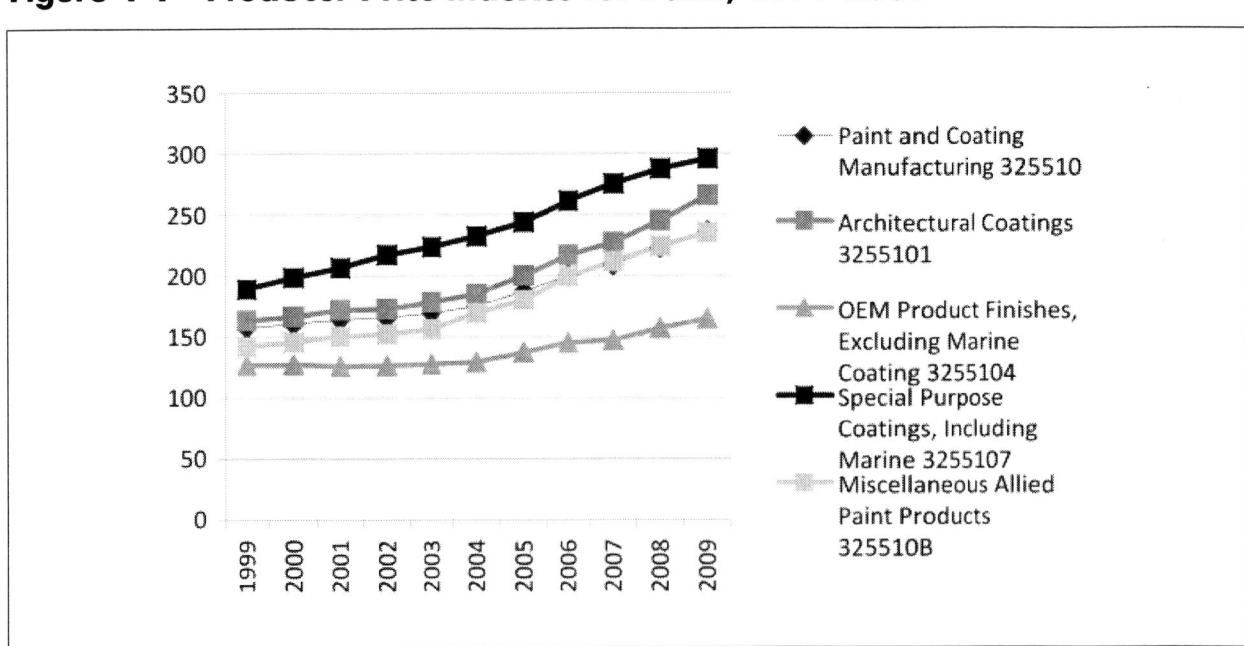

Figure 1-10 **Number of Firms, Number of Establishments, Employment, and Annual Payroll by Employment Size for Paint and Coating Manufacturing Enterprises, 2006**

NAICS CODE: 325510
NAICS DESCRIPTION: Paint and Coating Manufacturing

				Employment Size of the Enterprise				
	TOTAL	**0-4**	**5-9**	**10-19**	**<20**	**20-99**	**100-499**	**<500**	**500+**
Firms	1,093	346	205	189	740	237	65	1,042	51
Establishments	1,344	346	205	192	743	258	120	1,121	223
Employment	46,209	625	1,371	2,582	4,578	8,204	7,365	20,147	26,062
Annual Payroll ($1,000)	2,488,091	30,910	51,185	110,283	192,378	377,645	347,744	917,767	1,570,324

Source: Adapted from "Number of Firms, Number of Establishments, Employment, and Annual Payroll by Employment Size of the Enterprise for the United States, All Industries 2006," 2006 County Business Patterns, U.S. Census Bureau, December 2009, http://www.census.gov/econ/susb/ (accessed January 15, 2010)

of such allied products as sealers, putty, and glazing compounds.

Architectural paints are packaged primarily in one gallon, quart, and smaller metal cans and five-gallon pails. Two-gallon and one-gallon plastic containers are used for some latex sealers and primers.

Industrial OEM finishes are shipped mainly in 55-gallon drums but tote bins and tankwagons are used for larger consumers. In these cases, primers and topcoats are off-loaded into spray or electrocoat storage tanks for piping to applications area.

Special purpose coatings are shipped primarily in five-gallon pails with some high-volume paints, including traffic paints, shipped in drums, and at times, in tank wagons. Automotive refinishes are packaged primarily in one-gallon and smaller-size containers. Aerosols are also an important package type in special purpose coatings.

OPERATIONS/PRODUCTIVITY

In its Economic Census, taken every five years, the Census Bureau reports value added, a measure of relative economic health

Figure 1-11 **Industrial Production of Paints and Allied Products, 1990-2009**

Time Period	Industrial Production
1990	95.2697
1991	91.578
1992	94.1333
1993	99.5994
1994	106.8603
1995	103.5787
1996	103.37
1997	104.1297
1998	104.3461
1999	102.3218
2000	102.0023
2001	99.7432
2002	100
2003	98.6669
2004	104.5858
2005	102.0557
2006	95.9312
2007	94.5076
2008	87.0336
2009	70.1478

Source: Adapted from "G.17. Industrial Production and Capacity Utilization," Federal Reserve Board, January 15, 2010, http://www.federalreserve.gov/datadownload/Choose.aspx?rel=G17 (accessed January 27, 2010)

13

Figure 1-12 Major Producing States, 2007, and Operating Margin

Geographic Area Name	Number of establishments	Establishments with 20 employees or more	Number of employees	Annual payroll ($1,000)	Production workers avg per year	Production workers hours (1,000)	Production workers, nonleased employees wages ($1,000)	Value added ($1,000)	Total cost of materials ($1,000)	Total value of shipments ($1,000)	Total capital expenditures (new and used) ($1,000)	Operating Margin
Ohio	82	43	5,206	306,976	2,242	4,469	101,795	1,355,720	1,644,895	3,002,836	32,719	39.6%
Texas	106	35	3,595	188,183	2,204	4,685	95,768	977,375	1,420,810	2,385,164	32,550	32.5%
Illinois	94	45	4,279	232,000	2,647	5,127	108,168	1,112,643	1,197,822	2,308,193	28,825	38.1%
California	175	39	2,893	145,686	1,787	3,680	72,047	935,240	744,030	1,678,281	19,893	47.0%
Pennsylvania	65	24	2,399	123,224	1,235	2,387	53,627	697,966	785,036	1,493,375	17,515	39.2%
Michigan	62	20	2,219	124,166	1,197	2,466	49,948	700,316	497,731	1,207,852	21,851	48.5%
Georgia	38	12	1,072	49,870	850	1,665	35,802	464,122	610,657	1,075,785	15,276	38.6%
Kentucky	27	14	974	45,731	610	1,223	24,033	464,533	391,299	856,770	8,614	49.0%
North Carolina	46	18	1,601	80,957	969	1,944	39,930	356,622	462,575	830,298	12,213	34.5%
Virginia	19	7	789	44,093	469	954	25,766	430,170	399,212	827,134	6,832	46.4%

Source: Adapted from "Sector 31: ECO731A1: Manufacturing: Geographic Area Series: Industry Statistics for the States, Metropolitan and Micropolitan Statistical Areas, Counties, and Places: 2007," U.S. Census Bureau, April 2010, http://factfinder.census.gov/servlet/IBQTable?_bm=y&-dataitem=GEO_ID$|NAICS2007|NAICS2007$|FOOTID|RCPTOTI|RCPTOTI|ESTAB|ECTGE20|EMP|PAYANN|EMP AVPW|HOURS|PAYANPW|VALADD|CSTMTOT|RCPTOT|CEXTOT&-fds_name=EC0700A1&-defOrder=Y&-filter=&-ib_type=NAICS2007&-_lang=en&-geo_id=01000US&-NAICS2007=325510&-sortkey2=&-ds_name=ECO731A1&-sortkey1=&-sortkey0=-RCPTOT (accessed June 2, 2010)

of an industry. Value added is calculated by subtracting the cost of materials used and contract work required to produce a product from the value of the shipments. The Census Bureau indicates that paint manufacturing operations have been able to maintain value added at a relatively high level through the years. Value added has averaged between 45% and 50% of shipments over the past two decades. In 2007, the total value of shipments was $23,574 million, while value added was $11,503 million; therefore, value added was 48.8% of shipments in that year. The latest available segment data shows value added for architectural coatings at 39.8% in 2002, followed by OEM coatings at 25.9% and special purpose coatings at 18.9%.

Figure 1-10 lists the number of plants producing paints and coatings in 2006. In that year, 1,344 plants operated, down from 1,463 in 2002. Nearly 750 establishments employed fewer than twenty people; this small operations accounted for 55.3% of all paint and coating manufacturing establishments in that year. Comparatively few plants, just 223, employed more than five hundred people, accounting for 16.6% of all paint and coating manufacturing establishments in 2006.

Figure 1-11 shows the annual average production index from 1990 to 2009. Output between 2000 and 2009 decreased by 31.2%, or at an average annual rate of 3.1%. The decline between 2007 and 2009 was particularly severe due to the worldwide economic recession. Between 2007 and 2009, industrial production declined from 94.5 to 70.1, for an average annual decrease of 12.1%.

Figure 1-13 gives the industry capacity utilization rates for fourth quarters in selected years from 1990 to 2009. Plants operated at 63% to 69% of full capacity between 1990 and 2006; the utilization rate in 2007 jumped to about 79%. However, the global economic recession that began in the last quarter of 2008 had a significant impact on utilization rates in

the paint industry. In 2008, the fourth quarter utilization rate was only 55%; in 2009, it was only 47%.

Operating margin equals shipments less cost of materials and production labor and is expressed as a percentage of the value of shipments. In 2007, the operating margin for the industry averaged 39.6%, down from 43.1% in 2002. Operating margins for the largest paint-producing states are shown in Figure 1-12.

Inventories, measured at the end of the year, are comprised mainly of finished products, materials, supplies and fuels and work in progress. In 2007, industry inventories were $1,940.4 million, 56.7% in finished products, 37.6% in materials, supplies, and fuels, and 5.7% in work in progress. Inventory turnover grew from 7.8 times in 1980, to 7.8 times in 1990, 11.4 times in 2002, and reached 12.2 times in 2007, thus indicating an improvement in inventory management. Industry inventories by type for selected years are shown in Figure 1-14.

Figure 1-13 Capacity Utilization Rates at Plants Producing Paints and Related Products, Fourth Quarters of Selected Years, 1990-2009

Year	Capacity Utilization Rates
1990	69
1995	68
2000	64
2005	66
2006	63
2007 (estimated)-a	79
2008	55
2009	47

Source: Created from Annual Surveys of Plant Capacity Utilization and Quarterly Surveys of Plant Capacity Utilization, U.S. Census Bureau, http://www.census.gov/manufacturing/capacity/historical_data/index.html

Capital investment in buildings and machinery and equipment is necessary to support growth and provide improvement in productivity and profit. In 2002, capital expenditures totaled $332.96 million, or 1.4% of industry shipments—down significantly from 2002, when capital expenditures totaled $556.1 and constituted 2.9% of industry shipments. In 2007, capital expenditures as a percent of total sales hit a twenty-year low.

The industry has not been a large investor in research and development (R&D), with expenditures generally accounting for only 3-4% of sales. Typically many of the paint companies have relied on resin manufacturers and suppliers of pigments and fillers to assist in paint modifications or new product development. However, due to VOC regulations and market conditions, new product development needs have required higher levels of R&D efforts by all paint industry factors.

The paint and allied products industry typically spends about 2.5% of sales for advertising, with the percentage increasing over the years. The U.S. Census Bureau reported in the 2007 Economic Census that the industry spent approximately $29.4 million on advertising and promotion, less than one percent of total sales. Spending is primarily for architectural paints. The Internal Revenue Service reported that in 2007, corporations claimed $524.9 million in advertising expenditures, approximately 1.2% of overall sales. Figure 1-15 gives historical expenditures as provided by the Internal Revenue Service for selected years.

EMPLOYMENT/PRODUCTIVITY

The total number of employees in the paint and allied products industry is shown in Figure 1-16. Since peaking at 71,000 in 1970, total employment in the industry decreased to 41,893 in 2007, a decline of 41%. Production workers as a percent of total industry employment have declined from a high of 59% in 1980 to 56.8% in 2007, when the annual average of production workers in the industry was 23,777. Improvements in manufacturing productivity have seen output per production employee increase from 27,000 gallons in 1980 to 42,100 gallons in 1990, and 53,100 gallons in 2002.

Figure 1-14 Inventories of Paints and Allied Products Industry, Selected Years, 1987-2007

Year	Inventory of Materials, Supplies, Fuels (in millions of dollars)	Inventory of Work in Process (in millions of dollars)	Inventory of Finished Products (in millions of dollars)	Total (in millions of dollars)
1987	$567.2	$135.4	$846.1	$1,548.7
1992	$638.0	$110.8	$1,010.4	$1,759.2
1997	$856.8	$94.2	$1,229.5	$2,180.4
2002	$636.3	$76.5	$977.8	$1,690.6
2007	$729.0	$110.7	$1,100.4	$1,940.4
2005	759.3	410.1	211.1	1,380.5
2006	767.6	381.7	210.4	1,359.7
2007	776.7	369.7	206.9	1,353.3
2008	682.0	344.1	196.3	1,222.4

Sources: "Adapted from Sector 31: ECO73111: Manufacturing: Industry Series: Detailed Statistics by Industry for the United States," Economic Censuses 1987-2007, U.S. Census Bureau, http://factfinder.census.gov/servlet/IBQTable?_bm=y&-geo_id=01000US&-ds_name=EC073111&-NAICS2007=325510&-_lang=en.

As shown, the value of shipments per employee has increased steadily, reaching a high of $562,700 in 2007. Figure 1-16 also provides a 27-year listing of the industry's total payroll costs and expenditures for materials as a percentage of shipments. Payroll costs have steadily declined from a high of 17.4% of shipments in 1970 to 12% in 1970, 11.4% in 1990, 10.5% in 2002 and 9.3% in 2007. Material costs have likewise declined from 57.4% in 1980 to 51.1% in 2007.

Value added per worker man-hour provides a measure of industry productivity. As shown in Figure 1-17, value added per worker man-hour has more than quadrupled since 1980, reaching an estimated $240.33 per man-hour in 2007. By this measure, value added per man-hour increased by, on average, 8.1% per year between 1980 and 1990, 2.7% per year between 1990 and 2000, and 6.1% per year between 2000 and 2007.

The average number of gallons produced per man-hour is one means of measuring productivity. The industry had to improve manufacturing productivity in order to ensure profitability. Between 1980 and 2007, gallons

Figure 1-15 Advertising Expenditures for Paints and Allied Products, Selected Years, 1970-2007

Year	Advertising Expenditures (in millions of dollars)	Percent of sales
1970	$43.8	1.5%
1975	$55.1	1.2%
1980	$126.6	1.8%
1985	$228.1	2.1%
1990	$267.0	2.1%
1995	$442.3	2.5%
2000-estimated	$508.3	2.5%
2005	$531.3	1.4%
2007	$524.9	1.2%

Source: Adapted from "SOI Tax Stats," Corporation Source Book: Manufacturing (sector 31), Internal Revenue Service, http://www.irs.gov/taxstats/article/0,,id=168246,00.html (accessed June 2, 2010)

Figure 1-16 Employment and Expenditures in the Paints and Allied Products Industry, Selected Years, 1980-2007

Year	No. of Employees (in thousands)	Shipments (in millions of dollars)	Sales per Employee (in thousands of dollars)	Cost of Materials as Percent of Sales	Payroll as Percent of Sales
1980	62.3	$8,349	$133.9	57.4%	13.0%
1985	55.5	$11,562	$208.3	55.3%	11.8%
1990	53.9	$14,238	$264.2	52.3%	11.4%
1995	52.4	$17,943	$342.4	53.4%	11.0%
2000	53	$19,766	$372.9	53.8%	11.2%
2002	46.1	$19,257	$417.7	52.5%	10.5%
2007	41.9	$23,575	$562.7	51.1%	9.3%

Source: Adapted from "Sector 31: ECO73111: Manufacturing: Industry Series: Detailed Statistics by Industry for the United States," Economic Census 2007, U.S. Census Bureau, http://factfinder.census.gov/servlet/IBQTable?_bm=y&-geo_id=01000US&-ds_name=EC073111&-NAICS2007=325510&-_lang=en.

Figure 1-17   Productivity and Wages in the Paint Industry, Selected Years, 1980-2007

Year	Production Workers (thousands)	Average Weekly Hours	Gallons Produced per Man-Hour	Average Hourly Earnings	Annual Wage Bill (in millions of dollars)	Value Added per Man-Hour
1980	32.9	40.3	12.74	$7.39	$463	56.13
1985	30.3	41.4	14.26	10.04	597	89.72
1987	30.7	41.9	15.72	10.84	628	110.49
1992	25.7	40.1	23.23	12.71	676	134.55
1997	28.4	37.8	26.35	15.73	878	166.61
2002	25.2	37.6	27.13	17.69	872	184.1
2007	23.8	38.7	28.3	20.55	982	240.33

Source: Adapted from *Employment and Earnings, Current Industrial Reports, M28F, Annual Survey of Manufacturers,* and *2007 Economic Census,* U.S. Census Bureau.

produced per man-hour increased from 12.74 in 1980, to 19.78 in 1990, to 28.3 in 2007, an average annual increase of 3% each year. (See Figure 1-17.)

REGIONAL PATTERNS AND DISTRIBUTION

Due to high shipping costs and delivery requirements of end users, manufacturing of paints is centered in regions with the highest consumption. According to the 2007 Economic Census, Ohio is the leading producing state with a value added of nearly $1.4 billion, accounting for 5.8% of the value added in the industry as a whole, followed by Illinois with a value added of $1.1 billion and Texas with $95.8 million in value added. (See Figure 1-12.)

Distribution varies greatly depending on type of paint. Paints are not typically shipped long distances. OEM and most special purpose coatings are purchased directly by users, whereas wholesalers and retailers are important channels of distribution for architectural coatings. Most product finishes and special purpose coatings are sold directly to industrial, commercial, government and institutional users, although some products,

such as automotive and machinery refinishes, also go through wholesalers and retailers. Finishmaster, Inc. is the largest distributor, with 177 sales outlets and three major distribution centers in twenty-nine states in 2010. However, architectural coatings are shipped to consumers and professional end users through a variety of distribution channels.

The internet continues to play a growing role, as companies develop e-commerce sites to provide an alternative method of paint selection and ordering. Nearly all paint manufacturers and their suppliers have web sites where consumers can obtain information about their company's product lines, directly request information, and become informed about changing technologies.

Most architectural coatings are distributed through retail stores, including paint, glass and wallpaper stores, to consumers, contractors and for building maintenance. Direct sales from manufacturers are principally to contractors, governments, building and maintenance, and for export. Wholesales are most important for building maintenance. Overall, the professional market represents over half of volume and DIY consumers take about one-third of the total. Leading suppliers are Sherwin Williams and PPG, with each company selling many brand names. Behr and Valspar are sold through big box retailers and take up increasingly large shares of the architectural coatings market in the United States.

Figure 1-18 shows the geographical distribution of the sales of U.S. paint stores by state. As expected, sales by state follow population. There were 8,025 paint and wallpaper stores operating nationwide in 2007, with over 35,000 employees. Most paint stores are small, averaging 4.4 employees per store. The largest number of stores, 765, were in California, followed by Florida (627), Texas (574), Ohio and Pennsylvania (with 355 each). Increasingly, however, paint is being sold by big-box retail stores such as Wal-Mart, Lowes and Home Depot. In 2007 there were 7,150 of these stores nationwide.

Many producers of architectural coatings operate their own retail outlets which sell the company's paint brands, and also paint sundries, often wallpaper, and sometimes an array of other items. Sherwin Williams was by far the largest operator of retail paint stores, with 3,354 stores operating in 2009; its nearest competitor, the Comex Group, operated 380 company-owned stores in the United States and Canada.

GOVERNMENT REGULATIONS

Background

Since about 1970, all industries have been subject to increased government regulations, which were deemed necessary and appropriate to ensure environmental integrity, to conserve energy, and to protect public health and worker safety. Before that time, weak and largely unenforceable federal laws were based on aspects of interstate pollution: that a source of air or water pollution in one state adversely affected environmental integrity or created health hazards for those people living in another. Under such a system, even the most severe pollution abuses were extremely difficult to monitor accurately, and almost impossible to prosecute under law.

Intrastate pollution was considered to be essentially a "states rights" issue, subject to state laws, standards, regulation and enforcement. This policy proved unsatisfactory because of the diversity of rules and regulations. For example, some states kept laws pertaining to pollution intentionally weak in an attempt to attract heavy industry, create jobs and expand tax bases, and some companies would locate in states with minimal regulations.

In 1970, largely in response to political pressure from environmental lobbies and public consensus, the federal government stepped in to assume the leading role in environmental regulation. Instead of focusing on the intrastate elements of pollution, the federal laws of the 1970s and 1980s were founded upon the general power of the federal government to regulate businesses engaged in interstate commerce. In this way, uniform federal laws could theoretically regulate all pollution generated, regardless of location. This centralization of authority, regulation, enforcement and prosecution removed, to some degree, the loopholes from those industries that took advantage of inequalities of state laws.

Regulations and standards are in place for almost every aspect of the paint and coatings industry, from utilization of raw materials in formulation to workplace health and safety standards and disposal of by-product waste, through transport and distribution, to end-user applications. Effects on the industry range from the reduction in the use of solvents to replacement of propellants for spray paints, and from restrictions on heavy metals used as pigments to elimination of mercury compounds used for product production. In addition, there are limitations on a variety of other chemicals that are

Figure 1-18   Paint and Wallpaper Stores by State, 2007

"NOTE: Data based on the 2007 County Business Patterns. Data for counties may not add to state totals due to the exclusion of ""statewide"" county data. Statewide data are included in the CBP html tables and download files found at County Business Patterns Website. For information on confidentiality protection, sampling error, nonsampling error, and definitions, see Survey Methodology. Data in this table represent those available when this report was created; data may not be available for all NAICS industries or geographies. Excludes most government employees, railroad employees, and self-employed persons."

Geography	Establishments (number)	Paid employees for pay period including March 12 (number)	First quarter payroll ($1,000)	Annual payroll ($1,000)
United States	8,025	35,316	333,162	1,360,666
Alabama	134	522	4,824	19,566
Alaska	14	77	794	3,455
Arizona	124	774	6,746	27,187
Arkansas	91	281	2,581	10,641
California	765	4,968	47,768	188,500
Colorado	139	709	6,224	25,314
Connecticut	103	464	4,415	18,533
Delaware	31	101	1,027	4,104
District of Columbia	8b	D	D	
Florida	627	2,525	24,415	95,538
Georgia	313	1,189	11,133	44,958
Hawaii	30	142	1,455	5,905
Idaho	52c	S		6,878
Illinois	282	1,228	10,906	45,378
Indiana	209	876	8,009	34,265
Iowa	92	360	3,042	12,783
Kansas	88	290	2,897	11,928
Kentucky	126	401	3,320	14,052
Louisiana	125	552	5,345	22,566
Maine	39c		1,199	5,123
Maryland	128e	D	D	
Massachusetts	172	919	8,071	33,245
Michigan	234	901	8,038	33,356
Minnesota	142	684	5,397	22,235
Mississippi	103	315	2,993	12,631
Missouri	172	693	6,213	24,739
Montana	39	163	1,557	6,222
Nebraska	52	207	1,975	8,425
Nevada	49	406	5,099	17,406
New Hampshire	35	205	1,903	8,520
New Jersey	225	1,141	10,315	42,585
New Mexico	43	178	1,549	6,211
New York	348	1,971	21,811	92,685
North Carolina	276	935	9,010	36,715
North Dakota	15b		507	2,071
Ohio	355g		10,573	45,425
Oklahoma	91e	D	D	
Oregon	116f		7,951	34,278
Pennsylvania	355g		11,495	47,238
Rhode Island	31	118	1,059	4,374
South Carolina	144	514	5,115	20,364
South Dakota	22	91	679	3,115
Tennessee	199	669	6,163	25,887
Texas	574	2,300	22,645	92,366
Utah	58	298	2,558	9,804
Vermont	27c		867	3,577
Virginia	210	877	7,642	31,448
Washington	203	971	8,524	34,990
West Virginia	37c		933	3,977
Wisconsin	164	584	5,248	21,460
Wyoming	14b		485	1,955
Puerto Rico	142	431	3,022	13,059

Source: "Table 1. Selected Industry Statistics for the U.S. and States: 2007, NAICS 44412," *2007 County Business Patterns*, U.S. Census Bureau, 2010, http://factfinder.census.gov/servlet/IQRTable?_bm=y&-ds_name=CB0700A1&-NAICS2002=44412&-_lang=en (accessed June 10, 2010)

D: Withheld to avoid disclosing data for individual companies; data are included in higher level totals.
N: Not available or not comparable.

considered hazardous to health or harmful to the environment. Other effects include the research and development of new processes and products as technology is driven by regulations, improvement in hazardous waste exchange technology and a restructuring of the industry to achieve greater efficiency and productivity.

Federal regulatory activity has produced changes in the basic structure of the paints and coatings industry during the past 40 years. A major change is the trend toward consolidation and the acquisition of smaller, weaker, or marginal operations by larger, stronger, or more diversified corporations better adapted to survive the combination of stringent regulations. In addition to continued technical and economic challenges, the industry also faces continuing product liability and educational challenges. Because of this form of economic "natural selection," the paints and coatings industry is stronger than before, and ready to meet the challenges of the future.

Air Pollution Laws

The first major federal attempts to regulate, control and diminish atmospheric pollution occurred when Congress passed the Clean Air Act of 1963 and subsequent amendments. It was significantly rewritten in 1970, and there have been subsequent amendments in 1977 and 1990.

All legislation was preceded by earlier guidelines established by the County of Los Angeles in an attempt to overcome intolerable conditions that prevailed in that area. The resulting amendment, based on Los Angeles' regulations, including "Rule 66," was enacted in 1967. It restricted emissions of photochemically reactive hydrocarbons and oxidants that react with oxides of sulfur and nitrogen in the presence of ultraviolet radiation and water vapor to form smog.

As a result of such reactions, secondary atmospheric contaminants are formed which amplify health hazards to humans and other forms of animal and plant life and also cause corrosive damage to architectural and structural surfaces. The most damaging and harmful of these was the ground level ozone formed by reaction of sunlight, hydrocarbons, and atmospheric oxygen.

Although the situation and circumstances were in some ways unique to Los Angeles at the time, the fact that other urban and industrial areas had similar air quality problems prompted federal legislation geared toward preventative avoidance. The Clean Air Act of 1970 charged the newly formed Environmental Protection Agency (EPA) with creating standards which would define levels of air quality necessary to protect public health, and with developing a program by which the states would be responsible for implementation and enforcement of those standards.

This process was accomplished with two essential points of focus: developing emission standards and setting up a system of air quality management. Emission standards were written to clean up the two most obvious mobile and stationary "point sources" of air pollution, vehicular exhaust systems and industrial smokestacks. The air quality management system involved state regulatory activity intended to guarantee and protect against significant deterioration of air quality in any portion of any state.

The 1970 amendments provided for individual states to solve their air quality problems. States are required to file State Implementation Plans (SIP), which are essentially the ways and means by which air quality will be improved in non-attainment areas. Some areas in the United States are attainment areas; areas that do not meet national ambient air quality standards (NAAQS) are considered non-attainment regions. Since non-attainment areas—generally large cities and industrial areas--have poorer ambient air quality, restrictions for coating use are more stringent in these areas.

The attainment status of areas depends on the pollutant. An area may be in compliance for one pollutant, hence be an attainment area for that pollutant, but not be in attainment for another pollutant. The amendment provides for determination of major pollution sources--specific sites that exceed standards. The volume of each pollutant is measured each year to determine if the facility will be considered a major source.

Amendments to the Clean Air Act were enacted in 1977 and expanded in 1990. The 1990 Amendments to the law constitute a comprehensive law designed to improve and maintain air quality. Enactment affects all domestic industries, bringing new regulations pertaining to air quality, hazardous pollutants, acid rain, stratospheric ozone depletion and automotive emissions. The amendments provide for attainment of air quality by limiting emissions of air pollutants. These include suspected ozone depleting agents, nitrogen oxides and volatile organic compounds (VOC). For all these materials, NAAQS have been set. In 1998, the EPA issued the National Volatile Organic Compound Emission Standards for Consumer and Commercial Products which limited VOCs in most coatings to 450 g/L, a rule which substantially shifted the coatings market to water-borne systems and represented a turning point in the industry (Karsten Danielmeier, "The World Marketplace for Protective Coatings—Opportunities and Trends," *Paint & Coating Industry*, April 2010, pp. 38-46).

A variety of techniques are available to control pollution, including maximum achievable control technology (MACT), best available control technology (BACT), reasonably available control technology (RACT), and lowest achievable emission rate (LAER).

The required pollution control technology depends on many factors, including attainment/non-attainment status of an area, level of air quality, and specific pollutant. New and modified sources of pollution in ozone non-attainment areas are required by the amendments to include pollution control goals of meeting at least LAER standards. RACT is required on existing sources in non-attainment areas. BACT is required on major new or modified sources in attainment areas. The EPA, in the final rule for architectural and industrial maintenance coatings, requires BACT because reformulation to reduce VOC emissions has proven effective as a means of pollution prevention.

The Clean Air Act clearly outlines the EPA's permit procedure. New plants or modified plants are required to obtain construction permits before construction or modification. Prior to start-up, the plant must obtain an operating permit. The states review and issue permits and are responsible for maintaining emissions after start-up. After five years the permit must be reviewed before renewal. Assuming an operating permit is granted, states outline the emission thresholds by pollutant, dictate monitoring methods to determine pollutants, provide for plant entry by inspectors, and outline reporting procedures if emissions exceed threshold levels.

In addition to monitoring paint users, EPA has enforcement powers, including the notification of violations of either paint manufacturers or industrial consumers. If a violator is put on notice, he has a choice of altering the process or paint use, or of controlling emissions in any number of ways. After a meeting to devise compliance strategies, the EPA can issue an administrative order which outlines the remedial methods to be undertaken. Failure to comply with an administrative order could result in legal action. The amendments subject a wide range of violations to civil, criminal and administrative actions and costly fines.

Clean Air Act Amendments also impact manufacturers and users of OEM finishes and architectural, special purpose and industrial maintenance coatings. OEM finishes are usually proprietary products formulated specifically for a particular equipment manufacturer. Here, both the paint manufacturer and the industrial consumer need to be concerned with the amount of VOCs or hazardous air pollutants (HAPs) in any particular paint or coating product. Toxic, or hazardous air pollutants, are those pollutants known or suspected to cause cancer or other serious health effects as well as other environmental effects. HAPs can also cause health effects such as eye, nose, throat, and skin irritation, nausea, vomiting, headache, dizziness, or liver and kidney damage. The EPA has published a list of HAPs that are covered under the Clean Air Act and are subject to National Emission Standards (NES) when used in a manufacturing process or any manufactured product. When developing an NES, the EPA takes into account the presence of these chemicals in any process--for example, paint and coating manufacture or paint products. The list published by the EPA has 188 chemicals listed as HAPs. Figure 1-19 contains ninety chemicals listed as hazardous that are likely to be found in paint manufacturing or in the formulation of paint and coating products.

The EPA has developed final rules and regulations to control emissions of HAPs for a number of categories of industrial OEM manufacturing operations that are estimated to account for 95% of OEM paint consumption. Included in the HAP list are such compounds as benzene, toluene, xylenes (both individual and isomers), ethylbenzene, styrene, ethyl glycol monobutyl ether, glycol ethers, methyl ethylene ketone, methyl isobutyl ketone, isophorone, cumene, naphthalene, formaldehyde, hexane, methanol, methylene

chloride and methylene diphenyl isocyanate. Since many of the HAP chemicals are also volatile organic compounds, their inclusion might be considered an extension of volatile organic chemicals control. Control Technique Guidelines have been developed for coatings for shipbuilding and ship repair, aerospace and wood furniture. Since 2001, Control Technique Guidelines have been issued for coatings used for large appliances; auto and light duty truck manufacturing; wood building products, including siding, doors, flooring, interior wall paneling, and windows and miscellaneous wood building products; metal furniture; metal cans; metal coil coatings and miscellaneous metal products; and plastics. Paint makers must supply information on the VOC and HAP content of the product as shipped to industrial OEM consumers, so that the industry can comply with various local, state, and federal emissions regulations. These products represent nearly 95% of OEM equipment surface coatings that the industry produces. The rules establish material technology based emission standards, or Maximum Achievable Control Technology (MACT) that require add-on controls that are intended to capture HAP emissions.

HAP emissions for manufacturers of such home appliances as refrigerators, freezers, washers, dryers, ranges, air conditioners, hot water tanks and other miscellaneous appliances are limited to 0.022 kilogram per liter (0.022 kg/L) or 0.18 pounds per gallon of coatings solids. The limits apply to the sum of all coatings, thinners, and cleaning materials used at the affected site. The EPA estimated that the rule as issued would reduce HAP emissions by 45% at a cost to the industry of $1.63 billion in the fifth year ("National Emission Standards for Hazardous Air Pollutants: Surface Coating of Large Appliances; Final Rule," Federal Register, vol. 67, no. 141, July 23, 2002, http:// www.epa.gov/ttn/atw/lapp/fr23jy02.pdf).

Figure 1-19 Hazardous Air Pollutants Specified in the Clean Air Act

1,2-Dibromo-3-Propane	Ethylene Oxide
1,3-Dichloroprene	Formaldehyde
2-Chloroacetophenone	Glycol ethers
2-Nitropropane	Hexachlorocyclopentadiene
4-Nitrophenol	Hexachlorocyclopentadiene
Acetaldehyde	Hexamethyl phosphoramide
Acetonitrile	Hexane
Acetophenone	Hydroquinone
Acrolein	Maleic anhydride
Acrylamide	m-Cresol
Acrylic acid	Methanol
Acrylonitrile	Methoxychlor
Allyl Chloride	Methyl bromide
Aniline	Methyl ethyl Ketone
Benzene	Methyl isobutyl ketone
Benzotrichloride	Methyl isocyanate
Benzyl chloride	Methyl methacrylate
Bis (chloromethyl) ether	Methylene chloride
Butadiene	Methylene diphenyl diisocyanate
Caprolactam	Methyl-tert-butyl ether
Carbon tetrachloride	m-xylene
Catechol	N,N-Diethyl aniline
Chlorobenzene	Naphthalene
Chloroform	o-Anisidine
Chloromethyl methyl ether	o-Cresol
Chloroprene	o-Xylene
Cumene	p-Cresol
Di-2-ethylhexyl phthalate	Phenol
Dibutyl phthalate	Phthalic anhydride
Dichloroethyl ether	p-Phenylene diamine
Diethanolamine	Propionaldehyde
Diethyl sulfate	Propylene dichloride
Dimethyl formamide	p-Xylene
Dimethryl phthalate	Quinoline
Dimethyl sulfate	Quinone
Dioxane	Styrene
Epichlorohydrin	Styrene oxide
Ethyl acrylate	Tetrachloroethylene
Ethyl carbamate	Toluene
Ehtyl carbamate	Trichloroethylene
Ethyl chloride	Triethyl amine
Ethylbenzene	Vinyl acetate
Ethylene dibromide	Vinyl chloride
Theylene glycol	Xylenes (mixed)

The rule for automobile and light truck manufacturing facilities include HAP emissions limits for both new and reconstructed plants or source plants and for emission limits for existing sources. The rule established combined limits for all coatings and primers, including primers, electro deposition primer coatings, primer surfacers, top coats (both pigments and clear coat), glass bonding primers and glass bonding adhesives. The combined limits for all products at new or reconstructed facilities are 0.036 kg/L or 0.30 lb/gal. For existing plants, the combined limits for the same products are 0.072 kg/L or 0.60 lb/gal. The emission limits covers all primers and coatings used and also thinners, cleaning materials, and waste materials recovered in the painting operation. The rule also provides that all materials containing HAPs must be stored in closed containers, and the risk of spills minimized. The manufacturer must also develop and implement a work practice plan to minimize HAP emissions from cleaning and purging equipment associated with all coating operations for which emission limits have been proposed. The compliance date for the emission rule for existing plants was April 26, 2007 ("National Emission Standards for Hazardous Air Pollutants: Surface Coating of Automobiles and Light-Duty Trucks; Final Rule," Federal Register, vol. 69, no. 80, April 26, 2004, http://www.epa.gov/ttn/atw/auto/fr26ap04r.pdf).

The HAP limits for the manufacturing operations for metal furniture are extremely stringent for new or reconstructed or renovated plants. As issued, the rule allows for no HAP emissions in such plants. For existing metal furniture plants emission limits for HAP are set at 0.10 kg/L or 0.83 lb/gal. The limits apply to the emissions from all coatings, thinners and cleaning solvents or materials used in the coating operations at the affected source. The compliance date for existing plants was May 23, 2006 ("National

Emission Standards for Hazardous Air Pollutants: Surface Coating of Metal Furniture; Final Rule," Federal Register, vol. 68, no. 100, May 23, 2004, http://www.epa.gov/ttn/atw/mfurn/fr23my03.pdf).

The emission limits for manufacturing metal cans were issued for both new and reconstructed or renovated plants and for existing plants. All plants that use can coatings over 1,500 gallons (5,700 liters) per year are covered by the emission rule. The limits are established for all the individual components of metal cans. For example, limits were set for two-piece beverage cans, two-piece food cans, one-piece aerosol cans, sheet coating, three-piece cans and end coatings. The rule includes the coating for metal sheets for subsequent processing into cans or can parts, not for coating for metal coils for other end uses. The limits exclude the coating of pails and drums, which are covered in the emission rule for miscellaneous metal parts and products. The limits for each type are listed in Figure 1-20 for can coatings. The compliance date for existing plants was November 13, 2006 ("National Emission Standards for Hazardous Air Pollutants: Surface Coating

of Metal Cans; Final Rule," Federal Register, vol. 68, no. 219, November 13, 2003, http://www.epa.gov/ttn/atw/mcan/fr13no03.pdf).

HAP emission limits were set for metal coil coating operations. The emission limits were not more than 0.046 kg/L or 0.38 lb/gal of solids applied during each compliance period. Alternatively, the rule provided that HAP emission be no more than 2% of the organic HAP applied, or 98% overall control. Existing facilities were ordered to comply by June 10, 2005. New or reconstructed sources were to comply immediately upon start up of the affected source after June 10, 2002 ("National Emission Standards for Hazardous Air Pollutants: Surface Coating of Metal Coil; Final Rule," Federal Register, vol. 67, no. 111, June 10, 2002, http://www.epa.gov/ttn/atw/mcoil/fr10jn02.pdf).

HAP emission limits have also been established for wood building products manufacturers and are set for each of five different categories of products. The rule covers all plants and sources that use more than 1,100 gallons of coatings annually. The rule applies to existing facilities. The limits are shown in Figure 1-21. Manufacturers had three years to

Figure 1-20 HAP Emission Limits for Can Coatings

HAP EMISSION LIMITS FOR NEW OR RECONSTRUCTED SOURCES	
Two piece beverage cans – all coatings	0.04 kg/L – 0.31 lb/gal
Two piece food cans – all coatings	0.06 kg/L – 0.50 lb/gal
One piece aerosol cans – all coatings	0.08 kg/L – 0.65 lb/gal
Sheetcoating	0.02 kg/L – 0.17 lb/gal
Three piece cans – inside spray	0.12 kg/L – 1.03 lb/gal
HAP EMMISION LIMITS FOR EXISTING SOURCES	
Two piece beverage cans – all coatings	0.07 kg/L – 0.59 lb/gal
Two piece food cans – all coatings	0.06 kg/L – 0.51 lb/gal
One piece aerosol cans – all coatings	0.12 kg/L – 0.99 lb/gal
Sheeting coating	0.03 kg/L – 0.26 lb/gal
Three piece cans – inside spray	0.29 kg/L – 0243 lb/gal

Source: "National Emission Standards for Hazardous Air Pollutants: Surface Coating of Metal Cans; Final Rule," *Federal Register*, vol. 68, no. 219, November 13, 2003, http://www.epa.gov/ttn/atw/mcan/fr13no03.pdf

Figure 1-21   HAP Emission Limits for Wood Building Products

Exterior Siding and Primed Doorskins	0.07 kg/L – 0.06 lb/gal
Flooring	0.93 kg/L – 0.78 lb/gal
Interior Wall Paneling and Tileboard	0.18 kg/L – 1.52 lb/gal
Other Interior Panels	0.20 kg/L – 0.17 lb/gal
Doors, Windows, and Miscellaneous	0.23 kg/L – 1.93 lb/gal

Source: "National Emission Standards for Hazardous Air Pollutants: Surface Coating of Wood Building Products; Final Rule," Federal Register, vol. 68, no. 102, May 28, 2003, http://www.epa.gov/ttn/atw/wbldg/fr28my03r.pdf

comply with its requirements; the compliance date was May 28, 2003 ("National Emission Standards for Hazardous Air Pollutants: Surface Coating of Wood Building Products; Final Rule," Federal Register, vol. 68, no. 102, May 28, 2003, http://www.epa.gov/ttn/atw/wbldg/fr28my03r.pdf).

In December 2003, the EPA issued rules and regulations on National Emission Standards (NES) for miscellaneous coatings manufacturing. The affected sources of emissions that are subject to the rule are storage tanks, process vessels, equipment components, wastewater treatment and conveyance systems, and such ancillary sources as heat exchange systems. The final standards cover vents from and any leakage from such equipment. For stationary vessels at existing facilities with capacities of 0.94 cubic meters, or 250 gallons, the final rule requires an overall reduction of at least 75% by weight of HAP for chemicals with a vapor pressure of greater or equal to 0.09 pounds per square inch and at least 60% for any HAP chemical with a vapor pressure less than 0.9 pounds per square inch. Stationary vessels must be provided with vented covers so that at least 95% of the HAP emissions are reduced. HAP emissions from storage tanks must be lowered 90% by weight.

Any wastewater containing soluble or partially soluble HAP loads of 750 pounds annually and a concentration of 4,400 ppm or greater must be treated as a hazardous waste or by using an enhanced biological treatment unit. Standards for transfer operations require at least 75% control of HAP emissions from product loading into tank cars for trailers. As written, the rule will include manufacturing of paints, inks and adhesives.

OEM end users must prepare documents for reference by auditors and for submittal to various governmental bodies to characterize VOC content of paint as applied. VOC data sheets prepared by paint makers require specific information to satisfy regulations in effect at the facility. This information includes the test procedure used for the determination of VOC content, which is recorded as weight of solvent in pounds per gallon (lb/gal) and kilograms per liter (kg/liter) of paint. Furthermore, the solids and HAP contents, heavy metal content, destination of the coating, batch numbers of the coating and its identification must be stated, if required by applicable regulations. The data sheets require the user's name, the coating supplier, and the user's coating identification and also all properties of the coating as applied.

Architectural and industrial maintenance coatings are the responsibility of the paint manufacturer. Since their products can be used in attainment and non-attainment areas, the EPA established VOC content limits for all types of architectural and industrial maintenance coatings. The wide range of VOC's permitted in these coatings, as given in Figure 1-23, were published by the EPA as the Final Rule in 1998 and went into effect for coatings manufactured after September

1999 ("National Volatile Organic Compound Emission Standards for Architectural Coatings," Federal Register, vol. 63, no. 176, September 11, 1998, http://www.epa.gov/ttn/atw/183e/aim/fr1191.pdf).

Paint manufacturers are required to notify the EPA of the status of the coatings being sold to architectural and industrial maintenance coatings markets. Specific labeling requirements include a statement of VOC, date of manufacture, and type of coating, such as "for industrial use only." The category with the lowest VOC must be used for coatings used in the categories listed in Figure 1-23. Should a question of compliance arise, confirmation of VOC content is by EPA Test Method 24. Companies may utilize exceedance fees or tonnage exemptions as defined in the rule.

Figure 1-22 shows the rule that applies to automobile refinish coatings manufactured since 1999. Exceptions include OEM, non-refillable aerosols, lacquer topcoats and touchup coatings.

In 2010, Congress was considering amending the Clean Air Act that would reduce emissions from the burning of fossil fuels.

Water Quality

The first major federal law concerned with water quality standards was the Federal Water Pollution Control Act of 1948. It authorized federally funded studies on pollution control, but otherwise had little effect due to inherent weakness in the law in terms of implementation. In 1965 the government began to take a more active interest in pollution abatement with the passage of the Water Quality Act, followed by the Clean Water Act of 1972 and its subsequent amendments.

The Clean Water Act of 1977, reauthorized in 1987, established a time-schedule program to restore and maintain the chemical, physical, and biological integrity of

national waterways. Provisions required that industrial discharges were to be reduced to comply with limitations based on the application of the "best practical technology" (BPT) economically available and required compliance by July 1984.

The original intent of the act, to reduce the effluent pollutants discharged to zero by 1985, was impractical. However, substantial progress has been made. At the time the amendments were enacted, the EPA recommended several procedures to meet the BPT deadline. For paint manufacturing facilities, the procedures included the reduction of water use, recycling of rinse water back into production, and contract hauling to completely eliminate the discharge of pollutants, which was based on the assumption of the standard of zero discharge. Such a low level of discharge would require that waste water containing only traces of certain organic chemicals or metals be treated like concentrated hazardous wastes rather than by disposal through public treatment facilities.

After hearing practical arguments of the industry, the EPA began to withdraw some of the proposed guidelines pertaining to paint formulation and, in particular, for certain

Figure 1-22 VOC Content Standards for Automobile Refinish Coatings

Coating Category	VOC Content Grams/Liter (Pounds/Gallon)
Pretreatment Wash Primer	780 (6.5)
Primer/Primer Surfacer	580 (4.8)
Primer Sealer	550 (4.6)
Single / 2-Stage Topcoats	600 (5.0)
Topcoats of 3 of more stages	630 (5.2)
Multi-coloured topcoats	630 (5.2)
Specialty Coatings	840 (7.0)

Source: "National Volatile Organic Compound Emission Standards for Automobile Refinish Coatings," Federal Register, vol. 63, no. 176, September 11, 1998, http://www.epa.gov/ttn/atw/183e/aim/fr1194.pdf

Figure 1-23 Permitted VOC Emissions for Architectural Industrial Maintenance Coatings

Architectural Coatings	Grams VOC/Liter
Flat coatings	
Exterior	250
Interior	250
Non-flat coatings	
Exterior	380
Interior	380
Primers and undercoaters	350
Quick-dry coatings	
Primers, sealers, undercoaters	450
Enamels	450
Lacquers	680
Sanding sealers (other than lacquer sealers)	550
Sealers (including interior clear wood sealers)	400
Shellacs	
Clear	730
Opaque	550
Stains – Clear and Semitransparent	550
Stains – Opaque	350
Varnishes	450

Special Purpose Coatings and Industrial Maintenance Coatings

	Grams VOC/Liter
Anti-fouling coatings	450
Anti-graffiti coatings	600
Bituminous coatings and mastics	500
Concrete curing and sealing compounds	700

	Grams VOC/Liter
Concrete protective coatings	
Extreme high durability coatings	800
Floor coatings	400
Flow coatings	650
Fire-retardant/resistive coatings	
Clear	850
Opaque	450
Graphic arts coatings (sign paints)	500
Heat Resistant coating	420
High temperature coatings	650
Industrial maintenance coatings	450
Mastic texture coatings	300
Metallic pigments coatings	500
Multi-coloured coatings	580
Nuclear coatings	450
Pretreatment wash primers	780
Roof coatings	250
Rust preventative coatings	400
Swimming pool coatings	600
Traffic marking paints	150
Waterproofing sealers and treatments	600
Wood preservatives	
Clear and semitransparent	550
Below grounnd	550
Opaque	350
Zone marking coatings	450

Source: "National Volatile Organic Compound Emission Standards for Architectural Coatings," Federal Register, vol. 63, no. 176, September 11, 1998, http://www.epa.gov/ttn/atw/183e/aim/fr1191.pdf

wastewater and solvent wash subcategories. Considering that about 95% of industrial paint manufacturing facilities are in compliance with the BPT (economically-achievable) aspects of the Clean Water Act, and that new facilities have water pollution control technology built in, a certain amount of relief is justifiable from the potential economic hardships of complete compliance.

Hazardous Wastes

The Resource and Conservation and Recovery Act (RCRA), an amendment of The Clean Water Act, was enacted in 1975 and implemented in October 1980. The Act regulates and defines the manner in which hazardous wastes are generated, transported, treated, contained, labeled, stored and disposed. Waste is classified as hazardous, and is subject to federal regulation, if it exhibits one or more of the following characteristics: ignitability, corrosivity, reactivity, or toxicity. An ignitable waste poses a fire hazard during routine management. Corrosive wastes are capable of corroding standard containers and/or damaging human tissues. Reactive wastes include certain explosives and materials that tend to react violently when mixed with water. Toxic wastes are harmful or fatal when ingested or absorbed, or can leach toxic chemicals into the soil or ground water (as determined by TCLP Test Method 1311, the Toxic Characteristic Leaching Procedure).

The materials used in paint production, including certain resins and catalysts, solvents, pigments and dyes, the wash rinse waters, and adhesives and glues are all considered part of the hazardous waste category if they meet one of the characteristics. Since 2000 the EPA has been collecting information to determine if paint production wastes should be treated as "listed" hazardous wastes. Categories being considered by the EPA are solvent-cleaning water, water and caustic cleaning sludge, emission-control dust or sludge, and off-specification production waste.

A variety of management approaches to hazardous waste management exist. Source reduction, treatment, recycling and reuse, reclamation, and disposal are foremost.

Source reduction involves a careful assessment of ways to reduce hazardous waste at the source. This approach prevents generation of hazardous wastes, implements an approach of resource conservation, is more economical, is environmentally safe and is legally sound. Source reduction may involve modifying a process, substituting a safer material for hazardous materials, or replacing a product that creates a large quantity of hazardous wastes.

If source reduction is not feasible, the second optimum management strategy is to recycle or reuse the hazardous materials. Treatment is characterized as any physical,

chemical, biological or thermal process that destroys, detoxifies, or neutralizes hazardous waste, reduces its volume, or makes the waste amenable to recovery, storage, or transport.

Disposal techniques include land burial, underground injection wells, surface impoundments, or secure landfills, secure landfills meeting RCRA standards may, under temporary variances, be able to accept a few hazardous wastes for which alternative disposal methods have not been developed.

The 1984 amendments to RCRA, the Federal Hazardous and Solid Waste Amendments, required phasing out land disposal of hazardous wastes. RCRA established a comprehensive system whereby hazardous wastes must be packaged and labeled in accordance with rules established by the Department of Transportation prior to movement from the source site. A manifest is prepared identifying the producer and transporter, the location of the site of disposal, and a description of the type and quantity of waste being moved. The transporter must deliver to the prescribed site, and return a signed copy of the manifest to the producer indicating safe and proper disposal. The law, implemented by the EPA, also mandates that all producers and transporters of hazardous wastes apprise the EPA of their activities and that the owners of hazardous waste treatment, storage and disposal operations be required to obtain RCRA permits for their facilities. Some states have more stringent regulations, to which hazardous waste generators and transporters must comply.

In 2001, the EPA released a proposed rule that would list certain production wastes as hazardous, and be subject to Subtitle C of the RCRA. The chemicals involved, if released above a certain level, are acrylamide and acrylonitrile, both binders; antimony, a pigment; ethylbenzene and methyl isobutyl ketone, methylene chloride, N-butyl alcohol, toluene and xylene, all solvents; formaldehyde, a biocide; and methyl methacrylate, a binder. Had the rule been adopted, production of many latex paints could be considered hazardous wastes. On April 2, 2002, the EPA determined not to list these wastes as hazardous ("Paint Listing Final Rule, April 4, 2002, http://www.epa.gov/wastes/hazard/wastetypes/wasteid/paint/index.htm).

Toxic Substances

Prior to 1976 and the passage of the Toxic Substance Control Act (TSCA), all toxic substances were simply classified as hazardous and were subject to regulatory action by a number of state and federal agencies. With the enactment and implementation of TSCA, the EPA assumed the overall responsibility for identifying toxic substances and establishing standards to prevent unreasonable risks to health, safety, and the environment. The regulations would prevent damage to the environment associated with the manufacture, processing, distribution, use and disposal of by-product toxic residues. The law provided the EPA powers and authority to require industry to conduct testing for toxicity at its own expense, to compel manufacturers to give the agency ninety days' notice prior to the production of a toxic chemical substance, and to regulate specific toxic materials. The Office of Pollution Prevention and Toxics administers the law.

Because most paints and coatings are considered mixtures of component materials, many manufacturers are only indirectly affected by TSCA regulations concerning chemical substances used in the formulations. Both suppliers to the industry and manufacturers who produce their own chemicals and raw materials in reportable quantities are vitally influenced. An inventory list is required under law, and companies that produce paints and coatings components must report the name and location of production facilities as well as name and volume of substances manufactured. In 1978, an initial inventory of classes of toxic substances was published, and this is revised periodically. All new substances not on the list must be reported.

Under law, the TSCA Interagency Testing Committee is required to submit to the EPA the names of chemical substances it recommends for additional assessment and testing; those which seem especially harmful, or potentially so. The initial list, submitted by the committee, included ten chemical substances. Those widely used in the paint and coatings industry included toluene, alkyl epoxies and alkyl phthalates.

The use of lead in paints brought about the first toxic substance legislation that vitally affected the industry. It was instances of lead poisoning, primarily among children in depressed urban areas, which prompted the federal government to enact legislation regulating its use in paints and other products. The Lead-Based Paint Poisoning Prevention Act, enacted in January 1971, prohibited the manufacture and use of paints containing more than 1% lead (by weight, in the nonvolatile portion of liquid paints, or in the dried paint film residue) intended for application on interior or exterior surfaces accessible to children in residential structures.

The following year, the U.S. Food and Drug Administration (FDA), acting under the authority provided by the Federal Hazardous Substances Act of 1960, reduced allowable lead content in paints to be used in residential housing to 0.5%, effective January 1, 1973, and to 0.06% two years later. Responsibility for implementation of the act was transferred to the Consumer Products Safety Commission. In June 1976, the National Education and Disease Prevention Act was passed. Title II of this act includeds amendments to the Lead-Based Paint Poisoning Prevention Act, which used the 0.06% standard. In December 1976, the Consumer Products Safety Commission ruled that 0.06% should be the maximum level for lead in certain paints manufactured after February 27, 1978.

Since 1976, legislation by vaious other agencies has been adopted to prohibit the use of lead-based paints in specific instances, expanding to all types of paints and coatings. In 1992 the Residential Lead-Based Paint Hazard Reduction Act directed the EPA and the U.S. Department of Housing and Urban Development (HUD) to issue regulations regarding lead-based paint on older structures. In 1996, lead inspector certification program requirements began. Most paint companies had anticipated the prohibition on lead, and diminished or phased out its use in their products before the final ruling took effect. Due to the amount of lead remaining on coated surfaces it has become a continuing challenge to painting contractors and owners who must determine the appropriate remediation procedure. The coatings are hazardous to remove, and the procedure is highly regulated throughout the country, including required inspection by EPA-certified lead inspectors. The waste is considered toxic, and must be disposed of accordingly. Strict procedures must also be followed to protect workers from exposure during repair, removal and recoating.

A number of class action lawsuits have been brought against a wide range of paint manufacturers, lead pigment producers, some with only a peripheral or incidental association with paint production back as far as the 1950s. The suits are directed toward obtaining a verdict against the defendants to force them to pay for the cleanup of all houses in an area or city that might contain lead paints. The potential liability is estimated in any single area in the hundreds of millions of dollars for the cleanup of 40,000 to 50,000 houses and apartments. By mid-2010, scores of lawsuits had been filed that claimed

manufacturers were liable injury caused by lead paint, but most of them had been dismissed. In these cases, the plaintiffs were unable to identify a paint manufacturer or a specific paint product that had caused any injury to anybody or harm to the community. In 2008, the Supreme Court of Rhode Island was the latest of several state Supreme Courts to reject "public nuisance" lawsuits against manufacturers of lead paint.

Mercury, in the form of phenylmercuric salts of acetic, oleic, or propionic acid, had been used extensively by the industry as an effective mildewicide and preservative for latex paints. Derivatives of mercury were used in a large percentage of water-based paints as an in-can preservative to prevent bacterial degradation and its by-product effects, and mercury-based fungicides were used in most architectural exterior paints to prevent fungi damage to dried paint film. The EPA banned the use of mercury in interior paint in 1990, but most manufacturers had reduced or eliminated mercury in their products before that time.

More recently, the EPA has taken action to eliminate the use of tributyl tin compounds in marine antifouling paints. Tributyl tin compounds, as the tributyl tin ester of methacrylic acid, were used to make copolymers with monomers such as methyl methacrylate and styrene, to produce resins for lacquer type coatings applied below the water line. As the tributyl tin slowly hydrolyzed in salt water, it released the active ingredient tributyl tin oxide. The copolymer dissolved, keeping the surface free of marine growth. Studies showed that these compounds persisted in the water and harmed certain sea life. The International Maritime Organization's treaty to eliminate the compound took effect in January 2008, and paint manufacturers reduced or eliminated products containing the compound several years in advance (Tim Wright, "Marine Coatings Market: With the

International Maritime Organization's TBT Antifouling Treated Set to Take Effect January 2008, Along with the Continuing Surge in Copper Prices, Marine Paint Makers and Their Raw Material Suppliers are Adapting to Meet These Demands," *Coatings World*, May 2007, pp. 40-42). While cuprous oxide, an older technology, continues to be used, the industry is investigating new and novel approaches to this problem. Silicone-based coatings are another option being tried. In the small boat and yacht market, antifouling paints are available that produce thin film paint formulated with Teflon. Other products for ship bottoms are ablative or self-polishing coatings which wear away slowly and in the process remove any marine fouling that might be attached to the hull.

The Comprehensive Environmental Response, Compensation and Liability Act, commonly known as the Superfund, was enacted in 1980. The intent of the legislation was to establish jurisdiction and the means of cleaning thousands of chemical waste sites that pose health and environmental hazards, with primary attention being given to sites leaking highly toxic substances. The legislation gave rise to a number of questions, including responsibility—not only who was responsible for causing the problems that the Superfund seeks to solve, but also what methods could be used to determine the degree of financial liability and equitable division of expenses incurred. Each industry's obligation to the Superfund was legislated, and a total of $1.6 billion was raised through taxes on the chemical and petroleum industries, to be used to clean up abandoned waste sites for which no responsibility could be assigned.

With the enactment of the Superfund Amendments and Reauthorization Act of 1986, the money allocated to clean up hazardous waste sites was increased. The fund was financed by a tax on major petrochemical feedstocks such as benzene, toluene, and

xylene at about 2.5 cents a gallon for benzene and toluene and 4.5 cents a gallon for xylene. In essence, this raised the cost of these materials that are used as solvents or intermediates for the production of paints and coatings.

The Superfund has come under a great deal of criticism because only relatively few of the hundreds of identified waste sites have been cleaned up and much of the money has been spent on legal costs. In 2010, the EPA announced the "Integrated Cleanup Initiative," a new publicly reported performance measure as well as an increase in its commitments to complete remedial action projects in response to criticism of the program. By 2009, the EPA had controlled exposure to toxic substances in 1,320 sites and controlled the migration of contaminated ground water in 1,012 sites ("Superfund National Accomplishments Summary Fiscal Year 2009," EPA, 2010, http://www.epa.gov/superfund/accomp/numbers09.html).

Safety

The Occupational Safety and Health Administration (OSHA) was established as a division of the Department of Labor by the Occupational Safety and Health Act of 1970. It has the authority to set workplace standards relating to the handling and storage of hazardous materials, exposure to dust and vapor particles, fire prevention systems, noise levels, and a number of concerns pertinent to employee health and safety. The National Institute for Occupational Safety and Health was created as the research institute for OSHA. It is currently part of the Centers for Disease Control and Prevention (CDC).

OSHA set precise and definitive standards for acceptable occupational exposure levels to air borne particulates of various chemicals, including lead and benzene. OSHA published Permissible Exposure Limits in

1971, and they began a review and revision program in 1996. The American Conference of Governmental Industrial Hygienists publishes a separate list of exposure limits, called Threshold Limit Values, many more restrictive than OSHA. Both guides are normally listed on MSDS for paint raw materials. The Permissible Exposure Limits set by OSHA are enforceable under the law.

Another OSHA function and policy is responsibility for the identification, classification and regulation of confirmed or suspected carcinogens. Carcinogens are placed under an emergency standard, and companies are required to reduce exposure immediately while specific standards are determined. Suspected carcinogens would be regulated, but less stringently. Such proposals and policies have caused much concern and industry/government controversy in recent years, in terms of the definition of carcinogens and testing procedures and also in such gray areas as threshold levels of hazardous exposure. Some of the raw materials that have affected the paint industry are asbestos, coal tar and 4,4 methylene dianiline (MDA), which is used in urethanes and epoxies.

In an effort to assure the health and safety of those employed in the paint and coating industry, the Occupational Health Task Force of the National Paint and Coatings Association developed and implemented a Hazardous Materials Identification System. Although OSHA had suggested the need for new hazardous label warning regulations, no federal system was devised. The NPCA determined that an in-plant labeling program would be beneficial and promoted Paint Industry Labeling. It defined a method for plant operational safety, which allows for compliance with governmental regulations while assuring employee protection by means of a uniform, visual, label communication code that warns of potential on-the-job hazards and circumstances.

A large label was developed to warn workers of the three major hazards associated with any given raw material: danger to health, flammability, and reactivity. Numerical ratings codes, from zero to four, denote the degree of hazard, from minimal to severe, in each of the three categories. In addition, an alphabetical code is provided to indicate the appropriate personal protection equipment such as gloves, boots, safety glasses, aprons and respirators. In 1995, the Occupational Health Task Force revised and updated the Hazardous Material Identification System labels, coding system, and training program in response to the evolution of the OSHA Hazard Communication Standard.

Worker rights are covered under the Hazard Communication Standard. The Emergency Planning and Community Right to Know Act, Section 311, and OSHA regulations require material producers to prepare and distribute Material Safety Data Sheets (MSDS) for their products. Expanded hazard and toxicity labeling is also required and is the focus of specific regulations in various parts of the country, such as California's Proposition 65.

OUTLOOK & FORECAST

Governmental regulatory influence on the paint and coatings industry has been pervasive since 1970 and will continue to impact well into the future. Virtually every aspect of paint and coating production and use must comply with an expansion of regulations. In addition to federal laws, the growth of regulatory activity by individual states, local government entities and foreign governments creates significant problems for many paint companies. They lead to different standards that can impact manufacturers who operate on an interstate, regional, national or international basis. In many instance, these differing regulations reflect that some states or localities have more severe problems or a heavier concentration of polluting industries and much more stringent regulations are therefore necessary. The continuing implementation of existing or newly enacted laws, and those currently under consideration for legislative update, will have an impact on paint and coating manufacturers for many years.

Some of the most important regulatory issues confronting paint manufacturers are discussed below:

• VOCs continue to be one of the most important challenges with regard to formulations for all classes of paints and coatings. The inclusion of Hazardous Air Pollutants or chemicals subject to control extends VOC limits to more compounds.

• Waste disposal and continuing implementation of both the Resource Conservation and Recovery Act and Superfund influence factory operations and implementation of rework or recycling plans. The Emergency Planning and Community Right To Know Act places additional burdens based on Superfund legislation. Sections 311 and 312 cover chemicals on site, and Section 313 covers chemical releases from a site.

• Worker right to know forces a high level of compliance.

• Heavy metals and lead have contaminated sites and present abatement challenges in existing structures.

The South Coast Air Quality Management District in California enacted new, more restrictive VOC regulations that took effect in 2006 for Architectural and Industrial Maintenance paints and coatings. In addition, the Ozone Transport Commission, comprised of twelve Middle Atlantic and Northeastern states and the District of Columbia adopted more stringent VOC emissions limits. The EPA is expected to adopt new limits similar to the Ozone Transport Commission's limits in 2011. Figure 1-24 lists the types of coatings

covered, the current national VOC limits, the Ozone Transport Commission limits, and the South Coast Air Quality Management District limits.

In addition to environmental regulations, paint and coatings manufacturers continue to face a variety of other problems, including right-to-know laws, class action suits, and leakage from underground storage tanks. Community and worker right-to-know laws can put a burden on small paint manufacturers. Class actions suits against producers of lead-containing paints applied years, or even decades, ago on the interiors of residential homes and apartments indicate the problems facing the industry. Producers of chrome and cadmium pigments likewise face challenges concerning hazardous waste residues at plant sites. Some issues have enormous potential liabilities, including cost of removal and/or remediation. Leaking underground storage tanks and groundwater contamination are also becoming a primary target for federal regulatory activity.

Over the years the paint and coatings industry has responded to regulatory pressure by product and process innovations. These achievements and continuing efforts, often at great expense, indicate that the industry is committed to protecting the air, water, and soil from pollution. Paint and coatings manufacturers can apply for "green" certification for their plants, processes, and products from a variety of groups.

Technology has progressed on many fronts, resulting in a variety of newer finishes and equipment to apply them, and in the reduction of emissions. The use of high-solids and water-based coatings has significantly reduced the amount of VOCs emitted and brings many coatings into compliance. However, technical limitations still exist for producing paint formulations that are eight high solids or water-based for certain applications, such as stains and finishes for wood furniture. Duplicating the performance and long-term protection properties the customer needs with the newer technologies has presented a challenge that coatings manufacturers and raw material suppliers are still struggling to meet.

Powder coatings are emission free and an ideal alternative to liquid paints. Besides emission control, advantages include cleanliness, transfer efficiency, safety, and ease of cleanup, as well as reduced solvent-related fire hazards and hazardous waste disposal. Their use is limited to items that can be electrostatically charged for application and baked in an oven to cure. Furthermore, color changes can be difficult.

Radiation cured coatings are mostly 100% solids liquid coatings and present few or no VOC emission problems. Their high cost of equipment and materials is the major disadvantage. They produce excellent coatings with high-volume production runs and fast line speeds. Problems remain in curing three-dimensional substrates, as these often possess areas shaded from the radiation, so use is limited to niche markets.

Electrodeposition coatings are water-based coatings applied by dipping a charged substrate. Utilization rates are high and coating application is extremely efficient. Use is growing for critical components for automobiles and appliances.

Electrostatic spray and HVLP (high volume, low pressure) spray equipment offer better transfer efficiency and reduced overspray, and hence better compliance with regulations. They are being used with conventional VOC-compliant liquid coatings for applications not suited to powder or radiation cure.

Plural component spray, when used with epoxies or polyurethanes, can reduce solvent emissions as well as personal exposure and waste generation.

The ongoing high cost of reformulation to reduce VOCs and HAPs, as well as the growing potential liability for hazardous residues, worker health, lead and other heavy metal residues and plant site cleanup, have forced many smaller paint companies to sell to larger regional or national producers. The number of plants and producers will continue to decline in the years ahead.

Steve McDaniel and Phil Phillips point out that the value of the paint and coatings industry had declined significantly since 1975 compared to the Consumer Price Index—a 38% decline for coatings in general and a 78% decline for powder coatings—in large part because consumers saw little difference in paint quality and let price guide their buying decisions. Only very high-performance coatings could command premium prices. The authors point to the need for coatings

Figure 1-24   VOC Emission Limits: Current National Rule, South Coast Air Quality Management District Rule, Ozone Transport Commission Rule, 2010

Coating Type	National Rule (g/L)	OTC (g/L)	SCAQM (g/L)
Flat Coatings	250	100	50
Non-Flat Coatings, Except High Gloss)	380	150	50
Industrial Maintenance Coatings	450	340	100
Sealers	400	200	100
Primers and Undercoaters	350	200	100
Stains (Interior)	550		250

Source: Created by Melissa Doak for Grey House Publishing.

companies to embrace innovation in order to emerge from the recession unscathed and revitalize the industry ("A Platform for Revitalizing the Paint and Coatings Industry, *Coatings World*, February 2010).

Karsten Danielmeier reported on several key events that made the paint and coatings industry a truly global one: economic reform and the opening of the Chinese market to the West, beginning in 1978; the growth of Dubai in the United Arab Emirates, beginning in the 1970s; and the 1989 fall of the Berlin Wall. These shifts created a global coatings market. Danielmeier suggests that paint and coatings manufacturers who shift their manufacturing operations to emerging economies in Asia, Brazil, Russia or Mexico will have the opportunity to grow exponentially. In addition, focusing research and development monies on "green" products—which will meet ever-stricter new and pending environmental regulation worldwide—proves another opportunity for growth.

In June 2010, *Paint & Coatings Industry* reported on a study from The Freedonia Group, Inc., which forecast that the worldwide demand for architectural paint was forecast to rise 3.6 percent each year through 2013. Although that growth was slow compared to the 2003 to 2008 period because of the slowdown in building and construction, the gains were nonetheless strong. The most rapid gains would take place in Asia, particularly in China and India, but North America was also forecast to see above-average growth through 2013 as the housing and mortgage crisis abated ("Architectural Paint Demand to Reach 22.8 Million Metric Tons, June 2010, p. 8). *Coatings World* reported that the Freedonia Group had forecast that the demand for paint and coatings in the United States would grow to $23 billion by 2012 ("Demand for Paints and Coatings to Grow in the U.S.," November 2009, p. 11).

FOREIGN TRADE

U.S. foreign trade in paints and coatings represents a minor portion of domestic production and supply. Since 1989, trade data for paints and coatings has been reported in kilograms rather than gallons. In addition, the Census Bureau reclassified and reduced the number of paint and coating classifications, making comparisons with earlier years difficult if not impossible.

The Census Bureau reports foreign trade of paints and coatings. Figure 1-25 shows exports, imports, and growth rates of coatings for 1980 through 2008 in dollars. Imports grew 21% annually between 1980 and 1990, 16.4% annually between 1990 and 2000, and 6.1% annually between 2000 and 2008. Exports grew 7.4% annually between 1980 and 1990, 11.2% annually between 1990 and 2000, and 4.8% annually between 2000 and 2008. Exports at $1,521.9 million in 2008 represented 6.4% of industry shipments.

Canada is the leading source of imports into the United States and also the leading importer of U.S.-produced paints and coatings. Mexico ranks as the second-largest importer, and has provided steady growth. Both Canada and Mexico have benefitted since the passage of NAFTA legislation with its increasing cross-border trade in OEM products. China, with its growing manufacturing base, has also become a rapidly growing market for U.S.-produced paints and coatings. Chinese industries benefit from its specific exclusion from the Kyoto Protocol on Global Warming. Manufacturers from all over the world are moving production to China since there will be no restrictions and energy consumption that might involve carbon dioxide emissions.

WORLD PRODUCTION AND MARKETS

The economic downturn that began in late 2008 had a significant impact on the global paint & coatings industry. While the industry grew at an annual rate of nearly 5% in terms of volume and 7% in terms of revenue between 2002 and 2007, a disastrous fourth quarter in 2008 essentially flattened growth that year and the industry contracted by 2%-3% in 2009. In that year, Orr & bass estimated global paint and coatings revenues at US$90 billion with a volume of 26 billion liters (Scott Detiveaux, "The State of the Global Coatings Industry," *Coatings World*, March 2010, pp. 58-61.) The market in 2010 was forecast to be essentially flat, with slow declines continuing in the United States and Europe and a "robust rebound" in Asia.

Canada

The Canadian Paint Association estimates that Canadian paint shipments were worth C$1.8 billion in 2008, down 6.3% from 2007 (Preparing for Tomorrow: Annual Report 2008, 2009, http://www.cdnpaint.org/uploads/pdf/x7E-CPCA-AnRep2008.pdf). Canada imported C$917 million in paint in 2008 and exported approximately C$400 million. Of the Canadian demand for paint, 42.9% of the total dollar amount of shipments and imports was for architectural paint, OEM coatings garnered 26.1% and automotive paint garnered 21% of the total value.

A large amount of the export shipments to Canada are primers, electrodeposition coatings, color coats and clear coats for use on automobiles made in Canada for U.S. manufacturers. The North American Free Trade Agreement (NAFTA) has allowed auto manufacturers to integrate Canadian motor vehicle production with that conducted in the United States.

Canadian paint manufacturing is dominated by U.S. and European paint manufacturers. A number of major paint companies have affiliates in Canada, including BASF, Benjamin Moore, DuPont, PPG, and Valspar. Sico is the leading independent Canadian producer.

Japan

Japan is the largest producer of paints and coatings in Asia. The Japan Paint Manufacturers Association collects and reports Japanese production in metric tons and sales in million yen. Data are reported for solvent and water-thinable paints and coatings, nitrocellulose lacquers, and also non-solvent products (powder coatings and traffic paints) and a miscellaneous category which includes insulating enamels and varnishes and all other miscellaneous types. Figure 1-26 lists Japanese production and sales of paints and coatings in 2009.

Figure 1-25 U.S. Foreign Trade in Paints, Selected Years, 1980-2008

Year	Imports (in millions of dollars)	Exports (in millions of dollars)
1980	$12.3	$179.0
1985	$28.8	$247.0
1990	$83.0	$364.0
1995	$228.4	$673.7
2000	$380.0	$1,049.8
2003	$452.9	$1,165.6
2007	$662.4	$1,511.9
2008	$609.2	$1,521.9

Source: Adapted from "Table 3. Shipments, Exports, and Imports of Selected Paints: 2008 and 2007," Current Industrial Reports M325F, U.S. Census Bureau, http://www.census.gov/manufacturing/cir/historical_data/ma325f/index.html (accessed November 30, 2009).

China

By 2009 the market for paint in China had reached 6.4 million tons ("Chinese Paint Market Reaches 6.4 Million Tons," *Paint & Coatings Industry*, October 2009, p. 8). As the market in China matured and foreign companies opened raw material and paint manufacturing plants in the country, China became increasingly self-sufficient and had negligible imports by 2009 excepting in high-tech types of coatings. Meanwhile, strong car sales in 2009 and 2010 made China surpass the United States as the world's largest automobile market—great news for automobile coatings manufacturers in that country (Tim Wright, "Automotive Coatings Market: China's Engine Heats Up, Ends U.S.'s Reign as Largest Auto Market," *Coatings World*, March 2010, pp. 36-38). In 2009, while the automotive OEM coatings market dropped 22% in North America, it grew by 5.1% in China. Multinational corporations like PPG, Valspar and DuPont expanded their presence in China as a result.

Figure 1-26   Japanese Production and Sales of Paints and Coatings, 2009

Sales & Production of Paints in Japan 2009   2010/2/15
(1 Jan 2009 to 31 Dec 2009)

Type of Paint			Production Volume		Sales			
			Volume (ton)	2009/2008	Volume (ton)	2009/2008	Value (Million JPY)	2009/2008
Nitro cellulose lacquers			14,815	76.8	10,157	79.8	5,427	83.7
Insulating enamel & varnishes			21,636	73.6	21,053	73.9	14,219	80.4
Synthetic resin base	Organic solvent type	Alkyd resin enamels & varnishes	17,968	63.7	19,499	69.8	9,559	75.0
		Alkyd resin base paints (Household and maintenance use)	24,696	91.5	24,339	88.6	9,187	92.7
		Alkyd resin base anticorrosive paints	37,617	72.9	40,589	76.7	10,053	80.5
		Thermo setting amino-alkyd enamels & varnishes	55,313	74.1	56,771	75.1	29,102	78.0
		Acrylic resin enamels & varnishes: Air drying type	41,189	78.3	43,637	79.6	31,926	77.9
		Baking type	27,427	70.3	27,959	71.1	22,575	70.7
		Epoxy resin base paints	131,895	93.2	152,157	97.1	58,288	93.7
		Urethane base paints	106,119	78.3	120,914	78.9	87,493	81.3
		Unsaturated polyester enamels & varnishes	13,532	75.4	13,493	79.7	8,565	80.3
		Ship's bottom paints	16,506	88.0	19,283	92.7	14,339	90.3
		Others	93,775	82.7	90,606	85.9	64,711	87.3
		Sub-total	566,037	80.9	609,247	83.3	345,795	83.1
	Water thinnable type	Emulsion paints	155,975	90.2	149,197	90.1	47,167	92.9
		With aggregates	29,120	65.6	41,225	82.5	7,284	85.7
		Water-borne coatings (including ED.)	140,418	72.4	138,888	72.2	51,299	72.6
		Sub-total	325,513	79.1	329,310	80.8	105,748	81.4
	solvent type	Powder coatings	25,962	74.6	31,182	78.5	21,719	79.7
		Road-marking paints	58,772	104.7	65,538	103.8	6,487	106.0
		Sub-total	84,734	92.4	96,720	93.3	28,207	84.1
	Synthetic resin base Total		976,284	79.5	1,035,277	81.7	479,749	82.4
Miscellaneous			76,383	84.4	135,705	87.6	63,088	86.8
Thinners			395,307	82.4	435,352	82.5	71,457	74.1
Grand Total			1,484,425	80.8	1,637,544	82.6	633,945	81.8

Source: Industrial Statistics, "Ministry of Economy, Trade and Industry"
Note: Continuity Coefficients are applied to calculate 2009/2008 figure.

Source: "Sales and Production of Paints in Japan 2009," Japan Paint Manufacturers Association, February 15, 2010, http://www.toryo.or.jp/eng/data-e/eng09.pdf (accessed June 13, 2010)

The paint industry is unequaled in the variety and specialization of its products due to market and customer requirements for appearance and performance of the paint on the substrate, as well as regulations regarding its manufacture, raw materials and use. As a result, a typical paint manufacturer produces hundreds of different formulations, each with raw materials that vary by type and volume, and which are subject to numerous quality control checks.

Paints have two basic components: the vehicle and the pigments. The vehicle normally contains volatile and non-volatile components. The non-volatile portion includes the film-forming binder, consisting of resins or drying oils and such modifying resins as surfactants or plasticizers. In most paints the water or organic solvent is the volatile portion, which maintains fluidity during manufacture, application and film formation. It then evaporates from the film during the drying and curing process. The pigment system contributes such properties as color, opacity, corrosion inhibition and reinforcement, as well as simply extending or filling the voids. Most paints consist of all components, although certain clear coatings have no pigment, and powder coatings are 100% solids with no volatile vehicle.

Film formation and curing is achieved by chemical or physical mechanisms. In most solvent and some water-based paints, cure occurs by a catalyzed reaction of the resin with atmospheric oxygen after evaporation of the solvent. Water-based emulsion or latex paints and solvent lacquers form a film by the coalescence of the binder and pigment as the water or solvent evaporates. Baking enamels and powder coatings are cured at temperatures greater than 90C by condensation or other chemical reactions. Such two-component coatings as urethanes and epoxies contain components that react chemically, both after mixing and in the applied film.

MATERIALS AND MANUFACTURING

HIGHLIGHTS

Raw Materials
■
Binders/Resins
■
Solvents
■
Pigments
■
Fillers and Extenders
■
Additives
■
Prices

Radiation curing, another mechanism, uses ultraviolet light or electron beams to initiate curing.

What raw materials a paint manufacturer uses depends on many factors, including price, capacity, producer profitability, and foreign trade. The supply and demand situation is extremely dynamic and subject to continuous and at times abrupt changes due to mergers, consolidations, and product shortages. Within the United States, the chemical industry underwent significant restructuring and consolidations between 1980 and 2010. When plants operate at 85-90% of capacity or better, the industry can be subject to supply disruptions whenever such problems as plant outage occur. Titanium dioxide and acrylic acid and its esters are examples of raw materials that occasionally are in tight supply.

However, beginning in the mid-1990s, the chemical industry began operating at only 75-80% of capacity; in 2010, *Chemical News & Intelligence* reported that globally, the chemical industry remained in a state of oversupply that drove down profits ("World Chemical Industry Still 15-20% Over Capacity," February 11, 2010). The globalization of the chemical industry and the corresponding growth in foreign trade is a relatively new factor that presents both challenges and opportunities for growth. In 2010, shortages of titanium dioxide and methyl methacrylate were leading to a global paint shortage—especially of highway paints, leading to delays in U.S. highway construction. Meanwhile, the price of the raw materials in short supply were rising quickly ("Tight Supplies of MMA, TiO2 choke U.S. Paint Market," *ICIS News*, June 4, 2010). The U.S. supply of acrylates was threatened in 2010 with production and equipment problems that forced suppliers to place sales controls on their products (Larry Terry, "The U.S. Acrylates Market is Constrained by Ongoing Operational Woes.

How will Pent Up Demand Be Satisfied?" *ICIS Chemical Business*, April 5, 2010).

The global economic downturn that began in the United States in 2008 adversely affected the paint and coatings industry as new housing starts and home buying were down sharply. The decline in demand for paints and coatings translated into a downturn in demand for raw materials. The market for resins in the paint industry was down as much as forty percent, according to *Coatings World* (Tim Wright, "Resins Market Panel Discussion," *Coatings World*, April 2010, pp. 34-37). Resins suppliers did not expect the paint market to recover until the second half of 2011, although the do-it-yourself architectural paint market was not as severely depressed as the industrial and automotive paint markets, as homeowners redecorated their homes rather than buying or building new homes.

In the first decade of the twenty-first century, the rising cost of crude oil and natural gas and their impact on energy and petrochemical feedstock prices also adversely affected prices of paint raw materials. Such products include ethylene, propylene, benzene and xylene that are used to manufacture coatings resins, including vinyl acetate, acrylic acid and acrylate esters, epoxies, alkyds and polyurethanes. Organic solvents produced from petroleum feedstocks, including the aliphatics, aromatics, and such oxygenated solvents as butyl alcohol, isobutanol, ethanol, ethyl acetate, methyl ethyl ketone, ethylene glycol, and glycol ethers were also severely impacted. In March 2010, the most widely used index of petrochemicals prices, the Platts Global Petrochemical Index, rose 10.4% in one month, good news in that it signaled a strengthening economy, but bad news for manufacturers who saw their profit margins shrink as raw materials prices rose markedly ("Platts Global Petrochemical Index Shows Petrochemical Prices Hit 6-Month Highs in

March, Worsening Margin Squeeze," *Biotech Business Week*, April 26, 2010, p. 4001).

RAW MATERIALS

In 2007, paints and coatings consumed raw materials and related items valued at $11,094 million, or 47.1% of factory sales of paints and coatings of $23,575 million. Water, consumed in emulsion paints and coatings, is excluded from the data. Paint materials include binders or resins, solvents, pigments, dyes, and colorants, fillers and extenders, and additives.

While overall production of paint has generally increased in recent decades, consumption of raw materials has not kept pace. Such consumption is influenced by modified product design to meet changing performance and application requirements. However, the reduced use of solvents is the major factor in slower growth due to: (1) the long-term shift to water-based architectural paints; (2) regulation that have caused the industry to alter the use and emission of solvents by formulating higher-solvent coatings; (3) an increase in powder coatings; and (4) growing use of solvent-free or low-VOC radiation cured coatings.

Figure 2-1 shows the value of materials consumed by kind as collected by the Economic Census. (The Census Bureau discontinued reporting data on the volume of materials consumed by industry in 1997.) Also included are industry consumption of containers, plastic parts and other materials. The data reflect consumption of materials put into production by establishments classified in this industry, and therefore include materials consumed in the manufacture of other products, and exclude paint materials consumed by companies who are primarily in other industries. The cost of materials reported consumed in 2007 was $12,039 million.

Due to material shortages at times, price increases, competition, and consumer tastes for product types and quality, the use of such pigments as TiO2 and binders and their relative use ratios are frequently adjusted by paint manufacturers. Between the top and bottom lines of latex paints, it is not unusual for the resin, pigment and extender contents to vary by three to four times as the water content increases from 50% to over 70%. As shown on labels, the content of vinyl acrylics and TiO2 can vary from less than 10% in lowest grades to over 25% in top of the line grades.

BINDERS/RESINS

Film formers, such as natural resins and drying oils and synthetic resins, are normally blended with solvents to form the coating vehicle. When dried or cured, they hold the elements of the film and adhere to the substrate. The film formers, or binders, are largely responsible for the physical properties and the resistance to degradation by the environment or during use.

Binders were originally produced from such natural materials as linseed, soybean, tung and tall oils. Cellulose ntrate or nitrocellulose, a synthetic resin, was first used in lacquers in 1923. Since then, a wide range of resins have been developed and used as binders in paints, sometimes in combinations. Oils and natural resins are slower to dry and less durable than synthetics, and are now relegated to minor consumption in architectural varnishes. In 2010 the vast majority of binders are synthetic resins with natural resins making up the balance. The resin industry suffered from the global economic recession as did the industries it served; the American Chemistry Council reported that in 2008, as a result of the global economic recession, the U.S. plastic resins industry produced 98.7 billion pounds, down 2.8% from 2008 and the lowest production figures

Figure 2-1 Materials Consumed by Kind by the Paints and Allied Products Industry, 1997, 2002, and 2007

MATERIAL CONSUMED	Delivered Cost (in thousands of dollars)		
	1997	2002	2007
RESINS and OILS			
Vegetable Oils		50,437	58,310
Plastic Resins			
Acrylics, latex		452,641	830,899
Acrylics, other		143,775	146,568
Alkyds	310,878	410,480	286,061
Epoxies	231,697	258,815	271,089
Polyesters	211,067	180,423	210,068
Urethanes and isocyanates	214,259	292,420	218,926
Vinyl	166,259	150,366	236,750
Other plastic resins	337,349	342,573	210,515
PIGMENTS			
Titanium Dioxide	820,235	867,843	937,916
Other Inorganic Pigments (chrome colors, zinc oxide, etc.)	203,935	327,193	341,237
Organic Pigments, Lakes, Toners	504,812	453,216	278,820
Minerals and Earths, ground or otherwise treated	359,882	330,159	295,934
SOLVENTS			
Hydrocarbons (toluene, xylene, etc.)	223,480	206,437	350,892
Alcohols (butyl, ethyl, isopropyl, etc.)	77,710	62,522	103,788
Ketones (acetone, MEK, MIBK, etc.)	106,616	101,878	169,190
Esters (ethyl acetate, butyl acetate, etc.)	103,401	135,973	134,199
Glycol and Glycol Derivatives	107,974	141,831	121,141
Other Solvents	134,021	188,988	143,655
OTHER CHEMICALS (additives, driers, modifers, etc.)	543,399	729,090	1,148,258
CONTAINERS			
Metal	395,559	375,982	459,274
Plastic	140,897	149,084	184,816
Other Containers	33,072	40,234	183,083
ALL Other Materials/Components/Parts/Containers/Supplies	1,754,838	1,567,109	1,594,399
Materials/Ingredients/Containers/Supplies Not Specified by Kind	1,936,387	1,401,230	2,113,996
TOTAL			

Adapted from "Manufacturing: Industry Series: Materials Consumed by Kind: 2002 and 2007," in Economic Census 2002, U.S. Census Bureau; and "ECO73113: Manufacturing: Industry Series: Materials Consumed by Kind for the United States: 2007," Economic Census 2007, U.S. Census Bureau, 2010, http://www.census.gov/econ/ (accessed May 30, 2010)

in a decade ("In Wake of Global Recession, U.S. Plastic Resins Industry Struggled to Regain Ground During 2009," http://www.americanchemistry.com/s_acc/sec_policyissues.asp?CID=996&DID=9827).

Older resins, including alkyds, epoxies and such thermosetting resins as the phenolics account for a decreasing proportion of overall consumption in the paint industry. Figure 2-1 shows that in 2007 manufacturers spent $286 million on alkyds, down from $410 million in 2002, and the amount spent on epoxies was up only slightly during that period. In contrast, manufacturers spent increasing amounts on vinyls, polyesters, and especially latex acrylics. (Information on the pounds of raw materials consumed is no longer available in the Economic Census.)

Synthetic Resins

Alkyds. Alkyds, one of the first synthetic resins consumed in paints and coatings, are still one of the major ingredients in paints. Some of the advantages of alkyd resins are low cost, an excellent range of properties, and versatility of use. However, alkyds are not as weather resistant as such newer synthetic resins as the acrylics, polyvinyl acetates, and urethanes. In addition, polyester resins, which are similar in chemical composition to the alkyds, have become more important, particularly in OEM product finishes. Oil-free polyesters, for example, are now preferred in OEM baking enamels, displacing super alkyd-melamine enamels.

In 2007, paint producers spent $286.1 million on alkyds, down significantly from five years before, when the industry spent $410.5 million on alkyds. (See Figure 2-1.) This represented a 30.3% decline over the five-year period. Other plastic resins, particularly latex acrylics and vinyl, had gained in importance during that period.

Alkyd resins are reaction products of polybasic acids or anhydrides and polyhydric alcohols modified for solubility and curing with oils and fatty acids. Although a wide variety of resins or polyhydric alcohols and polybasic acids are included in the general term "alkyd," the most important being the oil-modified glycerol phthalate resins. These are reaction products of glycerol and phthalic anhydride, modified with drying, semi-drying, or non-drying oils. In most oil-based alkyds, the glycerol is contained as the triglyceride of the fatty acid that constitutes the vegetable oil and not added to the resin formulation as a distinct addition ("In the 1920s Alkyd Resin Roars into Prominence," *Paint & Coatings Industry*, March 2004).

Phthalic anhydride is the leading dibasic acid used to manufacture alkyd resins. Other ingredients include maleic anhydride and fumaric acid, both of which provide unsaturation as crosslinking sites for drier catalyzed curing systems. Isophthalic acid, which is used primarily in water-based alkyds, ranks as the second-largest alkyd raw material.

Pentaerythritol is the most important polyol followed by glycerin. Such oils as soybean oil and linseed oil are used to make airdried alkyds. The oils, which are triglycerides of fatty acids, provide both unsaturation in the fatty acid and glycerol.

Architectural coatings take some 45% of all alkyds consumed in the U.S. paint industry, although alkyds have lost market share to acrylics in many formulations. The largest uses include such products as sash, trim, porch and deck enamels and semi-gloss and gloss paints, which together account for about half of alkyds used in architectural paints. Other uses are in flat house and wall paints, primers and sealers, varnishes and stains.

Long-oil, air-drying alkyds have very good elasticity and exterior durability, making them suitable for architectural trim paints.

Medium-oil and short-oil alkyds are combined with other resins to make fast air-drying colored finishes, and are popular in interior solvent-based flat, semi-gloss, and gloss enamels. In addition, alkyds are used in exterior flat paints, enamels for trim, porch, floor and decks, and barn and roof paints, and some varnishes and stains. Some alkyd resins are still used in low solids (less than 50%) coatings. However, VOC regulations are forcing reformulation into medium solids (50%-60%) and high solids (greater than 60%) coatings. (See Section 1 for more information on VOC regulations.)

Although some alkyds are found in high-solids or water-based paints, they have not gained significant market share. However, research and development of alkyd-latexes was on the upswing by 2010 because of tightening environmental regulation as well as consumer demand for more environmentally-friendly paints (Jamie Dziczkowski, "Alkyd Latexes: Opening the Door for a Greener Tomorrow," *Paint & Coatings Industry*, April 2010, pp. 66-69). Carl Sullivan of *Paint & Coatings Industry* reported in 2008 that research into water-based alkyds had produced a soy-based resin that had the same glossiness, adhesion, and stain-blocking capabilities of traditional solvent-based alkyds ("Waterborne Alkyds Break through the Performance Barrier," May 2008). Phil Phillips of *Coatings World* reported that the new alkyds might represent "the most significant and revolutionary technology to come along since introduction of latex paints in the 1950s" ("Alkyds: A New Life and They Remain Very Relevant," February 15, 2008). Consumption of alkyds may again rise as a result of these new technologies.

While alkyds resins are still used in OEM product finishes, consumption has declined by half over the past two decades. These finishes still account for 40% of alkyds used by the paint industry. The largest applications are machinery and equipment enamels and wood and metal furniture coatings. Small amounts are used in automotive and truck underbody parts, insulation varnishes, appliances parts, paper, film and foil coatings, and miscellaneous use in household goods, sports equipment, and railroad paints.

Special purpose coatings account for about 15% of all alkyds consumed in paint production. They are formulated into traffic paints, industrial maintenance paints, aerosols, auto refinishes, and marine coatings. Consumption has declined significantly over the past decade as alkyds are being replaced in traffic paints by water-based acrylic emulsions. EPA regulations limiting VOC emissions were a primary motivator for the switch to water-based systems.

Alkyds are also used as modifiers with other resins. These include urethane-alkyds, chlorinated elastomers (especially for traffic paints), nitrocellulose lacquers, silicone-alkyds and acrylic enamels.

More than 25 companies produce alkyd resins, including a few paint companies that manufacture for captive consumption. Major merchant suppliers are Akzo-Nobel Resins, BASF, Cook Composites & Polymers (CCP Polymers), Reichhold, Eastman Chemical (McWhorter), PPG Industries, and Valspar. Reichhold, Worlee, and DSM offer near-zero VOC alkyd emulsions. In 2008, Cytec announced it was increasing production capacities for water-based alkyds in the United States ("Cytec Increases Capacity for Waterborne Alkyds in the Americas," *Paint & Coatings Industry*, July 2008).

Polyester Resins. The resins are normally saturated polyesters of branched and cross-linkable resins, based on phthalic anhydride or other dibasic acids which are esterified with diols, triols or tetrols and used in either solvent or water-based paint. Carboxylic or hydroxyl functional solid polyesters serve as vehicles for polyester powder coatings. Hybridization of the polyester with epoxy resins and crosslinking with amino resins is also used in the formulation of coatings. They can be used to formulate high solids coatings reducing VOC emissions. In 2007, paint producers spent $210.1 million on polyester resins, up from $180.4 in 2002—an increase of 16.4%--but essentially stagnant from 1997, when the industry spent $211.1 million on polyester resins. (See Figure 2-1.)

Polyester coating resins are similar to alkyd resins with the exception that no unsaturation or oils are used in their preparation. They are primarily used in baking-type finishes and not in architectural or special purpose coatings.

The largest uses are in metal furniture, appliances, coil coatings and machinery equipment, which together account for about 70% of consumption. Other uses are in insulation varnishes, automotive primers, container finishes, wood furniture and auto parts.

Polyesters are also used in blends with acrylic resins, particularly in overprint varnishes for beer and beverage containers. Approximately two-thirds of polyesters go into solvent-based, thermosetting coatings with another one-third used in formulation of powder coatings together with urethanes, epoxies, and triglycidyl isocynurate (TGIC). Metal furniture, appliances, automotive OEM, coil coatings machinery and equipment, magnet wire and insulating varnishes consume large amounts.

Producers of polyester resins include almost all of the suppliers of alkyl resins mentioned previously. Both resins can be made in the same equipment.

Acrylic Resins. These products, first used by the paint industry in the early 1950s, are now the leading resin. Acrylic resins are mainly polymers and copolymers of acrylate and methacrylate esters. They exclude polyvinyl acetate resins that contain 12-15% butyl or 2-ethylhexyl acrylate as comonomers. In 2007, the industry spent $830.9 million on latex acrylic resins and an additional $146.6 million on other types of acrylic resins. The amount spent on latex acrylics had increased by 83.5% since 2007. Part of this increase was due to raw materials shortages and price increases, but the use of acrylic resins in paint formulations is increasing quickly.

Acrylic resins are thermoplastic, addition-type polymers that range in physical properties from soft, sticky semi-liquids to hard, machinable solids, depending on their composition and molecular weight. With the range of properties obtainable by varying the alcohol side chains, and the additional opportunities for variation afforded by the copolymerization of changing ratios of acrylates and methacrylates, it is possible to produce resins having almost any degree of flexibility and hardness without the need for plasticizers. Through copolymerization, cross-linking, and modification, hundreds of different types of acrylics can be produced, an advantage since they possess clarity, resistance to discoloration on aging and exposure to heat and ultraviolet light unsurpassed by any other resin. The outstanding properties of acrylic-based products are high gloss, excellent clarity and color retention. They also feature excellent hardness, impact strength and resistance to chemicals and environmental degradation.

Because of their versatility and excellent combination of properties, acrylic resins find many applications in the paint industry. The most important types are water-based acrylic resins. As emulsion polymers they are used in exterior and interior architectural latex paints, including flat, satin, and eggshell exterior house paints and gloss and semigloss trim paints.

Approximately 20% of acrylic coatings resins are used to manufacture OEM product finishes, mainly solvent- and water-based enamels, with small amounts used in acrylic emulsion paints. Automobile, truck and bus coatings, the largest uses, account for approximately 8% of consumption. They are used in pigmented acrylic base coats and clear top coats. Water-based acrylic enamels dominate as automobile manufacturers convert their painting operations to meet stringent VOC emission limitations mandated by the EPA.

Acrylic solvent-based enamels and latexes are used to coat machinery and equipment, including farm and construction equipment. They are also used as topcoats on computers, business machines and electrical equipment. Approximately 4% of acrylic resins are used in such formulations.

Containers and closures coatings take another 2% of all acrylic resins. Water-based acrylic enamels are used as the exterior white base coat for aluminum beverage cans and ends. Some solvent-based acrylic enamel is consumed as interior coatings on vegetable and fruit cans to provide a clean, white appearance. Acrylics coatings are resistant to physical and color degradation resulting from high temperature processing of the filled container. Wood furniture, mainly kitchen cabinets, consumes another 2%, mainly as acrylic emulsions. Water-based coatings with short drying times allow finished goods to be stacked quickly off the production line. However, water-based acrylic topcoats are not always compatible with solvent-based stains and sealers, a major problem.

Acrylic water-based and solvent-based paint systems are used to coat aluminum sheet in coil form on automated, high speed, continuous production lines. The coated coil is then cured in an oven and recoiled, ready for shipment to the end user. Painted aluminum sheet is used in the fabrication of products for the building, transportation, appliance and furniture industries. They are used to fabricate such diverse products as truck trailers, metal signs, aluminum siding, trim, gutters and downspouts. Acrylics are noted for their excellent appearance, high gloss and good ability to withstand weather. Metal fabricators that use coated coils do not need their own paint operations, thereby eliminating the need to comply with EPA HAP rules, a major advantage ("Manage the Margin with Prepaint," *National Coil Coatings Association Newsletter*, Summer 2009, http://www.coilcoatinginstitute.org/misc/article1_0727.aspx).

Special purpose coatings account for approximately 10% of consumption of acrylic resins. Traffic paints, where water-based acrylics have largely replaced solvent-based alkyds since 1990, is the largest use and also the fastest growing, although severe shortages of several raw materials in 2010 limited the production of the resins used in traffic paint ("Study Finds Raw Material Shortages Hitting Paint Supply," *Chemical Week*, June 25, 2010). Other applications include automobile refinishes, industrial maintenance coatings, aerosol finishes, basecoats for antique finishes, and in fluorescent and luminescent coatings.

Acrylic resins are used in powders and radiation-curable coatings. Acrylic powders are applied electrostatically to form a thin protective film on a variety of metal parts, including washing machines, oven parts, refrigerators, microwave ovens and aluminum extrusions. Radiation cured coatings are solvent-free materials that cure by ultraviolet light or electron beam radiation. They are used as overprint varnishes, and on prefinished wood, metal containers and wood furniture.

The supply of acrylate monomers has been tight in recent years due to the rapid growth in demand for acrylate polymers in a wide variety of end uses. Acrylates are one of the more versatile plastic polymers available and their physical and chemical properties make them attractive in many end use markets, a trend that is expected to continue well into the future. Expansions should insure adequate supplies for many years.

Rohm and Haas, a subsidiary of Dow Chemical, is the largest broad line producer of acrylics. Other suppliers include Akzo Nobel, BASF, Cook Composites and Polymers, DuPont Polymers, Eastman Chemical (McWhorter), PPG Industries, Reichhold, Sherwin-Williams and Valspar. Some coatings companies produce resins for both captive consumption and merchant sales.

Vinyl Resins. In 2007, the paints and coatings industry used vinyl resins worth $236.8 million, up 57.4% from five years previously. This group of resins includes homo and copolymers of polyvinyl acetate (PVAc), its derivatives, polyvinyl alcohol (water-soluble), polyvinyl butyral (solutions), polyvinyl formal (solutions) and polyvinyl chloride (PVC). Structurally, vinyls are substituted ethylenes in which one or two atoms are replaced by chlorine, acetate radicals, hydroxyl groups or an acetal ring structure. Coatings from vinyl resins have good resistance to chemicals and water, fire-retardant properties, lack of odor or taste, durability, quick drying properties, and low cost. The most important vinyl esters are the polyvinyl acetate copolymers and polyvinyl chloride based resins.

The principal copolymers are butyl acrylate and smaller amounts of 2-ethylhexyl acrylate. In addition, vinyl propionate and vinyl versatate are also consumed. Combining vinyl acetate with these comonomers yields resins with good durability, stability, flexibility, and scrub resistance. Almost all of the polyvinyl acetate copolymer resins consumed

in paints are used in the production of architectural paints with 70% of consumption going into interior paints and the balance into exterior coatings. Smaller amounts, or less than 2%, are used in OEM coatings for factory finished wood products.

Polyvinyl acetate copolymers dominate in interior flat paints where performance is less demanding the cost is lower than the acrylics. Acrylics are the leaders in interior gloss and semigloss applications because of their ability to form high gloss coatings and their resistance to water and moisture exposure. Producers of vinyl acetate-acrylate copolymer coatings resins include Air Products and Polymers, Dow Chemical, Eastman Chemical, H.B. Fuller, National Starch and Chemical, Reichhold, and Rohm and Haas.

Vinyl chloride coating resins are predominantly solution, dispersion or powder-coating resins. The solution resins are thinned with organic solvents and usually copolymers of vinyl chloride with vinylidene chloride or vinyl ethers and normally produced by suspension polymerization. The resins are used to produce solvent-based paints for marine coatings, strippable coatings, paper and film coatings, and other general industrial coatings.

The dispersion coatings are produced by emulsion polymerization. After polymerization is complete, the resins are dried and formulated into 1) plastisols, which are liquid dispersions of finely divided resin in plasticizers that form into a homogenous mass when heated, or 2) organosols, which are resins in plasticizers that contain a mixture of the solvents necessary to obtain proper application viscosity. In order to achieve extra hardness organosols generally contain less plasticizer than plastisols.

Powder coating resins are 100% non-volatile mixtures of resins, plasticizers, pigments and additives that resemble PVC plastisols.

They are usually applied by a fluidized bed process or by electrostatic spray techniques.

PVC-based resins are used in container and coil coatings in the form of organosols and plastisols, automobile OEM coatings, industrial maintenance and marine and general industrial coatings. About 10% of vinyl resin consumption consists of polyvinyl formal and polyvinyl butyral resins, which are used in industrial application. Producers of polyvinyl chloride resins for surface coatings are Dow Chemical, Formosa Plastics, and Occidental Chemical.

Epoxy Resins. Epoxies, first introduced in 1946, are thermosetting resins characterized by the presence of a highly reactive epoxide or oxirane ring. The majority, or about 65%, is condensation products of epichlorohydrin with Bisphenol A. The primary reactive group is the terminal epoxide group. The higher molecular weight and modified epoxies can have side hydroxyl groups. The maximum adhesion, durability and resistance properties of the epoxies are realized with the higher molecular weight, unmodified resins. Epoxy resins can be esterified with fatty or or rosin acids to produce a variety of air dry or baking vehicles.

Other types of epoxy resins include low-viscosity aliphatic glycidal ethers, and cycloaliphatic and novolac epoxies. Cycloaliphatic epoxies have better weather resistance. Epoxidized novolacs offer high chemical resistance. In either form, epoxies provide excellent adhesion, flexibility, toughness and chemical resistance. Their tendency to yellow and chalk in sunlight is the principal disadvantage of epoxies.

Epoxies require a curing agent in order for cross-linking or curing to occur. Most commonly the reaction occurs at the terminal epoxide group which reacts with compounds containing active hydrogens such as amines, amides, phenols and acids. Cross-linking can also occur at hydroxyl groups. Most curing agents for epoxies are co-reactants. Various types of amines and polyamides are the most common curing agent.

The leading use for epoxy resins is in high-performance coatings (Elvira Greiner, Thomas Kaelin and Kazuaki Nakamura, "Epoxy Resins: Abstract," SRI Consulting, November 2007, http://www.sriconsulting.com/CEH/Public/Reports/580.0600/). In 2007, paint and coatings companies spent $271.1 million on epoxies. (See Figure 2-1.) Epoxies for non-coatings, or "structural" applications, account for less than 50% of U.S. production.

The major end uses for the coatings include primers and barrier coats for high-performance industrial maintenance paints (25%), linings for cans, drums and closures (13%), primers for automobiles (13%), powder coatings (28%), and coil coatings and general industrial products (10%). Epoxies are used as the primary resin in electrocoat primers, both anodic and cathodic types, for automobiles and appliances, and also in primers for coil coatings, appliances, and machinery and equipment. They are the principal resins in primers and special purpose coatings for chemical plants and refineries, storage tanks and pipelines, bridges, ocean-going marine vessels and offshore exploration rigs and auxiliary equipment. They are used in zinc-rich primers and coal tar epoxy coatings.

Epoxy-silane hybrids are a new type of "durable" epoxy for exterior use on commercial and industrial structures. Other epoxy hybrids such as epoxy polyester hybrids are used for powder coatings. Acrylated epoxy oligomers and cycloaliphatic epoxides, used in radiation curable coatings, represent a small percentage of consumption.

Solid epoxy powders account for about 28% of the metal decoration and industrial finish powder consumption. Principal uses are pipe coatings, general metal coatings, insulating varnishes, and miscellaneous automotive applications.

As high solids and water-based grades of paints continue to expand, epoxies are expected to grow. As metal fabricators are under pressure to reduce volatile organic compounds, powders are forecast to increase at 3.5% a year between 2008 and 2013 (Tim Wright, "Powder Coatings Demand in U.S. to Reach 445 Million Pounds in 2013," *Coatings World*, July 2, 2009). The first generation of water-based epoxies still had VOC content of 200-350 g/L. Because states are adopting increasingly stringent regulations, the use of these epoxies is limited. As of 2010, however, a low-VOC epoxy had been developed that offered high gloss, fast-cure, and durability (Wendy Zhao, "Zero-VOC, Water-Based Epoxy Topcoat," *Paint & Coatings Industry*, March 2010, pp. 58-65).

Dow Chemical, Hexion, and Huntsman Advanced Materials are basic suppliers of epoxy resins.

Polyurethanes (PU). In 2007, the paint and coatings industry consumed urethanes and isocynates with a value of $218.9 million. *Paint & Coatings Industry* reported that approximately 66,900 tons of polyurethane dispersions were produced in North America in 2009, with approximately 43,000 tons being used in industrial coatings. Growth in the industrial coatings sector was expected to be about 4.5% per year between 2010 and 2014, as the industry looks for alternatives to solvent-based coatings ("Global Polyurethane Dispersions Market Set for Growth," January 2010).

Polyurethanes are available in a wide variety of types. Coatings account for a small amount of polyurethane production overall—approximately 9% in the United States and Canada--with the majority share going into such plastics as rigid and flexible foam products used in furniture, mattresses, and automobiles (Christine Esposito, "Polyurethane Power," *Coatings World*, August 2005). The 2008 End-Use Market Survey on the Polyurethanes Industry found that production of polymethanes in the United States declined by 7.7% annually in 2007 and 2008. However, declines in the paint and coatings industry were less severe than in other end uses ("Polyurethane Market Evolution in United States and Canada; Mexican Polyurethane Industry Continues to Grow," *Paint & Coatings Industry*, April 2010).

PU is used to produce two component coatings, water-based systems, powder coatings, urethane alkyds, moisture cured coatings, lacquers and UV coatings. Two-component systems coatings are the largest end use for urethane resins followed by water-based systems and powder coatings. Industry professionals cited the low VOC-content, fast application and cure times, and their versatility as key factors in polyurethanes popularity (Mike Agosta, "Polyurethane Technology," *Coatings World*, June 2002.)

Products are formed by the reaction of isocyanates and polyols, and provide good corrosion resistance, film strength, durability, abrasion resistance and high gloss. The ratio of polyols to isocyanates is one to one. Polyols include hydroxyl terminated acrylics, polyester and polyether polyols. Polyester polyols are hydroxyl terminated polyesters made from a variety of dibasic acids and glycols with slightly more glycol than acid so that the resultant polyester has hydroxyl end groups. Polyethers are usually produced from the reaction of propylene oxide with a trifunctional or tetrafunctional polyhydroxy compounds to form a hydroxyl terminated polyether.

Both aliphatic and aromatic types of isocyanates are used to manufacture PU.

Hexamethylene diisocyanate (HMDI) is the most important of the aliphatic diisocyanates. Others include isophorone diisocyanate and hydrogenated dicyclohexyl methane 4,4'-diisocyanate, which is produced by hydrogenating methylene diphenyl diisocyanate (MDI). Aromatic diisocyanates include toluene diisocyanate (TDI) and methylene diphenyl diisocyanate. Aliphatic isocyanates are preferred for topcoat applications since they are more resistant to weathering than aromatic isocyanates, especially in combination with such durable polyols as acrylics.

Nonreactive urethanes, either air drying solvent-based or water-based, are used in architectural and other coatings. Architectural coatings account for 15% of urethane consumption in paints and coatings. Reactive one- and two- component urethane resin systems are used in OEM product finishes, particularly automobile coatings, wood finishes, and coil coatings. OEM finishes account for an estimated to 22% of urethane consumption by the paint industry. Special purpose coatings, the largest type with 50%, include auto refinishes, anticorrosion coatings, and general industrial maintenance. Approximately 10% of urethanes is consumed in powder coatings resins and radiation cured coatings.

Reactive urethane coatings take over two-thirds of all urethanes. Polyester types represent another one-third and consumed in architectural coatings, particularly high-gloss finishes, floor and gym coatings, and wood finishes. Water-based urethane technology is improving and its market growing. Moisture cured urethanes (ASTM Type II) are single package materials, usually aromatic isocyanates, which cure by reaction with moisture in the air. They tend to be surface-tolerant and find use in a variety of maintenance coating applications for steel structures.

Other OEM markets for urethanes include flexible plastics, wood furniture, wood flat stock, coil, aircraft, and machinery equipment. Some 28% of consumption is urethane alkyds, which are used mainly in architectural coatings. Polyurethanes are one of the leading resins used in bridge coatings, stain and graffiti resistant coatings and marine hull and topside paints. Auto refinishes are also an important outlet for urethane coatings. The remaining consumption is in a small quantity of urethane lacquers. Polyurethane powder coatings, generally polyester based, account for about 23% of powder coatings. Architectural paints, industrial maintenance and other special purpose coatings account for more than one-half of consumption of urethane resins.

Lanxess AG is the leading supplier of most types of isocyanates and of polyester polyols used by the industry. Other producers include Akzo Nobel, Cook Composites and Polymers, DuPont Polymers, Lyondell, and Eastman Chemical.

Amino Resins. The paint industry consumes aminos based on the reaction of melamine or urea with formaldehyde. Amine-functional resins are used primarily to cross-link such resins as acrylics, epoxies and polyesters. Elevated temperatures on baking allow the hydroxyl functionality on the amino resin to react. About 89% of amino resins used for this purpose are melamine-based and 11% are urea-based. Urea-formaldehyde resins are lower in cost, have good adhesion, and yield excellent white enamels with moderate baking temperatures. Melamine-formaldehyde resins are more expensive, faster drying, undergo less shrinkage during cure, have better color and gloss retention, and in elevated temperature applications have superior hardness, mar resistance, and better durability.

Automotive OEM coatings are the largest outlet for amino resins, followed by metal containers, metal furniture, coil coatings, machinery, appliances, general metal finishes, and overprint varnishes. Among the resins categories with which they are reacted, about one-third of the aminos are used with acrylics, followed by epoxies with one-fourth and polyesters with one-fifth. Many liquid epoxy OEM and special purpose coatings are cured at ambient temperatures with amine-functional curing agents.

Other Resins. Other synthetic resins consumed by the paint industry include such cellulosics as nitrocellulose, chlorosulfonated polyethylenes, chlorinated hydrocarbons, fluorocarbons, inorganic and ethyl silicates, petroleum hydrocarbon resins, phenolics, polyterpenes and gilsonite. The Census Bureau reported in the 2007 *Economic Census* that the paint and coatings industry spent $210.5 million on "other plastic resins" in that year. (See Figure 2-1.)

Cellulosic resins, principally nitrocellulose, are used in lacquers for wood furniture, paneling, aerosol paints, nail polishes and auto refinishes. Consumption will continue to decline due to the inability to formulate high solids coatings with low VOCs. Other cellulosic resins include cellulose acetate butyrate, hydroxyl ethyl cellulose and hydroxypropyl cellulose, all of which often serve as additives rather than as primary vehicles.

Chlorosulfonated polyethylene has largely displaced chlorinated rubbers, which are no longer produced domestically. A small amount is still used, principally for industrial maintenance coatings, swimming pool paints and pipe coatings. The principal uses were traffic paints. However, solvent-based traffic paints are losing market share to water-based products, particularly acrylics.

Ethyl silicates serve as the vehicle in inorganic zinc coatings and are widely used as primers for new structural steel in heavy industrial and marine construction. Inorganic zincs are topcoated with coal tar, epoxy and polyurethane to provide excellent corrosion protection in the most severe environments. They thus provide electrochemical protection to steel through the sacrificial action of the metallic zinc.

Petroleum resins, also referred to as hydrocarbon resins, comprise polymerization products of cracking streams isolated from petroleum by fractional distillation. They include cycloaliphatics, courmarone-indene resins, vinyl aromatics, and isoprene-rich fractions. Hydrocarbon resins are being used in products that are competitive with coal tar epoxies without its negative aspects. Principal applications include tank and deck coatings, packaging, and as tackifiers in adhesives.

Gilsonite is a natural hydrocarbon resin that can be used in metal parts for protection of auto body undercoats, steel structures, steel drums and seagoing cargo containers.

Phenolic resins serve either as modifiers for epoxies and other resins or as coating vehicles. The principal applications are metal container coatings, particularly interior coatings, pipe coatings, insulating varnishes and magnet wire coatings.

Silicone resins are used in low-volume but high-value coating products. Hybrids as silicone-acrylic, silicone-alkyd or silicone-polyester are also used in coating systems. Applications include heat-resistant industrial maintenance coatings, insulating varnishes, marine topcoats and coil coating systems. A newer polysiloxane technology is a high-build, durable topcoat that is finding uses in industrial maintenance applications. Adhesion of topcoats to silicone/siloxane or its hybrids tends to be poor.

A number of other resins are used to manufacture paints and coatings, mostly low-volume, high-value materials used for specialty applications. These include polytetrafluoroethylene (PTFE), polydifluoroethylene PTFE, and polyvinyl acetals. PTFE is formulated together with polyamidoimide into slurry, which is utilized to produce nonstick cookware surfaces. PTFE and several of its co-polymers are formulated into coil coatings and architectural coatings. Polyvinyl acetals, including polyvinyl formal and polyvinyl butyral, are utilized for magnet wire coatings.

Some coal tar coatings are formulated with epoxy resins to improve film hardness and chemical resistance, as well as reducing the tendency to sag and creep. Inexpensive bitumens such as asphalt and coal tar, used for waterproofing coatings and driveway sealers, are not included in the *Guide.*

Oils and Natural Resins

As stated earlier, consumption of oils and natural resins has declined to under 2% of all binders for paints. Such oils as soybean, linseed and tall oil fatty acids are used to manufacture alkyd resins. Other oils such as castor oil, tung oil, safflower oil, coconut and fish oil are consumed in small amounts in some specialized alkyd resins as drying resins.

In most cases, the oil provides both unsaturation in the fatty acid portion of the oil and glycerin as a tri-functional polyhydroxy ingredient. The oils and tall oil fatty acids can be used interchangeably if prices are subject to excessive volatility. The declining use of alkyd resins and the overall tendency to shorter oil alkyds, baked enamels, water-based and high solids coatings has led to a major decline in consumption of these materials over the past decade.

SOLVENTS

Both organic solvents—those that contain carbon--and water are used in large quantities in paints and coatings as the carrier or dispersion medium for nonvolatile binders, pigments, colorants and other additives that constitute the finished coating. They regulate viscosity as well as solubility and compatibility of the various components. The resultant low viscosity liquid can easily be applied and dried leaving a paint film that serves as protection, decoration, or both. Solvents also influence such application properties as consistency, flow, film build, potlife, and drying time.

Water is used in acrylic and vinyl latex paints to disperse the thermoplastic binders and emulsifying agents. Organic solvents dissolve oil or thermosetting resin-based products, and, as wash solvents and as thinners, are used to clean manufacturing equipment.

Solvents, available in a wide variety of different types, are characterized according to their strength, evaporation rates, solubility parameters and conductance ability. A list of major solvents is given in Figure 2-1. Almost all solvents used in the United States are one of two types—hydrocarbon or oxygenated solvents (American Solvents Council of the American Chemistry Council, "Formulating Fundamentals for Coatings," *Paint & Coatings Industry*, October 2006).

In 2007, paint companies spent some one billion dollars on organic solvents, including products that serve as coalescents in water-based paints. (See Figure 2-1.) Paints are one of the largest applications for solvents. Due to the increased use of water-based, high-solids, and solvent-free coating systems, consumption continues to decline. The Freedonia Group predicted that demand for chemical solvents would rise less than one percent per year between 2008 and 2012 in large part because manufacturers were continually reducing the VOC content of their products ("Freedonia Group Releases New Solvents Study," *Paint & Coatings Industry*, July 8, 2008).

Hydrocarbon Solvents

HAP emissions rules have necessitated the replacement of many hydrocarbon solvents in paints and coatings; the regulatory impact and a changing marketplace have caused the use of these solvents to decrease. Further declines are expected as manufacturers find better replacements (Jeannie Ramey, "Replacing HAP Solvents: Xylene and Toluene," *Paint & Coatings Industry*, April 2006). In 2007, the U.S. paint and coatings industry consumed hydrocarbon solvents valued at $350.9 million.

There are two types of hydrocarbon solvents, aliphatic and aromatic. Aliphatic hydrocarbons represent about 16% of organic solvents consumed by the U.S. paints and coatings industry. Included are mineral spirits, odorless mineral spirits, VM&P naphthas and pentane, hexane and heptanes. Aromatics account for about 24% of all organic solvents. They are comprised of the mixed xylenes and small amounts of toluene. Toluene finds wide application with many synthetic resins for coatings. Its rapid rate of evaporation makes it desirable in applications in which quick drying is essential. Paint applications represent less than 5% of toluene consumption. Xylene possesses high-solvent power for most synthetic resins, including epoxies. Paint consumes less than 5% of domestic xylene production. It has a slower evaporation rate than toluene and used where slower dry is required. Benzene is not used as a solvent in paint due to its toxicity.

OEM finishes, the largest application for hydrocarbon solvents, take slightly less than half of volume, excluding those used as thinners. Aromatics account for two-thirds of consumption. Wood furniture and fixtures, metal furniture and fixtures, and machinery and equipment, automotive, metal containers, coil coatings, magnetic media, overprint varnishes, general metal finishing and coatings for plastics are major consumers. Consumption is declining as organic solvents are classified as volatile organic compounds (VOCs) and in many cases as hazardous air pollutants (HAPs) and thus subject to emission limitations.

Architectural coatings, primarily exterior solvent-based paints, account for about one-third of all hydrocarbons consumed by the paint industry. They serve primarily in coatings based on alkyd resins. The acrylics, urethanes, epoxy, polyesters and cellulosics rank as the next leading uses for hydrocarbon resins. Semi-gloss and gloss enamels, flat paints, varnishes, and stains are the dominant uses for aliphatic hydrocarbons, although only minimal amounts are consumed. Controlled solvent evaporation is essential for spray, roller and brush application of architectural paints and coatings. In addition to direct use as a solvent in oil-based architectural coatings, such organic solvents as the glycol ethers are used as coalescing agents in water-based architectural paints and coatings.

Special purpose coatings account for the balance of hydrocarbon solvents. Aerosols, auto and machinery refinishes, and maintenance coatings are the largest consumers of both aliphatic and aromatic hydrocarbons. Hydrocarbon solvents for traffic marking paints have been eliminated as acrylic emulsion paints have nearly removed solvent-based paints in this application.

Oxygenated Solvents

These solvents, accounting for approximately 58% of the organic solvents, include ketones, glycols, glycol ethers and glycol esters, alcohols and esters. Oxygenated solvents are strong, polar compounds that have high solvent power for many organic polymers and resins. With some exceptions, paints and coatings account for only a small percentage of U.S. consumption.

Over two-thirds of oxygenated solvents are used in OEM coatings and finishes with the balance consumed in special purpose coatings and architectural coatings. They are also used in paint thinners and cleaners. Oxygenated solvents permit higher solids content than is possible with hydrocarbons and have higher solvency, lower viscosity, and well-defined evaporation rates. Blends of oxygenated solvents are commonly used in OEM and special purpose formulations to provide fast evaporation during spraying, slightly slower evaporation to allow the film to coalesce, and even slower evaporation to control viscosity while the binder cures by either chemical or thermal means. Consumption of oxygenated solvents will continue to grow so long as they maintain their reputation of being more environmentally friendly than the hydrocarbon or chlorinated solvents.

Ketones are leading oxygenated solvent used by the paint and coatings industry; in 2007, the industry consumed ketones valued at $169.2 million, up 66.1% from 2002. (See Figure 2-1.) Methyl ethyl ketone (MEK) is the leader. Other ketones include methyl isobutyl ketone (MIBK) and acetone. Acetone has been removed from EPA's VOC list in applications where its strong solvent characteristics as well as its extremely fast evaporation rate can be tolerated. The major applications are such OEM product finishes as automobiles, metal containers, especially in can liners, machinery equipment finishes. They are also used in some architectural and industrial maintenance paints and coatings.

Glycols, glycol ethers and glycol esters are also widely used in paints and coatings; in 2007, the industry spent $121.1 million on these solvents, down 14.6% from 2002. (See Figure 2-1.) The glycol ethers are chiefly made from ethylene glycol (EG) and propylene glycol (PG), diethylene glycol (DEG) and dipropylene glycol (DPG). Glycol ethers include ethylene glycol monomethyl ether (EGME), ethylene glycol monobutyl ether (MEBE), propylene glycol monoethyl ether (PGME) and propylene glycol monobutyl ether (PGBE). Ester derivatives of the glycol ethers include ethylene glycol methyl ether acetate and ethylene glycol monobutyl ether acetate, propylene glycol monomethyl ether acetate and propylene glycol monobutyl ether acetate. The propylene glycol ethers have been replacing the ethylene glycol ethers since some of them are believed to be carcinogenic. The glycol ethers are used in both solvent and water based paints using organic binders. The glycol ethers are soluble in water and also dissolve the paint resins. They are also used as coalescing agents in emulsion coatings.

Use of alcohol solvents have been increasing, as they are considered a "green" alternative to other solvents ("Another Look at Green Solvents," *Paint & Coatings Industry*, October 2, 2000). The paint and coatings industry spent $103.8 million on butanol, isobutanol, ethanol, propanol and ethanol and other alcohols in 2007, up 66% from 2002. (See Figure 2-1.) These solvents are used in all types of paints including architectural, OEM finishes and industrial maintenance coatings with wood finishes being a major consumer.

The paint and coatings industry spent about $134.2 million on esters in 2007, an amount that had remainded fairly steady since 2002. (See Figure 2-1). The principal esters are ethyl acetate, butyl acetate, isobutyl acetate and isobutyl acetate. Tert-butyl acetate is also used as a replacement for solvents that are classified as hazardous air pollutants (HAP). Ethyl and butyl propionate are also being consumed in paints and coatings.

Less than 2% of consumption of solvents comes from other low-volume chemicals, including such ethers as dimethyl ether, chlorinated hydrocarbons, nitropropanes, isophorone, tetrahydrofuran, n-methyl pyrrolidone and cresylic acid. However, exemption from VOC regulations is weighed against other possible risks. Methylene chloride is a carrier in aerosols and as a paint stripper.

Many companies supply solvents. Hydrocarbons are produced at oil refineries and distributed to industry. Some oil companies and several basic chemical companies produce oxygenated solvents.

Organic solvents are forecast to continue to continue their decline over the long term, due to VOC and HAPS regulations as well as safety concerns. The continued development of high solids coatings systems, powder coatings and UV cured coatings will also reduce the demand. Stronger solvents, such as aromatic hydrocarbons and oxygenated solvents, will mitigate the decline. The need for coalescing agents in water-based coatings will slow the decline of consumption of organic solvents.

PIGMENTS

Pigments, the third major group of raw materials, include inorganic and organic colorants, extenders and fillers, and such functional pigments as corrosion inhibitors, metallic flakes, and fluorescent materials. In 2007, the paint industry consumed pigments valued at $1.9 billion, down from $2 billion in 2002. (See Figure 2-1.)

Pigments are powders of fine particle size used in virtually all paints, except clears. Pigments add color and opacity to the coating, thus hiding the substrate. They also increase durability by screening out harmful light rays, controlling the transmission of moisture and gases through the film, imparting desirable mechanical properties and controlling such properties as corrosion inhibition, chalking and gloss. They are also used to control flow characteristics, improve scrub resistance and reduce formulation costs. The

characteristics transferred to the coating depend on the nature of the pigment and the concentration in which the pigment is used.

As stated, the primary purpose of pigments is to hide the substrate by preventing the transmission of light. Colored pigments accomplish this to a greater or lesser degree, by absorbing some of the light rays and reflecting others. However, white pigments absorb relatively little light so that their hiding power depends primarily on their ability to scatter and reflect the incident light. In turn, this depends on the particle size and the difference in refractive index between the pigment and the surrounding medium. The greater the refractive index of the pigment, the better its hiding power, if such other factors as particle size and shape are equal.

Color pigments include a wide variety of natural and synthetic materials, both organic and inorganic. The chief properties that govern the usefulness of a color pigment are: color (hue and brightness); durability (lightfastness, heat resistance, chemical resistance); bleeding resistance; tinting strength; and hiding power, or in some instances, transparency. White pigments are used heavily as a colorant for light hues and in most tints.

Approximately 40% of paint pigments, fillers and extenders is colors categorized as prime white pigments, colored and black inorganic pigments, and organic pigments. The number of white pigments having good hiding power is limited. The principal types still used are titanium dioxide in both the anatase and rutile forms and zinc oxide. Basic carbonate white lead, silica white lead, and antimony oxide have been largely discontinued due to health concerns.

Surface treatments are used to improve the wetability of the surface of the pigment particle. Either an aluminum oxide or silica coating, or an alumina coating can be used to help improve wetting and dispersion and inhibit coagulation.

White Pigments

Titanium dioxide (TiO_2), the largest paint pigment, is the most widely used paint pigment and accounts for nearly all white pigments. The paint industry consumed TiO_2 valued at $937.9 million in 2007 (see Figure 2-1), up 8.1% from 2002, largely because of rising prices ("Titanium Dioxide Producers Annouce Global Price Hikes," *Chemical Week*, May 29, 2009; "TiO_2 Producers Up Prices," *Chemical Week*, December 18, 2009). As Figure 2-2 shows, apparent consumption of TiO_2 decreased from 1,150,000 metric tons in 2000 to 1,130,000 metric tons in 2005 and still further to 979,000 metric tons in 2007 and only 800,000 metric tons in 2008. This was a drop in apparent consumption of 30.4% between 2000 and 2008, an average decrease of 3.4% per year. Paints take an estimated 52% of domestic consumption of TiO_2, with architectural coatings using 58% of this, OEM finishes 33%, and special purpose coatings the balance.

Titanium dioxide is a very stable pigment, soluble only in hot concentrated sulfuric acid, and inert to all the binders or resins used in paints and coatings. Its high refractive index produces the highest hiding power of all pigments. Titanium dioxide is a hydrophilic pigment and as such may present difficulties in dispersing in oil based paints.

TiO_2 pigments are shipped in 50-pound-bags, bulk bags (1 ton), 20 ton lots, and as dispersions in water (75% solids). Current levels of loading average about 0.88 lb per wet gallon.

When TiO_2 is in short supply or prices are high, some paint manufacturers adjust formulations by using TiO_2 spacers or replacements, such as calcined clay, followed by calcium carbonate, opaque polymers, and silica. Other materials utilized include buff TiO_2, hollow spheres, low-micron talc, barium sulfate or hydrous clay. In 2010, reduced inventories and production problems had led to shortages in TiO_2 worldwide.

Domestic production capacity for titanium dioxide in 2008 was 1,350,000 metric tons. The largest producer is DuPont. Other large producers include (20%) Cristal Global, and Huntsman-Kronos.

Figure 2-2 U.S. Production and Consumption of Titanium Dioxide, Selected Years, 1980-2008 (in metric tons)

Year	Production	Shipments	Imports	Exports	Stocks	Apparent consumption
1980	660,000	664,000	88,500	41,500	75,500	623,000
1985	783,000	862,000	178,000	93,600	51,500	831,000
1990	979,000	1,120,000	148,000	202,000	61,700	925,000
1995	1,250,000	1,330,000	183,000	342,000	120,000	1,080,000
2000	1,400,000	1,470,000	218,000	464,000	141,000	1,150,000
2005	1,310,000	1,420,000	341,000	524,000		1,130,000
2006	1,370,000	1,400,000	288,000	581,000		1,080,000
2007	1,440,000	1,480,000	221,000	682,000		979,000
2008	1,350,000	1,390,000	183,000	733,000		800,000

Compiled by D.A. Buckingham (retired) and J. Gambogi. Data are calculated, estimated, or reported. See notes for more information.

Source: Adapted from "Manufacturing: Industry Series: Materials Consumed by Kind: 2002 and 2007," in Economic Census 2002, U.S. Census Bureau; and "ECO73113: Manufacturing: Industry Series: Materials Consumed by Kind for the United States: 2007," Economic Census 2007, U.S. Census Bureau, 2010, http://www.census.gov/econ/ (accessed May 30, 2010)

The chloride process for making titanium dioxide now dominates U.S. production, having replaced the more expensive and environmentally damaging sulfate process. As the paint industry increases consolidation and globalization, the TiO_2 markets are consolidating, to satisfy demand by multinational paint companies.

Paint & Coatings Industry reported on a study on global demand for titanium dioxide. The study found that demand for the pigment will grow at an average of 3.5% between 2010 and 2016, reaching 6.8 million tons in 2016 ("Supply and Demand Balance Crucial to TiO_2 Industry," October 2009).

Carbon Black

Carbon black is a very finely divided, essentially non-porous type of carbonaceous material that is produced in a precisely controlled pyrolitic process. It is used in paints and coatings as a coloring agent, alone or in combination with white pigments to yield a range of grays. It is also used in conductive and anti-static paints. Tires and mechanical rubber goods take 88% of production, with printing inks consuming most of the remainder. Major producers of carbon black include Cabot Corp., Columbian Chemicals, Sid Richardson Carbon, Continental Carbon, Engineered Carbons and Evonik Industries.

Color Pigments

Color pigments include natural (inorganic earth colors) and synthetic inorganic and organic pigments. The impact of environmental and health and safety regulations is critical to all inorganic coloring pigments. Generally, use of any pigment containing lead, chromium (IV), cadmium, or any other heavy metal has greatly declined since 1990.

Iron oxides, the most important inorganic pigments, can contain a combination of siliceous materials and small amounts of oxides of manganese, aluminum, calcium and/or magnesium. Iron oxides can either be used in natural form or produced synthetically. Iron oxides are available in a variety of earth tones, such as red, yellow/orange and brown pigments.

Natural red iron oxides are obtained from ores high in hematite content and natural yellow iron oxides come from limonite ores. They lack brilliancy but are widely used for their low cost, durability, and excellent non-bleeding properties. However, because of their variable natural composition, they have, to a great extent, been replaced by synthetic iron oxides that offer greater uniformity, strength and brilliance.

Synthetic iron oxides with high purity are available as single oxides or blends of iron oxides in a range of colors that include yellow, orange, tan, red, maroon, brown and black. Synthetic red iron oxides are produced by thermal decomposition of ferrous sulfate followed by oxidation. Synthetic yellows are manufactured by precipitation of ferrous hydroxide followed by oxidation. Synthetic brown iron oxides are mixtures of synthetic reds, blacks and yellow/orange. The shade of the pure colors depends on the particle size and shape and their composition. The iron oxides are chemically resistant, inert, non-fading, bake resistant, non-bleeding, and low in cost. They are widely used in applications that require durability rather than brightness of color.

Micaceous iron oxide, long popular in Europe, is now widely used in anti-corrosive coatings in the United States.

In 2008, apparent U.S. consumption of iron oxides was 235,000 metric tons. (See Figure 2-3.) This was down nearly 10% from the year before but about the same amount as in 2000. Figure 2-3 shows domestic production and imports of natural and synthetic iron oxide pigments. Bayer is the world

Figure 2-3 U.S. Production and Consumption of Iron Oxide Pigments, Selected Years, 1980-2008 (in metric tons)

Year	Production	Imports	Exports	Apparent consumption
1980	114,000	35,800	4,580	145,000
1985	115,000	36,100	27,000	124,000
1990	125,000	34,100	9,540	150,000
1995	151,000	59,300	17,500	193,000
2000	154,000	91,300	9,640	236,000
2005	90,000	193,000	2,220	281,000
2006	70,300	199,000	3,100	266,000
2007	88,100	178,000	5,410	261,000
2008	85,100	155,000	4,740	235,000

Compiled by T.D. Kelly (retired), M.J. Potter (retired). Data are calculated, estimated, or reported. See notes for more information.

Source: Adapted from "Iron Oxide Pigments Statistics," U.S. Geological Survey, January 12, 2010, http://minerals.usgs.gov/ds/2005/140/ironoxide.pdf (accessed June 3, 2010)

leader in iron oxide production, followed by Elementis.

Chromate pigments comprise the chrome yellows, oranges, and molybdate orange. In general, the chromate pigments provide good hiding and durability at low cost, and excellent bleeding resistance. Medium chrome yellow is almost pure lead chromate, but the lighter shades contain lead sulfate. Its largest application is traffic paints. The volume of chrome yellows declined since 1990 because the products contain both lead and chromate. Molybdate chrome orange is a co-precipitated mixture of lead chromate, lead sulfate, and lead molybdate. Consumption of chrome orange has also declined.

Chrome greens are composites consisting of iron blue and chrome yellow. By varying the proportion of yellow and blue, a wide range of hues is possible. Chrome greens have high tinting strength, hiding power, and very good color permanency and durability. They are very stable in baking enamels.

Chrome oxides and their hydrates are green pigments of exceptional stability and color permanence. They are lower in tinting strength than the chrome green pigments but resist acids and alkalis and withstand high temperatures. While they are low in brightness, they are used in applications where their stability to light, heat and alkali is important.

Cadmium yellows and reds are essentially sulfides or sulfoselenides of cadmium combined with an inert based on barium sulfate. They are available in a wide range of colors, from light yellow to a deep maroon and possess good color brightness, light fastness, and resistance to acids. Their excellent alkali resistance makes them useful in emulsion paints and alkali resistant finishes. However, use of cadmium yellows and reds is decreasing as organic substitutes are found that lack environmental and health concerns. Cerium sulfate, being marketed as a replacement, is consumed in the plastics industry. In 2007, paint and coatings producers spent a combined $341.2 million on inorganic pigments other than TiO2, including the chrome colors and zinc oxide.

Iron blues are complex ferric-ferrocyanides with high hiding power and tinting strength and durability. They are low in cost and widely used in paints, lacquers and enamels.

Manganese Oxide Blue was accidentally discovered in 2009 at Oregon State University.

The vivid blue pigment represented a pigment that was durable, cheap, and environmentally sound. *Paint & Coatings Industry* commented that it was probably the best blue pigment in history and stood to be widely used in the paint industry (David Stanth, "New Blue Pigment," January 2010).

Synthetic organic pigments comprise a large, important, and growing group of colors prepared by the insolubilization or precipitation of organic dyestuffs. As with inorganic pigments, particle size and shape are important in determining color shade. They are high in price. New organic pigments are being developed to replace lead-, chromium- and cadmium-based pigments. The challenge has been to achieve comparable hiding, shades, brightness, heat stability and weathering durability (light fastness) at an acceptable cost. In 2007, the paint and coatings industry spent $278.8 million on organic pigments, down 38.5% from the year before.

The principal classes of synthetic organic pigments are reds, yellows, blues, violets, oranges and greens. Yellow pigments are chiefly acetoacetarylides, anthrapyrimidines and diarylides; oranges are dinitroanilines and diarylides; violet pigments are carbazoles and quinacridones; reds are toluidines, naphthols, perylenes, and quinacridones. Toluidine reds are insoluble azo dyestuffs in hues ranging from light red to medium reds with good hiding power, brightness and durability. They find applications in industrial and decorative enamels.

Blues and greens are phthalocyanines. The copper phthalocyanine blues and greens are chemically inert pigments with high tinting strength and excellent light fastness. They are resistant to acids and alkali, free from bleeding in oil and organic solvent paints, and treated with surface active agents to render them easily dispersed in water-based paints. Because of their strong, dark mass tones, the phthalocyanines are used chiefly in light tints, yielding clean, bright blues and greens of outstanding durability.

Suppliers of organic pigments include Ciba Specialty Chemicals, Clariant, BASF, and Sun Chemical.

A number of other pigments are added to paints and coatings for specific properties, performance or effects. These include corrosion inhibiting pigments, metallic pigments, magnetic pigments and fluorescent pigments (A. Nurhan Becidyan, "The Chemistry and Physics of Special-Effect Pigments and Colorants for Inks and Coatings," *Paint & Coatings Industry*, June 15, 2003).

- Corrosion inhibiting pigments include basic lead chromate, zinc chromate, strontium chromate, and lead silicochromate. Their effectiveness is due to their limited water solubility and ability to combine with metal surfaces to produce an impervious insulating film. Consumption of lead, chromium and cadmium anti-corrosive pigments is declining due to their negative impact on the environment as well as health issues. Newer anti-corrosive pigments are being used in their place, including molywhites (zinc-molybdenum complexes), nalzin (basic zinc hydroxyphosphite), zinc phosphates (hydrates, orthophosphates and polyphosphates), phosphosilicates, borosilicates, metaborates and calcium-, barium-or strontium-based phosphosilicates and Ferrinov pigments produces from furnaces used in steel production ("New, Active, Anti-Corrosion Pigments," *Paint & Coatings Industry*, October 2009, pp. 28-29). Anti-corrosive pigment are primarily used in industrial maintenance primers and marine coatings for protection of steel structures.
- Metallic pigments are added to paints and coatings for aesthetic purposes, such as in automotive finishes, and for practical reasons, such as the use of zinc dust as

a sacrificial pigment in marine coatings. Zinc dust accounts for about two-thirds of the total amount of metallic pigments used in the paint and coatings industry.

- Aluminum pigments are used primarily in flake form. The pigments are coated with a leafing agent so that they float to the surface where they become oriented to form a continuous, bright metallic surface resistant to passage of moisture and gases. They are also high in hiding power and light reflectance, and durable in exterior exposures.
- Bronze pigments range in shade from light brass to dark antique coppers. Consumption is probably less than 1 million lb.
- Magnetic pigments are used for coating magnetic media, including audio, video, and computer tapes including disks. Products include cobalt-doped iron oxides, chromium oxide, and undoped ferric oxides. Because most magnetic tape production has moved overseas and magnetic tapes are increasingly being replaced by compact disks and high-density disks, domestic demand is declining.
- Pearlescent or luster pigments are used in auto base coats, sporting goods and miscellaneous general decorative finishes. They are synthetic mixtures of titanium dioxide and mica or iron oxide and mica or can be derived from fish scale. In auto basecoats these pigments impart a polychromatic appearance because different colors are seen when viewed at different angles. They have a high refractive index owing to the titanium dioxide coating and the plate-like shape of mica.
- Miscellaneous metallic pigments include gold, silver and stainless steel.

About 65% of paint coloring is conducted at a retail outlet or a customer's choice from a pallet of choices that can number as high as 1,000 different colors and shades. Of this, about 80% is colored by using machine colorants, pigment dispersions or "color pastes" that are added by formula to three or four different types of tint bases. Some colorants are utilized at the plant for ready-mix colors. Machine colorants are tied to a color selection system program offered by the paint manufacturer. Independent suppliers, mainly Creanova and Elementis, supply over 80% of the machine colorants. Paint manufactures account for the balance. Point-of-sale tinting is usually performed with 12 colorants that can be added as prescribed by a formula, or color computer, to create a wide variety of hues.

The balance, about 35% of paint coloring, is conducted at the factory store by tinting a paint base by adding a pigment by grinding or a colorant. Of this, half is produced from purchased pigments, and the remainder from liquid dispersions produced by independent dispersion houses (75%) and pigment suppliers (25%).

The dispersions, including some chip and powder forms, are designed for a solvent-based or a water-based system but not for both. They can be manufactured for a particular resin system, such as epoxy or polyester, or for use with many resins, as for maintenance paints and general purpose finishes. Liquid dispersions, called machine colorants, are designed for use with water- or solvent-based architectural and maintenance paints. "Universal" colorants are usually glycol based. Creanova produces VOC-free architectural colorants.

The overall consumption of dispersions will increase as paint manufacturers choose to spend more time and capacity in making base paints, thus avoiding small color runs, equipment contamination, and toxic waste disposal problems. Speed and accuracy of color computers and spectrophotometers, as well as improved economics, have facilitated the color matching at all levels. With controlled bases and tints, and an established database, color matches can be done at the factory or throughout the distribution system.

FILLERS AND EXTENDERS

Extender pigments are white powders of relatively low refractive index approaching that of the paint vehicles, so that they have little hiding power at ordinary concentrations. However, they are useful in combination with the prime pigments. While generally lower in cost than the prime pigments, fillers and extenders contribute to paint properties by providing the proper consistency to prevent pigment settling and allowing for smooth application. They help to control the penetration of priming paints, are useful for diluting colored pigments, and assist in obtaining the desired surface appearance, such as gloss and hardness. Extenders can also inhibit the tendency toward film cracking on aging, and can improve mechanical properties, such as washability and abrasion resistance, as well as economics.

In 2007, paint and coatings companies spent $295.9 million on minerals and earths used as extenders and fillers. Among the most important products are calcium carbonate (natural chalk, limestone, and chemically precipitated grade), hydrated aluminum silicates (kaolin or china clays), talc, silica, mica, and barium sulfate (natural bartyes or precipitated blanc fixe).

Calcium Carbonate (CaCO$_3$)

CaCO$_3$ is the leading pigment in this group. It is used primarily in architectural coatings, industrial maintenance coatings and traffic paints. The low cost of calcium carbonate allows the production of a wide range of types varying in particle size and surface treatments. Coarse grades are used in putties,

other glazing compounds and sealants; intermediate sizes in flat and semi-gloss finishes; and ultrafine grades in gloss finishes to adjust consistency and to minimize sagging. Natural CaCO3 reduces costs without affecting coating properties in architectural and traffic paints. Use of synthetic calcium carbonate has decreased to minor levels. Paints consume about 15% of all types of grades. Major suppliers are Mineral Technologies (Specialty Minerals Inc.), Imerys (ECC and Georgia Marble), OMYA, and J.M. Huber.

Clays

Kaolins and other clays are consumed in paints to enhance hiding and whiteness. Most clay is added to architectural coatings, including many interior and exterior flat paints. They are versatile fillers that can be used in both water- and solvent-based finishes. Clays are very fine and soft in texture and have the property of forming a plastic thyrotrophic mass when mixed with water. In spite of ample availability and low relative cost, clay is not extensively used in some solvent- or oil-based formulations since it produces soft films with reduced water resistance.

Kaolin is basically a non-swelling type of clay and differs from such other clays as bentonite and attapulgite because its particles are colloidal in size. Although kaolin is not used as a thickener, it provides some body to systems, particularly at low pH or for highly pigmented paints.

Figure 2-4 shows total production and consumption of kaolin clay for selected years between 1980 and 2008. In 2008, approximately 3,650,000 metric tons were consumed by industry. Consumption in paints in 2008 is estimated at about five percent of all applications, or 182,500 metric tons. Major producers are Burgess Pigment, BASF, J.M. Huber, and Imerys, the largest producer of kaolin

Figure 2-4 U.S. Production and Consumption of Kaolin, Selected Years, 1980-2008 (in metric tons)

Year	Production	Imports	Exports	Apparent consumption
1980	7,150,000	14,400	1,260,000	5,900,000
1985	7,070,000	8,520	1,250,000	5,830,000
2000	8,800,000	62,500	3,690,000	5,170,000
2005	7,800,000	262,000	3,580,000	4,480,000
2006	7,470,000	303,000	3,540,000	4,230,000
2007	7,110,000	194,000	3,300,000	4,000,000
2008	6,280,000	211,000	2,960,000	3,650,000

Compiled by D.A. Buckingham (retired) and R.L. Virta. Data are calculated, estimated, or reported. See notes for more information.

Source: Adapted from "Kaolin Statistics," U.S. Geological Survey, November 24, 2009, http://minerals.usgs.gov/ds/2005/140/clay.pdf (accessed June 3, 2010).

worldwide. Georgia is the leading producing state. Brazil is the leading source of imports.

Attapulgite clay, a hydrated aluminum and aluminum/magnesium silicate, is added to latex and glossy solvent paints as a thickener, anti-sag agent, suspension stabilizer and viscosity controller. In powder form, attapulgite exists as millions of bundles of colloidal particles. The bundles are easily wetted and dispersed in aqueous systems and inert and non-swelling in aqueous applications. The network of finely dispersed colloidal particles causes attapulgite to develop desirable gels. Attapulgite is easy to use in powder form and can be added to the grind or high shear phase of the formulation without the need for added dispersants.

Talc

Talc, a form of hydrated magnesium silicate, ranks as the third leading extender pigment for paint. It is used as a fibrous extender to strengthen exterior house paints and also for some industrial coatings, such as panelboard, machinery and industrial maintenance products. Normally talc has a fibrous structure, although some grades are available with laminar properties. Since they are readily wetted and dispersed and tend to

inhibit hard settling of other pigments, they have excellent properties as extenders. The fibrous structure of talc contributes to mechanical strength and durability by leveling the stresses of expansion and contraction, minimizing cracking and reducing sagging.

Figure 2-5 shows U.S. production and apparent consumption of talc for selected years or 1980 to 2008. Almost all talc is produced in four states: Montana, New York, Texas and Vermont. Leading suppliers are Mineral Technologies (Specialty Minerals), Luzenac America and R.T. Vanderbilt. Kaolin clay and mica compete with talc for as an extended and filler pigment in paint.

Silica

Natural and synthetic silicas are used as a filler or extender. Only natural silica functions as a filler; precipitated or synthetic silica can be used as a rheological modifier or flatting agent. Architectural paints consume two-thirds of silica with the balance in OEM products and special purpose finishes. Major producers of natural silica are Unimin Corp. and U.S. Silica.

Figure 2-5   U.S. Production and Consumption of Talc and Pyrophyllite, Selected Years, 1980-2008 (in metric tons)

Year	Production	Shipments	Imports	Exports	Stocks	Apparent consumption
1980	1,120,000	1,210,000	18,700	249,000	155,000	977,000
1985	1,150,000	1,040,000	42,500	215,000	185,000	979,000
1990	1,270,000	1,100,000	65,100	238,000	82,000	1,050,000
1995	1,060,000	901,000	146,000	183,000	82,000	1,020,000
2000	851,000	821,000	270,000	154,000	1,900	967,000
2005	856,000	826,000	237,000	270,000		823,000
2006	895,000	900,000	314,000	253,000		956,000
2007	769,000	720,000	221,000	271,000		719,000
2008	706,000	667,000	193,000	244,000		655,000

Year	Production	Shipments	Imports	Exports	Stocks	Apparent consumption	Unit value ($/t)	Unit value (98$/t)	World production
2005	856,000	826,000	237,000	270,000		823,000	100	83.50	7,960,000
2006	895,000	900,000	314,000	253,000		956,000	106	85.70	7,790,000
2007	769,000	720,000	221,000	271,000		719,000	133	105	7,680,000
2008	706,000	667,000	193,000	244,000		655,000	143	108	7,510,000

Compiled by K.E. Porter (retired) and R.L. Virta. Data are calculated, estimated, or reported. See notes for more information.

Source: Adapted from "Talc and Pyrophyllite Statistics," U.S. Geological Survey, November 4, 2009, http://minerals.usgs.gov/ds/2005/140/talc.pdf (accessed May 27, 2010)

Barytes

Barytes, or barium sulfate, is extremely resistant to acids and alkalis and therefore used in chemical-resistant paints. It provides low oil absorption characteristics and hence has little effect on the consistency of paints and coatings. Applications are anti-corrosive primers, traffic paints, flat interior wall paints, and fillers.

Mica

The value of mica comes from unique physical properties, in which its crystalline structure forms layers that can be split or delaminated into thin sheets. Mica is chemically inert, dielectric, elastic, flexible, hydrophilic, insolute, platy, reflective, refractive, resilient, and transparent to opaque. Mica, a phyllosilicate mineral, is composed of crystal sheets, which are delaminate by grinding. It prevents water penetration and UV degradation because its platy structure inhibits penetration into the paint film, provides reinforcement, and promotes adhesion (Peter A. Ciullo, "Strength and Sheen," *Paint & Coatings Industry*, May 2003).

Figure 2-6 gives U.S. statistics on production, imports, and apparent consumption of mica for selected years from 1980 to 2008. About 30% of domestically produced ground mica is used in coatings formulations (Peter A. Ciullo, "Strength and Sheen," *Paint & Coatings Industry*, May 2003). Producers include General Chemical Industrial Products, Georgia Industrial Minerals, Santa Fe Gold Corp., and Zemex Industrial Minerals. Approximately 25,200 metric tons were consumed by the paint industry in 2008.

Figure 2-6   U.S Production and Consumption of Scrap and Flake Mica, Selected Years, 1980-2008 (in metric tons)

Year	Production	Imports	Exports	Stocks	Apparent consumption
1980	101,000	8,160	12,700	6,350	96,200
1985	123,000	9,070	8,160	6,350	124,000
1990	101,000	13,000	5,000	7,000	105,000
1995	98,000	22,000	7,000	13,000	112,000
2000	112,000	28,300	10,300		119,000
2005	78,000	36,000	9,000		105,000
2006	110,000	45,200	7,230		148,000
2007	96,600	41,000	7,700		130,000
2008	84,000	26,900	9,100		102,000

Compiled by C.A. DiFrancesco (retired) and J.B. Hedrick (retired). Data are calculated, estimated, or reported. See notes for more information.

Source: Adapted from "Mica (Natural), Scrap and Flake Statistics," U.S. Geological Survey, December 28, 2009, http://minerals.usgs.gov/ds/2005/140/micascrap.pdf (accessed May 27, 2010)

Other

Other fillers and extenders include diatomite, wollastonite, feldspar, sodium silicoaluminate, synthetic calcium silicate, pyrophyllite and hydrated alumina. Diatomite is used to increase flattening and hiding and to thicken and suspend pigments; leading producers are World Minerals (Celite) and Eagle-Picher. Wollastonite, a natural calcium silicate with an acicular or needle-like structure, has applications in architectural paints and water-based primers. It can provide reinforcement or act as a pH buffer, flatting, or suspending agent. Consumption of other fillers by the paint industry total less than 10 million pounds annually.

ADDITIVES

The paint industry is a large user of specialty chemicals employed as additives. In 2009, Kugumgar, Nerlfi & Growny estimated worldwide consumption for five leading additives was 1.72 million pounds, valued at $3.47 billion. This was down ten percent from 2008, with consumption in North America and Europe down the most ("Additives Consumption Study Released," *Paint & Coatings Industry*, June 2010).

Additives, while generally making up less than 5% of a paint formulation, are key components. They are incorporated into paint formulations to alleviate or eliminate problems that can arise, improve product quality, or prevent problems from occurring during manufacture, storage, or application. Many additives are multipurpose in nature. However, most often they function in very specific applications, which can vary from being independent of other ingredients or whose function is critical to the performance of the paint product. Some additives aid in the manufacturing process but yet add nothing to the final performance of the product. On the other hand, other additives contribute little to the manufacturing process but their presence is necessary for the final performance of the product. An additive usually functions in terms of its chemical or physical nature and behavior in the presence of other components of the coating (Joseph V. Koleski and Robert Springate, "Two Thousand Ten

Additives Handbook," *Paint & Coatings Industry*, June 2010).

Additives are used in the formulation of all types of paints and coatings. Typically, water-based formulations require more additives than solvent-based systems. Major types of additives include the following:

- Adhesion promoters
- Flow and leveling agents
- Antiblocking agents
- Freeze-thaw stabilizers
- Anti-foams -Humectants
- Anti-freezes
- Light stabilizers
- Antioxidants
- Lubricants
- Antifouling agents
- Optical brighteners
- Anti-skids
- Plasticizers
- Anti-skinning agents
- Protective colloids
- Biocides/fungicides
- Rheology modifiers or thickeners
- Catalysts
- Slip aids
- Coalescing agents
- Surfactants
- Corrosion inhibitors
- Suspension agents
- Crosslinking agents
- Tackifiers
- Dispersants
- Thixotropes
- Driers
- UV absorbers
- Flame retardants
- Waxes
- Flatting agents

Surfactants

Surfactants, or surface active agents, alter the surface performance of the ingredients in paint formulations. All three types of surfactants are used—anionic, cationic and non-ionic. They act to reduce surface tension and improve wetting and spreading, aid in dispersion of pigments in formulated products, inhibit foam formation, or, in latex paints, help stabilize foams and improve emulsion formation. Their major application is water-based coatings where they emulsify oil and water systems, serve as wetting agents, disperse solids in liquids, and act as deformers.

Surfactants are compounds with both a hydrophilic, or water seeking portion, and another portion or radical that is hydrophobic or water hating. Water-based coatings at times require surfactants with multiple functionalities, like wetting and coalescing, to meet the requirements of low- or zero-VOC products.

Dispersants are added to the paint formulation to increase the stability of a suspension of powders or pigments in a liquid medium. They are used primarily before colorants are added to the formulation. Dispersants are usually surfactants that prevent reassociation of such particles as fillers, extenders and pigments that have been dissociated in a grinding operation. Typical dispersants are polyacrylates, polyphospates, sulfosuccinates, polycarboxylates, and lecithin, natural phospholipids.

Non-ionic surfactants are made by the condensation reaction of ethylene oxide with alcohols, acids and phenols. Non-ionic surfactants do not ionize, but instead hydrate in water and hydrogen, thus bonding the ether oxygen sites as well as the interaction with the hydroxyl groups. Many non-ionic surfactants also function as wetting agents. They improve wetting of the resins particles and prevent pigments from agglomerating with the resin. They also improve adhesion to the substrate, a trait especially necessary in exterior coatings where surfaces are often dirty and older coating might be chalky.

Anionic surfactants carry a negative charge in the hydrophilic portion of the molecule. They are usually phosphates, sulfates and sulfonate compounds. They are good emulsifiers and wetting agents. Anionics can also contain an oxyethylene chain in their structure.

Cationic surfactants carry a positive charge, and amphoteric surfactants contain both a positive and a negative charge. They have limited applications in paints and coatings. When used, they assist pigment dispersion and wetting in acidic formulations.

Surfactants are the leading additive used by the industry. Suppliers of surfactants include Air Products, Bayer Chemical, Clariant, and Dow Chemical.

Rheology Modifiers

Rheology modifiers, often referred to as thickeners, are added to both water-based (70%) and solvent-based (30%) paints. The products have become important as water-based paints have grown, especially for architectural coatings. They also provide pigments dispersion and also rheology control or modification in water-based OEM product finishes, thus continuing to spur growth. Specialized rheology control additives are necessary in radiation curable coatings, which are converted very rapidly from fluid products to cured films. The additive chosen for rheology control or modification cannot interfere or block the specific radiation wavelength that initiates the cure. Associative thickeners, or emulsifiers, are polymeric compounds that provide consistent and reliable control of paint rheology during manufacturing and consumption. They are particularly useful in controlling the spattering of latex paints during application. Modifiers also provide excellent leveling and promote one-coat coverage.

Rheology modifiers alter the deformation and flow characteristics of matter when it is under the influence of stress. They also function as suspending agents, anti-sag agents, and emulsion stabilizers by increasing the viscosity of the water phase of the paint. Rheology modifiers comprise such compounds as hydroxyl ethyl cellulose, hydroxypropyl cellulose, sodium carboxycellulose, and methyl cellulose. HASE thickeners are copolymers of ethyl acrylate, methacylic acid, and other monomers. The polymer, which consists of 10 to 100 ethylene oxide units, is considered as an associative thickener, and provides better application properties. HEUR thickeners are based on modified ethylene oxide-based urethane linkages coupled to the ends or sides of a polyethylene oxide polymer. The rheology modifiers are much improved over the original materials that were based on starches and subject to attack by microorganisms.

Suppliers of rheology modifiers include Dow Chemical, Rohm and Haas, and Hercules Chemical.

Plasticizers

Plasticizers, the third-largest category of additives, are used mainly in solvent-based lacquers and plastisols. They increase the flexibility of films that are inherently brittle, improve the flow and processability of paints or coatings, and reduce brittleness in the final product. They also provide impact resistance, toughness, and adhesion. Basically, plasticizers lower the glass transition temperature of paint films so that they can flex and withstand shock or impact in use.

Phthalate esters, the general purpose plasticizers used most widely, include dibutyl and dioctyl phthalates. Other plasiticizers are the dialkyl adipates, a number of alkyl benzoate esters, castor oil, alkyl and aryl phosphates, polymeric phthalates, and sebacates.

Epoxidized soybean, linseed or tall oil fatty esters are used, although soybean oils dominate. Plasticizers are not permanently bonded to the coating film and can be extracted and are used in solvent based plastisols, principally ones based on PVC polymers. Major applications are automotive OEM plastisols, coil coatings, powder coatings, and acrylic resin systems.

Use of plasticizers has been declining due to the drop in solvent-based lacquers and emission limits on volatile organic compounds (VOCs). Some suppliers are Dow Chemical, Bayer, and Rohm and Haas.

Antifoulants

Antifoulants protect underwater marine hulls from the harmful effects of marine life, which attach themselves to the hull. These organisms cause reduce slippage when the vessel is under way, reducing speed and increasing fuel consumption. Copper sheeting was used on wooden vessels before the steel hulls became common. At that time cuprous oxide pigments, which are fungicides that deter attachment of such marine organisms as barnacles and mussels, were used. The pigments are typically used with other co-biocides to enhance paint performance and improve the coating's resistance against algae and attachment of slime.

Tributyl tin (TBT) compounds were used for decades as the most effective antifouling additive. However, most formulations containing TBT are ablative coatings, which wear away from the hull, thus releasing the TBT into the water. However, tin compounds have been found to be harmful to other marine life. In 2001, the International Maritime Organization (IMO) approved a ban on the application of antifouling marine paints containing TBT that went into effect at the start of 2003. The IMO agreement also required removal of all TBT-based coatings

from vessels by January 2008, and the U.S. EPA followed suit. Paint manufacturers reduced or eliminated products containing the compound several years in advance (Tim Wright, "Marine Coatings Market: With the International Maritime Organization's TBT Antifouling Treated Set to Take Effect January 2008, Along with the Continuing Surge in Copper Prices, Marine Paint Makers and Their Raw Material Suppliers are Adapting to Meet These Demands," *Coatings World*, May 2007, pp. 40-42). While cuprous oxide, an older technology, continues to be used, the industry is investigating new and novel approaches to this problem. Silicone-based coatings are another option being tried. Tin-free compounds based on isothiazolone chemistry were also used as replacements. However, they last only three years as opposed to the tin compounds, which can remain effective for five years.

Driers

Driers are used in paints and varnishes to promote the crosslinking of polymers or drying oils. The most common products are catalysts, which initiate the polymerization or crosslinking reaction. Driers are metallic soaps or salts of monocarboxylic acids, usually C8-C10 branched acids, such as naphthenic acids and neodecanoic acids, tall oils. They are usually cobalt, manganese, vanadium or iron salts. Crosslinking driers are based on zirconium, lanthanum, neodymium, bismuth, strontium, and barium. Auxiliary driers are calcium, potassium, lithium and zinc salts. Cobalt and manganese are considered "surface driers", which cure only at the top of the coating film. Zirconium, aluminum and the rare earths are "through driers", which act by curing the interior of the film. Calcium, barium and tin are considered "auxiliary driers" that speed up drying.

Typical application levels are at 0.02-0.05% metal concentration based on vehicle solids.

Biocides/Fungicides

These products are used to protect paints and coatings from microorganisms that can cause degradation of organic materials in paint formulations, particularly the resins and polymers. Microorganisms can cause deterioration of viscosity, undesirable odors, gas formation, emulsion breakdown, and other physical and chemical changes.

Biocidal agents are available to protect paints during storage and in the dried film. A variety of these agents are used, including algaecides, bactericides, fungicides, and mildewicides.

Typical biocides include organic compounds based on isothiazolinones, oxazolidines, formaldehyde donors, chlorothalonil, carbamates, zinc pyrithone and benzinidozoles and dithiocarbamates.

Suppliers of biocides include Buckman Laboratories, Cognis Corp., Rohm & Haas, Troy Corp., and R.T. Vanderbilt.

UV Light Stabilizers

These products, also known as UV absorbers, are free radicals scavengers that function by chemical mechanisms. Since the stabilizers are regenerated rather than consumed in the stabilization process, they are efficient and long lived. Typical light absorbers are the benzotriazoles, and the hydroxyl phenyl triazines.

Coalescing agents, or leveling agents, are additives that aid in the transition from liquid to solid state during the latex drying and film formation process. In latex paints, the film resin is comprised of tiny solid polymers particles dispersed in water. As the film dries, water evaporates and the particles are forced closer until they overcome the repulsive forces that kept them separated. As the particles

come together, the emulsion collapses and the particles coalesce or solidify to form a film. The coalescing agents keep the polymer sufficiently soft so that they can fuse into a film. Typical coalescing agents include ethylene glycol monobutyl ether, propylene glycol monobutyl ether, and a variety of other ethylene and propylene glycol monoalkyl ethers.

Suppliers of coalescing agents include Clariant Corp/, Akzo Nobel, and Ciba Specialty Chemicals.

Other Additives

A variety of other additives are used in paints and coatings, including adhesion promoters, antioxidants, flatting agents, freeze-thaw additives, and slip aids.

Adhesion promoters improve the ability of the coating to withstand mechanical separation from the substrate. Examples are the silanes, titanates, and chromium compounds.

Antioxidants prevent oxygen from reacting with other compounds that are susceptible to oxidation. They suppress degradation by oxygen, ozone or UV radiation attack. Oxygen attack can occur under ambient or elevated temperatures during application or use. Effective antioxidants include the p-phenylenediamine derivatives, hindered phenols, and octyl and high alkylphenols and phospites.

Flatting agents, both natural and synthetic materials, are added to coatings that affect the gloss of the film. When light is reflected from a smooth surface, the surface appears to be glossy. If light is scattered as it hits the surface, instead of being reflected, a matte appearance will be created. Flatting agents reduce gloss by imparting micro-roughness to the paint surface as it dries and cures. They are available in different chemical compounds, primarily inorganic materials, including silicas for clear coatings, and clays, talcs, and carbonates for pigmented systems. Silicas are typically consumed in both solvent and water-based systems.

Freeze-thaw additives have become important as water-based paints have come to dominate the industry product lines. The additives impart freeze-thaw resistance to water-based paints by preventing the product from coalescing irreversibly when subjected to a freeze-thaw cycle. Such compounds as ethylene or propylene glycol andoxygenated solvents are used most frequently. Most of the additives are found in aqueous emulsion systems to maintain latex equilibrium. They function by lowering the freezing point of the aqueous medium and inhibiting the desorption of water from the emulsion particle that constitute the resin portion of the paint.

Slip aids are chemical compounds that migrate to the surface of the coating during and after application and curing. They coat the surface and provide lubricity to lower the coefficient of friction to improve slip characteristics of the paint. Some slip aids also function as anti-mar agents or abrasion-resistant additives. All types of waxes are used as solid slip aids. Waxes include carnauba, paraffin and microcrystalline waxes, polyethylene

and polypropylene waxes, and polytetrafluoroethylene (PTFE). The waxes are added to the formulation during manufacture as emulsions or micronized powders. Liquid slip additives, normally based on silicon, are used in both solvent and aqueous systems. Normally they are polydimethyl siloxane. Silicon fluids have low surface tension, repel water, have good thermal resistance, and improve gloss and surface smoothness.

Miscellaneous additives include anti-skinning agents that retard skin formation in oil-based paints, waxes to help the coating resist marring and to act as slip aids and other uses, and anti-static agents.

As newer and tougher regulations are promulgated for coatings products, challenges and opportunities are created for formulators and suppliers. These include products to meet the new VOC and HAP requirements while avoiding hazardous materials and maintaining product performance at competitive costs.

PRICES

Beginning in the 1970s, price indices based on list prices of a broad list of

Figure 2-7 Price Indexes of Selected Paint Raw Materials, 2000-2009

	1983=100									
	2000	2001	2002	2003	2004	2005	2006	2007	2008	2009
Paint colors	159.9	156.2	146.3	146.2	152.7	162.3	168.7	178.9	190.3	180.1
Organic Pigments	133.8	129.4	122.2	121.4	120.4	121.4	120.8	123.6	139.4	132.6
Titanium Dioxide	164.7	160.9	146.1	146.7	149.5	164.3	169.2	163.3	168.6	163.2
Iron oxides	174.9	167.4	178	178.1	180.2	191.3	202	204.6	209.8	200.2
All other inorganic pigments	136.3	136.8	132.9	131.9	161.7	168.4	188.7	251.4	268.2	244.2
Paint fillers	113.6	120.1	119.4	121.6	123.6	127.1	135.3	147.2	157.1	177.1
Kaolin Clay	130.3	137.7	136.8	139.5	141.7	145.8	155.1	168.8	180.2	203.1
Average All Materials	148.5	149.8	165.9	172.9	179.7	190.4	198.6	211.3	224.9	218.7

Source: Adapted from "Producer Price Index, Commodities, Not Seasonally Adjusted," Bureau of Labor Statistics, 2010, http://www.bls.gov/ppi (accessed May 16, 2010).

paint materials have been available from the Bureau of Labor Statistics. Over the years the Bureau has greatly reduced the number of reported materials and the items on the list. The items in the current list of paint materials are shown in Figure 2-7, which gives historical price indexes for paint raw material from 2000 through 2009. As shown, prices for all paint materials have increased by an average 4.4% a year through the decade. The Bureau has

eliminated the price indexes for resins, the most important ingredient in paint formulations, as well as organic solvents.

Prices for resins and organic solvents depend highly on the price of crude oil and refined petroleum products. Price indexes for paint colors increased by only an average of 1.3% per year over the 2000 to 2009 period, and prices for titanium dioxide remained fairly stable. Overcapacity has been a problem in recent years, putting pressure on producers.

Paints have a broad spectrum of end uses and are used on a variety of surfaces, including metal, wood, plastic, concrete, and wallboard. Paints are used to decorate, protect, preserve, and mark for safety in most sectors of the U.S. economy, including the manufacture of durable goods, and in construction and maintenance. Despite their widespread use, the paint industry represents only a small fraction of the total GDP, estimated at less than 0.15%.

Paints are produced predominantly as a diluted liquid mixture, but alternative forms such as high-solids and solvent-free liquids and powders have gained in importance mainly as a result of environmental concerns and increasingly stringent regulations. Products are available in containers ranging in size from ½ pint cans to one, two and five gallon pails, drums, tote bins, and tank wagons. Consumers, professional contractors, original equipment manufacturers (OEMs) and other service-related personnel purchase paints and coatings.

Although there are a myriad of types and grades, for statistical and marketing purposes, paints are categorized as (1) architectural coatings, (2) OEM coatings, and (3) special purpose coatings. The U.S. Census Bureau adopted these categories in 1978 to replace the older categories of trade sales paints and industrial finishes. Excluded from this *Guide* are such allied products as wood fillers and sealers, putty and glazing compounds, thinners, paint and varnish removers and peripheral coatings used on masonry surfaces, roofs, textiles, paper and film such as that used for packaging and graphic arts, and as electrical insulation.

ARCHITECTURAL COATINGS

Paints for building decoration and general maintenance are the largest segment of the paint market and are described by the U.S.

PRODUCTS AND MARKETS

HIGHLIGHTS

Architectural Coatings
■
Industrial OEM Coatings
■
Special Purpose Coatings

Census Bureau as "coatings for onsite application to interior or exterior surfaces of residential, commercial, institutional, or industrial buildings." They are protective and decorative finishes applied at ambient temperatures for ordinary use and exposure. The products are normally distributed through wholesale and/or retail channels and purchased by the general public, painters, building contractors, and governmental bodies. They are sold in containers in sizes of five-gallon pails, one-gallon pails, one-half gallon containers, pints, and a few other sizes for application by brush, roller or spray.

U.S. shipments of architectural coatings in 2008 were 682 million gallons, or 55.8% of the volume for all paints. (See Figure 3-3.) Architectural coating shipped had a value that year of $8,669 million, or 45.8% of dollar shipments. (See Figure 3-1.) The percent of both volume and dollar shares

of architectural paints had dropped since 2004, mainly because of the drastic slowdown in new home starts and in the rise of foreclosures.

Between 1985 and 2007, dollar shipments of architectural paints increased at an average of 1.9% year before dropping 4.4% in 2009. Unit shipments grew by an average of 2.2% annually between 1985 and 2007, before dropping 12.2% in 2008. (See Figure 3-3.)

From 1986 to 2007 the prices for architectural paints increased by an average of 1.8% annually. However, during that time solvent-based paints, which are 15-16% more expensive per gallon than water-based paints, declined as a percentage of the total. Thus, the data are somewhat misleading. The average price per gallon in 2007 compared to 1986 is shown in Figure 3-2.

Figure 3-1 Shipments of Architectural Coatings in Millions of Dollars, 1985-2008

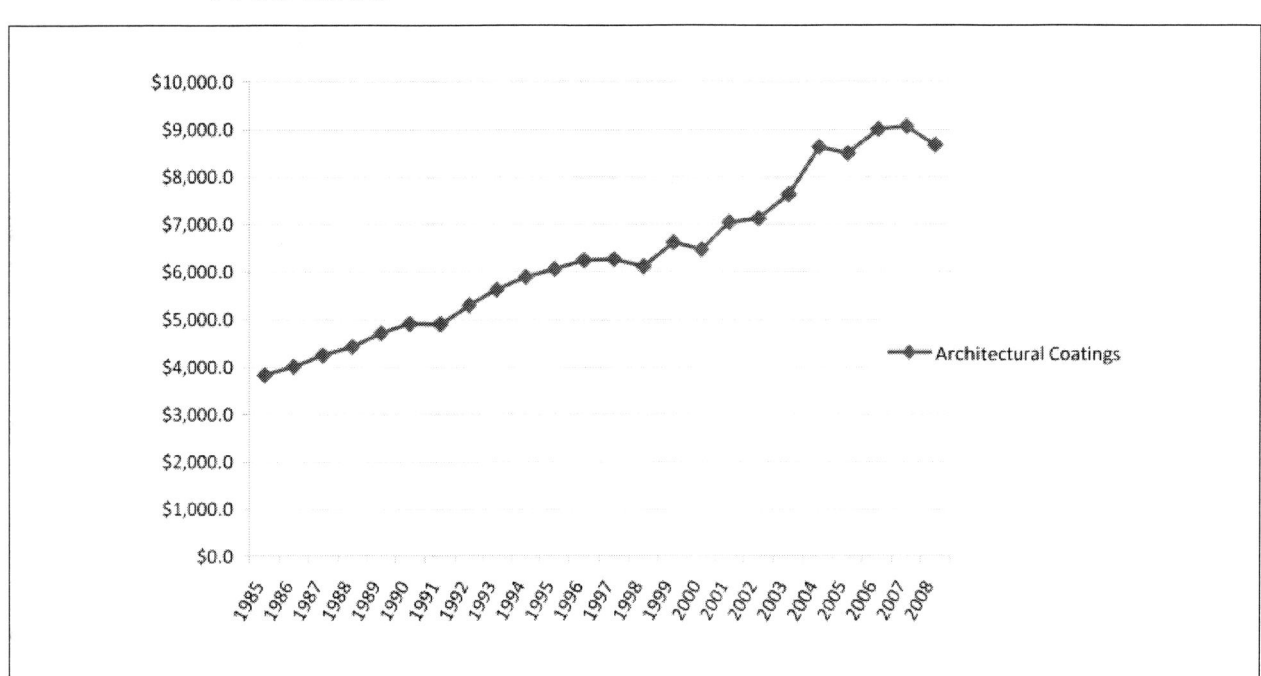

Source: Adapted from "Sector 31: EC073111: Manufacturing: Industry Series: Detailed Statistics by Industry for the United States: 2007," 2007 Economic Census, U.S. Census Bureau, 2009, http://factfinder.census.gov/servlet/IBQTable?_bm=y&-geo_id=01000US&-ds_name=EC073111&-NAICS2007=325510&-_lang=en (accessed November 30, 2009)

The sales of architectural paints mirror new housing starts, which are shown in Figure 3-4. After the recession of 1991-92, industry sales improved steadily as housing starts recovered and the economy improved. Housing starts declined slightly in 1995 and sales fell. Then with a strong recovery in 1996 and 1997, sales rose again. As the Federal Reserve Board lowered interest rates in 2001, housing starts increased, rising by 31.8% from 2000 and 2005. Housing starts then declined dramatically each year—by 12.9% in 2006, 24.8% in 2007, 33.2% in 2008, and 38.8% in 2009—for a total decline of 73.2% between 2005 and 2009.

Some signs in 2010 pointed toward economic recovery in the paint industry. *Paint & Coatings Industry* reported in November 2009 that demand for wood coatings would increase 2.2% per year between 2010 and 2013 ("U.S. Demand for Wood Coatings to Reach $3.0 Billion," p. 8). The magazine also reported on a study from The Freedonia Group, Inc.

Figure 3-2 Average Price per Gallon of Paint, by Type of Paint, 1986 and 2007

Type of Paint	1986	2007
Exterior		
Solvent-Type	$9.95	$13.43
Water-Type	$7.47	$12.72
Interior		
Solvent-Type	$10.40	$12.28
Water-Type	$6.98	$10.89
Lacquers	$7.39	$9.82
Average	$8.02	$11.67

Source: Compiled from Current Industrial Reports, MA325F—Paints and Allied Products, U.S. Census Bureau, http://www.census.gov/manufacturing/cir/historical_data/ma325f/index.html.

Figure 3-3 Shipments of Architectural Coatings in Gallons, 1985-2008

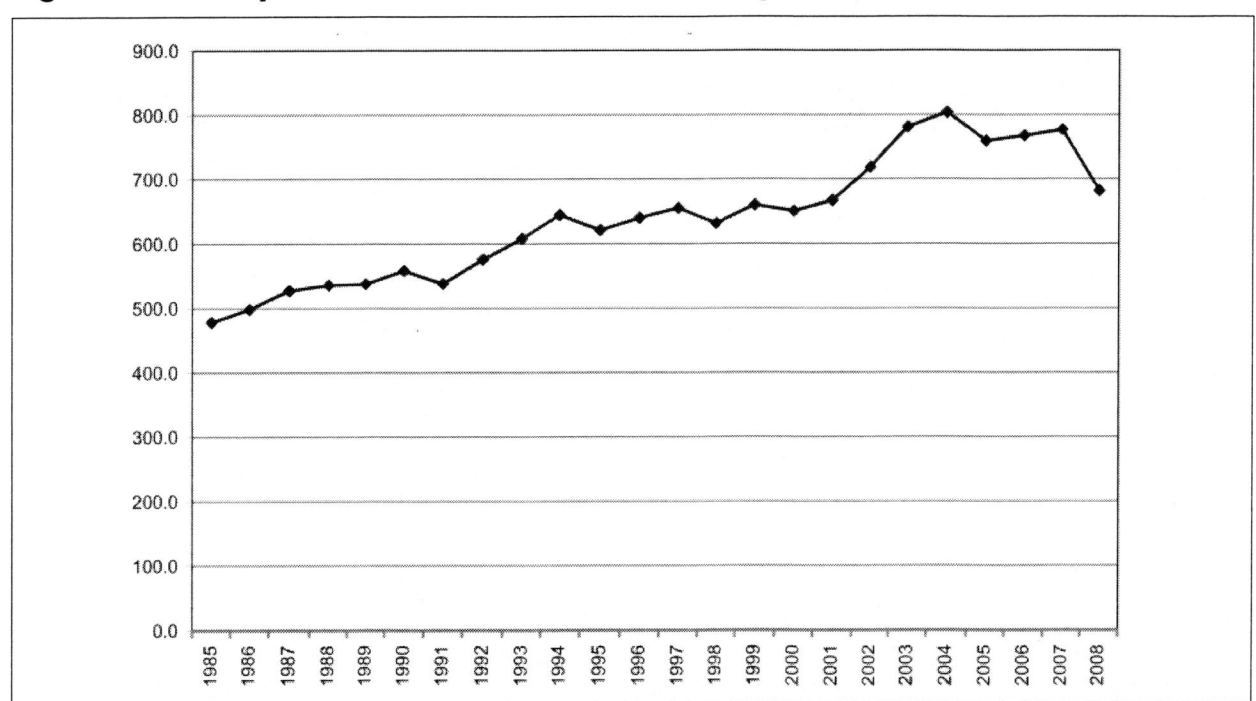

Source: Adapted from "Table 1. Summary of Estimated United States Quantity and Value of Shipments of Paint and Allied Products: 2004-2008," Current Industrial Reports M325F, U.S. Census Bureau, http://www.census.gov/manufacturing/cir/historical_data/ma325f/index.html (accessed November 30, 2009).

Figure 3-4   New Privately-Owned Housing Units Started, 1980-2009

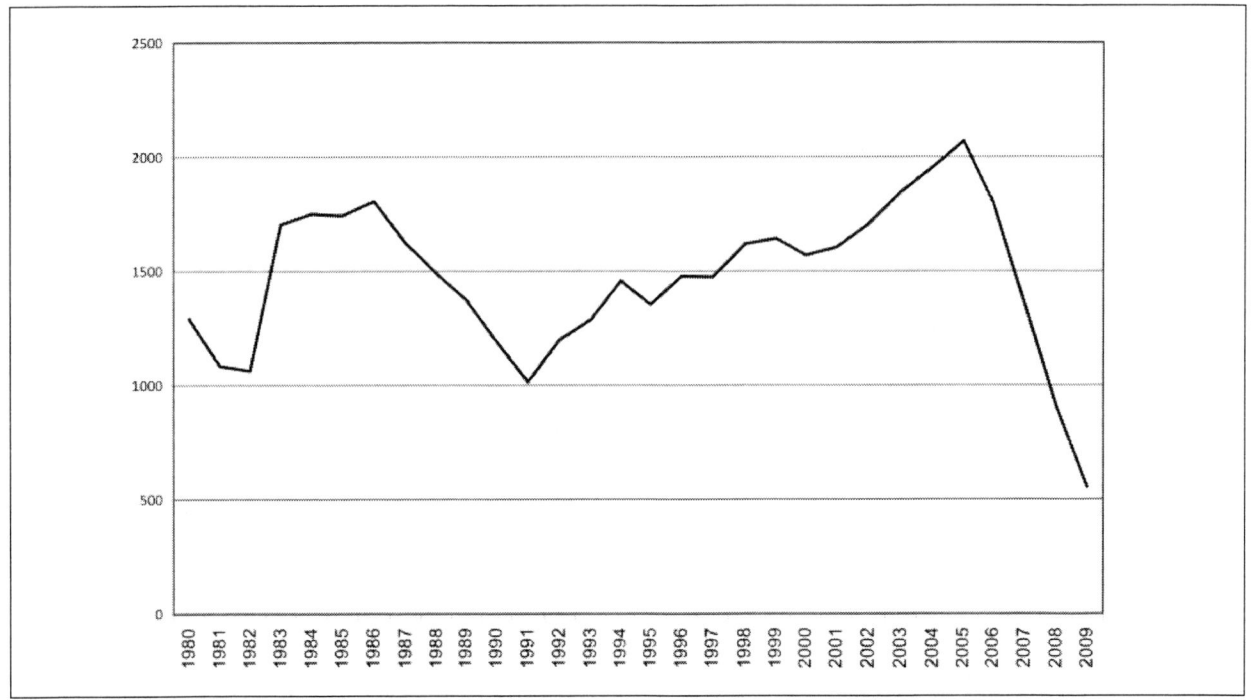

Source: Adapted from "New Privately Owned Housing Units Started: Annual Data," C20 Housing Starts, Historical, U.S. Census Bureau. 2010, http://www.census.gov/const/startsan.pdf (accessed June 20, 2010)

that forecast that worldwide demand for architectural paint would begin to rise again at an average of 3.6% each year between 2010 and 2013 as the housing and mortgage crisis abated. Although that growth was slow compared to the growth during the 2003 to 2008 period because of the slowdown in building and construction, the gains were nonetheless strong ("Architectural Paint Demand to Reach 22.8 Million Metric Tons," June 2010, p. 8).

Types of Architectural Coatings

Architectural coatings are classified primarily as exterior and interior paints, either solvent or water-based, with minor amounts of lacquers and other miscellaneous paints and coatings. Shipments in 2007 and 2008 are given in Figure 3-7.

Interior paints continue as the leading architectural product in 2008; 398.9 million gallons were shipped that year, 59.2% of

the total shipments of architectural paints. Exterior paints made up the balance of shipments (architectural lacquers were unreported that year), with 275 million gallons shipped, 40.8% of the total.

Figure 3-7 shows that consumption of water-based architectural coatings, estimated at 516.4 million gallons in 2008, had grown to 76.6% of the total gallons of architectural coatings shipped; water-based paints accounted for 98.4% of all interior flat paint and 92.1% of all interior gloss, semigloss, eggshell, and satin paints shipped. The popularity of water-based paints is based on such features as ease of application and clean-up, low odor, fast dry and excellent durability.

The growth of water-based paints and coatings is shown in Figure 3-5 for interior use and in Figure 3-6 for exterior use. The share of water-based paints in each architectural segment increased steadily between 1964 and 2008, although growth slowed after the mid-1990s. Since penetration of water-based paints in the architectural paint market is already well advanced, the shift to water-based paint has likely reached its highest level, particularly for interior paints.

Declines in solvent-based paints for both interior and exterior surfaces are due in large part to regulations limiting volatile organic compounds (VOC) that these paints emit. Figure 1-23 in Section 1 shows solvent limits for each type of solvent-based architectural paint. In addition to national limits imposed by the U.S. Environmental Protection Agency (EPA), a number of states have imposed even stricter limits.

Wood has steadily lost its share of exterior residential surfaces to sheet metal and plastic sidings, which require less upkeep and, in the case of vinyl and PVC sidings and brick, no painting. Continued use of siding, particularly for exterior use, will limit the rate of

Figure 3-5 Percent of All Interior Architectural Paints that were Water-Based, 1964-2008

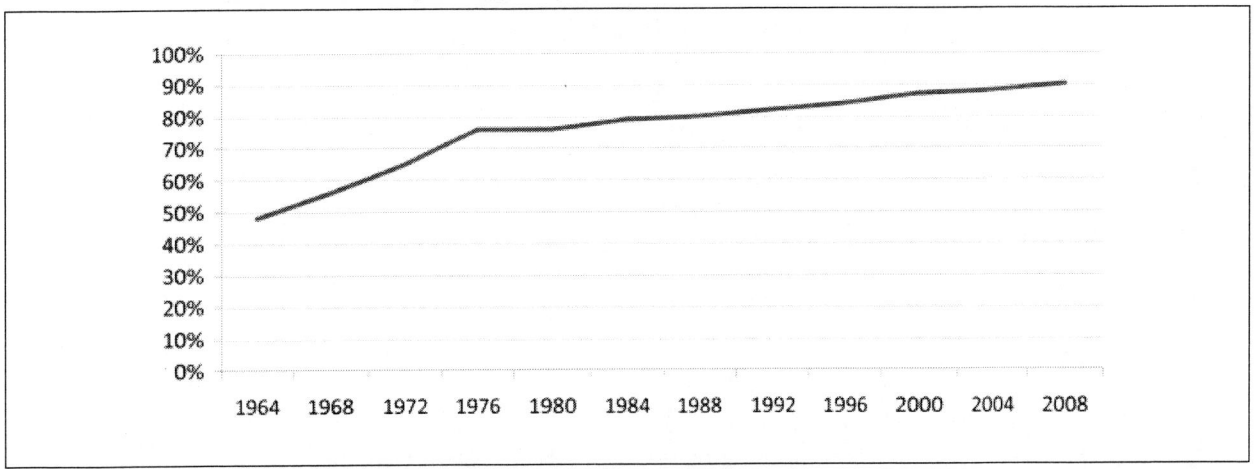

Source: Adapted from Current Industrial Reports M325F, U.S. Census Bureau, 1964-2008

Figure 3-6 Percent of All Exterior Architectural Paints that were Water-Based, 1964-2008

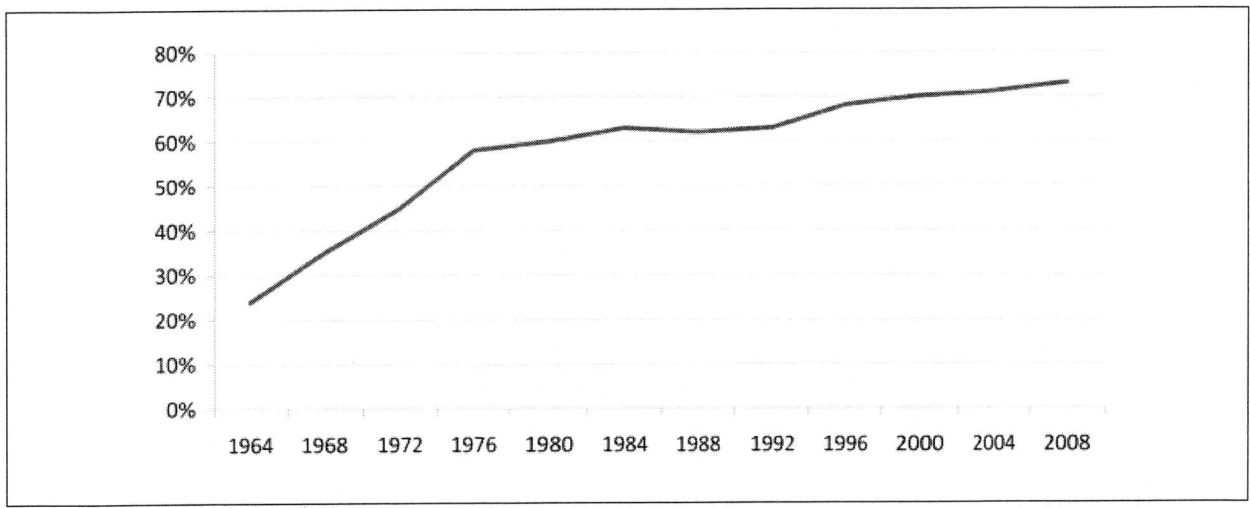

Source: Adapted from Current Industrial Reports M325F, U.S. Census Bureau, 1964-2008

Figure 3-7 Quantity and Value of Shipments of Architectural Coatings and Allied Products, 2007 and 2008

Product code	Product description	Year	No. of Cos.		Quantity		Value
3255101	Architectural coatings	2008	(X)	a/	673,908	a/	8,566,199
		2007			767,488		8,957,724
	EXTERIOR SOLVENT TYPES						
3255101111	Exterior, solvent thinned paints and tinted bases, including barn	2008	63	b/	16,454	b/	205,051
	and roof paints	2007			18,430		216,000
3255101115	Exterior, solvent thinned enamels and tinted bases, including	2008	71	c/	13,922	b/	277,814
	exterior-interior floor enamels	2007		a/	16,907	a/	247,768
3255101119	Exterior, solvent thinned undercoaters and primers	2008	75	c/	7,017	c/	103,371
		2007			7,781	a/	102,083
3255101121	Exterior, solvent thinned clear finishes and sealers	2008	64	b/	4,562	a/	68,184
		2007			5,669		84,303
3255101125	Exterior solvent thinned stains, including shingle and shake	2008	58	a/	10,182	a/	146,859
		2007			12,946		173,716
3255101129	Exterior, other solvent thinned coatings, including	2008	32	a/	5,674	b/	85,507
	bituminous paints	2007			6,498		92,837
	EXTERIOR WATER TYPES						
3255101131	Exterior, water thinned paints and tinted bases, including barn	2008	114	a/	96,136	a/	1,305,923
	and roof paints	2007		a/	111,870	a/	1,444,862
3255101135	Exterior, water thinned exterior-interior deck and floor enamels	2008	52	a/	5,926	a/	83,004
		2007		a/	5,011	r/a/	61,043
3255101139	Exterior, water thinned undercoaters and primers	2008	80	c/	12,840	c/	168,020
		2007			30,819	a/	354,940
3255101141	Exterior, water thinned stains and sealers	2008	59		19,512		279,374
		2007			22,501		306,003
3255101145	Exterior, other exterior water thinned coatings	2008	69		21,641		289,933
		2007			23,806		300,301

(Continued)

Figure 3-7 (Continued)

Product code	Product description	Year	No. of Cos.		Quantity		Value
	INTERIOR SOLVENT TYPES						
3255101211	Interior, flat solvent thinned wall paint and tinting bases, including mill white paints	2008	27	c/	2,411	a/	70,242
		2007		c/	2,774	a/	79,067
3255101215	Interior, gloss and quick drying enamels and other gloss solvent thinned paints and enamels	2008	30	c/	3,163	b/	50,358
		2007		b/	3,674	a/	54,118
3255101219	Interior, semigloss, eggshell, satin solvent thinned paints and tinting bases	2008	50	b/	11,206	b/	187,848
		2007			11,893		160,083
3255101221	Interior, solvent thinned undercoaters and primers	2008	50	b/	21,702	b/	224,278
		2007			22,949		205,049
3255101225	Interior, solvent thinned clear finishes and sealers	2008	69	c/	(S)	c/	101,266
		2007		b/	7,842	b/	97,888
3255101229	Interior, solvent thinned stains	2008	43		(D)		(D)
		2007			(D)		(D)
3255101231	Interior, other solvent thinned coatings	2008	25		(D)		(D)
		2007			(D)		(D)
	INTERIOR WATER TYPES						
3255101235	Interior, flat water thinned paints and tinting bases	2008	95	a/	145,497	a/	1,487,974
		2007			169,545		1,576,527
3255101239	Interior, semigloss, eggshell, satin, and other water thinned paints and tinting bases	2008	96		166,405		2,234,038
		2007			194,130		2,358,815
3255101241	Interior, water thinned undercoaters and primers	2008	79	b/	48,479	c/	476,316
		2007			31,708		279,176
3255101245	Interior, other interior water thinned coatings, stains, and sealers	2008	61		(D)		(D)
		2007			46,803		599,119
3255101249	Architectural lacquers	2008	21		(S)		(S)
		2007		a/	6,009	a/	59,296

Source: Adapted from "Table 2. Quantity and Value of Shipments of Paint and Allied Products: 2008 and 2007," Current Industrial Reports M325F, U.S. Census Bureau, http://www.census.gov/manufacturing/cir/historical_data/ma325f/index.html (accessed November 30, 2009).

growth for exterior house and trim paints. Use of PVC windows and sashes also impacts the demand for gloss trim paints.

Interior Paints. The interior paint category is composed mainly of water-based types with the balance solvent-based grades. Approximately 398.9 million gallons of interior paints were produced in 2008, comprised of 360.4 million gallons of water-based and 38.5 million gallons of solvent-based products.

Water-based paints. There are four groups of water-based interior paints: 1) flat water-based paints and tinting bases; 2) semigloss, eggshell, satin and other water-thinned paints and tinting bases; 3) undercoats and primers; and 4) stains and sealers.

In 2008, production of flat water-based paints and tinting bases totaled 145.5 million gallons, or 36.5% of all interior paints, valued at $1,488 million. (See Figure 3-7.) Prices averaged of $10.23 a gallon at the manufacturers' level. Vinyl-acrylic (80% vinyl acetate, 20% butyl acrylate) resin-based paints account for 90% of all vehicles used in flat paints. About 6% are straight acrylic (50% methyl methacrylate, 50% butyl acrylate) with the balance based on vinyl acetate-ethylene copolymer resins. A typical gallon of water-based interior flat paint or tinting base weighs 10 to 11 pounds a gallon and contains 42-50% solids by weight. The vehicle or resin accounts for 20-25% of the solids.

Semigloss, eggshell, satin and other water thinned paints and tinting bases accounted for 166.4 million gallons valued at $2,234 million in 2008, an average of $13.43 per gallon. (See Figure 3-7.) The leading vehicle is a blend of vinyl-acrylic and acrylic resins with a typical formulation containing two-thirds vinyl-acrylic and one-third straight acrylic. Blends provide improved gloss and scrub resistance. Vinyl-acrylic resins rank next followed by terpolymers of vinyl acetate-vinyl chloride-butyl acrylate. Small amounts of

straight acrylics are also used to produce high quality, interior semigloss paints. They have excellent gloss as well as mar and scrub resistance. Semigloss paints weigh 10-11 pounds a gallon, and contain 48-50% solids by weight. The vehicle accounts for about 40% of the solids.

Approximately 48.5 million gallons of water-thinned interior undercoats and primers with a value of $476.3 million, or an average value of $9.83 a gallon, were produced in 2008. (See Figure 3-7.) This type of coating almost always contains vinyl-acrylic resin as the vehicle. A typical formulation weighs 9 to 10 pounds per gallon and contains 38-40% solids by weight, of which only 20-23% is the vehicle.

The latest production figures for water-based stains and sealers were in 2007. In that year, 46.8 million gallons of water-based stains and sealers were shipped. These products were valued at $451.7 million; price per gallon averaged $12.80. (See Figure 3-7.)

Solvent-based paints. Production of solvent-based interior paints and coatings totaled 38.5 million gallons in 2008 with a value of $634 million, or an average value of $16.47 per gallon. There are four major classes: 1) gloss; 2) semigloss, eggshell and satin finish; 3) flat; and 4) undercoats and primers.

Gloss, semigloss, eggshell and satin finish paints account for 37.3% of the volume of solvent-based interior paints. Nearly 3.2 million gallons of solvent-based gloss paint was shipped with a total value of $50.4 million in 2008. (See Figure 3-7.) Average price per gallon was $15.92. Over 11.2 gallons of solvent-based semigloss, eggshell, and satin interior paints were shipped that year with a total value of $187.8 million. Average price per gallon was $16.76. Alkyd resins, the major vehicle in this class of paints, are a well-known vehicle for gloss coatings, but they continue to lose market share to water-based products. A number of factors are responsible for the decline, including cost, VOC restrictions, improved performance and application characteristics of newer water-based formulations, and the basic trend away from solvent-based paints.

Production of flat solvent-based interior paints was just 2.4 million gallons valued at $70.2 million in 2008, or an average of $29.13 per gallon. (See Figure 3-7.) Alkyd and its relatives are the only significant resin used in interior solvent-based paints.

Solvent-based undercoats and primers totaled 21.7 million gallons valued at $224.3 million in 2008, or an average value of $10.33 a gallon. (See Figure 3-7.) Alkyd resins are also used in this class of paints.

Exterior paints. Until 1997 water-based paints continued to make significant inroads into the exterior paint segment as they replaced solvent-based alkyds and linseed oil coatings. Since then growth has slowed. In 2008, some 213.9 million gallons of exterior paints were produced, with water-based paints accounting for 156.1 million gallons or 73% of the total.

Water-based products. There are four major classes of exterior water-based paints: 1) water-thinned paints and tinting bases; 2) water-thinned deck and floor enamels; 3) water-thinned undercoats and primers; and 4) water-thinned stains and sealers.

More water-thinned paints and tinting bases, including barn and roof paints, are shipped than any other water-based exterior paint. In 2008, production totaled 96.1 million gallons valued at $1,305.9 million, or an average of $13.58 per gallon. (See Figure 3-7.)

Straight acrylics are the leading resin for water-based flat exterior paints and tinting bases, followed by vinyl-acrylic and small amounts of vinyl acetate-vinyl chloride-butyl acrylate resins. The paints weigh about 11-12 pounds per gallon and contain 50-55% solids by weight with 2.2 to 2.4 pounds

of vehicle. A small amount of alkyd resin is blended into many exterior paints to provide adhesion on previously painted surfaces that have chalked.

The balance of water-based exterior paints includes water-thinned deck and floor enamels, stains and sealers, and undercoats and primers. In 2008, 5.9 million gallons of water-based deck and floor enamels, 12.8 million gallons of undercoaters and primers, and 19.5 million gallons of stains and sealers were produced. (See Figure 3-7.) Deck and floor enamels were valued at $83 million (an average price per gallon of $14.00); undercoaters and primers were valued at $168 million (an average price per gallon of $13.09); and stains and sealers were valued at $279.9 million (an average price per gallon of $14.32). These water-based exterior coatings are primarily based on straight acrylic resins, average 10.5 to 11 pounds per gallon, and contain 50-52% solids, of which 2.4 pounds is vehicle.

Solvent-based products. Approximately 57.8 million gallons of solvent-based exterior paints valued at $886.8 million were produced in 2008, at an average value of $15.34 per gallon. Paints and tinting bases, enamels and tinted bases, undercoats and primers, finishes and sealers, and stains are the five primary categories of solvent-based exterior coatings.

Paints and tinting bases, including barn and roof paints, enamels and floor enamels, account for over half of all solvent-based exterior paints; in 2008, 30.4 million gallons were shipped with a value of $482.9 million. (See Figure 3-7.) Semigloss and gloss paints, which largely use alkyd resins with small amounts of polyurethanes and acrylics, are the largest types. Due to VOC restrictions coupled with the trend toward low odor, easy clean-up water systems continue to erode sales of gloss and semigloss paints.

Seven million gallons of solvent-based undercoats and primers valued at $103.4 million were shipped in 2008, with an average value of $14.73 per gallon. (See Figure 3-7.) VOC restrictions for primers are not as severe as those for flat paints, but sales will continue to decline due to the overall trend toward water-based products. Alkyd resins still dominate in most products. The balance of solvent-based paints is comprised of stains, including products for shingles and shakes, and clear finishes and coatings. Alkyd resin and oil/oleoresinous vehicles are used in stains, while clear finishes are usually polyurethane systems.

Suppliers. According to the trade journal *Paint & Coatings Industry*, in 2008 (twenty-four North American coatings companies) twenty-two of them based in the United States, had sales of $100 million or more (Karen Parker, "PCI 25 Reflects Industry Consolidation," July 1, 2009, http://www.pcimag.com/Articles/Feature_Article/BNP_GUID_9-5-2006_A_10000000000000618036). PPG Industries Inc., based in Pittsburgh, was the leading U.S. paint company, with sales of $10.1 billion; however most of this company's sales were in OEM coatings. The leading U.S. architectural coatings supplier is Sherwin-Williams; the company had $5.98 billion in sales in 2008.

Significant changes occurred in the 1990s and early 2000s as mergers and acquisitions in the maturing paint industry were frequent. However, none of the major U.S. companies had been acquired in 2008, and the pace overall had slowed due to the effects of the global economic recession (Sean Milmo, "Acquisitions and Divestments... Or the Lack of Them," *Coatings World*, March 2010, pp. 30-31).

Figure 3-8 shows price indexes for architectural paint by type from 2000 to 2009. Prices increased steadily over this time spurred by sharply rising prices for interior products.

On average, prices for architectural coatings increased by 5.4% a year between 2000 and 2009.

Architectural paints are sold to do-it-yourself (DIY) consumers, painting contractors, and commercial and industrial maintenance users through a variety of channels. They are distributed at 8,025 independent paint and wallpaper dealers, although big-box stores such as Wal-Mart and Lowes claim increasing shares of paint customers. (See Figure 1-18 in Section 1.) Hardware stores, building material and lumber dealers, and general merchandise stores also sell paint.

The professional market consists of contractors, decorators and remodelers. According to the 2002 Economic Census, the latest data available, approximately 39,477 companies were active in Painting and Wall Covering (NAICS 235210), employing 239,381 people. The value of painting and paper hanging was $17.8 billion, up from $13.1 billion in 2002.

The penetration of water-based products into the architectural paint sector achieved maturity in the 1990s. Since then only minor changes in formulations have been made,

Figure 3-8 Producer Price Indexes for Architectural Paint, 2000-2009

Year	Annual
2000	168.7
2001	174.3
2002	175.2
2003	180.6
2004	187.4
2005	203.3
2006	220.2
2007	230.5
2008	249.0
2009	269.7

Source: "Producer Price Index, Commodities, Not Seasonally Adjusted--Architectural Coatings," Bureau of Labor Statistics, 2010, http://www.bls.gov/ppi (accessed May 16, 2010)

particularly for the resin systems used in interior and exterior products. As a result, producers rely heavily on aggressive marketing and advertising programs, including computerized color matching and tinting programs.

Computerized tinting systems help assure reliability in color matching between wall and trim paints, as well as between batches. In addition, the system allows paint colors and shades to match with carpeting, drapery or furniture, and has become an integral part of paint merchandising. In addition, paint companies are constantly searching for ways to use technology to market their products. Architectural paint retailer Benjamin Moore even introduced a free iPhone and iPod Touch application that enabled users to match any colors in a photograph to one of the company's paint colors in 2009 (Rima Suqi, "On Your iPhone: Point and Paint," *New York Times*, May 20, 2009, http://www.nytimes.com/2009/05/21/garden/21apps.html). Other merchandising programs include computerized systems for visualizing paint colors on exterior surfaces or interior walls. Varying the color of trim and other flat surfaces enables the consumer to preview paint colors on realistic images of interior and exteriors. Fandecks, color cards or color collections are produced by Colwell Industries, Kendallville, Indiana and Color Communications, Chicago, Illinois. Many leading producers of architectural paints offer color cards to customers.

Some 80% of architectural paints are colored in-store or by the painter by mixing precise volumes of 12 liquid "universal" colorants by formula into one of five grades of water- or solvent-based tint bases, including deep tone, medium tone, pastel, clear and chromatic. The remaining 20% of architectural paints are colored at the factory, by using aqueous or solvent-based dispersions.

INDUSTRIAL OEM COATINGS

Paints, coatings and powders for Original Equipment Manufactures (OEM), the second largest segment of the paint industry, accounted for 344.1 million gallons of finished product in 2008. (See Figure 3-10.) The U.S. Census Bureau describes OEM coatings as "coatings formulated specifically for OEM to meet conditions of application and product requirements, and applied to such products during the manufacturing process."

This important segment is highly fragmented by type of coating, the variety of application techniques, and a large number of formulations resulting in a high degree of product specialization. Over 200 companies compete intensely with products requiring customer pre-purchase technical approval. As noted previously, such OEM coating segments as electrical insulation, paper, film, paperboard and other specialty coatings are not covered in this *Guide*.

Due to the changing character of coating formulations, with the trend towards high-solids, solvent-free and powder coatings, and to the impact of different and improved application equipment with improved transfer efficiency, statistics for OEM finishes consumption are sometimes reported in dry gallons, that is, gallons less volatile solvent and or water, equivalent to dry weight. Currently, consumption in dry gallons is about half reported gallons.

Resins used in OEM coatings have improved, and include alkyds, polyesters, epoxies, acrylics, vinyls, urethanes and combination resins, such as epoxy-acrylic or acrylic-polyurethane. Water-based products are chiefly acrylics (48%), vinyls (15%) and epoxies (20%). They dominate in metal decorating and in electrodeposition (ED) primers, both cathodic and anodic types. Water-based coatings are also making inroads into coil

81

coatings, and coatings for wood flat stock and paper and paperboard.

In 2008, production of OEM coatings totaled 344.1 million gallons, about 28.1% of all paints in shipped. (See Figure 3-10.) OEM product coatings in that year were worth $5,662.5 million, about 29.9% of the total value of all paint shipments that year. (See Figure 3-9.) The volume of OEM coatings shipped declined 6.9% and the value declined 5% from the previous year because of the global economic recession that began late in 2008.

Figure 3-9 illustrates the long-term pattern of shipments of OEM coatings. Growth in dollars was strong until 1998; after a decline in the first five years of the new century, growth rebounded before drastically declining in 2008. Shipments of gallons have been more erratic over the long term, although they generally declined after 2000. (See Figure 3-10.)

Paint & Coatings Industry reported that in 2008, PPG Industries was the largest U.S. supplier of OEM product finishes; the company had coatings sales of approximately $10.1 billion in 2008. DuPont Coatings & Color Technologies Group was the second largest OEM product finish supplier in the United States; in 2008, that company's coatings sales were $6.6 billion.

Figure 3-12 shows production indexes for OEM product finishes compared to selected end uses for 1999 to 2009. Production of paints and coatings generally increased until 2004, when it began to slide, dropping below 1999 levels in 2006 and continuing the decline through 2009. Between 2004 and 2009, production decreased by an average of 6.3% each year. All but two end uses, farm machinery/equipment and aircraft and parts, were consuming lower volumes of coatings in 2009 than in 1999.

Figure 3-11 shows producer prices for OEM Product Coatings, excluding marine coatings for 2000 to 2009. Prices increased, on average, 2.9% annually during the decade, generally at a slower rate than increases in architectural coatings producer prices (which averaged a 5.8% increase annually) and special purpose coatings producer prices (which averaged a 4.5% increase annually). Much of the product price increases were due to new formulations required to meet environmental standards set by the EPA as well as to increasing costs for raw materials.

OEM finishes are classified by end-uses, both in pre-finished (wood or metal), or finished form. Figure 3-13 groups data for OEM product finishes into the leading categories. Figure 3-14 shows dollar shipments by major end use in 2007. Machinery and equipment consumed the largest dollar amount of OEM product finishes in that year. Industries that provide details to the Census Bureau on their consumption of paints are listed in Figure 3-15. The metal coating industry consumed

Figure 3-11 Producer Price Index for OEM Product Coatings, 2000-2009

Year	Annual
2000	127.0
2001	125.5
2002	126.2
2003	127.4
2004	129.0
2005	137.1
2006	145.0
2007	147.0
2008	157.0
2009	164.8

Source: "Producer Price Index, Commodities, Not Seasonally Adjusted--Architectural Coatings," Bureau of Labor Statistics, 2010, http://www.bls.gov/ppi (accessed May 16, 2010)

Figure 3-9   Shipments of OEM Coatings, 1985-2008 (in millions of dollars)

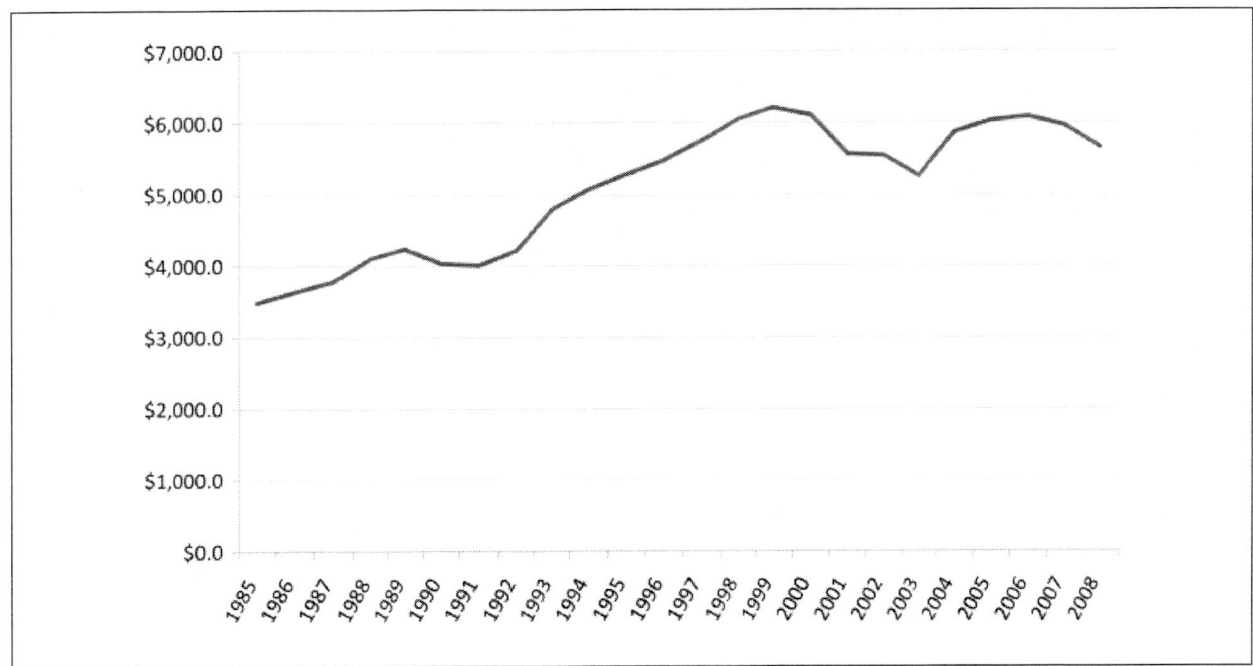

Source: Adapted from "Sector 31: EC073111: Manufacturing: Industry Series: Detailed Statistics by Industry for the United States: 2007," 2007 Economic Census, U.S. Census Bureau, 2009, http://factfinder.census.gov/servlet/IBQTable?_bm=y&-geo_id=01000US&-ds_name=EC073111&-NAICS2007=325510&-_lang=en (accessed November 30, 2009)

Figure 3-10   Shipments of OEM Coatings, 1985-2008 (in millions of gallons)

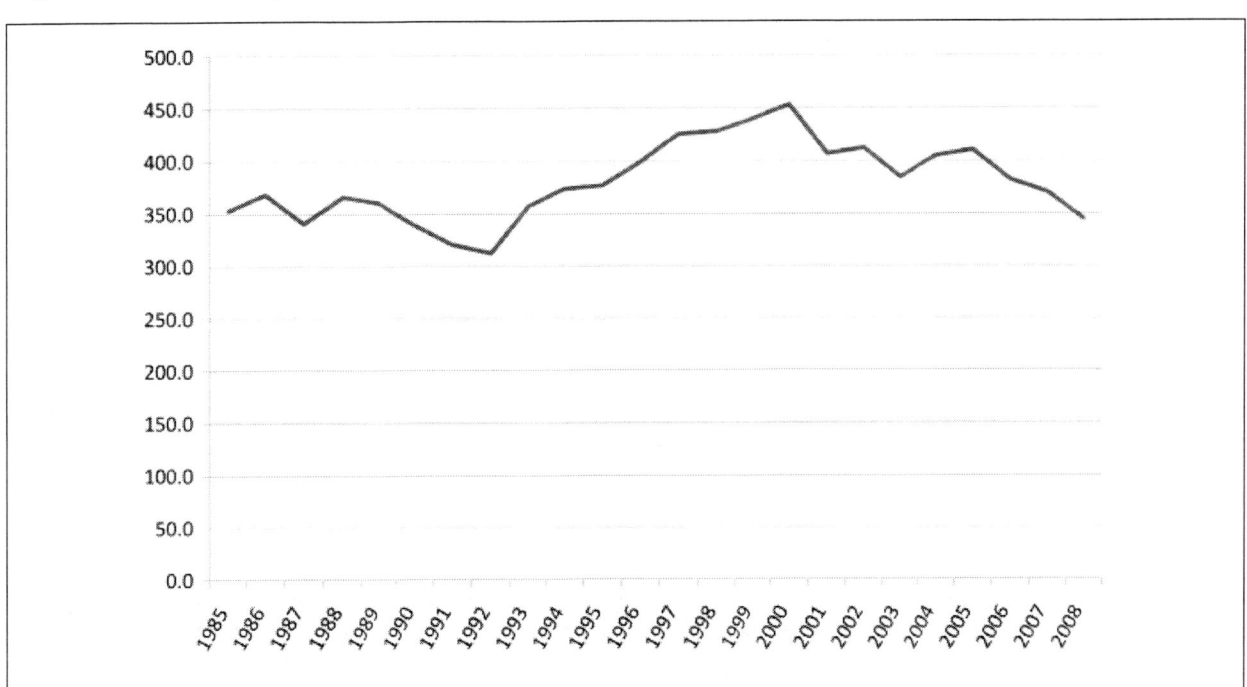

Source: Adapted from "Sector 31: EC073111: Manufacturing: Industry Series: Detailed Statistics by Industry for the United States: 2007," 2007 Economic Census, U.S. Census Bureau, 2009, http://factfinder.census.gov/servlet/IBQTable?_bm=y&-geo_id=01000US&-ds_name=EC073111&-NAICS2007=325510&-_lang=en (accessed November 30, 2009)

Figure 3-12   Industrial Production Indexes for OEM Product Finishes and Select End Use Industries, 1999-2009

Descriptions:	1999	2000	2001	2002	2003	2004	2005	2006	2007	2008	2009
Paint and coating NAICS=32551, nsa	108.3	108.0	105.6	106.6	105.3	112.4	109.4	104.8	100.0	89.5	72.3
Farm machinery and equipment NAICS=333111, nsa	64.7	76.2	76.8	78.9	81.2	91.4	97.7	93.8	100.0	111.7	103.3
Construction machinery NAICS=33312, nsa	73.0	75.8	66.7	59.1	62.2	76.2	89.1	98.2	100.0	95.6	66.5
Household appliance NAICS=3352, nsa	96.0	101.6	97.9	96.3	100.4	105.2	103.8	101.4	100.0	91.0	81.1
Automobile NAICS=336111, nsa	117.1	114.9	101.1	105.0	102.8	102.1	104.0	110.0	100.0	97.9	57.3
Heavy duty truck NAICS=33612, nsa	135.8	117.2	74.3	90.1	86.6	115.4	141.8	156.2	100.0	93.0	56.8
Motor vehicle parts NAICS=3363, nsa	106.0	106.7	96.1	105.0	104.4	103.5	104.6	100.3	100.0	83.1	68.5
Aircraft and parts NAICS=336411-3, nsa	87.7	77.7	84.3	75.7	69.4	68.8	74.7	84.8	100.0	92.1	95.6
Ship and boat building NAICS=3366, nsa	83.9	86.4	82.7	91.0	93.0	94.7	94.6	94.3	100.0	102.9	82.8
Office and other furniture NAICS=3372,9, nsa	100.2	103.4	93.8	95.6	95.3	97.8	101.2	100.1	100.0	92.7	79.7
Railroad rolling stock NAICS=3365, nsa	94.9	89.1	76.4	70.8	64.7	74.9	83.0	95.1	100.0	117.3	76.1
Household and institutional furniture and kitchen cabinet NAICS=3371, nsa	102.2	102.5	98.4	102.9	100.0	103.1	107.0	104.8	100.0	89.4	68.2
Total index, nsa	88.4	92.0	88.9	89.1	90.2	92.3	95.3	97.4	100.0	96.7	87.7
Durable consumer goods, nsa	88.6	91.4	87.3	92.6	95.7	97.1	97.8	98.2	100.0	89.7	74.5

Source: Derived from "Monthly Report of Industrial Production," not seasonally adjusted, G17, Federal Reserve Board, http://www.federalreserve.gov/datadownload/Download.aspx?rel=G17&series=22dea0fad47de931142cdbb9f4166802&filetype=spreadsheetml&label=include&layout=seriesrow&from=01/01/1999&to=12/31/2009 (accessed June 25, 2009)

Figure 3-13 U.S. Shipments of OEM Product Finishes by End Use, 2007 and 2008

Product code	Product description	Year	Quantity	Value
3255104	Product finishes for original equipment manufacturers (OEM), excluding marine coatings	2008	343,441	5,651,190
		2007	368,922	5,948,121
3255104111	Automobile, light truck, van, and sport utility vehicle finishes	2008	(S)	(S)
		2007	53,077	1,190,747
3255104121	Automobile parts finishes	2008	3,115	118,603
		2007	4,132	157,161
3255104131	Heavy duty truck, bus, and recreational vehicle finishes	2008	7,115	(S)
		2007	6,688	148,438
3255104141	Other transportation equipment finishes, including aircraft and railroad	2008	8,799	195,131
		2007	8,591	181,458
3255104211	Appliance, heating equipment, and air-conditioner finishes	2008	7,074	87,013
		2007	6,557	84,489
3255104215	Wood furniture, cabinet, and fixture finishes	2008	33,762	520,310
		2007	39,060	549,521
3255104219	Wood and composition board flat stock finishes	2008	8,372	109,503
		2007	9,334	107,022
3255104221	Metal building product finishes (including coatings for aluminum extrusions and siding)	2008	28,304	628,406
		2007	27,764	591,749
3255104225	Container and closure finishes	2008	34,030	511,550
		2007	33,072	472,510
3255104229	Machinery and equipment finishes, including road building equipment and farm implement	2008	21,905	564,703
		2007	22,146	551,529
3255104231	Nonwood furniture and fixture finishes, including business equipment finishes	2008	27,413	368,946
		2007	30,315	400,475
3255104235	Paper, paper board, film, and foil finishes, excluding pigment binders	2008	13,840	149,686
		2007	13,471	135,096
3255104239	Electrical insulating coatings	2008	804	23,527
		2007	787	22,597
3255104241	Thermoset general decorative, appliance powder coatings 1/	2008	9,140	195,168
		2007	8,804	180,776
3255104245	Thermoset general decorative, automotive powder coatings 1/	2008	3,273	70,522
		2007	3,561	73,796
3255104249	Thermoset general decorative, architectural powder coatings (such as aluminum extrusions) 1/	2008	1,703	27,834
		2007	1,790	25,169
3255104251	Thermoset general decorative, lawn and garden powder coatings 1/	2008	795	11,918
		2007	1,170	17,392
3255104255	Thermoset general decorative, general metal finishing powder coatings 1/	2008	16,884	293,532
		2007	20,476	352,841
3255104259	Thermoset functional powder coatings (for pipe, rebar, electrical insulation, etc.) 1/	2008	(D)	(D)
		2007	(D)	(D)
3255104261	Thermoplastic powder coatings (all) 1/	2008	(D)	(D)
		2007	(D)	(D)
3255104263	Other powder coatings	2008	(D)	(D)
		2007	(D)	(D)
3255104265	Other industrial product finishes	2008	31,744	392,512
		2007	33,177	400,980

Source: Adapted from "Table 2. Quantity and Value of Shipments of Paint and Allied Products: 2008 and 2007," Current Industrial Reports M325F, U.S. Census Bureau, http://www.census.gov/manufacturing/cir/historical_data/ma325f/index.html (accessed November 30, 2009)

Figure 3-14   U.S. Consumption of OEM Industrial Finishes by Use in 2007

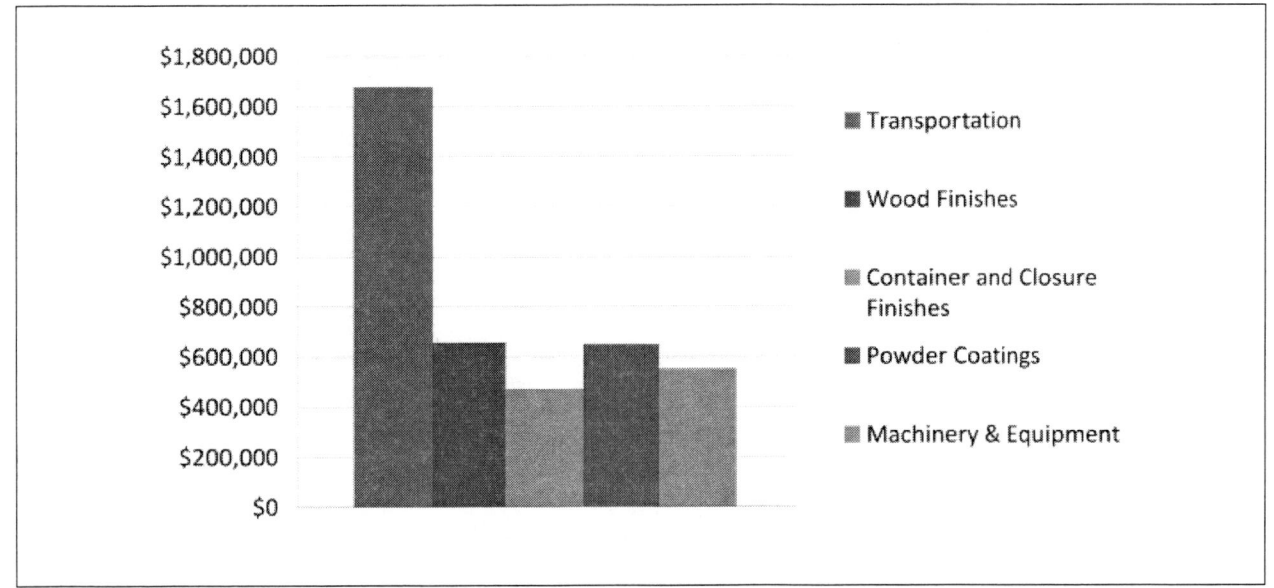

Source: Adapted from "Table 2. Quantity and Value of Shipments of Paint and Allied Products: 2008 and 2007," Current Industrial Reports M325F, U.S. Census Bureau, http://www.census.gov/manufacturing/cir/historical_data/ma325f/index.html (accessed November 30, 2009)

the largest amount (in dollars) of paint in 2007.

Transportation

The U.S. transportation industry consumed 76 million gallons of coatings (including powder coatings) valued at $1,751.6 million in 2007, representing 22.2% of all OEM product finishes (by volume) in that year.

Motor vehicles. Motor vehicle finishes (excluding powder coatings), the largest application for OEM transportation coatings, accounted for estimated consumption of 68.4 million gallons valued at $1,520.6 million in 2007. Included in these data are 57.2 million gallons of finishes valued at $1,347.9 million for automobiles, light trucks, vans and sport utility vehicles (SUVs) and automobile parts. The balance, 6.7 million gallons valued at $148,438 million, was for heavy-duty trucks, buses, recreation vehicles and related items. (See Figure 3-13.)

In 2008, 3.3 million pounds of automotive powder coatings were consumed with a value

of $70.5 million. (See Figure 3-13.) Among the parts coated with powder coatings are roof racks, door handles, rear view mirror backs, window clips, mirror housings, oil and air filters, wheels, engines, seatbelt tracks, value covers, carburetors, struts, shock absorbers, master cylinders, wiper blades holders, radiators, radiator fan blades, roll bars, deflectors, and stabilizer bars. Top coats and full body primers are growing in importance for powders.

Automobiles and trucks. An important factor in the production of motor vehicles in North America was the passage of the North American Free Trade Agreement (NAFTA) in the mid 1990s. As a result, production of motor vehicles slowed in the United States and increased in Canada and Mexico. With the increased production of passenger cars and trucks these countries, the U.S. paint industry is exporting increasing quantities of finishes for passenger cars and trucks. In addition to assembled motor vehicles, some parts for motor vehicles are produced in Canada and

Figure 3-15 Value of Industrial OEM Paints Consumed by Reporting Industries, 2007

2007 NAICS code	Meaning of 2007 NAICS code	Delivered cost ($1,000)
321219	Reconstituted wood product manufacturing	41,633
321999	All other miscellaneous wood product manufacturing	25,522
332114	Custom roll forming	24,652
332115	Crown and closure manufacturing	29,139
332116	Metal stamping	47,631
332311	Prefabricated metal building and component manufacturing	32,606
332312	Fabricated structural metal manufacturing	253,987
332313	Plate work manufacturing	32,141
332322	Sheet metal work manufacturing	100,807
332323	Ornamental and architectural metal work manufacturing	130,880
332410	Power boiler and heat exchanger manufacturing	4,563
332420	Metal tank (heavy gauge) manufacturing	46,293
332431	Metal can manufacturing	239,722
332439	Other metal container manufacturing	51,039
332812	Metal coating and nonprecious engraving	1,582,286
332813	Electroplating, plating, polishing, anodizing, and coloring	75,364
333111	Farm machinery and equipment manufacturing	110,493
333112	Lawn and garden equipment manufacturing	68,318
333120	Construction machinery manufacturing	93,789
333311	Automatic vending machine manufacturing	2,422
333921	Elevator and moving stairway manufacturing	6,564
333922	Conveyor and conveying equipment manufacturing	39,069
333923	Overhead cranes, hoists, and monorail systems	D
333924	Industrial truck, trailer, and stacker mfg.	D
335211	Electric housewares and household fan manufacturing	8,439
335221	Household cooking appliance manufacturing	65,712
335222	Household refrigerator and home freezer manufacturing	80,767
335224	Household laundry equipment manufacturing	85,127
335228	Other major household appliance manufacturing	48,044
337110	Wood kitchen cabinet and countertop manufacturing	175,116
337121	Upholstered household furniture manufacturing	7,931
337122	Nonupholstered wood household furniture manufacturing	76,072
337124	Metal household furniture manufacturing	4,639
337125	Household furniture (except wood and metal) manufacturing	1,935
337127	Institutional furniture manufacturing	28,371
337129	Wood television, radio, and sewing machine cabinet manufacturing	1,226
337211	Wood office furniture manufacturing	30,082
337212	Custom architectural woodwork and millwork manufacturing	34,631
337214	Office furniture (except wood) manufacturing	46,003
337215	Showcase, partition, shelving, and locker manufacturing	74,291
339920	Sporting and athletic goods manufacturing	34,964
339950	Sign manufacturing	52,298
339995	Burial casket manufacturing	8,315

Source: Derived from "Sector 31: EC073113: Manufacturing: Industry Series: Materials Consumed by Kind for the United States: 2007," 2007 Economic Census, U.S. Census Bureau, 2009, http://factfinder.census.gov/servlet/DatasetMainPageServlet?_lang=en&_ts=295950014473&_ds_name=AM0831VS101&_program=EAS (accessed June 25, 2010)

shipped to the United States for assembling. For exterior parts, color matching is essential, requiring export of U.S. produced auto finishes to Canada for the parts.

Typically, an automobile exterior is first coated with an electrodeposition (ED) primer based on epoxy resins. After deposition of the paint as positively charged particles onto the grounded auto body in an ED tank, the entire body is baked to cure the epoxy resins. Approximately 1.8-2.0 gal of ED primer are consumed per unit. A number of top-of-the-line auto bodies are then coated with a primer/surfacer which smoothes out the surface by filling in any voids, improves adhesion between the ED primer and topcoats, and provides for a better overall finish. They are also used when an ED primer coat has been damaged. Primer/surfacers are high solids materials which use epoxy, polyester or urethane resins. Electrocoat primers and primer/surfacers account for about 40% of coating consumption on auto bodies.

Basecoats or color coats are applied either to the ED coat or to the primer/surfacer, if used. Approximately 0.9 gallon is applied per unit. Base coats contain the colored and metallic pigments and other additives that provide the basic color and corrosion protection for the system. Both solvent- and water-based acrylics are used as basecoats, which provide color and film build that contributes to the overall appeal of the automobile. Due to the pressure to reduce VOCs, water-based base coats have become the dominant material.

A clear coat is then applied onto the slightly wet basecoat. Clear coats give autos their lustrous look and protect the basecoat from environmental attack. Solvent-based acrylics are the leading clear coat. Two-part solvent-based urethane clear coats are also used, representing about 30% of volume. Urethane clear coats have a deeper luster and possess better environmental resistance and are more resistant to road salt, acid rain and

bird excrement. They also have lower VOCs than acrylics, a major driving force for their use. Aliphatic isocyanates are used along with a hydroxy functional acrylic or polyester polyol. Aliphatic isocyanates are more resistant to sunlight than are organic isocyanates. Base coats and clear coats account for 30% of the volume of coatings used on automobiles and electrodeposition coatings accounting for 25%.

New technology is introduced regularly as increasingly stringent environmental regulations push automakers to find alternatives to solvent-based coatings. For example, a two-coat E-coat system called *Power-Prime* was developed by PPG in which a second coat replaces the conventional primer-surfacer. Paint films are increasingly used to coat auto bodies and automobile parts because of their low VOC-emissions and durability as compared to traditional paint applications (Teri Chouinard, "Changing the Way We Color Our World: Dry Paint Film—the 'Green' Alternative to Paint Gains Momentum," *Paint & Coatings Industry*, June 2006, pp. 26-29). In 2009, Ford rolled out a "3-Wet" paint technology that used a solvent-based, high-solid paint that produces fewer emissions than even current water-based auto-paint technologies, as well as a savings in the amount of time—and cost—of paint processes ("Ford's Innovative, Sustainable Paint Technology Goes Global," *Coatings World*, October 2009, p. 20).

Most autos also have an anti-chip coating applied on lower body parts, such as rocker panels, to provide protection against nicking from stones and other road debris. Either solvent-based PVC plastisols or solvent-based urethanes are applied. Other coatings are used as underbody coatings and sound deadeners, including PVC plastisol and emulsion and solvent-based asphalt coatings. Alkyds are employed for miscellaneous metal parts found under the hood.

On April 26, 2004, the EPA rule limiting Hazardous Air Pollutants (HAP) for automobile and light truck manufacturing plants went into effect. The rule set limits for all coatings and primers used in automobile manufacturing including electrodeposition primers, primer surfacers, base coats, and clear coats. The combined limits for Hazardous Air Pollutants (HAPs) for new or rebuilt plants for all coatings used were set at 0.30 lb/gal. For existing plants the limits were set at 0.60 lb/gal; these plants had an additional three years to meet those limits. The rule also set limits for all cleaning and purging equipment and solvents associated with the coating operation ("National Emission Standards for Hazardous Air Pollutants: Surface Coating of Automobiles and Light-Duty Trucks; Final Rule," *Federal Register*, vol. 69, no. 80, April 26, 2004, http://www.epa.gov/ttn/atw/auto/fr26ap04r.pdf).

The growing use of plastic parts and components on the exterior of automobiles has led to the development of a wide variety of new paints and coatings. These include in-mold coatings for both thermoset and thermoplastic parts, such as those used in hoods, door panels, and fascias. Other coatings applied over plastic substrates include conductive primers needed for applying coatings by electrostatic spray onto exterior thermoplastics, base coat/clear coat coatings for urethane (PU), thermoplastic olefins (TPO) which are harder to coat, paint films, and flexible plastics.

UV-cured coatings are finding increasing uses for applications where VOCs and HAPs are strictly regulated. Control Technique Guidelines (CTGs) are in place for auto and light duty truck manufacturing, and the EPA also regulates HAPs for automobile refinish coatings (see Figure 1-22 in Section 1). UV-cured coatings significantly reduce hazardous emissions as well as energy consumption at automobile factories, and also enable plastic parts to be on the vehicle during coating application and cure.

Coatings for plastics are subject to emission limits established by the EPA in their final rule for plastic coatings, issued April 19, 2004. The rule limits emissions for different products and substrates, as shown in Figure 3-17. The rule affected manufacturers and industries producing steel furniture, office machines, radio and telephone equipment (cell phones), motor homes, motor vehicle body parts, medical equipment and supplies, sporting and athletic goods, signs and advertising specialties.

Three companies—PPG, DuPont, and BASF—dominate global sales of motor vehicle coatings, including electrodeposition coatings, base coats, clear coats and primer surfacers.

Other Transportation. Other types of transportation equipment together consumed 8.8 million gallons of coatings valued at $195.1 million in 2008. (See Figure 3-13.) This group includes principally aircraft and railroads.

Solvent-based, two-component epoxies are used as aircraft primers followed by solvent-based, two-component aliphatic isocyanate polyurethane coatings. Aliphatic isocyanates are used because aromatic types yellow and degrade in the intense UV light of the upper atmosphere. PPG and Akzo-Nobel dominate sales of aircraft coatings. Solvent-based alkyds, polyurethanes and epoxies account for the vast majority of the volume of coatings used by railroad equipment and truck trailers.

Metal Finishes

Metal finishes are used to decorate and protect a variety of steel and aluminum products including beverage and food cans, bottle closures, office and household furniture and other metal parts or components. Epoxy

89

Figure 3-16   U.S. Consumption of Metal Cans by End Use, Selected Years, 1980-2005 (in billion units)

Year	Beverages	Food	General Packaging	Total
1980	55.2	30.0	4.9	90.1
1985	70.2	27.8	3.9	101.9
1990	90.1	30.1	4.0	124.2
1995	98.1	31.3	4.3	133.7
2000	100.2	31.5	4.4	136.1
2001	100.8	30.8	4.2	135.8
2002	100.5	31.3	4.3	136.1
2003	99.7	30.5	4.4	134.6
2004	99.8	30.5	4.5	134.8
2005	99.2	29.5	4.3	133.0

Source: Adapted from "General Line Can Shipments," "CMI Shipments by Category," and "Beverage Can Data," Can Manufacturers Institute, 2006, http://www.cancentral.com/content.cfm (accessed June 25, 2010)

resins are used as primers, when needed, and in finishes. Alkyds, acrylics, polyesters, urea and melamine formaldehydes and urethanes are also major factors. Conventional low-solids finishes continue to be used, but high-solids and solvent-free finishes and powder coatings are growing rapidly.

Metal Containers. The use of coatings on metal cans and closures, collapsible tubes, pails and drums is one of the larger end uses for product finishes. It is a specialty application requiring uniform-quality coatings used on interior and/or exterior surfaces, container ends, and closures. Interior can linings protect the integrity, taste and flavor of foods and beverages packaged in metal cans. Consumption in 2008 totaled 34 million gallons valued at $511.6 million. (See Figure 3-13.) Over 90% of the total is applied to metal cans as a protection for inner surfaces and as a base coat for overprint varnishes in exterior graphics. Pails and drums account for 7% of consumption and metal closures (caps, crowns) for 3%.

According to the Can Manufacturers Institute, about 133 billion cans were produced in 2005, down by about 1.3% from the year before and down 2.3% from the peak of 136.1 billion units shipped in 2002. (See Figure 3-16.) Competition from plastic containers for beverages, especially soft drinks, and some shift to plastic containers for foods, have impacted the demand for metal cans.

In 2005, 74.6% of cans were used for beverages, primarily beer and soft drinks, 22.2% were used for food products, and the balance for the general packaging of variety of non-food products. (See Figure 3-16) Two-piece cans dominate aluminum beverage containers whereas three-piece steel cans still dominate among food containers. However, two-piece construction is becoming more common.

Over the years the trend to aluminum cans served to moderate the growth of coatings, particularly for interior linings, since thinner applications are used to coat aluminum than for steel cans. The steel can maintains its position as the leading packaging material for foods.

Beverage cans and containers use water-based coatings almost exclusively. Overprint varnishes on beverage cans are primarily water-based acrylics with small amounts of polyester and UV cured epoxy acrylates also used.

Approximately two-thirds of food can coatings are applied to interior surfaces, primarily solvent-based epoxy phenolics, epoxy-aminos, epoxy-esters, oleoresinous, acrylics and vinyls. Small amounts of water-based epoxy-phenolics are also consumed. A variety of coatings systems are used on food can exteriors, including epoxy aminos, alkyds, acrylics and polyesters. Since epoxy-phenolics provide chemical resistance and resistance to high temperature sterilization after food is packed in cans, they are commonly used on the interior, bottom and filler end of food cans. Vinyls are flexible and provide chemical and corrosion resistance for the interior of beer and beverage can ends (lids) and aluminum. Acrylics, applied by spray or roll coating and subjected to a short bake cure, are used on the interior of food cans and bottle crowns, and to cover the weld area on three-piece food cans. Coil coatings for food cans are pre-coated with vinyl or polyester then fabricated later.

Metal closures use solvent-based coatings consisting of vinyls and epoxies for interior surfaces and acrylics, alkyds and vinyls for exterior surfaces. Pails and drums consume predominantly solvent-based coatings. Phenolic and epoxy phenolics are the leading system for interior surfaces. Solvent-based alkyds are applied to exterior surfaces, with water-based alkyds gaining market share.

The EPA issued HAP emission limits for metal cans on November 13, 2003. All plants using 1,500 gallons annually are covered, including new and reconstructed plants and also existing facilities. The limits vary depending on the type of can produced, as shown in Figure 3-17.

Coil Coatings. The coating of pre-finished metal, called coil coating, is commonly accomplished through high-speed application of liquid coatings to continuous sheet, strip or coils of aluminum or cold-rolled steel, galvanized steel and aluminum/zinc coated steel. Steel accounts for about 65% of consumption and aluminum the balance. Using coil coated metal is attractive to manufacturers because it saves time and space on the factory floor, eliminates the need to keep inventories-in-process, and helps companies meet EPA rules ("Manage the Margin with Prepaint," *National Coil Coatings Association Newsletter*, Summer 2009, http://www.coilcoatinginstitute.org/misc/article1_0727.aspx).

The pre-painted or pre-coated metal coils are bent and shaped by manufacturers of such construction products as wall and roof panels, doors and siding for residential homes and prefabricated buildings. Coil coated metal is also used to manufacture transportation equipment, including truck trailers and RV's, and also in the production of metal furniture, appliances, containers and a variety of miscellaneous metal products.

Once the sheet has been cleaned, it is roller or curtain coated, cured and re-rolled for shipping. Dry film thickness (dft) of coatings ranges from 0.1 mil to over 4 mils, with the most common 0.7 to 1.0 mil. Plastisols are generally applied at 4 to 10 mils dft. Coating line speeds are typically 200 to 400 feet per minute (fpm), but can go as high as 900 fpm.

Solvent-based polyesters, the leading type of coil coatings, account for nearly one-third of the total. However, consumption is flat as systems based on water-based acrylics and polyvinyl difluoride/acrylic (PVDF) are gaining market share. PVDF, with about an 18% share, provides extraordinary long life to building products, which is especially desirable when used on panels for high rise buildings. Epoxies, with a 24% share, are the preferred primer for both steel and aluminum, and the fastest-growing type of coil coating products. Other systems are vinyl organosols and vinyl plastisols.

Figure 3-17   EPA Emission Limits for Existing and New Sources for Metal Can Coatings, Final Rule, November 13, 2003

If you apply surface coatings to metal cans or metal can parts in this subcategory . . .		For all coatings of this type . . .	Then, you must meet the following organic HAP emission limit in kilograms (kg) HAP/liter solids (lb HAP/gal solids):[1,2]
1.	One- and two-piece D&I can body coating	a. Two-piece beverage cans—all coatings b. Two-piece food cans—all coatings c. One-piece aerosol cans—all coatings	0.04 (0.31). 0.06 (0.50). 0.08 (0.65).
2.	Sheetcoating	Sheetcoating	0.02 (0.17).
3.	Three-piece can assembly	a. Inside spray b. Aseptic side seam stripes on food cans c. Nonaseptic side seam stripes on food cans d. Side seam stripes on general line nonfood cans. e. Side seam stripes on aerosol cans	0.12 (1.03). 1.48 (12.37). 0.72 (5.96). 1.18 (9.84).
4.	End coating	a. Aseptic end seal compounds b. Nonaseptic end seal compounds c. Repair sprays	
1.	One- and two-piece D&I can body coating	a. Two-piece beverage cans—all coatings b. Two-piece food cans—all coatings c. One-piece aerosol cans—all coatings	0.07 (0.59). 0.06 (0.51). 0.12 (0.99).
2.	Sheetcoating	Sheetcoating	0.03 (0.26).
3.	Three-piece can assembly	a. Inside spray b. Aseptic side seam stripes on food cans c. Nonaseptic side seam stripes on food cans d. Side seam stripes on general line nonfood cans e. Side seam stripes on aerosol cans	0.29 (2.43). 1.94 (16.16). 0.79 (6.57). 1.18 (9.84). 1.46 (12.14).
4.	End coating	a. Aseptic end seal compounds b. Nonaseptic end seal compounds c. Repair sprays	0.06 (0.54). 0.00 (0.00). 2.06 (17.17).

[1] If you apply surface coatings of more than one type within any one subcategory, you may calculate an overall subcategory emission limit according to 40 CFR 63.3531(i).

[2] Rounding differences in specific emission limits are attributable to unit conversions.

Source: "Table 2. Emission Limits for Existing Affected Sources," and "Table 3. Emission Limits for New or Reconstructed Affected Sources," in National E mission Standards for Hazardous Air Pollutants: Surface Coating of Metal Cans; Final Rule," Federal Register, 40 CFR Part 63, November 13, 2003, http://www.epa.gov/ttn/atw/mcan/fr13no03.pdf (accessed June 25, 2010)

Metal building product finishes, which included coil coatings for building products (such as aluminum extrusions and siding), reached 28.3 million gallons in 2008, with a total value of $628.4 million. (See Figure 3-13.) The Census Bureau does not separate coil coatings from other metal coatings, however. Other uses for coil coating include pre-engineered building materials, roof decking, metal doors and windows, soffit, trim, and awnings and canopies. Some 80% of the coil coatings for building applications are applied to steel with the balance on aluminum substrates.

The appliance industry, a moderate to small consumer of paints and coatings overall, was hard hit by restrictions on VOC emissions and found pre-coated metal an attractive alternative to on-site application of coatings. In addition, small amounts of pre-coated steel and aluminum are used in metal furniture including desks, cabinets, shelving, stands and some household furniture. Solvent-based epoxies are used as primers with solvent-based polyesters the dominant topcoat. Steel substrates dominate in this segment.

HAP emission limits were issued on June 10, 2002 for metal coil coating operations. The emission limits are 0.38 lb/gal of solids applied during each period. The rule also provides that HAP emissions be no more than 2% of the organic HAP applied, or 98% overall control. Existing facilities had to comply by June 2005, while new or renovated plants had to comply immediately upon start up ("National Emission Standards for Hazardous Air Pollutants: Surface Coating of Metal Coil; Final Rule," *Federal Register*, vol. 67, no. 111, June 10, 2002, http://www.epa.gov/ttn/atw/mcoil/fr10jn02.pdf).

Fabricated Metal

Products in this industry include metal furniture, fixtures and appliances. Consumption of appliance, heating equipment, and air-conditioner finishes was 7.1 million gallons in 2008, with a total value of $87 million. (See Figure 3-13.) Consumption of nonwood furniture and fixture finishes was 27.4 million gallons in 2008, with a total value of $368.9 million. Volume excludes powder coatings and coil coatings, which are covered separately.

Metal furniture and fixtures include metal household and office furniture as well as metal partitions, fixtures, and doors. Metal furniture and fixtures used an estimated 27.4 million gallons of coatings valued at $368.9 million in 2008. (See Figure 3-13.) Shipments of metal furniture and fixtures from 2002 through 2008 are shown in Figure 3-18.

High-solids, solvent-based polyester coatings account for approximately half of the coatings consumed by metal furniture and fixtures. High solids polyesters provide excellent wear, chemical resistance, and coffee and water resistance necessary for office and household furniture. Solvent-based alkyds, the second largest coating system, are losing market share to powder coatings. Alkyds provide a hard finish at low cost. Small amounts of water-based alkyds are also used, but long drying times are a disadvantage. Other systems used include water-based acrylics, solvent-based acrylics, acrylic lacquers and small amounts of polyurethanes.

HAP limits for metal furniture manufacturing operations are extremely stringent for new or renovated plants. The rule as issued does not allow for any HAP emissions in these plants. For existing plants, HAP emission limits are set at 0.83 lb/gal. These limits apply to the emissions from all coatings, thinners, solvents or materials used in the coating operation at the affected source. These limits are expected to encourage manufacturers to improve coating efficiency or turn to pre-coated metals or powder coatings ("National Emission Standards for Hazardous Air Pollutants: Surface Coating of Metal

Figure 3-18   U.S. Shipments of Metal Furniture and Fixtures, 2002-2008 (shipment value in thousands of dollars)

	2002	2003	2004	2005	2006	2007	2008
Household furniture	1,923,215	1,676,403	1,863,720	1,910,483	1,946,860	2,329,510	2,264,480
Office furniture	7,158,873	7,126,280	7,779,193	8,394,498	7,754,780	7,772,678	8,107,141
Partitions and lockers	257,969	237,893	233,017	237,027	416,828	521,402	559,362

Source: Adapted from "Sector 31: Annual Survey of Manufactures: Value of Product Shipments: Value of Shipments for Product Classes," *Annual Survey of Manufactures*, 2004-2008, U.S. Census Bureau, http://factfinder.census.gov/servlet/DatasetMainPageServlet?_lang=en&_ts=295950014473&_ds_name=AM0831VS101&_program=EAS (accessed June 25, 2010)

Figure 3-19   EPA Emission Limits for Existing and New Sources for Wood Furniture Manufacturing Operations, Final Rule, December 7, 1995

Emission Point	Existing Source	New Source
Finishing operations:		
(a) Achieve a weighted average VHAP content across all coatings (maximum kg VHAP/kg solids [lb VHAP/lb solids], as applied);	a 1.0	a 0.8
(b) Use compliant finishing materials (maximum kg VHAP/kg solids [lb VHAP/lb solids], as applied);		
— Stains	a 1.0	a 1.0
— washcoats	ab 1.0	ab 0.8
— sealers	a 1.0	a 0.8
— topcoats	a 1.0	a 0.8
— basecoats	ab 1.0	ab 0.8
— enamels	ab 1.0	ab 0.8
— thinners (maximum % HAP allowable); or	10.0	10.0
(c) As an alternative, use control device; or	c 1.0	c 0.8
(d) Use any combination of (a), (b), and (c)	1.0	0.8
Cleaning operations:		
Strippable spray booth material (maximum VOC content, kg VOC/kg solids [lb VOC/lb solids])	0.8	0.8
Contact adhesives:		
(a) Use compliant contact adhesives (maximum kg VHAP/kg solids [lb VHAP/lb solids], as applied) based on following criteria:		
i. For aerosol adhesives, and for contact adhesives applied to nonporous substrates	d NA	d NA
ii. For foam adhesives used in products that meet flammability requirements	1.8	0.2
iii. For all other contact adhesives (including foam adhesives used in products that do not meet flammabil¬ity requirements); or	1.0	0.2
(b) Use a control device	e 1.0	e 0.2

a The limits refer to the VHAP content of the coating, as applied.

b Washcoats, basecoats, and enamels must comply with the limits presented in this table if they are purchased premade, that is, if they are not formulated onsite by thinning other finishing materials. If they are formulated onsite, they must be formulated using compliant finishing materials, i.e., those that meet the limits specified in this table, and thinners containing no more than 3.0 percent HAP by weight.

c The control device must operate at an efficiency that is equivalent to no greater than 1.0 kilogram (or 0.8 kilogram) of VHAP being emitted from the affected emission source per kilogram of solids used.

d There is no limit on the VHAP content of these adhesives.

e The control device must operate at an efficiency that is equivalent to no greater than 1.0 kilogram (or 0.2 kilogram) of VHAP being emitted from the affected emission source per kilogram of solids used.

Source: "Table 1. Summary of Emission Limits," Federal Register, 40 CFR Parts 9 and 63, December 7, 1995, http://www.epa.gov/ttn/atw/wood/fr07de95.pdf (accessed June 25, 2010)

Furniture; Final Rule," *Federal Register*, vol. 68, no. 100, May 23, 2004, http://www.epa.gov/ttn/atw/mfurn/fr23my03.pdf).

The appliances industry consumed an estimated 7.1 million gallons of coatings valued at $87 million in 2008. Appliances include refrigerators and freezers, stoves and ranges, washers and dryers, microwave ovens, air conditioners, dishwashers, water heaters and furnaces. Liquid coatings for appliances are declining as powder coatings and pre-coated metals continue to gain market share. Solvent-based polyester is the dominant topcoat for appliances, with small amounts of acrylics also used. Primers are primarily electrodeposited epoxies.

HAP limits are a maximum of 0.18 lb/gal of coating solids for manufacturers of home appliances. The limits apply to all coatings, thinners and cleaning materials used in coating operations at the affected site ("National Emission Standards for Hazardous Air Pollutants: Surface Coating of Large Appliances; Final Rule," *Federal Register*, vol. 67, no. 141, July 23, 2002, http://www.epa.gov/ttn/atw/lapp/fr23jy02.pdf).

Figure 3-20 gives unit shipments of major household appliances for the 2002 to 2007 period. In 2007, 60.4% of appliances shipped were used in the kitchen, 19.6% were used in the laundry, and the balance (20%) was made up of other utility appliances. Each segment represents a sizable application for OEM finishes or as the end use for pre-finished metal.

Wood

Coatings for wood materials and products, another sizable application for OEM coatings, include coatings for wood furniture, fixtures, and flat wood stock. Wood furniture, cabinets, and fixtures was the largest segment; nearly 33.8 million gallons of coatings were shipped for use on these products in 2008, with a total value of $520.3 million. (See Figure 3-13.) Figure 3-21 shows shipments of wooden household non-upholstered and upholstered furniture, wood office furniture, and wood partitions and fixtures from 2002 through 2008.

An EPA rule, published December 7, 1995, regulates VOC and HAP emissions in the wood furniture and fixtures industry. A summary of emission limits for the industry is listed in Figure 3-19. Despite the increased regulatory pressure of the past thirty years,

Figure 3-20 U.S. Shipments of Major Household Appliances, 2002-2007 (shipment value in thousands of dollars)

	2002	2003	2004	2005	2006	2007
Small electrical appliance manufacturing	1,309,978	1,152,063	1,066,704	1,238,253	1,328,113	3,509,826
Household cooking appliance manufacturing	4,129,322	4,369,141	4,242,477	4,618,303	4,745,567	4,427,581
Household refrigerator and home freezer manufacturing	5,354,924	5,757,764	5,760,810	6,064,134	6,128,554	5,666,088
Household laundry equipment manufacturing	4,352,179	4,658,154	4,986,523	5,185,321	5,087,524	4,423,364
Other major household appliance manufacturing	3,126,360	3,215,821	3,565,345	3,953,257	3,944,090	4,500,056

Source: Adapted from "Sector 31: Annual Survey of Manufactures: Value of Product Shipments: Value of Shipments for Product Classes," Annual Survey of Manufactures, 2004-2008, U.S. Census Bureau, http://factfinder.census.gov/servlet/DatasetMainPageServlet?_lang=en&_ts=295950014473&_ds_name=AM0831VS101&_program=EAS (accessed June 25, 2010)

Figure 3-21 U.S. Shipments of Wood Furniture and Fixtures, 2002-2008 (shipment value in thousands of dollars)

	2002	2003	2004	2005	2006	2007	2008
Household nonupholstered furniture	10,441,977	9,396,855	9,736,331	8,895,677	8,560,985	6,727,694	6,474,655
Household upholstered furniture	8,708,520	8,362,032	8,711,535	8,444,471	8,352,070	8,575,483	7,993,294
Office furniture	2,957,507	3,096,855	3,114,122	3,526,093	3,439,508	3,196,146	2,945,924
Partitions and lockers	166,677	177,376	180,307	209,694	244,057	222,397	268,879

Source: Adapted from "Sector 31: Annual Survey of Manufactures: Value of Product Shipments: Value of Shipments for Product Classes," Annual Survey of Manufactures, 2004-2008, U.S. Census Bureau, http://factfinder.census.gov/servlet/DatasetMainPageServlet?_lang=en&_ts=295950014473&_ds_name=AM0831VS101&_program=EAS (accessed June 25, 2010)

low-solids, solvent-based coatings dominated the coatings consumed on wood furniture and fixtures for many years. The emissions standards forced a reduction in solvent emissions. Powder coatings are being developed with lower temperature cures, so that they can be used on wood. Radiation cured coatings are also increasing, mainly acrylated resin types. Water-based technologies for wood are being developed, including one- and two-component systems.

Solvent-based stains and nitrocellulose lacquers account for the majority of coatings for wood furniture. Nitrocellulose lacquers are normally low solids materials (18-25% solids) used as a sealer coat after the solvent-based stain (3-5% solids) has been applied. Nitrocellulose finishes have high optical clarity, excellent gloss, ease of application, and are readily repaired. De-listing of acetone by the EPA in 1995, no longer counted as a VOC, allowed continued use of lacquers.

Such other coatings as curable alkyd-UF products are used for kitchen cabinets, which require chemical resistance. They have good resistance to water, soaps and detergents, and food residues. Acrylic lacquers are used on wood or molded plastic components, particularly when colored furniture is produced. Polyurethane, epoxy and polyester materials are available for specialized use.

Wood composition board and flat stock products consumed an estimated 8.4 million gallons of coatings valued at $109.5 million in 2008. (See Figure 3-13.) Wood products included in this category are hardboard, hardwood plywood, particleboard, medium density fibreboard (MDF), softwood plywood, oriented strand board (OSB) and a variety of miscellaneous flat wood products. Hardboard is used for exterior siding, interior tileboard, and wall paneling. The majority of the coatings applied to hardboard are water-based acrylics, with some solvent-based acrylics also used.

Although small amounts of coatings are applied to wood composition board, most of these products, such as those used for furniture and fixtures, are covered with coated paper or vinyl film products. Hardwood plywood is the second-largest outlet for coatings, especially water- and solvent-based acrylics. Systems employed include epoxy acrylates, polyesters and epoxy acrylates.

The EPA has issued more stringent HAP regulations on most building products. Specifically, it requires water-based coatings on tileboard, now coated with solvent-based thermosetting materials. The agency is concerned with cure volatiles, such as formaldehyde and methanol. To date, water-based coatings have not been an effective substitute.

The limits for coatings are set for all each of five different categories of wood building products and for all plants that use more than 1,100 gallons of coatings a year. Companies could also meet requirements of the rule by installing emissions-control equipment. The rule took effect for existing manufacturing facilities in February 2006. HAP emission limits for wood building products are shown in Figure 1-21 in Section 1.

Machinery and Equipment

This segment is comprised of farm and construction equipment manufacturers, which includes tractors, planters, harvesting machinery, sprayers, haying and mowing equipment, cranes, graders, earth movers, and shovel loaders; electrical equipment manufacturers, which comprises motors and generators, transformers, panel boards, junction boxes, control devices, and switchgear; industrial machinery, which includes metal cutting and forming machinery, packaging machinery, paper industry machinery, and mining machinery; and miscellaneous products, which includes containers, baskets, tool boxes, fire extinguishers, exercise equipment, lawn and garden equipment, and vending machines. A summary of 2007 and 2008 shipments is given in Figure 3-22. Manufacturers of machinery and equipment consumed an estimated 21.9 million gallons of coatings valued at $564.7 million in 2008. (See Figure 3-13.)

Figure 3-22 Value of Shipments for Product Classes of Machinery and Equipment, 2007 and 2008 (in thousands of dollars)

NAICS	Meaning of Products and services code	2007	2008
333111	Farm machinery and equipment manufacturing	19,726,529	23,998,153
333112	Lawn and garden equipment manufacturing	7,480,401	7,064,711
333120	Construction machinery manufacturing	31,404,210	31,424,193
333131	Mining machinery and equipment manufacturing	4,828,000	5,018,648
333132	Oil and gas field machinery and equipment	16,231,536	18,989,319
333210	Sawmill and woodworking machinery	871,359	832,498
333220	Plastics and rubber industry machinery	3,194,668	3,481,799
333291	Paper industry machinery manufacturing	2,172,994	2,366,072
333292	Textile machinery manufacturing	1,022,114	944,109
333293	Printing machinery and equipment mfg.	2,876,155	2,755,820
333294	Food product machinery manufacturing	3,659,114	3,815,206
333295	Semiconductor machinery manufacturing	13,365,682	9,044,817
333298	All other industrial machinery manufacturing	8,545,344	8,661,199
333511	Industrial mold manufacturing	5,614,862	5,471,666
333512	Metal cutting machine tool manufacturing	4,244,244	4,343,456
333513	Metal forming machine tool manufacturing	1,519,591	1,589,870
333515	Cutting tool and machine tool accessory mfg.	4,747,858	4,624,901
334111	Electronic computer manufacturing	37,921,321	40,356,884
334112	Computer storage device manufacturing	9,962,081	9,134,882
334113	Computer terminal manufacturing	375,821	354,585
334119	Other computer peripheral equipment manufacturing	11,750,181	11,323,620

Source: Adapted from "Sector 31: Annual Survey of Manufactures: Value of Product Shipments: Value of Shipments for Product Classes," Annual Survey of Manufactures, 2008, U.S. Census Bureau, http://factfinder.census.gov/servlet/DatasetMainPageServlet?_lang=en&_ts=295950014473&_ds_name=AM0831VS101&_program=EAS (accessed June 25, 2010)

Due to the relatively small number of items manufactured in most categories, as well as the use of heavy, thick metal substrates, air-dried coatings account for two-thirds of consumption. In addition, since most of the items are used indoors, solvent-based alkyds are satisfactory, and as a result dominate. For most such systems, two-part epoxy primers are also used. Epoxy systems are also utilized as one-coat systems where chemical resistance is necessary. Polyurethane coatings can serve as topcoats over epoxy primers when gloss and appearance is desirable or some weather resistance is required. Acrylic lacquers and enamels are also used to some extent. Powder coatings are making inroads into machinery and equipment finishes, particularly for small, relatively high volume times such as lawn and garden equipment.

Powder Coatings

Powder coatings are 100%-solid materials comprised of a pigment, resin, crosslinker and a flow agent. They are applied to form highly durable and attractive finishes and manufactured and applied without organic solvents. Powders are used for decoration or protection in and on several hundred different types of consumer and industrial products and have the advantage of a 95-98% utilization rate (transfer efficiency) compared to only 60-70% for sprayed liquid coatings. Any overspray of powder coatings can be recovered and recycled, contributing to the efficiency of the coating operation.

At one time powder coatings were applied by fluidized bed techniques whereby the substrate was heated and then immersed in a bed of powder coatings. The process was a thermoplastic coating system suspended by air. The coating was flocked onto the surface and melted to form a continuous film. Powder coatings were later applied by electrostatic spray, a superior process to other application techniques in that thinner (1-3 mils) can be easily applied to the part. Currently 80-90% of powder coatings are applied by this technique.

Powder coatings are comprised of four key raw materials, film formers or binders, which include resins and curing agents, pigments, fillers and additives. The binder is the backbone of the system, serving to bind the pigment particles to the surface of the substrate.

The most common resins include epoxies, epoxies and carboxyl terminated polyesters, polyesters, hydroxyl terminated polyesters, which are used in urethanes, and acrylics. They are glycidyl methacrylates hybrids. Epoxies are preferred because of their toughness, flexibility, resistance to chemicals and corrosion and adhesion to the substrate. Polyesters possess excellent exterior weatherability and hybrids, based on epoxies and polyesters, combine the desirable properties of each binder. Acrylics display excellent film appearance and clarity, improved weatherability and lower curing temperatures than polyesters but are brittle and expensive.

Thermosetting powders, the larger, faster growing type, including low-molecular weight epoxy, TGIC-polyester, epoxy polyester hybrids, polyurethanes, and acrylics, are applied by electrostatic spray and cured to a thinner film (0.75-2.0 mil). They are generally used for decorative purposes. Thermoplastic powders, primarily vinyl but also nylon, polyolefin, and fluorocarbon types, represent about 30% of powder coating consumption. The thermoplastic powders are tough, flexible, and chemically resistant and form thick films, and are generally applied by a fluidized bed process.

The U.S. Census Bureau began using a factor of 5 lb = 1 gallon in 1999 to replace the outdated factor of 3 pounds= 1 gallon. In 2008, about 31.8 million gallons of powder coatings were shipped with a value of $599 million. (See Figure 3-13.) Tim Wright reported in *Coatings World* that the global economic recession beginning in 2008 hit powder coatings especially hard, with a decline of as much as 30% ("AkzoNobel Widens its Powder Coatings Reach," December 2009, pp. 20-23).

Nearly two-thirds (61%) of all powder coatings is used in general metal decorating, including stadium seating, shelving, lawn and garden furniture and equipment, all types of manufacturing machinery and equipment, electrical equipment, and for architectural uses such as window and door frames. Coatings are primarily epoxy and TGIC and hybrid polyurethanes. Metal furniture is one of fastest-growing end uses since powder coatings provide durable chip-resistant coatings in a wide array of colors. In addition, furniture manufacturers find that powder coating technology is cost efficient and provides more consistent quality than liquid coatings.

Appliances, the second largest end use, used 9.1 million gallons in 2008 and accounted for about 28.7% of consumption. (See Figure 3-13.) Powders are used on refrigerators, freezers, washers and dryers, ranges, water heaters, air conditioners, vacuum cleaners, electric heaters and fans. Epoxy and polyurethane and TGIC coatings are widely used.

In 2008, powder coatings accounted for about 10.6% of all OEM finished in the United States as measured in dollars, down from about 14% in 2003. While the imposition of new HAP emission limits on automobile and truck coatings, appliances, metal furniture, and coil coatings was expected to spur the growth of powder coatings, such growth did not materialize in part because powder coatings are being produced elsewhere in the world and because of the impact of the global economic recession on the industry. However, Tim Wright of *Coatings*

World reported in 2009 that the demand for U.S. powder coatings was projected to expand 3.5% annually from 2010 to 2013, although prices commanded for powder coatings were declining ("Powder Coatings Demand in U.S. to Reach 445 Million Pounds in 2013," July 2009.)

Epoxy powders are the leading resin system among powder coatings. Epoxies feature excellent chemical and corrosion resistance and hardness, a good balance of mechanical properties, high gloss and a low cure temperature of 250F. While epoxies have good initial gloss, they are poor in gloss and color retention in exterior finishes and used primarily for metal furniture, underbody auto parts, pipe coatings, major appliance parts, microwave ovens, shelving and power tools. In addition they are part of the formulation of hybrid systems.

Polyester-urethane types, the second-largest category of powder coatings, can be applied in thinner coatings, and are thus the best choice for many outdoor applications. The most popular type (also called a urethane powder) is cured with a urethane crosslinker. They have good chemical and corrosion resistance, good mechanical properties and excellent gloss and color retention in exterior applications. They can readily be produced in both pigmented and clear coatings, and are used on automotive wheels and trim, playground equipment, garden tractors, and fence fittings.

Polyesters, the third type, are TGIC and polyester resin crosslinked with a glycidal functional curing agent. They account for about a quarter of all powder coatings consumed. This grade is popular in Europe for its excellent exterior durability. It has good chemical and corrosion resistance, good mechanicals, and excellent color and gloss retention. Polyesters are widely used for architectural aluminum, outdoor furniture, farm equipment, fence poles, and air conditioning units.

Hybrids, representing 20% of the total, are epoxy/polyester mixtures used as primers. They have good chemical and corrosion resistance, and a good balance of properties. They are applied to water heaters, radiators, transformers, office furniture, fire extinguishers, and toys.

Acrylic thermosetting powders account for the balance of sales of powders. They are used on washing machines, oven parts, refrigerators, microwave ovens, and aluminum extrusions. Acrylics have good chemical and corrosion resistance, good color and gloss retention and also detergent and alkali resistance for use in washing machine parts and components.

Thermoplastic technology was introduced after World War II but commands a lessening share of the powder coatings market, now about 5% ("Major Resin Types," SpecialChem4Coatings.com). Thermosetting powders were commercialized in the late 1950s. The industry developed improved processing, such as melt-mixing and spraying in the 1960s. Alternate resins and raw materials and application equipment were introduced in the 1970s. Formulations and equipment are being continually refined.

Radiation Cured Coatings

Radiation cured (rad-cure) formulations are mainly 100% solids liquid coatings, which present few or no environmental problems. They are used in paints and coatings, inks, adhesives and a variety of miscellaneous applications. While the global economic recession hit this market hard, Coatings World reported that rad-cure coatings were 1.9% of the global coatings market in 2009 and were projected to increase their market share to 3% by 2013. Demand in North America was strongest in 2009, with products valued

at $538.5 million (Tim Wright, "Radcure Coatings Market is Growing," May 2010).

Products are formulated with liquid unsaturated resins. They crosslink when the polymerization reaction is initiated with photoiniated catalysts activated by ultraviolet light or electron beam irradiation. Unsaturated polyesters dissolved in styrene, the first systems, are still used due to their cost advantages. However, acrylates now dominate because of their improved reactivity and the chemical and weathering resistance of the final coatings. At present a wide variety of low molecular weight resins are used, including epoxy acrylates and polyurethane oligomers dissolved in acrylate ester monomers. Overall, acrylate resins and monomer technology account for 80-85% of radiation curable applications.

In addition to the environmental advantages, with no or very low solvent emissions, major advantages include the ability to coat heat-sensitive materials, better overall quality of finished products, and near instantaneous cure which allows for faster production throughput. The application of radiation cured products also contributes to space savings since they eliminate the need for drying ovens and solvent collection equipment.

The main disadvantages to using rad-cure coatings are the high initial coat of investment in equipment and materials, although the ultraviolet UV and electron beam (EB) cures requires lower cure temperatures than powder coatings. In addition, radiation curing requires a direct line of sight for the UV or EB rays, and applications have been limited primarily to flat surfaces. The average cost of coatings is about $40-42 a gallon with some products priced as high as $150-160 a gallon.

RadTech International estimates North American consumption of rad-cure coatings at about 95 million pounds in 2006 ("Status of UV & EB in North America 2006," http://www.radtech.org/ind_overview/pdf-files/

RadT_UVStatusRpt8_8_06.pdf). Coatings, the largest segment, account for about 45% of all uses. Rad-cure coatings are consumed principally by the wood, metal can, and automotive industries. In 2005, about 6,000 metric tons of clear wood finishes were used; 8,000 metric tons were used for plastics coatings, and 3,000 metric tons were used for metal coatings. Suppliers are looking at new applications, especially for "shaped" surfaces and on plastic substrates, where opportunities exist in auto OEM and even the aftermarket.

Graphic arts coatings, the largest application for radiation cured coatings, account for about a quarter of all rad-cure products. They are used to coat plastic and paper products, which are heat sensitive. The coatings can be applied at high line speeds and provide high gloss, blocking and surface protection. Uses include magazine covers, leather finishes, upscale shopping bags, specialty coated papers, release coatings, and overprint varnishes. Graphic products are not included in the market data in this *Guide*.

Plastics coatings, especially for automotive applications, including plastic wheel covers, side body molding strips, tail lens assemblies, vinyl wrapped interior parts, flexible trim, door handles, pillar posts, forward and rear lighting systems such as scratch-resistant hard coats for polycarbonate head lamp lenses, are the second-largest application for rad-cure coatings. A fast growing market, and potentially major end use, is UV coatings for auto body refinishes. Rapid cure allows for rapid turnaround in a segment of the coatings industry that has relied on air-dried and ambient temperature curing of refinish paints. Development work is underway on coating system for OEM automobile coatings. Approximately 8,000 metric tons of rad-cure coatings were used on plastics in 2005.

Wood products like paneling and prefinished wood flooring are the third-largest end use for radiation cured coatings. Because they allow for high production runs and fast line speeds they are ideal for wood flatstock. Radiation cured products for these end use markets include stains, sealers, and clear coatings. The finished coats provide excellent mar, scratch and chemical resistance compared to the more established lacquers traditionally used on wood products. Wood furniture is a fast growing end use, accounting for approximately 4% of consumption of radiation cured coatings. Similar products to those used on wood paneling are applied to coating wood furniture. In 2005, about 6,000 metric tons of clear wood finishes were used. Rad-cure coatings may soon be used more widely on wood cabinets.

Radiation cured coatings are increasingly used for metal and coil coatings. Demand topped 2,800 metric tons in 2005. Possible applications include coatings for pipes, hardware, metal parts, and other small metal products.

Leading producers of radiation-cured paints are Akzo Nobel, BASF, PPG, Sherwin-Williams and Valspar.

Other OEM Coatings

A variety of other coatings are used, but are not covered in this *Guide*, as they are not considered "paints." "Other industrial product finishes" reported in the 2008 Current Industrial Report totaled 31.7 million gallons valued at $392.5 million in 2008. They include some of the products discussed below.

Magnet wire coatings are used mostly in coils of motors, generators and transformers. To prevent short circuits, the wires are coated with a thin layer of varnish. Most products are liquid enamels, but a small volume of powders are also used. Insulating varnishes are used to insulated slot cells in motors and generators, and also to insulate bus wires. Both liquids (solvent and water-based) and powders are used.

Conformal coatings are primarily liquid products used for printed circuit boards to protect them from mechanical and environmental damage. Some powders are used on such electrical components as resistors and capacitors.

Conductive coatings serve as primers in automotive parts, EMI shielding coatings and electrographic-type copying paper. Carbon black, copper, silver and nickel and cationic resins are used in the coating for conductivity.

Packaging uses extruded and coextruded coatings applied to paper, paperboard, film and foil. Additionally, the industry consumes such solid coatings as clay and calcium carbonate.

Overprint varnishes are applied over imprinted surfaces for protection and to improve appearance. Basically, the products are clear inks. Paper and paperboard account for 90% of the total, with the balance applied to packaging film, foil and wallpaper.

Release coatings are used on all release liners, with the protective covering placed over the adhesive layer. They are also coated on non-adhesive surfaces of self-wound tape and other pressure-sensitive products to promote separation. Silicones, which account for about 50% of the volume and 80% of the value, are used on all release liner materials whereas such other coatings as acrylic emulsions and vinyl acetates are used on topcoat self-wound tapes.

Pipe coatings are primarily bituminous types, with a limited volume of epoxies and polyurethanes.

Other coatings such as acrylic emulsions and vinyl acetates are used on topcoat self-wound tapes.

SPECIAL PURPOSE COATINGS

This category, adopted by the Census Bureau in 1979, is a collection of specialty coatings previously reported under Trade Sales. It includes coatings for the refinishing of machinery and automobiles. Special purpose coatings are described by the Census Bureau as stock or shelf goods that differ from architectural coatings because they are formulated for special applications and/or special environmental conditions, such as extreme temperatures, chemicals or fumes. Included are paints for new construction and maintenance of industrial facilities or plants; traffic marking paints; marine paints, for ships, offshore construction, and maintenance; pool maintenance coatings; aerosol paints; athletic markings; concrete and roof coatings; and fire retardant paints. Some 225 companies compete in this varied industry segment.

A constant and continuing problem with special purpose coatings is that some products can be used in both this category as well as in architectural and OEM products in some instances. Such a situation can result in volatility of statistics for special purpose coating.

In 2008, shipments of special purpose coatings were 196.3 million gallons valued at $4,604.8 million. This product category represents 16.1% of all paints, as measured in dollar value, down from 23% in 1997. Figure 3-23 illustrates the pattern of shipments in millions of dollars between 19085 and 2008, while Figure 3-24 illustrates the unit volume of shipments during the same period. Special purpose coatings endured a mild slump in response to the mild recession of the early 2000s, but beginning in 2003 this segment saw spectacular growth. This growth leveled off in response to the global economic recession that began in late 2008, especially in terms of volume.

**Figure 3-23   Shipments of Special Purpose Coatings, 1985-2008
(in millions of dollars)**

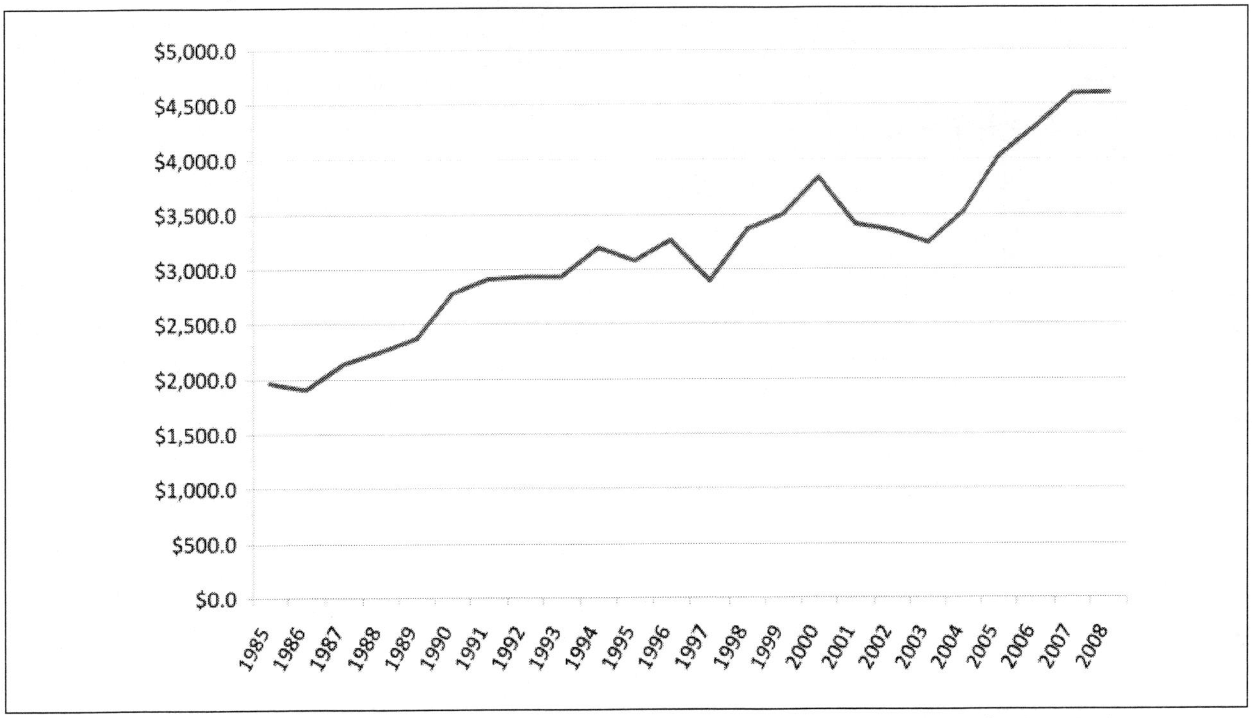

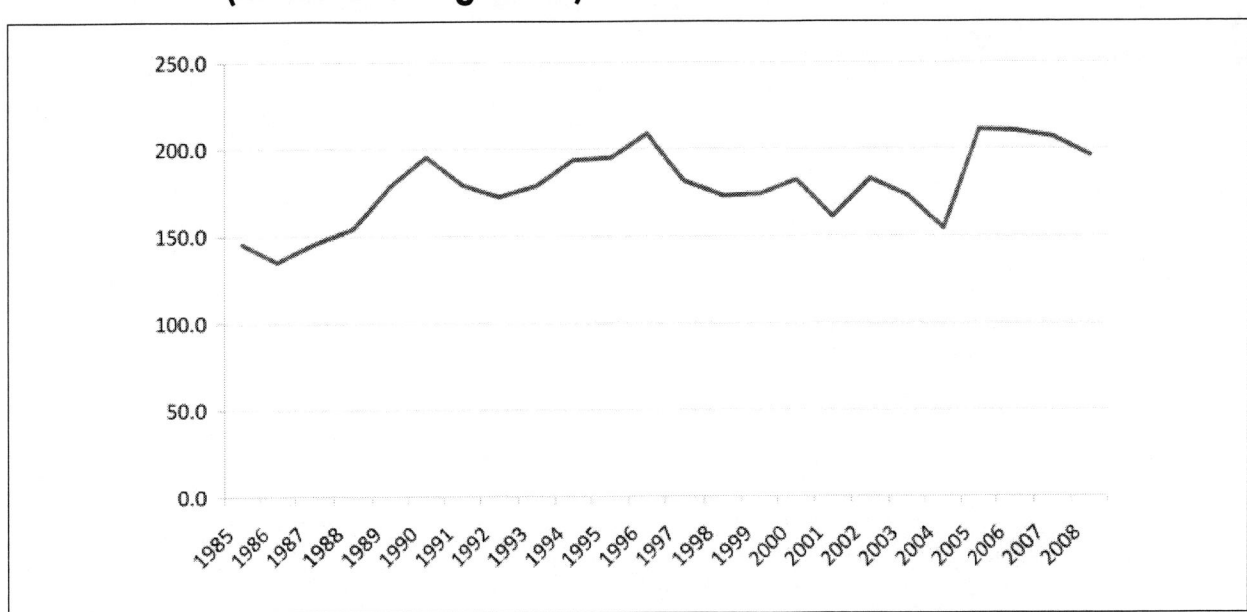

Source: Adapted from "Sector 31: EC073111: Manufacturing: Industry Series: Detailed Statistics by Industry for the United States: 2007," 2007 Economic Census, U.S. Census Bureau, 2009, http://factfinder.census.gov/servlet/IBQTable?_bm=y&-geo_id=01000US&-ds_name=EC073111&-NAICS2007=325510&-_lang=en (accessed November 30, 2009)

**Figure 3-24   Shipments of Special Purpose Coatings, 1985-2008
(in millions of gallons)**

Source: Adapted from "Sector 31: EC073111: Manufacturing: Industry Series: Detailed Statistics by Industry for the United States: 2007," 2007 Economic Census, U.S. Census Bureau, 2009, http://factfinder.census.gov/servlet/IBQTable?_bm=y&-geo_id=01000US&-ds_name=EC073111&-NAICS2007=325510&-_lang=en (accessed November 30, 2009)

Figure 3-25 Producer Price Index for Special Purpose Coatings, 2000-2010

Year	Jan	Feb	Mar	Apr	May	Jun	Jul	Aug	Sep	Oct	Nov	Dec	Annual
2000	195.8	196.1	196.1	197.7	197.7	197.7	197.9	197.9	200.2	200.6	201.8	203.7	198.6
2001	204.8	206.7	205.7	206.7	207.0	208.2	207.8	209.1	208.0	204.7	207.4	207.1	206.9
2002	212.0	212.3	215.2	220.1	216.4	218.8	217.2	217.9	220.6	218.9	221.3	220.3	217.6
2003	221.5	223.0	224.3	223.8	221.7	221.6	224.8	223.9	223.4	223.5	228.6	228.1	224.0
2004	229.5	229.8	229.9	231.1	230.6	231.8	234.2	234.8	234.5	234.7	234.8	234.3	232.5
2005	239.8	240.0	240.4	240.2	245.0	245.6	246.1	247.4	245.0	246.8	247.2	249.2	244.4
2006	251.5	254.9	254.8	257.8	262.0	262.3	262.9	263.4	264.7	268.1	268.3	269.7	261.7
2007	270.6	274.1	274.1	274.6	274.6	277.2	277.7	277.7	276.8	277.3	277.0	276.8	275.7
2008	279.8	280.6	283.0	283.9	283.5	285.3	290.0	291.7	292.3	295.8	296.4	296.1	288.2
2009	295.8	297.0	296.7	298.5	298.0	298.3	297.4	295.1	292.9	293.7	292.0	295.2	295.9
2010	297.8	297.6	302.0	303.9	301.6								

Source: "Producer Price Index, Commodities, Not Seasonally Adjusted--Special Purpose Coatings," Bureau of Labor Statistics, 2010, http://www.bls.gov/ppi (accessed May 16, 2010)

Figure 3-26   Consumption of Special Purpose Coatings by Selected End Use, 2007

End Use	Million Gallons	Million Dollars	Average Price/Gallon
Automotive, transportation, and machinery refinishes	62.1	2,438.1	39.26
Industrial Maintenance			
Exterior	33.0	747.9	22.66
Interior	42.6	494.2	11.60
Total	75.6	1,242.1	16.42
Highway and Traffic Marking	32.9	338.6	10.29
Miscellaneous	173.1	1,499.3	8.66

Source: Adapted from "Table 2. Quantity and Value of Shipments of Paint and Allied Products: 2008 and 2007," Current Industrial Reports M325F, U.S. Census Bureau, http://www.census.gov/manufacturing/cir/historical_data/ma325f/index.html (accessed November 30, 2009)

Sales of special purpose coatings for 2007 are shown in Figure 3-26. The average prices for 2007 varied from a high of $39.26 a gallon for auto refinish paints to only $10.29 for traffic paint.

Figure 3-25 gives the annual price index for special purpose coatings, including marine coatings, from 2000 to 2009. The value of special purpose coatings increased by an average of 4.5% per year during that period.

Auto, transportation and machinery refinishes accounted for sales of $2,438.1 million in 2007, or about 44.2% of segment value. Industrial maintenance coatings, valued at $1,242.1 million, represented another 22.5%. (See Figure 3-26.)

Automotive, Transportation and Machinery

Automotive, transportation and machinery refinishes include specially designed base coat/clear coats (BC/CC) (40%) and include solvent-based acrylic and polyester-base coats followed by acrylic urethane clean coats. Single-stage coatings systems are acrylic enamels and acrylic urethane enamels, acrylic lacquers, urethanes and the balance in miscellaneous systems including epoxy, polyester and nitrocellulose systems.

Topcoats and topcoat systems account for 70 to 72% of materials and primers the balance. The reported quantities of auto and machinery refinishes are only for paint sales, and not the amount of coating applied by end users. Historically, each gallon of refinish paints is diluted with as much as one gallon of thinner before application.

Sales of automotive, transportation, and machinery refinishes in 2007 were 62.1 million gallons valued at $2,438.1 million, or an average value of $39.25 per gallon. (See Figure 3-28.) Growth between 2002 and 2007 averaged 6.2% per year in volume and 8.4% per year in value. Refinishes have a high price because suppliers must develop new formulations to duplicate the color changes that occur each model year as well as any new coatings systems developed by OEM paint producers. In addition, automotive refinish manufacturers work closely with OEM paint producers to insure compatibility with original equipment auto finishes. Refinish paint producers are also committed to have each color in inventory or available for ten model years. With color changes, however slight, occurring almost annually, inventory costs can be quite high.

Consumption of auto refinishes accounts for 75% of this category with the balance

Figure 3-28   Shipments of Special Purpose Coatings and Miscellaneous Allied Paint Products, 2007 and 2008

Product code	Product description	Year	Quantity	Value
3255107	Special purpose coatings, including all marine coatings	2008 2007	193,813 204,241	4,545,755 4,538,206
3255107111	Industrial new construction and maintenance paints, interior	2008 2007	40,841 42,616	492,385 494,247
3255107115	Industrial new construction and maintenance paints, exterior	2008 2007	(S) 33,042	(S) 747,859
3255107121	Traffic marking paints (all types; shelf goods and highway department)	2008 2007	34,039 32,894	341,258 338,625
3255107131	Automotive, other transportation and machinery refinish paints and enamels, including primers	2008 2007	(S) 62,111	(S) 2,438,100
3255107141	Marine paints, ship and off-shore facilities and shelf goods for both new construction and marine refinish and mainte-nance. Excludes spar varnish	2008 2007	(S) (D)	(S) (D)
3255107151	Marine paints for yacht and pleasure craft, new construc-tion, refinish and maintenance	2008 2007	(D) (D)	(D) (D)
3255107161	Aerosol - paint concentrates produced for packaging in aerosol containers	2008 2007	(D) (D)	(D) (D)
325510B	Miscellaneous allied paint products	2008 2007	(S) 173,057	(S) 1,499,254
325510B111	Paint and varnish removers	2008 2007	(S) 5,583	(S) 37,050
325510B121	Thinners for lacquers and other solvent based paint prod-ucts	2008 2007	(S) 36,060	(S) 204,605
325510B131	Pigment dispersions	2008 2007	33,804 46,800	602,561 658,313
325510B141	Other miscellaneous allied paint products, including brush cleaners, ink vehicles, putty and glazing compounds, etc.	2008 2007	(S) 84,614	629,411 599,286

Footnote: 1/ Data for powder coatings are collected in pounds and converted to gallons by using a conversion factor of 5 (5 lbs. = 1 gallon). The total quantity of Powder Coatings collected in pounds amounted to 352,715 thousand pounds in 2008 and 363,153 thousand pounds in 2007.

Source: Adapted from "Table 2. Quantity and Value of Shipments of Paint and Allied Products: 2008 and 2007," Current Industrial Reports M325F, U.S. Census Bureau, http://www.census.gov/manufacturing/cir/historical_data/ma325f/index.html (accessed November 30, 2009)

going to other transportation, including trucks, buses, vans, motorcycles (17%) and machinery refinishing (8%). Of the auto refinish volume, approximately 30% is for fleet refinishing where the consumers are professional refinishing operators who coat such fleet equipment as trucks and taxis and buy paint directly from manufacturers in bulk. Body shops, both those independently owned and operated (about 42,129 establishments in 2007), or facilities located at automobile dealerships, account for the balance

Much of the paint goes through distributors who usually carry only one manufacturer's line of refinishes. Do-it-yourself users, which are a minor portion of the segment, include farmers, boat owners, and auto racing teams, as well as individuals who refinish their own cars and trucks.

Refinishes are sold direct through factory branches or such distributors as Finishmaster to end users. Major U.S. suppliers are PPG (reportedly the largest), Akzo Nobel, BASF, DuPont, Sherwin-Williams, and Valspar. Several of the leaders also operate regional refinish training centers.

Industrial Maintenance

Industrial maintenance paints and coatings are high-performance products for corrosion control of the interior and exterior of industrial plants and facilities and some highway structures. They are applied to steel and concrete structures to provide protection from corrosive environments. The products are designed to withstand fumes, salt spray, abrasion, acids, bases, elevated temperatures, galvanic action, and general environmental conditions.

Industrial maintenance coatings represent about 5% of the total volume of paint sold in the United States. Major consumers of industrial maintenance coatings include the oil and gas, petrochemical and chemical

industries, such public utilities as power generation and gas distribution industries, government agencies responsible for highway and bridge construction and maintenance, and such public services as water, sewage and waste disposal utilities. Tim Wright of *Coatings World* reported that commercial architectural uses are the fastest growing segment of industrial maintenance coatings and that the segment was forecast to grow by about 3.9% per year between 2010 and 2015 ("Industrial Maintenance Coatings," June 2010).

Shipments of industrial maintenance coatings (interior and exterior) in 2007 were 75.7 million gallons valued at $1,242.1 million. Of this amount, 42.6 million gallons, worth $494.2 million, were interior paint, with an average price of $11.60 per gallon; 33 million gallons, valued at $747.9 million, were exterior paints, with an average price of $22.63 per gallon. (See Figure 3-28.) Between 2002 and 2007 the volume of industrial maintenance coatings shipped increased at an average of 5.6% per year, while the value of these shipments increased at an even faster rate of 9.6% per year.

Solvent-based primers and topcoats dominate the industrial maintenance segment, although they are losing market share to water-based acrylics and alkyd coatings. The systems are generally considered as anticorrosion coatings and based primarily on epoxy, urethane, ethyl silicate, and vinyl binders. Other coating systems include silicones, silicone alkyds, coat tar epoxies, and alkyds. Epoxies and inorganic zinc are the primary coatings applied as primers for anticorrosion coating systems and acrylics and epoxy systems the principal resins in water-based coatings.

Among the solvent-based paints, alkyds are losing share while polyurethanes are growing at an above-average rate. Zinc-filled inorganic coatings and epoxies are also growing but at a lower rate. The need to reduce VOC has forced consumers to use higher solids formulations and improved coatings are becoming increasingly popular and generally are more cost effective by providing longer term performance (Wright, Industrial Maintenance Coatings," *Coatings World*, June 2010).

Solvent-based alkyds are lower in cost compared to other coatings systems. They can be used as both primers and topcoats. Alkyds are easy to apply, have good durability and color retention in mild environments. Furthermore, they provide decent tolerance to poorly prepared surfaces, a problem for the higher-cost industrial maintenance coatings that are very sensitive to surface preparation for long-term performance. Because of their low cost, solvent-based alkyds still hold approximately a 10% share of sales of industrial maintenance coatings.

Epoxies are generally two-component systems that have excellent resistance to petroleum, petroleum products and most chemicals. They are used as primers and topcoats that have excellent adhesion, film hardness, and chemical resistance. Epoxies are the largest binder system used. They are easy to apply and can be produced as high solids, solvent free, solvent-based and water-based coatings. Solids content range is generally from 65 to 80%.

Epoxies control the largest category of industrial maintenance coatings. They can be modified with other resins such as coumarone indene, xylene and terpene phenol. Epoxy esters are made from a combination of epoxy resin with a fatty acid and offer better adhesion and chemical resistance compared to alkyds but are more costly. Epoxies coating systems are widely used on the exterior of storage tanks, the interior of water storage tanks, pipe coatings, and for general industrial maintenance.

Zinc-filled primers contain high levels of powdered zinc, which protect steel surfaces by galvanic action. They are considered as the universal primer coatings for almost all high performance coatings. There are two types of zinc coatings; those that use such inorganic binders as ethyl silicate and products that employ an organic binder, usually an epoxy. The organic zinc rich coatings are more tolerant to surface preparation conditions and easier to topcoat than the inorganic zinc-rich systems. When applied properly, zinc-rich primers are excellent corrosion controlling materials. Zinc systems account for about 10% of the industrial maintenance market based on their wide use as primers for almost all other topcoats.

Coal tar epoxies are two-component systems with an epoxy binder to harden the tar. They can be used as both primers and topcoats. The systems have excellent water resistance and can be formulated in high film build coatings that can go as high as 10 mils. They provide excellent service for dams, canals and other similar structures. Coal tar epoxies are low-cost coatings systems which are very cost effective over the long term. They have excellent resistance to acids, alkalis, and other corrosive materials.

Polyurethanes using aliphatic isocyanates are the leading topcoats for exterior applications. They have outstanding color and gloss retention and are resistant to the yellowing that can be a problem with epoxies. They provide superior weatherability as well as resistance to acids and alkalis. Polyurethanes have high hardness, abrasion, chemical and solvent resistance. Disadvantages are their high cost and the highly toxic isocyanates that are used as curing agents. Solids content for polyurethane coatings systems can be up to 90%. Urethanes are used to coat bridges, water tanks, structural steel, architectural structures, and for general maintenance. Urethanes account for 27% of the industrial maintenance market with resins based on aliphatic isocyanates representing two-thirds of the end use and aromatic isocyanates one-third.

Solvent-based silicones are used primarily as high temperature coatings for continuous service up to 1000F. They also have good UV, electrical, color and gloss retention and water resistance. A disadvantage is their high cost. Silicone resins can be used to modify the properties of other binders. Solvent-based silicone alkyds are used when temperature requirements are less severe and permit a compromise, for a lower price.

Vinyl coating systems have good durability, flexibility, and toughness as well as resistance to chemicals and salt water. They are the preferred binder for acidic environments but suffer from poor performance to most organic solvents, such as the aliphatic and aromatic hydrocarbons, ketones and esters. They are only made in solvent-based systems of low solids content. However, they account for 1% or less of the binders in the high-performance coating systems.

Water-based paints are growing, although they are not as efficient as solvent-based materials. Improved formulations are continuing to be developed so growth might be above average. Acrylic latex coatings, the leading water-based product, have excellent light and weathering resistance but are not efficient for inhibiting corrosion. They are used on bridges, cargo containers, and general non-immersion service. In addition, water-based products are not as tolerant of the temperature ranges and substrate conditions encountered during maintenance and construction of machinery and structures that require high performance coatings.

Approximately 20% of industrial maintenance coatings are consumed by such plants as chemical and oil producing and refining facilities. Some 25% are used by food, water and waste treatment, pulp and paper mills, and power plants. The balance is applied to bridges, storage tanks, government applications, marine, institutional and other industrial facilities.

Distribution of industrial maintenance coatings is primarily through painting contractors. The leading U.S. companies—RPM, Sherwin-Williams, AkzoNobel, and PPG—account for approximately 60% of the market. The top nine companies control about 90% of the market (Wright, Industrial Maintenance Coatings," *Coatings World*, June 2010).

Highway and Traffic Marking

Consumption of traffic paints, the fourth largest type of special purpose coatings, totaled 34 million gallons valued at $341.3 million in 2008, with an average value of $10.03 per gallon. Between 2002 and 2008 the volume of traffic paints decreased by an average of 2.2% per year while its value increased by an average of 6% per year, despite a shift from solvent- to water-based paints. In 2010, a shortage of traffic paints due to scaled back production during the recession and shortage of methyl methacrylate, a crucial ingredient in traffic paints, delayed roadwork around the United States (Michael Cooper, "Traffic Paint Shortage Threatens Roadwork," *New York Times*, May 23, 2010).

Both solvent-and water-based paints are used to formulate traffic marking paints. Solvent-based alkyds and alkyd-chlorosulfonated polyethylene resins, the leading binders, declined in importance due to restrictions on VOC's in all areas of the country. Alkyd-chlorosulfonated polyethylene is a relatively new binder since chlorosulfonated polyethylene is replacing chlorinated rubber, which is no longer produced in the United States.

Water-based acrylics now account for about 85% of the volume of traffic paints and will continue to increase their share of the market, although longer drying times are a drawback compared with competitive striping materials. Other traffic paints consumed in small quantities include two-component epoxies, unsaturated polyesters and water-based vinyl acrylics. Paint and coating striping materials compete against hot melt thermoplastic marking materials that are 100% solids and require special equipment for melting at temperatures of about 400F. Alkyd and hydrocarbon resins are used in these systems. Traffic marking coatings were included in the Final Rule for VOC content limits for architectural and industrial maintenance (AIM) coatings.

State governments and authorities purchase some 50% of marking paints by competitive bid. They are then applied by government agencies themselves, or by contractors. The largest producer of traffic paints is Ennis Paint.

Marine

Marine coatings are used during shipbuilding and for repair during dry-docking primarily for ocean-going vessels. The products are considered high-performance coatings which must withstand the salt water environments. The repair and maintenance of commercial oceangoing vessels, offshore structures, and naval vessels account for about 75% of this segment with the remainder used for the construction of new oceangoing and naval vessels, offshore rigs and platforms, and inland marine and harbor facilities.

In 2006, the U.S. market for marine paints was $251.9 million (*Paints and Allied products: 2006*, U.S. Census Bureau, MA325F(06)-1, June 2007, http://www.census.gov/industry/1/ma325f06.pdf). This represented about 10% of the global market for marine paints. The value of marine paints had stayed fairly steady for the previous decade, although annual production and sales can be extremely volatile due to the impact

new construction spending can have on demand in any one year. The U.S. produces very few commercial ocean going vessels or naval vessels so that one or two new construction projects can have an impact on sales. In addition, such large naval vessels as aircraft carriers can take 3-4 years to build. In 2008-09, the market for marine paints was down considerably due to the deferral of maintenance on government-owned ships and the inability of prospective owners to obtain financing for new ship purchases (Kerry Pianoforte, "Marine & Offshore Coatings Market," *Coatings World*, May 2010).

Zinc-rich primers are the favored undercoat for steel hulls and offshore rigs and platforms. Inorganic zincs are the major type, followed by organic zinc coatings. An epoxy primer or tie-coat is then applied over the zinc-rich primer. Afterwards, the epoxy tie coat can be coated with an epoxy or polyurethane topcoat at the above-water areas. Polyurethanes are now preferred as topcoats since they have excellent weatherability and gloss retention compared to epoxy topcoats, which tend to chalk in strong sunlight.

Alkyds are not widely used on oceangoing vessels due to their poor performance in salty environments, but are applied in such non-critical areas as cabins, engine rooms, and cargo holds, or on fishing vessels, scows, tugboats, and other small craft. Silicone-alkyds are also used on naval vessels and some merchant vessels.

Coal tar epoxy and hydrocarbon epoxy coatings are applied as bottom paints and underwater coatings on oceangoing vessels and stationary structures. They are relatively cheap and easy to apply in one coat at a high film thickness.

Antifouling paints are used on all oceangoing commercial and naval vessels to provide protection against such animal growth as barnacles and plant life like sea grasses. A variety of coatings are used, including self-polishing tin methacrylate polymer binders and ablative copper oxide coatings. Both vinyl and acrylic polymers are used in the ablative coatings, which degrade over time.

The leading suppliers of marine coatings are Ameron (the largest), Akzo Nobel, RPM, Sherwin-Williams, Hempel Coatings, Jotun and Sigma Coatings USA.

Aerosols

Concentrates for aerosol paints are the fifth major segment of this industry group. Aerosol paints are solvent based, low-solids coatings, a formulation that is necessary to permit atomization of the paint. Aerosols are prepared by paint manufacturers who produce the concentrate, which is subsequently reduced with an equal volume of solvent. In 2006, 18.2 million gallons of aerosol paint concentrate valued at $227.8 million were produced (*Paints and Allied products: 2006*, U.S. Census Bureau, MA325F(06)-1, June 2007, http://www.census.gov/industry/1/ma325f06.pdf). This volume represented a significant decline of 32% from 2006. The number of aerosol paint cans filled continued to decline as well. The Consumer Specialty Products Association reported that the number of cans of aerosol paints and finishes sold in 2008 decreased 14.1% from the year before (Press Release, "Aerosol Industry Weathers Economic Storm," May 7, 2009, http://www.cspa.org/public/media/press/aerosol_survey.html).

Most aerosol paints are colored enamels for general decorating and touch up of small items. Lacquers for automotive touch up, rust preventatives and high-temperature application are also packaged in aerosol spray cans. Aerosol paints are a convenient way to coat small objects, or to mark surfaces that require defining. The aerosol coating only requires shaking of the can before use. The predominant resins in aerosols are alkyds, acrylic and nitrocellulose. Nearly all aerosols are solvent-based products, although some water-based products are used at times. A typical formulation weights 7 to 8 pounds per gallon and contains 12-15% solids by weight.

Aerosol paints consist of the metal can, valve, valve assembly, propellant, paints, reducing solvent and air agitator. The chemicals serving as reducing solvents are such low-boiling materials as dichoromethane, acetone and MEK. Propellants are usually mixtures of hydrocarbons such as propane, isobutane and butane. Fluorocarbon propellants have not been used for over 20 years.

The aerosol market is split into two types of producers. Approximately 50% of aerosol paint is packaged by contract fillers that do not manufacture paints, and the balance produced by companies that both manufacture paint and fill their own cans. The leading supplier of aerosol coatings is Sherwin-Williams (Krylon, Red Devil, Dupli-Color) with about one-half of the market. RPM (Rust-Oleum) and Valspar (PlastiKote) combined control another 30-35%.

Government

Various government documents can be obtained by ordering from the issuing departments. Most documents can be accessed from their web sites.

Manufacturing and Trade Department of Commerce
1401 Constitution Avenue, NW
Washington, DC 20230
Web: www.commerce.gov

Employment and Earnings, Producer Price Index
U.S. Department of Labor
200 Constitution Avenue, NW
Washington, DC 20210
Web: www.dol.gov

Economic Census, Annual Survey of Manufactures, Current Industrial Reports, Statistical Abstracts, Foreign Trade
Bureau of Census
Web: www.census.gov

Trade Statistics
International Trade Commission
500 E Street, SW
Washington, DC 20436
Phone: (202) 205-2000
Web: www.usitc.gov

Environmental Protection Agency
Ariel Rios Building
1200 Pennsylvania Avenue NW
Washington, DC 20460
Phone: (202) 260-4700
Web: www.epa.gov

Company data are available from the Security and Exchange Commission on its web site: www.sec.gov. The SEC's Edgar Data base, which dates to 1994, provides 10-K's and other financial data for publicly owned companies, and also for companies with public debt.

United States government statistical data on the production and utilization of paints is somewhat limited compared with other industries of comparable size. The Economic Census gives production and sales statistics, by major category and type of paint, every five years (those encling

INDUSTRY ACTIVITIES, ORGANIZATIONS AND SOURCES OF INFORMATION

HIGHLIGHTS

Government

■

Canada

■

Trade Associations and Professional Societies

■

Trade and Technical Publications

■

Industry Events and Trade Shows

in 2 and 7). The Census of Retail Trade and the Census of Wholesale Trade provide additional information on paints and allied products.

The *Consumers Specialty Products Association* provides an annual survey with data for the number of aerosol paint containers utilized each year in the United States and Puerto Rico. Web: www.cspa.org The Can Manufacturers Institute produces an annual survey of metal can production. Web: www.cancentral.com.

Canada

Annual Census of Manufactures, Paint and Varnish Manufacturers Catalog No. 46-210 Statistics Canada, Publication Sales Ottawa, ON KIA OV7, CN

The survey gives a summary of the Canadian paint industry, including paint shipments by type, comprehensive data on consumption of raw materials, and a directory of Canadian paint and varnish manufacturers. Web: www.statcan.ca.

Trade Associations and Professional Societies

American Craft Council
72 Spring Street
New York, NY 10012
Phone: (212) 274-0630
Fax: (212) 274-0650
Web: www.craftcouncil.org
Email: council@craftcouncil.org
Executive Director: Chris Amundsen

Association of the Wall and Ceiling Industry
513 W Broad Street
Suite 210
Falls Church, VA 22046
Phone: (703) 534-8300
Fax: 703-534-8307
Web: www.awci.org
EVP/CEO: Steven Etkin
Members: 2,000+

Association for Finishing Processes (AFP) chapter of SME
One SME Drive
Dearborn, MI 4812
Phone: (313) 425-3000
Web: www.sme.org
Pres: Barbara Fossum
Members: 2,000

Associated Builders and Contractors
4250 N Fairfax Drive 9th Floor
Arlington, VA 22203-1607
(703) 812-2000
Web: www.abc.org
Email: gotquestions@abc.org
President/CEO: M. Kirk Pickerel
National convention

American Brush Manufacturers Association
2111 Plum Street Suite 274
Aurora, IL 60506
Phone: (630) 631-5217
Fax: 866-837-8450
Web: www.abma.org
Email: info@abma.org
President: Mark F Godfrey

International Code Council
4051 W Flossmoor Road
Country Club Hills, IL 60478
Phone: (888) 422-7233
Fax: (708) 799-4981
Web: www.iccsafe.org
CEO: Richard P Weiland

Chemical Coaters Association International (CCAI)
5040 Old Taylor Mill Road PMB 13
Taylor Mill, KY 41015
Phone: (859) 356-1030
Fax: (859) 356-0908
Anne Goyer, Executive Director
Web Page: www.ccaiweb.com
16 Chapters

**Consumers Specialty Products
Association (CSPA)**
900 17th St. NW Suite 1300
Washington, DC 20006
Phone: (202) 872-8110
Fax: (202) 872-8114
Web: www.cspa.org
Email: info@cspa.org
President: Christopher Cathcart
Semiannual conference and trade show.

Colored Pigment Manufacturers Association
300 N. Washington St., Suite 105
Alexandria, VA 22314
Phone: (703) 684-4044
Fax: (703) 684-1795
Web: www.cpma.com
Email: cpma@cpma.com

American Coatings Association
1500 Rhode Island Avenue NW
Washington, DC 20005
Phone: (202) 462-6272
Fax: (202)462-8549
Web: www.paint.org
Email: npca@paint.org
President/CEO: J Andrew Doyle

International Paint & Printing Ink Council
1500 Rhode Island Avenue NW
Washington DC 20005-5503
Phone: (202) 462-6272
Fax: (202) 462-8549
Web: www.ippic.org
Email: ippic@paint.org

**National Association of Corrosion
Engineers (NACE)**
1440 South Creek Drive
Houston, TX. 77084-4906
Phone: (281) 228-6200
Fax: (281) 228-6300
Web Page: www.nace.org
Email: firstservice@nace.org
Regional conferences

**National Association of Pipe Coating
Applicators (NAPCA)**
100 Louisiana Suite 3400
Houston, TX 77002
Phone: (713) 276-5306
Fax: (713) 276-6206
Web: www.napca.com
Managing Director: Merritt B. Chastain, III

National Coil Coating Association
1300 Sumner Ave.
Cleveland, OH 44115
Phone: (216) 241-7333
Fax: (216) 241-0105
Web: www.coilcoating.org
Email: ncca@coilcoating.org

**National Paint and Coatings
Association (NPCA)**
1500 Rhode Island Ave. N.W.
Washington, DC 20005
Phone: (202) 462-6272
Web Page: www.paint.org
Executive Director: J. Andrew Doyle
Members: 350

**Paint and Decorating Retailers
Association (PDRA)**
1401 Triad Center Drive
Fenton, MO 63376
Phone: (636) 326-2636
Web: www.pdra.org
Email: info@pdra.org
Annual trade show

**Painting and Decorating Contractors
of America (PDCA)**
1801 Park 270 Drive, Suite 220
St. Louis, MO 63146
Phone: (314) 514-7322
Fax: (314) 514-9417
Web: www.pdca.com
CEO: Richard Greene
Annual Expo

Powder Coatings Institute
2170 Buckthorne Place Suite 250
The Woodlands, TX 77380
Phone: (703) 684-1770
Fax: (832) 585-0220
Web: www.powdercoating.org
Email: pci-info@powdercoating.org
Executive Director: Steve Houston
Annual Trade show

RadTech International North America
7986 Old Georgetown Road Unit 8D
Bethesda, MD 20814
Phone: (240) 497-1242
Fax: (240) 209-2340
Web: www.radtech.org
Email: uveb@radtech.org
Members: 200

The Society for Protective Coatings (SSPC)
40 24th Street 6th Floor
Pittsburgh, PA 15222-4656
Phone: (412) 281-2331
Fax: (412) 281-9992
Web Page: www.sspc.org
Executive Director: William Shoup
Members: 7,221

Trade and Technical Publications

Advanced Coatings and Surface Technology
Monthly
John Wiley & Sons
111 River Street
Hoboken, NJ 7030
(201)748-6000
Web: www.wiley.com
Publisher Alan Brown

Advanced Coatings and Surface Technology
Full-text
John Wiley & Sons
111 River Street
Hoboken, NY 07030
(201) 748-6000
www.wiley.com

**Furniture Executive American
Home Furnishings Alliance**
317 W High Avenue PO Box HP-7
High Point, NC 27261
Phone: (336)884-5000
Fax: (336) 884-5303
Web: www.afma4u.org
CEO: Andy Counts
Subscribers: 2,000

American Painting Contractor
Monthly
Briefings Media Group
PO Box 787 Williamsport,
PA 17703
Phone: (800) 791- 8699
Fax: (570) 320-2079
Web: www.briefingsmediagroup.com
Email: briefingsweborders@publishersservicess-
sociates.com
Publisher: Andrew Dwyer
Subscribers: 25,000

Brushware
Brushware/12Twelve Media
PO Box 98
Southern Pines, NC 28387
Phone: (910) 693-2644
Fax: (910) 246-1681
Web: www.brushwaremag.com
Email: editors@brushwaremag.com
Publisher: Karen Grinter
Subscribers: 2,000

Chemical Marketing Reporter
Weekly
Schnell Publishing Co.
Two Rector Street St.
New York, NY 10004
Phone: (212) 248-4177
Web: www.chernicalmarketreporter.com
Editor: Helga Tilton

Chemical & Engineering News
Weekly
American Chemical Society
1155 Sixteenth St. N.W.
Washington, DC 20036
Phone: (202) 872-4600
Web: www.acs.org
Editor-in-Chief: Rudy M Baum

Chemical Week
Weekly
Chemical Week Associates
110 William Street New York,
NY 10038
Phone: (212) 621-4900
Fax: (212) 621-4800
Web: www.chemweek.com
Group VP/Publisher: Lyn Tattum

Coatings World
Monthly
Rodman Publications
70 Hilltop Rd.
Ramsey, NJ 07446
Phone: (201) 825-2552
Web Page: www.coatingsworld.com
Editor: Tim Wright
Circulation: 18,000

DesignSource: Official Specifying and
Annual
PO Box 5059
Hoboken, NJ 07030
Phone: (201) 963-9000
Circulation: 4,000

Directory of Decorating Products
Paint and Decorating Retailers Association
403 Axminister Drive
Fenton, MO 63026
(636) 326-2636
Web: www.pdra.org
Executive VP: Ernest W Stewart

Finishers' Management
10 per year
Publication Management
4350 Di Paolo Center
Glenview, IL 60025
(847) 699-1700
Web: www.finishers-management.com
Publisher: David Friedman
Circulation: 12000

JCT Research and JCT CoatingsTech
Monthly
Federation of Society for Coatings Technology
492 Norristown Rd.
Blue Bell, Pa 19422
Phone: (610) 940-0777
Web: www.coatingstech.org

Journal of the National Spray Equipment Manufacturers
550 Randall Road
Elyria, OH 44035
(440) 366-6808
Executive Secretary: Don R Scarbrough

Journal of Protective Coatings & Linings
Monthly
Technology Publishing Company
2100 Wharton Street Suite 310
Pittsburgh, PA 15203–1951
Phone: (412) 431-8300
Fax: (412) 431-5428
TF: (800) 837-8303
Web: www.paintsquare.com
Email: webmaster@paintsquare.com
Publisher: Marian Welsh

Metal Finishing
Monthly
360 Park Avenue South
New York, NY 10010-1710
Phone: (212) 633-3100
Fax: (212) 633-3140
Web: www.metalfmishing.com
Email: metalfinishing@elsevier.com
Publisher: Reginald Tucker

Modem Paint & Coatings
Monthly
110 William Street
New York, NY 10038
Phone: (212) 621-4900
Fax: (212) 521-4800
TF: (800) 774-5733
Web: www.chemweek.com
Group VP/Publisher: Lyn Tattum

Modem Paint & Coatings
Monthly
Cygnus Publishing
445 Broad Hollow Road
Melville, NY 11747
Phone: (631) 845-2700
Web: www.cygnuspub.com
Editor Esther D'Amico
Circulation: 14,000

Paint & Coatings Industry (PCI)
Monthly
Business News Publishing Co.
2401 W. Big Beaver Rd.
Troy, MI 48084
Phone: (906) 779-9498
Fax: (906) 779-9787
Web: www.pcimag.com
Email: darpaint@aol.com
Editor: Darlene Brezinski PhD

Painting and Wallcovering Contractor
Technology Publishing/PaintSquare
2100 Wharton Street Suite 310
Pittsburgh, PA 15203-1951
Phone: (412) 431-8300
Fax: (412) 431-5428
Web: www.pwc-magazine.com
Email: webmaster@paintsquare.com
Publisher: Sharon Steele

PaintSquare
PaintSquare
2100 Wharton Street Suite
310 Pittsburgh, PA 15203
(412) 431-8300
(800) 837-8303
Web: www.paintsquare.com
Publisher: Harol Hower

Products Finishing
Monthly
Gardner Publications
6915 Valley Ave.
Cincinnati, OH 45244
Phone: (513) 527-8800
Fax: (513) 527-8801
TF: (800) 950-8020
Web Page: www.pfonline.com
Publisher: Don Kline

Tole World
Quarterly
EGW.com
1041 Shary Circle
Concord, CA 94518
925-671-9852
Web: www.toleworld.com
Circulation Director Chris Slaughter
Circulation: 85,956

Walls & Ceilings
Monthly
BNP Media
2401 W Big Beaver Road Suite 700
Troy, MI 48084
Phone: (248) 362-3700
Fax: (248) 362-5103
Web: www.bnpmedia.com
Publisher: Amy Tuttle
Circulation: 30,000

Weekend Woodcrafts
Monthly
EGW.com
1041 Shary Circle
Concord, CA 94518
(925) 671-9852
Web: www.weekendwoodcrafts.com
Circulation Director: Chris Slaughter

Wood Strokes
EGW.com
1041 Shary Circle
Concord, CA 94518
(925) 671-9852
Web: www.egw.com
Circulation Manager Chris Slaughter

Industry Events and Trade Shows

Fall Home Improvement Expo
September
Coral Productions Show Management Company
100 Bickford Street
Rochester, NY 14606
Phone: (585) 254-2580 ext. 200
Fax: (585) 458-1511
Web: www.fallhomeimprovementexpo.com
Email: shows@coralproductions.com
Show Manager: Patti Cartwright

National Hardware Show
May
Reed Exhibitions
383 Main Avenue Norwalk, CT 06851
Phone: (203) 840-5622
(888) 425-9377
Fax: (203) 840-9622
Web: www.nationalhardwareshow.com
Email: inquiry@hardware.reedexpo.com
Group VP: Ed Several

Paint & Decorating Show
May
Paint and Decorating Retailers Association
1401 Triad Center Drive
St. Peters, MO 63376
Phone: (636) 326-2636
Web: www.pdra.org
Email: info@pdra.org

Paint Industries Show
October
492 Norristown Road
Blue Bell, PA 19422
(610) 940-0777
Show Manager: Robert F Ziegler

Painting & Decorating Expo
Painting and Decorating Contractors of America
Feb-March
1801 Park 270 Drive, Ste 220
St. Louis, MO 63146
Phone: (314) 514-7322
TF: (800) 332-7322
Fax: (314) 514-9417
Web: www.pdca.org

National Decorating Products Show
Paint & Decorating Retailers Association
403 Axminster Drive
Fenton, MO 63206-2941
(636) 326-2636
Executive Director: James Savens

5

THE LEADING U.S. PAINT COMPANIES

Alphabetical by Company Name

3M

3M Center
Minneapolis MN 55144-1000
Phone: 651-733-1110
Toll Free: 888-364-3577
Fax: 651-733-1771
Web: http://www.3m.com/

Annual Sales: $23.1 Billion
Number of Employees: 74,835
President: George W. Buckley
Research & Development: Frederick J. Palensky
Marketing Manager: Robert D. MacDonald
Sales Manager: Robert D. MacDonald

3M's Energy and Advanced Materials sector provides solutions for the industry including fluoro surfactants which serve as ideal wetting and leveling agents for paints, stains, primers, inks, coil coatings, adhesives, clearcoats, resins and floor coverings; ceramic microspheres for enhanced high filler loading/low viscosity, reduced VOCs, abrasion resistance, corrosion resistance, gloss control and hardness; and stain resistant additives that can be used in concentrate form as an additive for coatings and sealers.

A - Line Products

2955 Bellevue Street
Detroit MI 48207
Phone: 313-571-8300
Fax: 313-571-0417
Web: http://www.a-line.com

Annual Sales: $1.8 Million
Number of Employees: 15
President: Kevin Laura
Manufacturing Operations Manager: Gary Laura

Serves the automotive OEM, steel mills and CASE industries across the United States, Canada and Mexico offering a full line of natural oil polyols, waterborne and solvent borne coatings, plastic adhesion promoters, refractory releasing coatings, cleaners, chemical intermediates, and a variety of low VOC containing products.

A D M Tronics Unlimited

224 South Pegasus Avenue
Northvale NJ 07647
Phone: 201-767-6040
Toll Free:
Fax: 201-784-0620
Web: http://www.admtronics.com/
Email: sales@admtronics.com

Annual Sales: $1.1 Million
Number of Employees: 12
President: Andre' DiMino
Marketing Manager: Thomas Kistler
Manufacturing Operations Manager: Vincent DiMino

The Aqua Based Technologies division provides environmentally safe, water-based primers, coatings, adhesives and additives for medical and food packaging, graphic arts, converting and wall covering industries. It also produces specialty conductive paints, coatings, and other products for the computer, pharmaceutical and chemical fields for the prevention of static electricity damage to personnel, operating plants and to expensive computers & electronic equipment and parts.

A P S Materials

4011 Riverside Drive
Dayton OH 45405
Phone: 937-278-6547
Toll Free: 800-652-1510
Fax: 937-278-4352
Web: http://www.apsmaterials.com/

Annual Sales: $21 Million
Number of Employees: 65
CEO: Steve Shaw
Manufacturing Operations Manager: Mike Willson

The company manufactures thermal spray coatings for a variety of applications and for diverse clientele and industries including aerospace (coatings for aircraft engine manufacturers), materials processing, biomedical (porous and bioactive coatings for the orthopedic market), automotive (wear and corrosion of power train and chassis components), and electronics (silicon wafers and semiconductors).

A. P. Nonweiler

3321 County Road A
PO Box 1007
Oshkosh WI 54903
Phone: 920-231-0850
Toll Free: 800-792-7126
Fax: 920-231-8085
Web: http://www.apnonweiler.com
Email: dennis@apnonweiler.com

Annual Sales: $6.5 Million
Number of Employees: 10-49
President: Mark Nonweiler
Sales Manager: Dennis Lewandowski

Industrial and sustainable coatings, protective coatings, custom coatings and vacuum metalizing.

A. W. Chesterton

500 Unicorn Park Drive
Woburn MA 01801-3345
Phone: 781-438-7000
Fax: 781-438-8971
Web: http://www.chesterton.com

Annual Sales: $200 Million
Number of Employees: 1,200
President: Brian O'Donnell
Research & Development:

Chesterton is primarily a producer of seals and packings. For the marine industry it also manufactures ceramic reinforced corrosion and abrasion-resistant coatings for ballast tanks.

Abatron

5501 75th Avenue
Kenosha WI 53144
Phone: 414-653-2000
Toll Free: 800-445-1754
Fax: 262-653-2019
Web: http://www.abatron.com
Email: info@abatron.com

Annual Sales: $1 - 4.9 Million
Number of Employees: 10-49
President: John J.P. Caporaso
CEO: Marsha Caporaso
Sales Manager: Richard Ahlstrom

Coatings, adhesives, sealants, urethanes, acrylics, and other compounds for Electronics, Marine & Industrial Use. Several products are GREENGUARD Certified for low, non-toxic emissions.

Absolute Coatings

38 Portman Road
New Rochelle NY 10801
Phone: 914-636-0700
Toll Free: 800-221-8010
Fax: 914-636-0822
Web: http://www.absolutecoatings.com
Email: info@absolutecoatings.com

Annual Sales: $9 Million
Number of Employees: 40
President: David K. Sherman

The company manufactures polyurethane coatings, wood and concrete sealers, and varnish removers. It has three divisions. The Trade Sales Division produces polyurethane wood finishes, interior wood stains, exterior spar varnishes, and floor maintenance products. Products are sold in paint and hardware stores, home centers and lumberyards. The Professional Flooring Division produces wood floor finishes for the professional market. The Private Label/Specialty Coating Division manufactures products to customer specifications. This division manages the export business.

AC Products

Quaker Chemical
172 East LaJolla Street
Placentia CA 92870
Phone: 714-630-7311
Web: http://www.quakerchem.com

AC Products, Inc., Placentia, CA, a subsidiary of Quaker Chemical, manufactures specialty coatings, elastomeric wall coatings, and roof adhesives and coatings.

Ace Hardware

2200 Kensington Court
Oak Brook IL 60523
Phone: 630-990-6600
Toll Free: 877-223-4391
Fax: 630-990-6572
Web: http://www.acehardware.com
Email: media@acehardware.com

Annual Sales: $3.8 Billion
Number of Employees: 4500
President: Ray Griffith
CEO: Ray Griffith
Marketing Manager: Brian Wiborg
Manufacturing Operations Manager: Pat Laughran

Ace Paint Division produces an entire line of interior and exterior water-, latex-, oil- and solvent-based paints, stains, varnishes and coatings for sale through more than 4,600 independent dealers . It consists of two manufacturing locations—one in Matteson, IL, and the other in Chicago Heights, IL.

Acheson

Henkel
1600 Washington Avenue
Port Huron MI 48060
Phone: 810-984-5581
Toll Free: 800-255-1908
Fax: 810-984-3135
Web: http://www.achesonindustries.com
Email: web.mail@nstarch.com

Annual Sales: $8.1 Billion
Number of Employees: 206
CEO: Thomas Geitner
Sales Manager: Jim Vorderbrueggen

Acheson Colloids manufactures lubricants, specialty energy storage and anti-friction coatings which fight friction and protect from weather damage and are applied to everything from gaskets to injection seats in jets. Founded in 1908, Acheson is a part of German adhesives titan Henkel. It had joined with Ablestik Laboratories to make up National Starch and Chemical's Electronic and Engineering Materials division until a 2008 deal led to the breakup of National Starch's parent company, ICI. As a result of Henkel's acquisition of the National Starch businesses in April 2008, Henkel has expanded its metal solutions with the addition of the Acheson product lines. Acheson specialty coatings, process lubricants and lubricant application systems are now exclusively available through Henkel.

Aegeon Coatings

Exousia Advanced Materials
350 Fifth Ave, Suite 5720
New York NY 10118-5720
Phone: 212-796-4333
Web: http://www.exousiacorp.com
Email: info@exousia.com

Exousia industrial coatings are a family of high-performance epoxies, alkyd resin systems, polyurethanes and primers, many of which are formulated with VISTAMER® Rubber, ideal for heavy duty, highly corrosive environments, such as marine, petrochemical, infrastructure and energy.

Acrylux Paint Manufacturing

6010 Powerline Road
Fort Lauderdale FL 33309
Phone: 954-772-0300
Toll Free:
Fax: 954-771-4198
Web: http://www.acrylux.com/
Email: sales@acrylux.com

Number of Employees: 5-9
President: William C. Riedesel

Waterproofing products- acrylic roof paint, house paint, elastomeric roof paint, waterproof roof coatings, roof tile sealers, power sealers and green products.

AcryTech Coatings

3601 Northeast 5th Avenue
Fort Lauderdale FL 33334
Phone: 954-565-6001
Toll Free: 800-771-6001
Fax: 954-565-2864
Web: http://www.acrytech.com
Email: sales@acrytech.com

Number of Employees: 1-9
President: Dan Hittenberger
CEO: Mike Dobulis

Acrylic coatings for surfaces from roofs to floors. Industrial roof and metal paint primers, coatings, cleansers, and sealers.

Adams Paint Company

1416 North University Avenue
PO Box 5276
Lubbock TX 79415-1114
Phone: 806-763-2944
Toll Free:
Fax: 806-763-7856
Web: http://www.adamspaintmfg.com

Annual Sales: $1 - 4.9 Million
Number of Employees: 18172
President: James Adams

Quality architectural paints and durable industrial coatings including APCO performance coatings.

Advanced Coating Systems

2230 Towne Lake Parkway
Building 1000/140
Woodstock GA 30189
Phone: 678-445-0040
Toll Free: 800-587-3758
Fax: 678-445-0399
Web: http://www.advanced-coatings.com

Number of Employees: 8
President: Steve McGuinness
CEO: Steve McGuinness
Marketing Manager: Michael McGuinness

Elastomeric roofing coatings.

Advanced Polymer Coatings

951 Jaycox Road
Avon Ohio 44011
Phone: 440-937-6218
Toll Free: 800-334-7193
Fax: 440-937-5046
Web: http://www.adv-polymer.com
Email: apc@adv-polymer.com

Annual Sales: $18 Million
Number of Employees: 22
President: Don Keehan
CEO: Melissa Hoyt
Marketing Manager: Melissa Hoyt

High performance protective coatings for industry with patented polymer technology.

Advanced Protective Products

17-12 River Road
Fair Lawn NJ 07410
Phone: 201-796-3508
Toll Free: 800-787-8007
Fax: 201-548-5100
Web: http://www.rust007.com
Email: th00747@hotmail.com

Annual Sales: $1.5 Million
Number of Employees: 11
Sales Manager: Tom Heiss

Rust protection and corrosion prevention coatings.

Aegis Technologies Inc

PO Box 747
4 Industrial Drive
Pelham NH 03076
Phone: 603-889-7608
Fax: 603-889-7951

Number of Employees: 10-49
President: Jan Maczuba

Coatings for electronics industry

Aero-Marine Engineering

PO Box 189
708 Highway 380W
Bryson TX 76427
Phone: 940-392-3333
Toll Free: 800-874-4543
Fax: 940-392-2058
Web: http://www.ame-technicoat.com
Email: info@ame-technicoat.com

Number of Employees: 18
President: Don Jones
CEO: Don Jones
Research & Development: Denis Sutherland

The company produces corrosion-control coatings for the HVAC industry with added UV protection and that are environmentally friendly.

Aervoe Industries

1100 Mark Circle
Gardnerville NV 89410
Phone: 775-783-3100
Toll Free: 800-227-0196
Fax: 775-782-5687
Web: http://www.aervoe.com
Email: mailbox@aervoe.com

Annual Sales: $40 Million
Number of Employees: 160
President: David A. Williams
CEO: David A. Williams

The company manufactures paints and specialty coatings; cleaners; lubricants; MRO products; and recycling equipment for industrial use. Paints include camouflage, tree marking, varnishes, and primers.

Aexcel

7373 Production Drive
Mentor OH 44060
Phone: 440-974-3800
Toll Free: 800-854-0782
Fax: 440-974-3808
Web: http://www.aexcelcorp.com

Number of Employees: 45
President: John S. Milgram
Research & Development: Vince Genora
Manufacturing Operations Manager: M. G. Amiro

Aexcel produces acrylic, waterborne-latex, polyester, alkyd, and chlorinated-rubber formulations of traffic, safety and road marking paints. It also manufactures OEM industrial coatings for metals, wood, plastics and composites, and private label products. The company operates a 70,000 sq ft plant.

Agate Lacquer Tri-Nat

824 South Avenue
Middlesex NJ 08846
Phone: 732-968-1080
Toll Free: 800-452-4735
Fax: 732-968-1269
Web: http://www.agatelacquer.com
Email: april.morlock@verizon.net

Annual Sales: $1 Million
Number of Employees: 5
President: Les Trinity
CEO: Les Trinity
Marketing Manager: Les Trinity
Sales Manager: April Morlock

Lacquer coatings used in both domestic and international markets. Includes low VOC lacquers.

APV Engineered Coatings

1390 Firestone Parkway
Akron OH 44301
Phone: 330-773-8911
Toll Free: 800-772-3452
Fax: 330-773-1028
Web: http://www.apvcoatings.com
Email: kziprik@apvcoatings.com

Annual Sales: $21.1 Million
Number of Employees: 90
President: David Venarge
Marketing Manager: Mike Couchie
Sales Manager: Paul Bluman
Manufacturing Operations Manager: Ed Atsega

High performance low VOC chassis enamel, enamels- air dry coatings, stencil paints for rubber used to enhance race tire sidewalls and any other cured rubber surface with a logo or brand name, marine upholstery topcoats, a full line of high performance primers and basecoats for various TPO (Olefins, Plastics, polyolefin, and polyethylene) materials, vinyl topcoats for flexible vinyls. (Formerly Akron Paint & Varnish)

Akzo Nobel Coatings

Akzo Nobel NV (Netherlands)
2031 Nelson Miller Parkway
Louisville KY 40223
Phone: 502-254-0470
Fax: 502-253-5765
Web: http://www.akzonobel.com
Email: ifnewsupdate@akzonobel.com

Annual Sales: $18.1 Billion
Number of Employees: 57,060
CEO: Hans Wijers
Marketing Manager: David Knapp

Worldwide coatings sales of the parent are $18.1 billion in 2009. Decorative paints represent 34% of the corporate total; performance coatings 29%; and specialty chemicals 37%. The company is reportedly the largest coating company in the world. The Decorative Paints division: paints, lacquers and varnishes, adhesives and floor leveling compounds, mixing machines, color concepts and training courses for the building and renovation industry, specialty coatings for metal, concrete and other critical building materials. The Performance Coatings division: car refinishes, marine and protective coatings, powder coatings, industrial coatings, and wood finishes and adhesives.

Aladdin Laminating

438 West 37th Street
New York NY 10018
Phone: 212-279-1222
Fax: 212-268-5273
Web: http://www.aladdinfinishing.com

Number of Employees: 25
President: Hank Ruggiero
Sales Manager: Frank Cundari

Aqueous coating, UV coating, and film lamination.

Albi Manufacturing

Stanchem
401 Berlin Street
E. Berlin CT 06023
Phone: 860-828-0571
Fax: 860-828-3297
Web: http://www.stanchem-inc.com
Email: info@stanchem-inc.com

Annual Sales: $17.8 Million
Number of Employees: 50
President: D. Robert Albi
CEO: D. Robert Albi
Research & Development: Bridget Hanafin
Sales Manager: W. Casey West
Manufacturing Operations Manager: Robert Paradis

The Division of Stanchem produces intumescent coating for fireproofing structural steel, wood, wallboard and other interior and exterior surfaces. Stanchem develops and manufactures adhesives, coatings and emulsion polymers.

All City Paint & Hardware

18105 Northeast 19th Avenue
N. Miami Beach FL 33162
Phone: 305-947-5511

Annual Sales: Under $1 Million
Number of Employees: 3
President: Jose Drinidev
CEO: Jose Drinidev
Marketing Manager: Sergio Luna

Paints

Allans Paint

917 West 18th Street
Chicago IL 60608
Phone: 312-829-3200

Number of Employees: 5-9

House paints.

Allied Manufacturing

3100 South Glen
Springfield MO 65807
Phone: 417-883-9927
Fax: 417-886-9432
Web: http://www.alliedmfgco.com
Email: info@alliedmfgco.com

Number of Employees: 10-49
President: Norman Hill

Architectural paints.

Altawood

420 South 11th Avenue
Upland CA 91786
Phone: 909-931-1531
Fax: 909-931-1536
Web: http://www.altawood.com
Email: Sales@altawood.com

Annual Sales: $5 Million
Number of Employees: 10-50
President: Herbert Gleicke
CEO: Herbert Gleicke
Research & Development: Tony Velasquez

Altawood manufactures automotive and industrial aerosol spray paints, primers, finishes and chemical products that fit virtually every application.

American Home Paint

Talon Paint Products.
207 Bright Street
Jersey City NJ 7302
Phone: 201-433-8554
Fax: 201-401-7066
Email: talonpaint@verizon.net

President: George Picia

Architectural and industrial paints.

American Powder Coatings

420 South 38th Avenue
St. Charles IL 60174
Phone: 630-762-0100
Fax: 630-762-0111
Web: http://www.americanpowder.com
Email: sales@americanpowder.com

Number of Employees: 25
President: Dave Suvagia
Marketing Manager: Brett Suvagia

Powder coatings. Custom color matching available.

AmeriCoats

3429 North Runge Street
Franklin Park IL 60131
Phone: 847-455-1400
Toll Free: 866-455-2628
Fax: 847-455-2797
Web: http://www.americoats.com
Email: sales@americoats.com

Annual Sales: $7.7 Million
Number of Employees: 50-99
President: Raj Patel

High temperature and functional powder coatings.

Amsterdam Color Works

3326 Merritt Avenue
Bronx NY 10475
Phone: 718-231-8626
Fax: 718-231-8631
Web: http://www.amsterdamcolorworks.com/
Email: amsterdamcolorworks@hotmail.com

Annual Sales: $2-5 Million
Number of Employees: 30
President: Stephen Offerman
CEO: Stephen Offerman
Manufacturing Operations Manager: Naheem Ilahi

Full line of architectural, industrial maintenance, and general purpose paints, enamels, and varnishes.

Anchor Paint Manufacturing

6707 East 14th Street
Tulsa OK 74112
Phone: 918-836-4626
Toll Free: 800-999-4626
Fax: 918-836-6421
Web: http://www.anchorpaint.com
Email: info@anchorpaint.com

Annual Sales: $22 Million
Number of Employees: 60-120
President: Chuck Taylor
CEO: Chip Meade

Anchor produces architectural, protective and industrial coatings for metal surfaces, and also wholesales and retails these and similar products. It operates six retail stores.

Anvil Paints & Coatings

1255 Starkey Road
Largo FL 33771
Phone: 727-535-1411
Toll Free: 800-822-6776
Fax: 727-535-1413
Web: http://www.anvilpaints.com
Email: contact@anvilpaints.com

Number of Employees: 20-49
President: Chuck Garver
Research & Development: Chuck Garver
Sales Manager: Tony Anderson

Roofing, flooring, primers, wall coatings.

Ardex Engineered Cements

400 Ardex Park Drive
Aliquippa PA 15001
Phone: 724-203-5000
Toll Free: 888-512-7339
Fax: 724-203-5001
Web: http://www.ardex.com
Email: info@ardex.com

Annual Sales: $85 Million
Number of Employees: 525
President: Stephan M. Liozu
CEO: Mark Eslamlooy
Marketing Manager: John Nixon
Sales Manager: Jesse David
Manufacturing Operations Manager: Mark Litton

Specialty cements and substrate preparation products for flooring and building professionals.

Arma Coatings

5555 W. 11th Avenue
Eugene OR 97402
Phone: 541-688-3500
Toll Free: 800-524-2762
Fax: 541-688-0519
Web: http://www.armacoatings.com/
Email: arma@armacoatings.com

Number of Employees: 20-49
President: David Lucchetti
CEO: David Lucchetti

Manufactures spray on protective coatings for marine, automotive, and industrial applications.

Arrowhead Paint Products

24 N 39th Avenue West
Duluth MN 55807
Phone: 218-628-2819
Fax: 218-628-2819
Web: http://www.arrowheadpaint.com
Email: arrowheadpaint@yahoo.com

Annual Sales: Under $1 Million
Number of Employees: 3
President: Tom Lavato
CEO: Tom Lavato

Paints

Asheville Paint & Powder Coating

16 Old Charlotte Highway
Asheville NC 28803
Phone: 828-298-9844
Fax: 828-299-1779
Web: http://www.tlf-inc.com
Email: TomAtTLF@aol.com

Annual Sales: $1 - 4.9 Million
Number of Employees: 10-49
CEO: Tom Finger

Sales Manager: Patrick McClure

Custom and environmentally controlled powder coatings.

Ashland Performance Materials

Ashland
5200 Blazer Memorial Parkway
Dublin OH 43017
Phone: 614-790-3333
Web: http://www.ashchem.com

CEO: James J. O'Brien
Manufacturing Operations Manager: Lamar M. Chambers

Raw materials for paint and coatings applications.

Associated Chemists

4401 Southeast Johnson Creek Boulevard
Portland OR 97222
Phone: 503-659-1708
Toll Free: 800-554-4666
Fax: 503-653-0409
Web: http://www.achemists.com/
Email: info@achemists.com

Annual Sales: $9 Million
Number of Employees: 70-99
President: Richard M. Wilch

Paint and coating defoamers, maintenance paints, stencils and marking ink.

Atlas Minerals & Chemicals

PO Box 38
1227 Valley Road
Mertztown PA 19539
Phone: 610-682-7171
Toll Free: 800-523-8269
Fax: 610-682-9200
Web: http://www.atlasmin.com
Email: sales@atlasmin.com

Annual Sales: $18 Million
Number of Employees: 95
President: Frank X. Hanson
CEO: Frank Hanson
Research & Development: Mario Nazarro
Marketing Manager: Scott Gallagher
Sales Manager: Scott Gallagher
Manufacturing Operations Manager: Mario Nazarro

Atlas produces corrosion-resistant mortars, grouts, floorings and linings. The Chemical Construction Materials (CCM) group manufactures some concrete and steel coatings.

BASF Admixtures

BASF Construction Chemicals
23700 Chagrin Boulevard
Cleveland OH 44122
Phone: 216-839-7500
Toll Free: 800-628-9990
Fax: 216-839-8821
Web: http://www.construction-chemicals.basf.com
Email: admixtures@basf.com

CEO: John Salvatore

The Construction Chemicals division of BASF includes Master Builders Technologies. Their well-known construction industry products include joint sealants, waterproofing, grout, concrete repair, water repellent, performance flooring, surface adhesives and wall coating solutions.

BASF Building Systems

BASF Construction Chemicals
889 Valley Park Drive South
Shakopee MN 55379
Phone: 952-496-6000
Toll Free: 800-433-9517
Fax: 952-496-6063
Web: http://www.buildingsystems.basf.com

President: Doug MacRae
CEO: Doug MacRae

Formerly Degussa Building Sytems, it manufactures sealants and adhesives, waterproofing membranes, concrete repair products, grouts, cementitious/polyurethane and polymer-based (epoxy, polyurethane, acrylic and neoprene) flooring systems, architectural coatings, and low-e paint for the construction industry.

BASF North America

BASF Group
100 Campus Drive
Florham Park NJ 07932
Phone: 973-245-6000
Toll Free: 800-526-1072
Fax: 973-895-8002
Web: http://www.basf.us

Annual Sales: $13 Billion
Number of Employees: 15,945
President: Joseph C. Breunig

Operations in North America include BASF's entire product range: Coatings, Plastics, Chemicals, Care Chemicals, and Agricultural Products. The Coatings Division of the BASF Group, develops, produces and markets a high-quality range of innovative automotive OEM coatings, automotive refinishes and industrial coatings as well as decorative paints. The Performance Product segment produces dispersions, pigments and coating chemicals. The Functional Solutions segment produces environmentally friendly and innovative coatings solutions for automotive and industrial applications. The Automotive Group is headquartered in Southfield, MI.

Basic Coatings

Atlas Products
1001 Brown Avenue
PO Box 3126 Toledo OH 50321
Phone: 800-247-5471
Toll Free: 800-441-1934
Fax: 800-942-2007
Web: http://www.basiccoatings.com
Email: bcinfo@basiccoatings.com

Annual Sales: $25 Million
Number of Employees: 100

Basic manufactures clear wood finishes coatings and maintenance products for residential, commercial, and sports floors. Products are sold to contractors and the general public.

Bates & Company

PO Drawer 1328
2244 McArthur Drive
Orange TX 43607
Phone: 409-883-0384
Fax: 409-886-0795
Web: http://www.cdbates.com
Email: wsmith@cdbates.com

Annual Sales: $9 Million
Number of Employees: 5-10
President: Jim Gilliam

Manufactures specialty puttys for the wood products industry.

Bel-Mar Paint

14735 Northwest 24th Court
Opa Locka FL 33054
Phone: 305-769-0017
Fax: 305-769-2442

Number of Employees: 10
President: Rafael Behmoiras

Architectural paints, stains.

Benjamin Moore

Berkshire Hathaway
101 Paragon Drive
Montvale NJ 07645
Phone: 201-573-9600
Toll Free: 800-344-0400
Fax: 201-573-0046
Web: http://www.benjaminmoore.com
Email: info@benjaminmoore.com

Annual Sales: $900 Million
Number of Employees: 3,151
President: Denis Abrams

Marketing Manager: Bruce Zeh

Benjamin Moore produces a broad line of general-purpose paints, stains, and coatings, primarily for architectural applications. Products are sold through about 4,000 independent paint and decorating stores, mass merchandisers, discount stores and other retail outlets, and also through about 95 company-owned stores. Most sales are in North America. Brand names include Benjamin Moore, Moore's, Moorglo, Moorgard, Impervo, Regal Wall Satin, A Stroke of Brilliance, and Benwood. The company also manufactures industrial finishes for such applications as wood flooring, tanks, roof decking, coils, furniture and shelving, window blinds, and flatwood products. Through recent acquisitions Benjamin Moore began operating retail stores. Berkshire Hathaway, the parent, purchased the company for about $1 billion in 2001.

Bennette Paint Manufacturing

401 Industry Drive
PO Box 9088
Hampton VA 23670
Phone: 757-838-7777
Toll Free: 800-869-2929
Fax: 757-827-0529
Web: http://www.bennette.com
Email: info@bennette.com

Annual Sales: $8 Million
Number of Employees: 52
President: Howard Jordan
Sales Manager: M. Palmer

Bennette produces mostly architectural paints. It also offers a limited volume of industrial coatings, including swimming pool paints, masonry coatings, traffic paints, and marine paints. Products are sold through company owned stores or dealers in Virginia, N. Carolina, and S. Carolina. The Bennette Equipment Co., a subsidiary, sells and rents paint spraying and pressure cleaning equipment.

Berkley Products

405 South 7th Street
Akron PA 17501
Phone: 717-859-1105
Toll Free: 800-869-1104
Fax: 717-859-5678
Web: http://www.berkleyproducts.com
Email: contact@berkleyproducts.com

Annual Sales: $1 Million
Number of Employees: 10-49
Sales Manager: Dennis Scianna
Manufacturing Operations Manager: Thomas Faut

Industrial finishes and coatings for steel, wood, roof, and concrete.

Best Paint

1728 4th Avenue South
Seattle WA 98134-1502
Phone: 206-783-9938
Fax: 206-783-5017
Web: http://www.bestpaintco.com/
Email: paint@bestpaintco.com

Number of Employees: 5-9

Environmentally-safe consumer paints.

Black & Puryear Paint Manufacturing

13 Northeast 13th Street
Oklahoma City OK 73104
Phone: 405-236-5588
Fax: 405-232-0153

Annual Sales: Under $1 Million
Number of Employees: 9
President: John Puryear
CEO: John Puryear
Marketing Manager: Joe Johnson
Manufacturing Operations Manager: Stephen Holder

Paint, varnish, paint removers.

BLP Mobile Paint Manufacturing

4775 Hamilton Boulevard
Theodore AL 36582
Phone: 251-443-6110
Fax: 251-408-0410
Web: http://www.blpmobilepaint.com
Email: salesservice@blpmobilepaint.com

Annual Sales: $65 Million
Number of Employees: 475

The company, also known as Mobile Paint Co., produces architectural coatings and related products under the BLP name for sale both through 17 retail outlets in 12 states and to other retailers and contractors in the south and southeast and also in the Caribbean, Europe and Asia. Additionally, it manufactures such industrial coatings as UV coatings, traffic paints, aerosols, high-solids coatings and primers. Production of paints exceeds 3 million gal annually. It operates a 200,000 sq ft manufacturing facility.

Bona US

Bona AB (Sweden)
2550 South Parker Road
Suite 600
Aurora CO 80014
Phone: 303-371-1411
Toll Free: 800-872-5515
Fax: 303-371-6958
Web: http://www.bona.com
Email: usadmin@bona.com

Annual Sales: $134.5 Million
Number of Employees: 100
President: Kerstin Lindell
Research & Development: Nils-Erik Persson
Marketing Manager: Ilene LeBlanc
Sales Manager: John Ravoula
Manufacturing Operations Manager: Anders Karstensson

Hardwood floor finishes, fillers, abrasives, sealers, and floor care products.

Boro Paint & Hardware

1227 51st Street
Ste A7 Brooklyn NY 11219
Phone: 718-438-5500
Fax: 718-438-9280

Annual Sales: Under $1 Million

Paints and varnishes.

Bradley Coatings Group

Lockhart
2873 West Hardies Road
Gibsonia PA 15044
Phone: 724-628-9100
Toll Free: 800-245-4190
Fax: 724-628-0929
Web: http://www.bradleycoatings.com

Annual Sales: Under $1 Million
Number of Employees: 18
CEO: John Domonkos
Research & Development: Derek Crawford
Marketing Manager: Phil Capriotti

Urethane top coats, epoxy primers, undercoatings and general industrial coatings for the transportation, rail and general OEM markets.

Bradley-Van Holm Chemical

C.E. Bradley Laboratories.
PO Box 8238
Brattleboro VT 5304
Phone: 802-257-7971
Fax: 802-257-7070
Web: http://www.cebradley.com
Email: info@cebradley.com

Number of Employees: 40
President: Rashed Kanaan
CEO: Hisham Kanaan
Marketing Manager: Edward Rochford
Sales Manager: Robert Rowinski

Industrial coatings and thinners.

Bredero Shaw

ShawCor Ltd. (Canada)-P
3838 North Sam Houston Parkway East
Suite 300
Houston TX 77032
Phone: 281-886-2350
Toll Free: 800-367-7617
Fax: 281-886-2353
Web: http://www.brederoshaw.com
Email: solutions@brederoshaw.com

Annual Sales: $500 Million
Number of Employees: 3,400
President: W.P. Buckley
CEO: G. Hyland

The company claims to be the leading worldwide applicator of pipeline coatings for the oil and gas industry. It operates in 14 countries and has eight facilities in the United States.

Bridges Smith

118 East Main Street
Louisville KY 40202
Phone: 502-584-4173
Fax: 502-581-0390

Annual Sales: $16.3 Million
Number of Employees: 10-49
President: Harry Frampton

Paints and enamels.

Brite Products

14650 Dequindre
Detroit MI 48212
Phone: 313-865-4380
Toll Free: 888-992-7483
Fax: 313-883-4930
Web: http://www.briteproducts.com
Email: info@briteproducts.com

Annual Sales: $2.3 Million
President: John Campbell

Zinc coatings for galvanized steel-- rust protection.

Burke Industrial Coatings

600 S. 74th Place
Suite 108
Ridgefield WA 98642
Phone: 360-887-8819
Toll Free: 800-348-3245
Fax: 360-887-8825
Web: http://www.burkeindustrialcoatings.com
Email: info@burkeindustrialcoatings.com

Annual Sales: $1 - 4.9 Million
Number of Employees: 1-9
President: James P. Harris
Manufacturing Operations Manager: Darrell Badertscher

Industrial powder coatings, copolymer acrylic paint formulations.

C. DeSantis Paint Manufacturing

4101 East 116th Street
Cleveland OH 44105
Phone: 216-883-8422

Architectural paints, industrial finishes, maintenance coatings.

C. F. Jameson

72 South Kimball Street, Box 5197
Bradford MA 1835
Phone: 978-374-4731
Fax: 978-374-1492

Number of Employees: 10-49

Protective and decorative finishes for flexible and rigid substrates.

C.A. Reeve Paint

619 West Fayette Street
Syracuse NY 13204
Phone: 315-475-9923
Fax: 315-472-1643
Email: donal-martin@aol.com

Annual Sales: $1 - 4.9 Million
Number of Employees: 10-49
Sales Manager: Donald Martin

Industrial paints

CAAP

152 Pepes Farm Road
Milford CT 06460
Phone: 203-877-0375
Fax: 203-874-6072
Web: http://www.caapco.com/
Email: email@caapco.com

Annual Sales: $7.7 Million
Number of Employees: 20
Manufacturing Operations Manager: Bruce Moore

Erosion resistant aircraft coatings.

Cal Western Paint

11748 Slauson Avenue
Santa Fe Springs CA 90670
Phone: 562-693-0872
Toll Free: 800-559-5525
Fax: 562-696-9932

Annual Sales: $4.1 Million
Number of Employees: 25
Sales Manager: Aleta Zak

Produces architectural and industrial paints. Sales estimated at $3 million.

California Paints

California Products Corp.
150 Dascomb Road
Andover MA 01810
Phone: 978-623-9980
Toll Free: 800-225-1141
Fax: 800-533-6788
Web: http://www.californiapaints.com
Email: info@californiapaints.com

Annual Sales: $50 Million
Number of Employees: 145
President: David Lohr
CEO: Peter Longo
Research & Development: Ron Boyajian

California Paints produces paints and coatings for home and office uses under the Fres-Coat, and Pacific names; ceiling whites and enamels for hard wall interiors under Pro 2000; and acrylic latex finishes and primers under Storm Stain and Wipe Out. The Plexipave, Sports Surfacing Systems, Fiberlock Technologies and Deco Surfacing Systems divisions manufacture acrylic surfacing systems, such as pool paints and rust-resistant enamels.

Caloric Color

176 Saddle River Avenue
Garfield NJ 07026
Phone: 973-471-4748

Annual Sales: $1.1 Million
Number of Employees: 10
President: June Anton

Plastic colors.

Camger Coatings Systems

364 Main Street
Norfolk MA 2056
Phone: 508-528-5787
Fax: 508-520-1430
Web: http://www.camger.com
Email: info@camger.com

Number of Employees: 20-35
Manufacturing Operations Manager: Sarah Traham

Industrial coatings and adhesives for wood, metal, plastics, and specialty applications.

Cansto Paint & Varnish

9320 Woodland Avenue
Cleveland OH 44104
Phone: 216-231-6115
Fax: 216-231-6117

Annual Sales: Under $ 1 Million
Number of Employees: 7

Varnish, lacquers, paint.

Capitol Coating & Chemical

3002 Shallowford Road NE
Chamblee GA 30341
Phone: 770-457-1164

Number of Employees: 3
President: Al Filsoof

Paint

Capitol Paint Manufacturing

722 Southwest 23rd Street
Oklahoma City OK 73109
Phone: 405-634-3383
Toll Free: 800-405-3383
Fax: 405-632-8436
Web: http://www.capitolpaintmfg.com
Email: info@capitolpaintmfg.com

Annual Sales: $1 Million
Number of Employees: 10-49
President: Stanton Ballew

Acrylics, alkyd-bake dry enamels, urethanes, rust prevention coatings for industrial and residential applications.

Carbit Paint

927 West Blackhawk Street
Chicago IL 60642
Phone: 312-280-2300
Fax: 312-280-7326
Web: http://www.carbit.com
Email: info@carbit.com

Annual Sales: $6 Million
Number of Employees: 50
President: Jim Westerman
Sales Manager: David L. Westerman
Manufacturing Operations Manager: David T. Westerman

Carbit manufactures architectural paints, varnishes, and specialty and industrial coatings.

Carbolineum Wood Preserving

6683 North 40th Street
PO Box 090348
Milwaukee WI 53209
Phone: 414-353-5040
Toll Free: 800-671-0093
Fax: 414-353-3325
Web: http://www.carbolineum.com
Email: sales@carbolineum.com

Annual Sales: $1 Million
Number of Employees: 10
President: Frederick Leypoldt

Stains and wood preservatives.

Cardinal Industrial Finishes

1329 Potrero Avenue
South El Monte CA 91733
Phone: 626-444-9274
Toll Free: 800-696-5244
Fax: 626-444-0382
Web: http://www.cardinalpaint.com/
Email: Terryl@cardinalpaint.com

Annual Sales: $10-25 Million
Number of Employees: 200
Research & Development: Mike Mitchinson
Sales Manager: Bob Daiker
Manufacturing Operations Manager: Paul Bonani

The company produces alkyd and acrylic industrial coatings in South El Monte and powder coatings, including primers, at City of Industry, CA. Other facilities are in Phoenix, AZ; Denver, CO; Warren, PA; Lakeville, MN; Charlotte, NC; Dallas, TX; Maryland Heights, MO; Woodinville, WA; and San Jose, CA.

Caribbean Paint

5295 Northwest 79th Avenue
Miami FL 33166
Phone: 305-594-4500
Toll Free: 800-242-4100
Fax: 305-594-1800

Annual Sales: $5 - 9.9 Million
Number of Employees: 12
President: George Sixto

Traffic paints, tennis court paints, other specialties.

Carlisle Coatings & Waterproofing

Carlisle Companies
900 Hensley Lane
Wylie TX 75098
Phone: 972-442-6545
Toll Free: 800-527-7092
Fax: 972-442-0076
Web: http://www.ccwcompanies.com
Email: info@ccwi.com

President: Rick D. McKinnish

Sheet, liquid, and spray waterproofing coatings; pedestrian, specialty deck and vehicle coatings; moisture protection.

Carroll Coatings

150 Earnest Street
Providence RI 2905
Phone: 401-450-5500
Toll Free: 800-633-1154
Fax: 401-450-5510
Web: http://www.carrollcoatings.com
Email: info@carrollcoatings.com

Annual Sales: $4.5 Million
Number of Employees: 14
President: William Rooks
CEO: William Rooks
Marketing Manager: Neil J. Stubbers

Industrial paints.

Century Industrial Coatings

PO Box 830
Highway 69 South
Jacksonville TX 75766
Phone: 903-586-9197
Toll Free: 800-945-1241
Fax: 903-586-9291
Web: http://www.centurypaint.com

Annual Sales: $5 Million
Number of Employees: 20
President: Dean Harvey
CEO: Don Harvey
Research & Development: Gary C. Swindler
Sales Manager: Brian Martin

The company produces coatings and paints for structural steel, hardboard, steel (coil coatings), and OEM's.

Century Industries

5331 State Route 7
New Waterford OH 44445
Phone: 330-457-2367
Toll Free: 800-955-8443
Fax: 330-457-7362
Web: http://www.thecenturygroup.net
Email: sales@centuryemail.com

Annual Sales: $16 Million
Number of Employees: 85
President: Bruce W. Marlow
CEO: Bruce W. Marlow

The company produces roof coatings, decorative textures and driveway sealers.

Ceramic Industrial Coatings

325 Highway 81
PO Box 245
Osseo MN 55369
Phone: 763-424-2044
Fax: 763-424-1014
Web: http://www.paints.com

Annual Sales: $8 Million
Number of Employees: 55
President: Craig Morrison
CEO: Craig Morrison
Marketing Manager: Kathrine T. Leighton

The company manufactures industrial coatings for metal, wood, and plastics for sale in the Upper Midwest.

Ceramic-to-Metal-Seals

78 Stone Place
Melrose MA 02176
Phone: 781-665-5002
Fax: 781-662-4925
Web: http://www.kellysearch.com/us-company-300000745.ht

Annual Sales: $2.4 Million
President: David Broderick
Sales Manager: Stephen Ingemi

Waterproof industrial coatings.

Ceratech Coatings

3000 Chesser Boyer Boulevard
Fort Worth TX 76111
Phone: 817-831-1232
Toll Free: 888-686-1232
Fax: 817-831-1236
Web: http://www.ceratechcoatings.com

Annual Sales: Under $1 Mil
Number of Employees: 1-9
CEO: Tony King

Aerosol paints.

CFC International

ITW 500 State Street
Chicago Heights IL 60411
Phone: 708-891-3456
Fax: 708-758-5989
Web: http://www.cfcintl.com
Email: cfcinfo@cfcintl.co

Number of Employees: 357
CEO: David B. Speer

C F C Produces chemically complex, transferable and multi-layer coatings. Applications are primarily on plastic products, including credit cards, blow molded bottles, automobile batteries, automotive gauges, copier panels, garbage cans, industrial signage, golfing accessories, house wares, lipstick tubes, mud flaps, pens, personal care products, recycle bins, squeeze tube and toys.

Champion Coatings

77403 Wright Road
Houston TX 77041
Phone: 713-466-7593
Fax: 713-466-7499
Web: http://www.championcoatings.com

Annual Sales: $10 Million
Number of Employees: 50
President: Mike Stamps
Manufacturing Operations Manager: Gunter Warnke

The company produces coatings primarily for the rail and other transportation industries.

Chase

Bethany House
26 Summer Street
Bridgewater MA 02324
Phone: 508-279-1789
Fax: 508-697-6419
Web: http://www.chasecorp.com
Email: pmyers@chasecorp.com

Annual Sales: $87 Million
Number of Employees: 362
President: Peter R. Chase
CEO: Peter R. Chase

Principal products include protective coatings and tape products. In November 2001, Chase acquired the Tapecoat Division of T.C. Manufacturing Co., Evanston, IL, for cash and 40,000 shares of Chase common stock. Tapecoat produces protective coatings for above and below ground pipelines and metal surfaces at a 100,000 sq ft plant.

Chase Products

2727 Gardner Road
Broadview IL 60153
Phone: 708-865-1000
Toll Free: 800-242-7326
Fax: 708-865-7041
Web: http://www.chaseproducts.com
Email: sales@chaseproducts.com

Number of Employees: 200-499
CEO: Peter R. Chase

Metal, wood and plastic industrial coatings; latex paints; special purpose coatings.

Chemcoat

2790 Cansfields Lane
PO BOX 188
Montoursville PA 17754
Phone: 570-368-8631
Toll Free: 800-326-9471
Fax: 570-368-8635
Web: http://www.chemcoat.com

Annual Sales: $1 Million
Number of Employees: 30
President: James O'Brien
CEO: James O'Brien
Research & Development: James O'Brien
Marketing Manager: James O'Brien
Sales Manager: James O'Brien
Manufacturing Operations Manager: James O'Brien

Cement-based waterproof coating for concrete and masonry.

Chemcraft

Akzo Nobel Coatings
1431 Progress Avenue
High Point NC 27261
Phone: 336-841-5111
Web: http://www.chemcraft.com
Email: chemcraft.us@akzonobel.com

The Chemcraft brand is now part of the AkzoNobel family. It is known for quality wood coatings and finishes.

ChemMasters

300 Edwards Street
Madison OH 44057
Phone: 440-428-2105
Toll Free: 800-486-7866
Fax: 440-428-7091
Web: http://www.chemmasters.net
Email: chemmastersvp@hotmail.com

Annual Sales: $7.1 Million
President: Hank Vavrik

Marine paints, stains.

Chilton Paint

109-09 15th Avenue
College Point NY 11356
Phone: 718-359-0438

Cintech Industrial Coatings

2217 Langdon Farm Road
Cincinnati OH 45237
Phone: 513-631-4270
Toll Free: 877-894-4622
Fax: 513-366-4444
Web: http://www.cintechindustrial.com
Email: info@cintechindustrial.com

Wood and metal coatings.

Annual Sales: $2.4 Million
Sales Manager: Patrick Foy

Clausen Company

PO Drawer 140
Fords NJ 08863
Phone: 732-738-1165
Toll Free: 800-223-0893
Fax: 732-738-1618
Web: http://www.clausenautobody.com
Email: clausenco@aol.com

Automotive refinishing paints, polyester primers, glazing putties, and body shop supplies.

Annual Sales: $2.2 Million
Number of Employees: 20-49
Sales Manager: Donald Peck

Clifton Adhesive

480 Burgess Place
Wayne NJ 07470
Phone: 973-694-0845
Fax: 973-694-5678
Web: http://www.cliftonadhesive.com
Email: sales@cliftonadhesive.com

Heat seal coatings; textile coatings.

Annual Sales: $8.4 million
President: Robert Lefelar
CEO: Robert Lefelar

Cloverdale Paints

6950 King George Boulevard
Surrey BC V3W 4Z1
Phone: 604-596-6261
Fax: 604-597-2677
Web: http://www.cloverdalepaint.com
Email: helpdesk@cloverdalepaint.

Annual Sales: C$87 Million
Number of Employees: 650
President: Al Mordy
CEO: Al Mordy
Marketing Manager: Brian Carpentar
Sales Manager: Kevin Belton
Manufacturing Operations Manager: Stu Eaton

The company operates factories in British Columbia and Alberta and markets architectural and maintenance coatings in the Northwestern United States. It has 62 company-owned stored in North America, including seven in Washington State. In 2004 Cloverdale greed to merge with Rodda Paint Co. Business will be conducted under the Rodda name in the United States and under the Cloverdale name in Canada.

CMP Coatings

108 Longboat
Williamsburg VA 23081
Phone: 757-258-0520
Web: http://www.cmp.co.jp/
Email: cmpcoatings@worldnet.att.net

Annual Sales: $575.2 Million
President: Joseph Cross
CEO: Joseph Cross

Industrial coatings.

Coal Enterprises

8721 5th Street
Frisco TX 75034
Phone: 972-712-9280

Architectural paints and stains, non-skid floor coatings.

Coating Development Group

PO Box 14817
Philadelphia PA 19134
Phone: 215-426-6216
Fax: 215-426-6219
Web: http://www.cdgkonig.com
Email: info@cdgkonig.com

Annual Sales: $5-10 Million
Number of Employees: 19
President: Richard Greene
CEO: Richard Greene
Research & Development: Michael Bornisin
Manufacturing Operations Manager: Paul Lafautain

Water- and solvent-based coatings for kitchen cabinets, furniture and other surfaces.

Coatings for Industry

319 Township Line Road
Souderton PA 18964
Phone: 215-723-0919
Fax: 215-723-0911
Web: http://www.coatingsforindustry.com
Email: cfi@coatingsforindustry.com

Number of Employees: 10-49
President: Kevin Klotz
CEO: Kevin Klotz
Research & Development: Brian Klotz

Industrial, aerospace, and architectural coatings.

Coatings Resource

5582 McFadden Avenue
Huntington Beach CA 92649
Phone: 714-894-5252
Toll Free: 866-894-5252
Fax: 714-893-2322
Web: http://www.coatingsresource.com
Email: info@coatingsresource.com

Annual Sales: $10-25 Million
Number of Employees: 50-99
President: Edwin Laird
CEO: Edwin Laird

The company manufactures protective and decorative finishes for plastics, wood, specialty metals, and industrial maintenance.

Color Wheel Paint

Comex Group (Mexico)
2814 Silver Star Road
Orlando FL 32808
Phone: 407-293-6810
Toll Free: 800 749-6810
Fax: 407-293-0945
Web: http://www.colorwheel.com

Annual Sales: $50 Million
Number of Employees: 230
President: Gene Ponder
Marketing Manager: Jerry Droll
Sales Manager: Brad Worthington

Color Wheel manufactures architectural and industrial coatings and related equipment for sale primarily in Florida. It operates more than 30 paint stores.

Colorado Paint

4747 Holly Street
Denver CO 80216
Phone: 303-388-9265
Toll Free: 800-449-7587
Fax: 303-388-0881
Web: http://www.coloradopaint.com
Email: sales@coloradopaint.com

Annual Sales: $6 Million
Number of Employees: 15
President: Kevin Valis
Research & Development: Gary Stettin
Marketing Manager: Mark Vafquez
Sales Manager: Mark Vafquez
Manufacturing Operations Manager: Gary Stettin

Colorado Paint produces architectural and striping finishes. It also distributes paint, stains, spray and line-striping equipment, and sundries from other manufacturers.

Columbia Paint

641 Jackson Avenue
Huntington WV 25728
Phone: 304-529-3237
Fax: 304-525-2921

Annual Sales: $6 Million
Number of Employees: 45
President: HH Larison
CEO: HH Larison
Sales Manager: Brett Larrick

The company produces architectural coatings

Columbia Paint & Coating

North 112 Haven Street
Spokane WA 99202
Phone: 509-535-9741
Fax: 509-535-8114
Web: http://www.columbiapaint.com
Email: salesinfo@columbiapaint.com

Number of Employees: 225
President: Larry Warson
CEO: Larry Warson
Sales Manager: Porthos Jim Huang

The company manufactures, wholesales, and retails architectural paints, conventional traffic coatings, and maintenance and industrial coatings. It has 41 retail stores in the Pacific Northwest and Mountain West of the U.S.

Columbia Paint Labs

452 Communipaw Avenue
Jersey City NJ 07304
Phone: 201-435-4884
Fax: 201-435-0440

Number of Employees: 10-49
Sales Manager: George Pahiakos

Water-based paints.

Consolidated Color

131 Sumit Street
Peabody MA 01960
Phone: 978-531-2605

Annual Sales: $2-4.9 Million
Number of Employees: 20-49
CEO: Richard Sommers

Industrial finishes, lacquer thinners, leather finishing agents.

Continental Coatings

10938 Beech Avenue
Fontana CA 92337
Phone: 909-355-1200
Toll Free: 800-305-5869
Fax: 909-355-2061
Web: http://www.continentalprod.com
Email: info@continentalprod.com

Annual Sales: $5 Million
Number of Employees: 19
President: Bob Wang
CEO: Bob Wang
Manufacturing Operations Manager: Joe Seaton

Continental Coatings manufactures coatings for such diverse markets as automotive/truck, greenhouse, log homes and OEM-related industries.

Continental Industries

20757 Southwest 105th Avenue
Tualatin OR 97062
Phone: 503-692-3400
Fax: 503-692-3401
Web: http://www.continentalcompanies.com
Email: cii@teleport.com

Annual Sales: $1 - 4.9 Million
Number of Employees: 10-49
President: Mitch Behrens
Sales Manager: Vic Goudima
Manufacturing Operations Manager: Ryan Mellott

Powder coatings, dip coatings, and dry-spin coatings.

Continental Products

1150 East 222nd Street
St. Euclid OH 44117
Phone: 216-531-0710
Toll Free: 800-305-5869
Fax: 216-289-1745
Web: http://www.continentalprod.com
Email: info@continentalprod.com

Annual Sales: $5 - 9.9 Million
Number of Employees: 35
President: Miriam Strebek

The company manufactures water-borne and high solids product finishes and specialty coatings for such markets as automotive/truck, greenhouse, log homes and OEM-related industries.

Contract Coatings

706 East Main Street
Stockton CA 95202
Phone: 209-465-2634
Fax: 209-465-1338

Number of Employees: 200-499
CEO: Arlen Williams

Maintenance coatings, industrial finishes.

Copps Industries

10600 North Industrial Drive
Mequon WI 53092
Phone: 262-238-1700
Toll Free: 800-672-2622
Fax: 262-238-1701
Web: http://www.coppsindustries.com
Email: coppsind@coppsindustries.com

Annual Sales: $11.7 Million
Number of Employees: 35
President: Patrick Copps
CEO: Patrick Copps
Research & Development: Alex Kasoow
Manufacturing Operations Manager: Greg Palmer

Copps manufactures concrete floor coatings, adhesives, potting compounds, insulating varnishes, encapsulation products, and pre-cast concrete forms.

Corchem

PO Box 130160
Carlsbad CA 92013
Phone: 760-804-8550
Fax: 760-804-8551
Web: http://www.corchem.com
Email: jcwoods@corchem.com

Annual Sales: $50 Million
President: Carlos Guzman
Sales Manager: Jonathan C. Woods

Protective coatings.

Coronado Paint

INSL-X Products
308 Old County Road
Edgewater FL 32132
Phone: 386-428-6461
Toll Free: 800-883-4193
Fax: 800-394-9022
Web: http://www.coronadopaint.com

Annual Sales: $70 Million
Number of Employees: 200
President: James Weil
Manufacturing Operations Manager: Dave Dill

The company produces architectural paints; primers, finishes and specialty industrial coatings; and lacquers, which are sold to independent paint and decorating stores. In July 2004 both Lenmar and Coronado Paint were sold to INSUL-X Products of Berkshire Hathaway's Benjamin Moore.

Corroseal

Joan T Geiger Enterprises
26 Northwest Front Street
Coupeville WA 98239
Phone: 360-678-1905
Toll Free: 800-237-1573
Fax: 425-837-0300
Web: http://www.corroseal.com
Email: info@corroseal.com

Number of Employees: 1-9
CEO: Joan Geiger

Marine and industrial primers, rust – control products, water proofers, and coatings.

Corrosion Control Technologies

833 E Gulf Boulevard
Indian Rocks Beach FL 33755
Phone: 727-595-6192

Industrial corrosion-control coatings.

Cortec

4119 White Bear Parkway
St. Paul MN 55110
Phone: 651-429-1100
Toll Free: 800-426-7832
Fax: 651-429-1122
Web: http://www.cortecvci.com
Email: info@cortecvci.com

Annual Sales: $18.3 Million
Number of Employees: 60
CEO: Boris Miksic
Sales Manager: John Wiermaa
Manufacturing Operations Manager: Cliff Cracauer

Cortec produces corrosion- and rust-inhibiting products, including water- and oil-based coatings, corrosion inhibitors, cleaners, metal working fluids, and paint strippers.

Cote-L Industries

1542 Jefferson Street
Teaneck NJ 07666
Phone: 201-836-0733
Fax: 201-836-5220
Web: http://www.cotelind.com
Email: prodinfo@cotelind.com

Annual Sales: $1 - 4.9 Million
Number of Employees: 10-49
CEO: Avi Aviner

Non-slip, safety, waterproof, intumescent, fire-protective and flame preventive coatings.

Covalence Adhesives

Berry Plastics
25 Forge Parkway
Franklin MA 02035
Phone: 508-918-1600
Toll Free: 800-248-7659
Fax: 800-328-4822
Web: http://www.covalenceadhesives.com
Email: cpg@berryplastics.com

Annual Sales: $36.38 Billion
Number of Employees: 1,000

Corrosion prevention products serving the oil, gas, water, wastewater and district heating industries. (Formerly Tyco Adhesives.)

Coventry Coatings

89 Taft Avenue
Newburgh NY 12550
Phone: 845-562-5666
Toll Free: 800-307-7951
Fax: 845-562-8986
Web: http://www.kirkerautomotive.com
Email: info@kirkerautomotive.com

Number of Employees: 15
President: Bruce Sklak

Coventry Coatings Corp is the parent company of it's flagship brand Kirker Automotive Finishes which manufactures a wide variety of products for the automotive, fleet and equipment refinish market; North American Technologies, a manufacturer of high-performance industrial coatings and specialty finishes; and Trylanger, specialty finishes for CD, DVD and optical disc manufacturers. Coventry also manufactures a variety of other product types including protective coatings designed for use in pharmaceutical, food, beverage, and cosmetics production equipment.

CP

South Second & Water Street
PO Box 1049
Connersville IN 47331
Phone: 765-825-4111
Fax: 765-825-1581
Web: http://www.cpincpaints.com
Email: sales@cpincpaints.com

Annual Sales: $45 Million
Number of Employees: 200
President: Harold Findley
CEO: Orvall Spawn

C.P. Inc. manufactures an extensive line of industrial paints and compliant solventbase coatings, waterbase coatings, powder coatings and solvents; and a full line of waterbase, solventbase and powder coating for the Casket Industry. Custom coatings can also be developed to meet any process. The company has a modern manufacturing plant, research laboratory, central warehouse and general offices located in Connersville, Indiana.

Crawford Laboratories

4165 South Emerald Ave
Chicago IL 60609
Phone: 773-376-7132
Toll Free: 800-356-7625
Fax: 773-376-0945
Web: http://www.florock.net
Email: web@florock.net

Annual Sales: $12.6 Million
President: David Schmetterer
Research & Development: Tom Lux

Florock brand epoxy and polyurethane floor coatings. Decorative concrete floor paint for industrial and commercial applications.

Creative Coatings

428 North Longview Street
Kilgore TX 75662
Phone: 903-984-8454
Toll Free: 800-256-8184
Fax: 903-983-2125
Email: ccietp@verizon.net

Number of Employees: 20-49
President: Lisa J. Turner
CEO: Lisa J. Turner

Industrial finishes.

Creative Coatings

7505 Freedom Way
Fort Wayne IN 46818
Phone: 260-489-3580
Fax: 260-489-3643
Web: http://www.creativecoatingsinc.com
Email: info@creativecoatingsinc.com

Powder coatings.

Cross Link Powder Coating

1108 Abbott Street
Salinas CA 93901
Phone: 831-422-7600
Toll Free: 800-366-7155
Fax: 831-422-7571
Web: http://www.crosslink-powder-coating.com
Email: MRLOCICERO@aol.com

Number of Employees: 10-49
President: George Jacobs

Powder coatings

Crossfield Products

140 Valley Road
Roselle Park NJ 07204
Phone: 908-245-2800
Fax: 908-245-0659
Web: http://www.dexotex.com

Annual Sales: $20 Million
Number of Employees: 90
President: Brad Watt
CEO: Brad Watt

The Dex-O-Tex Division manufactures specialty materials for seamless epoxy and polyurethane flooring and wall coatings, waterproof deck surfacing systems, waterproof membranes and concrete repair materials.

Crow River Industrial Coatings

860 Norway Drive
Annandale MN 55302
Phone: 320-274-3059

Industrial finishes.

Crowe Industrial Coatings

875 Progress Center Avenue
Lawrenceville GA 30043
Phone: 770-963-1200
Fax: 770-963-2183
Web: http://www.croweindustrial.com/
Email: info@croweindustrial.com

Number of Employees: 10-49
Sales Manager: Mark Crowe

Industrial finishes, powder coatings.

Crown Metro Chemical

S- Alva.
315 Echelon Road
Greenville SC 29605
Phone: 864-299-2800
Fax: 864-299-1678

Annual Sales: $8 Million
Number of Employees: 55
President: Jeff McClelland
Marketing Manager: Robert A. Spurling
Sales Manager: Tracy Garrett Jr.,

The company produces wood coatings.

Crown Paint

1801 West Sheridan Avenue
Oklahoma City OK 73106
Phone: 405-232-8580
Toll Free: 800-877-7246
Fax: 405-232-4729
Web: http://www.crownpaint.co.uk

Number of Employees: 10-49
President: Nick Nicholson
CEO: Nick Nicholson
Research & Development: Nick Nicholson
Marketing Manager: Nick Nicholson
Sales Manager: Nick Nicholson
Manufacturing Operations Manager: Nick Nicholson

Paints and lacquers.

Custom-Pak Products

N118 W18981 Bunsen Drive
Germantown WI 53022
Phone: 262-251-6180
Fax: 262-251-6243
Web: http://www.custompakproducts.com
Email: info@custompakproducts.com

Number of Employees: 10-49
President: James Berg
Sales Manager: Daniel J. Berg

Aerosol and brush-top paints.

D&L Industrial Finishes

215 Brownsville Avenue
Liberty IN 47353
Phone: 765-458-5157
Toll Free: 800-313-1335
Fax: 765-458-5159

Annual Sales: $5 Million
Number of Employees: 35
President: Doug Hartman
Sales Manager: Harry Frnka

D&L produces industrial finishes.

Daly's Wood Finishing Materials

3525 Stone Way North
Seattle WA 98103
Phone: 206-633-4200
Toll Free: 800-735-7019
Fax: 206-632-2565
Web: http://www.dalyspaint.com
Email: info@dalyspaint.com

Annual Sales: $14.4 Million
Number of Employees: 45
President: Herb Paulson
CEO: Herb Paulson
Marketing Manager: Robin Daly
Sales Manager: Robin Daly

The company produces wood finishes and also distributes products from other paint companies. It has two retail locations in the Seattle area.

Dampney

85 Paris Street
Everett MA 02149
Phone: 617-389-2805
Toll Free: 800-537-7023
Fax: 617-389-0484
Web: http://www.dampney.com
Email: mail@dampney.com

Annual Sales: $1 - 4.9 Million
Number of Employees: 10-49
Sales Manager: Tom Trane

Marking paints, floor coatings, high-temp coatings Sales about $4 million.

Dan-Tex Paint & Coating Manufacturing

444 Aston Drive
Mesquite TX 75182
Phone: 214-226-0984

Paints and enamels.

Daubert Chemical

Daubert Industries
4700 S. Central Avenue
Chicago IL 60638
Phone: 708-496-7350
Toll Free: 800-688-0459
Fax: 708-496-7367
Web: http://www.daubertchemical.com/

Annual Sales: $36 Million
Number of Employees: 250
President: Larry Garman
CEO: Larry Garman

Daubert produces corrosion-control and metal-protection coatings for such industrial applications as steel, automotive, marine, aerospace, transportation, furniture and wood working, and general manufacturing. Applications include corrosion protection, industrial anti-skid, and sound deadening. The company also manufactures aerosol concentrates, cutting oils, grinding fluids, and adhesives and sealants. Plants are in Cullman, AL and Dixon, IL. The parent also manufactures automotive protective products (ECP, Inc.) and corrosion-protective products (Daubert VCI).

Davies Imperial Coatings

PO Box 790
1275 State Street
Hammond IN 46325
Phone: 219-933-0877
Fax: 219-932-4201
Web: http://www.daviesimperial.com
Email: bimes@daviesimperial.com

Annual Sales: $10.8 Million
Number of Employees: 30
President: MP. Davis Donn

Manufactures traffic paints and other industrial coatings.

Davis Paint

1311 Iron Street
PO Box 7589
North Kansas City MO 64116
Phone: 816-471-4447
Toll Free: 800-821-2029
Fax: 816-471-1460
Web: http://www.davispaint.com

Annual Sales: $12 Million
Number of Employees: 66
President: Kevin Ostby
CEO: Kevin Ostby
Research & Development: Bob Willhite
Marketing Manager: Kevin Ostby
Sales Manager: Kevin Ostby
Manufacturing Operations Manager: Bill Cliadourn

The company manufactures Davis industrial coatings, SAHARA waterproof masonry coatings, Cook consumer Paint, Eli Weatherby's exterior wood stains, Eventone wood finishes, Master Painter contractor coatings, Hold-Tite house paint, and Cold-Tite low temperature house paint. Products are sold through some four stores in the Midwest.

Davlin Coatings

700 Allston Way
Berkeley CA 94710
Phone: 510-848-2863
Toll Free: 800-709-5919
Fax: 510-848-1464
Web: www.davlincoatings.com
Email: info@davlincoatings.com

Annual Sales: $1 - 4.9 Mil
Number of Employees: 10-49
President: Brad DeReuiter
Marketing Manager: Scott Shannon
Sales Manager: Perter Bibby

Waterproofing coatings, architectural paints, specialty paints.

Deft

17451 Von Karman Avenue
PO Box 19507
Irvine CA 92614
Phone: 949-474-0400
Fax: 949-474-7269
Web: http://www.deftfinishes.com/
Email: proservice@deftfinishes.com

Annual Sales: $41 Million
Number of Employees: 200
President: William A. Desmond
CEO: William A. Desmond
Sales Manager: Janet Sauerwald

The company produces interior and exterior wood stains and finishes and also commercial and military specification primers and coatings for the aerospace industry. It operates a branch plant in Alliance, OH (30 employees).

Del Technical Coatings

1801 W. Reno Avenue
Oklahoma City OK 73106
Phone: 405-672-1431
Fax: 405-672-0804

Annual Sales: $3.1 Million
Number of Employees: 20
President: Sean Childers
Manufacturing Operations Manager: Bill Williams

Architectural, special purpose and industrial paints.

Delta Coatings

1529 N. 31st Avenue
Melrose Park IL 60160
Phone: 708-216-9800
Toll Free: 888-216-3600
Fax: 708-216-9895
Web: http://www.deltacoating.com
Email: paint@deltacoating.com

Annual Sales: $1.5 Million
Number of Employees: 5-9
President: John Bittle
Marketing Manager: Bob Madura
Sales Manager: Bob Madura

Water-based paints and coatings and primers for OEM's, coil coating, and job shops. The transportation industry is major end use. Acquired Federated Paint and Midwest Lacquer.

Delta Industrial Coatings

5700 Commander Drive
PO Box 444 Arlington TN 38002
Phone: 901-867-9000
Toll Free: 800-242-8454
Fax: 901-867-9222
Web: http://www.deltapolymers.com

Annual Sales: $7.2 Million
Number of Employees: 20-49
Sales Manager: Philip Starr

Industrial finishes.

Delta Laboratories

3710 Northwest SR326
Ocala FL 34470
Phone: 352-629-8101
Fax: 352-629-1268
Email: delta@ocf.com

Annual Sales: $10 Million
Number of Employees: 75

Delta manufactures a variety of industrial coatings and special purpose coatings, including traffic paint, UV curable products, glass coatings, and also adhesives and sealants at plants in Ocala and in Hialeah, FL.

Delta Polymers

130 South Second Street
N. Bay Shore NY 11706
Phone: 631-254-6240
Toll Free: 800-966 5142
Fax: 631-595 2537
Web: http://www.deltapolymers.com
Email: sales@deltapolymers.com

Annual Sales: $1 - 4.9 Million
Number of Employees: 20-49
Sales Manager: George Smilow

Epoxy and urethane coatings for the construction industry.Adhesives

Delta Creative

Diethelm & Keller (Switzerland)
2690 Pellissier Place
City of Industry CA 90601
Toll Free: 800-423-4135
Fax: 562-695-4227
Web: http://www.deltacreative.com

Annual Sales: $19 Million
Number of Employees: 135
President: Andreas Keller

Delta's Ceramcoat brand paint is recognized as one of the creamiest acrylic paint available in the marketplace and is available in every color for crafting, home décor and decorative painting.

Diamond Vogel Paint

1110 Albany Place Southeast
PO Box 380
Orange City IA 51041
Phone: 712-737-8880
Toll Free: 800-72VOGEL
Fax: 712-737-4998
Web: http://www.diamondvogel.com

Annual Sales: $133 Million
Number of Employees: 800
President: Drew Vogel
CEO: Drew Vogel
Sales Manager: Gary Sale

The company produces architectural paints, paint removers, wood stains, varnishes and a line of industrial paints, including powder coatings. In late 2003 the company acquired the industrial coatings business of Davis-Frost Paint Co., Lynchburg, VA. Assets include plants in Minneapolis, IN and Tulsa, OK. The facility in Minneapolis will be closed and operations consolidated in the existing plant of Diamond-Vogel here. In March 2004 Diamond-Vogel purchased Four Seasons Paint Co., Lincoln NE, a manufacturer of industrial coatings, which are distributed in a six state region. It will be combined with Van Sickle Paint Co.), a subsidiary, also in Lincoln.

Dick Blick

Blick Art Materials
PO Box 1267
Galesburg IL 61402-1267
Phone: 309-343-6181
Toll Free: 800-828-4548
Fax: 309-343-5785
Web: http://www.dickblick.com
Email: info@dickblick.com

Annual Sales: $120 Million
Number of Employees: 750
President: Bob Buchsbaum
CEO: Bob Buchsbaum
Sales Manager: Debbie Damon

The company produces arts and craft supplies, including oil and alkyd paints. It operates branches in Allentown, PA and Henderson, NV.

Drew Paints

PO Box 29139
Portland OR 97296-9139
Phone: 503-227-6497
Toll Free: 800-924-7874
Fax: 503-227-1609
Web: http://www.drewpaints.com
Email: ktarbell@drewpaints.com

Number of Employees: 10-49
President: Keith DiBrino
Sales Manager: Pat Moran
Manufacturing Operations Manager: Thomas Mitchell

OEM coatings and private-label. finishes

Dolphin Company

922 Locust Street
Toledo OH 43604
Phone: 419-241-8267
Toll Free: 800-525-8098
Fax: 419-241-4146
Web: http://www.dolphin-company.com
Email: lew@Dolphin-Company.com

Number of Employees: 25
President: Lew Smith
CEO: Lew Smith

Industrial finishes.

Duncan Enterprises

5673 East Shields Avenue
Fresno CA 93727
Phone: 559-291-4444
Toll Free: 800-438-6226
Fax: 559-291-9444
Web: http://www.duncanceramics.com
Email: consumer@duncanmail.com

Annual Sales: $28 Million
Number of Employees: 235
President: Larry Duncan

Duncan Enterprises manufactures crafts and hobby ceramics products, including dimensional/fabric acrylic paints craft glue, and a line of industrial strength adhesives.

Dunn-Edwards Paints

4885 East 52nd Place
Los Angeles CA 90040
Phone: 323-771-3330
Toll Free: 888-337-2468
Fax: 323-771-2095
Web: http://www.dunnedwards.com

Annual Sales: $300 Million
Number of Employees: 1,500
President: Karl Altergott
Marketing Manager: Timothy Bosveld
Manufacturing Operations Manager: Nicholas J. Hess

Dunn-Edwards manufactures architectural paints, painting supplies and equipment. It operates plants in Los Angeles, CA and Tempe, AZ. It operates over 100 stores in the Pacific and Southwest U.S. with over 1,300 owner-employees.

DuPont

1007 Market Street
Wilmington DE 19898
Phone: 302-774-1000
Toll Free: 800-441-7515
Web: http://www.dupont.com

Annual Sales: $26.1 Billion
Number of Employees: 58,000
CEO: Ellen J. Kullman

The Paints, Coatings & Finishes segment includes automotive custom finishes, OEM coatings, refinish coatings; aviation coatings; ceramic coatings; commercial transportation coatings; industrial coatings; powder coatings; recreational transportation coatings; and surface preparations.

Dur-A-Flex

95 Goodwin Street
East Hartford CT 06108
Phone: 860-528-9838
Toll Free: 800-253-3539
Fax: 860-528-2802
Web: http://www.dur-a-flex.com
Email: info@dur-a-flex.com

Annual Sales: $10 Million
Number of Employees: 70
President: Bob Smith
CEO: Bob Smith
Research & Development: Marcus Gray
Marketing Manager: Mark Taggioli

The company produces flooring primers, sealers, crack fillers, topcoats, for flooring and epoxy, urethane and methyl methacrylate (MMA) polymer components. It also manufactures colored quartz aggregates.

Durant Paints

112 Railroad Street
Revere MA 02151
Phone: 781-289-1400
Toll Free: 800-420-0021
Fax: 781-289-1405
Web: http://www.durantpaints.com

Annual Sales: $1 - 4.9 Million
Number of Employees: 10-49
President: Ronald A. Yannetti
CEO: Ronald A. Yannetti
Manufacturing Operations Manager: Al Losanno

Architectural and industrial applications, roadway sealants, and marine construction.

Duromar

35 Pond Park
Hingham MA 02043
Phone: 781-749-6992
Web: http://www.duromar.com
Email: information@duromar.com .com>

Annual Sales: $1 - 4.9 Mil
Number of Employees: 10-49
President: Wes Langeland

Resurfacing, concrete repair and other maintenance coatings.

Duron Paints & Wallcoverings

10406 Tucker Street
Beltsville MD 20705
Phone: 800-723-8766
Fax: 301- 595-3919
Web: http://www.duron.com
Email: information@duron.com

Architectural paint. Now a business unit of Sherwin-Williams.

Dyco Paints

5850 Ulmerton Road
Clearwater FL 33760
Phone: 727-536-2763
Toll Free: 800-282-7901
Fax: 727-536-0561
Web: http://www.dycopaints.com
Email: customerservice@dycopaints.com

Annual Sales: $7 Million
Number of Employees: 48
President: Maxie Quinn

Dyco manufactures architectural coatings, specialty paints, elastomeric coatings, gloss acrylic, caulks, mobile home and RV roof coatings, traffic paints, caulk sealers, and concrete stains and sealers. It has five stores in Florida. It also distributes Benjamin Moore paints.

E - Bond Epoxies

501 Northeast 33rd Street
Ft. Lauderdale FL 33307
Phone: 954-566-6555
Fax: 954-566-6663
Web: http://www.ebondepoxies.com
Email: info@ebondepoxies.com

Annual Sales: $5 Million
Number of Employees: 15
President: Mark Sugar
Research & Development: Mark Sugar
Marketing Manager: Mark Sugar
Sales Manager: Mark Sugar
Manufacturing Operations Manager: Mark Sugar

Epoxy finishes, for marine, OEM, bridges and other uses.

E. E. Zimmerman

PO Box 111254
Pittsburgh PA 15238
Phone: 412-963-0949
Fax: 412-963-0229
Web: http://www.eezimmermanco.com
Email: info@eezimmermanco.com

Number of Employees: 60
President: Ed Zimmerman

Zimmerman produces paint thinners, paint solvents, paint removers, wood finishes, and a variety of other products, which are sold under the EZ brand name

Eagle-Bridges

Highway 49 West
Byron GA 31008
Phone: 478-956-5605
Web: http://www.eaglebridges.com

Number of Employees: 10-49
President: Kevin Bridges
Sales Manager: Joelle Scarborough

Architectural and industrial finishes.

Earl Scheib

15206 Ventura Boulevard Suite 200
Sherman Oaks CA 91403-3397
Phone: 818-981-9992
Toll Free: 800-639-3275
Fax: 818-981-8803
Web: http://www.earlscheib.com/
Email: earlscheib@earlscheib.com

Annual Sales: $47 Million
Number of Employees: 850
President: Christian Bement
CEO: Christian Bement
Sales Manager: Victor Spinetti

Precision Coatings, Inc., a subsidiary, produces automotive paints in Springfield, MO, primarily for captive use in 124 paint and body repair shops, with a limited volume of sales ($456,000 in 2003) to small body repair shops.

Eastern Chem-Lac

1100 Eastern Avenue
Malden MA 02148
Phone: 781-322-8000
Toll Free: 800-492-2277
Fax: 781-322-8673
Web: http://www.easternchemlac.com
Email: info@easternchemlac.com

Annual Sales: $25 Million
Number of Employees: 150
President: David Liebman
CEO: David Liebman

The company manufactures industrial coatings, including powder coatings.

Eastwood

263 Shoemaker Road
Pottstown PA 19464
Phone: 800-343-9353
Toll Free: 800-343-9353
Web: http://www.eastwoodcompany.com

Annual Sales: $41 Million
President: Mr. Davis

HotCoat brand powder coatings, and specialty coatings for automotive applications.

Edison Coatings

3 Northwest Drive
Plainville CT 06062
Phone: 860-747-2220
Toll Free: 800-697-8055
Fax: 860-747-2280
Web: http://www.edisoncoatings.com

Annual Sales: $1 - 4.9 Million
Number of Employees: 10
President: Michael Edison
CEO: Michael Edison
Marketing Manager: Michael Edison
Sales Manager: Michael Edison
Manufacturing Operations Manager: Michael Edison

Concrete coatings.

Egyptian Lacquer Manufacturing

113 Fort Granger Drive
Franklin TN 37064
Phone: 615-790-3881
Fax: 615-790-3831
Web: http://www.egyptcoat.com
Email: egyptian@egyptcoat.com

Annual Sales: Under $1 Million
Number of Employees: 50-99
President: George Bruner
Marketing Manager: Lyn Daunheimer
Sales Manager: Todd Nelson
Manufacturing Operations Manager: Kerry Mattox

Finishes and coatings for metals, plastics and wood.

Elantas PDG

Altana (Germany)
5200 North Second Street
St Louis MO 63147
Phone: 314.621.5700
Toll Free: 866-376-9954
Fax: 314.436.1030
Web: http://www.elantas.com
Email: info.elantas.pdg@altana.com

Number of Employees: 500-999
President: Dr. Susan W. Graham
CEO: Dr. Susan W. Graham

Coatings for electric motors in various colors.

Electo Tech CP

Structural Group
354 Cypress Drive
Suite 10
Tequesta FL 33469
Phone: 561-744-2258
Toll Free: 800-445-9543
Fax: 561-747-1290
Web: http://www.crt-norust.com
Email: sales@crt-norust.com

Number of Employees: 6
President: Jorge Costa

Corrosion control coatings.

Electro Chemical Engineering and Manufacturing

P O BOX 509
750 Broad Street
Emmaus PA 18049
Phone: 610-965-9061
Toll Free: 800-235-1885
Fax: 610-965-2595
Web: http://www.electrochemical.net
Email: info@electrochemical.net

Number of Employees: 20-49
Research & Development: Jeffrey Reimer
Manufacturing Operations Manager: Dennis Dees

Fluoropolymer coatings.

Elite Coatings

Eagle Bridges
120 Tremon Street
Gordon GA 31031
Phone: 478-956-5605
Toll Free: 800-659-0908
Fax: 478-628-5870
Web: whttp://www.elitecoatings.com
Email: kbridges@eaglebridges.com

Number of Employees: 10-49
President: Kevin Bridges
Sales Manager: Kevin Bridges
Manufacturing Operation's Manager: Frank Sweatt

Industrial maintenance coatings: general and specialty advanced coatings and linings for steel and concrete substrate protection.

Elixir Industries

17925 South Broadway
Gardena CA 90247
Phone: 310-767-3400
Toll Free: 800-421-1942
Fax: 310-767-3443
Web: http://www.elixirind.com/

Annual Sales: $170 Million
Number of Employees: 1,300
President: Christopher A. Sahm
CEO: Christopher A. Sahm
Marketing Manager: Tim Suttles
Sales Manager: Julie Cameron

The company manufactures a variety of fabricated aluminum, plastic and steel products, tapes, and also aluminum and roof coatings.

Ellis Paint

C- Berg Lacquer Co.
3150 East Pico Boulevard
Los Angeles CA 90023
Phone: 323-261-8114
Toll Free: 800-325 3148
Fax: 323-780 9940
Web: http://www.ellispaint.com
Email: info@ellispaint.com

Annual Sales: $20 Million
Number of Employees: 100
President: Sandra Berg
Sales Manager: Robert O. Berg Jr

Ellis Paint produces industrial and maintenance paints and coatings, including pool and deck coatings. The company also collects waste solvents for auto body repair shops and returns distilled and reused material to manufacturing plants in California.

El Paco

PO Box 50256
St. Louis MO 63105
Phone: 314-725-6800
Toll Free: 800-325-8153
Fax: 314-725-7228
Web: http://www.tritechcoatings.com

Annual Sales: $4 Million
Number of Employees: 20
President: Michael Peter

The company produces liquid and powder coatings, including marine coatings and high-temperature automotive and industrial finishes. (Formerly TriTech it changed company name back to El paco in March of 2010.)

Empire State Varnish

117 Wiiliam Street
Williston Park NY 11596
Phone: 516-747-2949
Fax: 718-388-6385

Annual Sales: $1.5 Million
Number of Employees: 13
President: Richard Stark

Varnishes.

Enerfab

4955 Spring Grove Avenue
Cincinnati OH 45232
Phone: 513-641-0500
Toll Free: 800-966-7322
Fax: 513-482-7767
Web: http://www.enerfab.com
Email: sean.ballinger@enerfab.com

Annual Sales: $84.3 Million
Number of Employees: 500-999
President: Wendell Bell
Sales Manager: Sean Ballinger

Heavy-duty tank paints.

Ennis Traffic Safety Solutions

1509 South Kaufmann Street
PO Box 404Ennis TX 75119
Phone: 972-875-7272
Toll Free: 800-331-8118
Fax: 800-555-0217
Web: http://www.ennistraffic.com

Annual Sales: $37.30 Million
Number of Employees: 300
CEO: Bryce Anderson

In 2010 Ennis Paint Inc., its subsidiaries and partners abroad changed their name to Ennis Traffic Safety Solutions, to better reflect their mission to offer cost effective, engineered solutions to the industry. It is a leading global provider of pavement marking materials and traffic safety products. Products include water borne and solvent borne traffic paint; thermoplastic (alkyd and hydrocarbon materials); preformed thermoplastics; poly urea; epoxies, methacylates, and markers.

Environmental Coatings

6450 Hanna Lake Southeast
Caledonia MI 49316
Phone: 616-698-8102
Toll Free: 866-698-8102
Fax: 616-698-7911
Web:

Annual Sales: $20 Million
Number of Employees: 130
President: Michael Allister
Manufacturing Operations Manager: Ronald Henderson

Environmental Coatings manufactures water-based baking enamels for metal and wood finishes.

Environmental Coatings Systems

668 North Coast Highway #511
Laguna Beach CA 92651
Phone: 949-497-4562
Toll Free: 800-255-3325
Fax: 949-497-8493
Web: http://www.alldeck.com
Email: info@alldeck.com

Number of Employees: 92
President: Stephen R. Johnson
CEO: Stephen R. Johnson

Water-based wood finishes, deck and walking-surface coatings and related products.

Environmental Protective Coatings

2035 Regency Road
Lexington KY 40503
Phone: 859-277-0014
Fax: 859-278-4973
Web: http://www.enviroprotectcoatings.com
Email: sales@enviroprotectcoatings.com

Annual Sales: Under $1 Million
Number of Employees: 3
President: Holmer O'Hart
CEO: Holmer O'Hart
Research & Development: Holmer O'Hart
Marketing Manager: William Gardener
Sales Manager: William Gardener
Manufacturing Operations Manager: Holmer O'Hart

Steel coatings.

Erie Powder Coating

The Cummings Group, Ltd
227 Hathaway Street East Girard
Girard Pa 16417
Phone: 814-774-8238
Fax: 814-774-9372
Web: http://www.powdercoater.net/
Email: EriePowderCoating@netzero.com

Annual Sales: Under $1 Million
Number of Employees: 10-49
President: John Cummings
Manufacturing Operations Manager: Bart Cummings

Powder coatings

Eutectic USA

S- Castolin GmbH
N94 W14355 Garwin Drive
Menomonee Falls WI 53051
Phone: 262-255-5520
Toll Free: 800-558-8524
Fax: 262-255-5542
Web: http://www.eutectic-na.com
Email: marketing@messer-mg.com

Annual Sales: $3716 Million
Number of Employees: 2,000
President: John Kirkwood
CEO: John Kirkwood
Marketing Manager: Carlos Esteves
Sales Manager: Carlos Esteves

The company produces protective coatings, including powder coatings. Other activities include welding, brazing, carbon and graphite products and services

Excelsior Coatings

Harrison Paint
1329 Harrison Avenue SW
Canton OH 44706
Phone: 330-455-5125
Toll Free: 800-292-5755
Fax: 330-454-1750
Web: http://www.harrisonpaint.com
Email: info@excelsiorcoatings.com

Annual Sales: $1 Million
Number of Employees: 40
President: Patrick Lauber
Marketing Manager: Guy Braun
Sales Manager: Guy Braun

Industrial finishes, deck and floor finishes.Also maintenance products, petroleum and lubricant products and water treatment chemicals. Sales about $2 million.

Farrell-Calhoun

221 East Carolina
Memphis TN 38126
Phone: 901-526-2211
Fax: 901-525-8574
Web: http://www.farrellcalhoun.com

Annual Sales: $22 Million
Number of Employees: 140

Farrell-Calhoun produces architectural paints and primers. It operates 14 company stores and sells through some 300 dealers in the mid-south.

Farwest Paint Manufacturing

4522 South 133rd Street
Tukwila WA 98108
Phone: 206-244-8844
Toll Free: 800-727-9694
Fax: 206-246-7691
Web: http://www.farwestpaint.com
Email: mrmichaelhuber@yahoo.com

Annual Sales: $5 Million
Number of Employees: 25
President: Paul Sheehan
CEO: Paul Sheehan
Sales Manager: Michael Huber

The company produces architectural paints and primers, marine paints, and industrial coatings, and also manufactures paints under military specs. It operates a retail store in Tukwila.

Fasse Paint

851 Forest Avenue
Sheboygan Falls WI 53081
Phone: 920-467-7850
Fax: 920-467-7851
Web: http://www.fassepaint.com/
Email: info@fassepaint.com

Annual Sales: $5-10 Million
Number of Employees: 35
President: James Fasse
CEO: James Fasse
Sales Manager: James Fasse
Manufacturing Operations Manager: James Fasse

Fasse produces wood, metal, and OEM coatings; architectural coatings, including industrial maintenance products; automotive aerosol touch-up paints, and provides aerosol filling. It operates four retail outlets in the Sheboygan area.

Faux Effects

3435 Aviation Boulevard, A-4
Vero Beach FL 32960
Phone: 772-778-9044
Toll Free: 800-270-8871
Fax: 772-778-9653
Web: http://www.fauxfx.com
Email: info@fauxfx.com

Number of Employees: 10-49
President: Raymond P. Sandor

Specialty architectural paints.

Fiberlock Technologies

150 Dascomb Road
Andover MA 01810
Phone: 978-623-9987
Toll Free: 800-342-3755
Fax: 978-475-6205
Web: http://www.fiberlock.com
Email: info@fiberlock.com

Number of Employees: 4,000
President: Joseph Connor
CEO: Joseph Connor

Sales Manager: Andre Weker

Asbestos and lead containment paints; strippers; and other.Repair and specialty products.

Fields

Gardner-Gibson
2240 Taylor Way
Tacoma WA 98421
Phone: 253-627-4098
Toll Free: 800-627-4098
Fax: 253-383-2181
Web: http://www.fieldscorp.com
Email: sales@fieldscorp.com

Annual Sales: $17 Million
Number of Employees: 100
President: Don Field
CEO: Don Field
Marketing Manager: Matt Field
Sales Manager: Matt Field
Manufacturing Operations Manager: Sandy McArthur

Roofing and waterproofing products. Fields has three manufacturing divisions including: (1) Coatings & Mastics, (2) Hot Asphalts, and (3) Roll Roofing. Products are marketed through distributors and dealers domestically and in other locations worldwide.

Finishes Unlimited

PO Box 69
Sugar Grove IL 60554
Phone: 630-466-4881
Fax: 630-466-1064
Web: http://www.finishesunlimited.com
Email: sales@finishesunlimited.com

Annual Sales: $4.5 Million
Number of Employees: 17
President: Ken Burton
Research & Development: Tyotr Smelyansky
Sales Manager: Frank Grimm
Manufacturing Operations Manager: John Schwartz

The company produces waterborne coatings to coat iron, steel, aluminum, wood and glass such products as folding chairs, agricultural equipment, computer cabinets, storage racks, tool boxes, factory furniture, compressors and glass candle holders.

Finnaren & Haley Paint & Coatings

901 Washington Street
Conshohocken PA 19428
Phone: 610-825-1900
Toll Free: 800-225-5554
Fax: 610-825-1184
Web: http://www.fhpaint.com

Annual Sales: $30 Million
Number of Employees: 80
President: Dan Haley, Jr.
CEO: Robert A. Haley, Jr
Research & Development: Tom Feneis
Sales Manager: Peter McManus
Manufacturing Operations Manager: Daniel J. McManus

Finnaren & Haley has four divisions: Architectural Paints & Coatings; Industrial Coatings; Marine Coatings; and Weather Barrier, Inc. Products are distributed through 24 stores, with 15 in Pennsylvania, eight in New Jersey and one in Delaware, and also through direct sales and distributors.

Fire-Tect

26951 Ruether Avenue, Unit D
Canyon Country CA 91351
Phone: 661-298-8801
Toll Free: 800-380-8801
Fax: 661-298-8851
Web: http://www.firetect.com
Email: info@firetect.com

Number of Employees: 10-49
President: Mr. Randy Newman

Fireproof and fire-retardant paints and coatings.

Flame Control Coatings

PO Box 786
Niagara Falls NY 14302
Phone: 716-282-1399
Fax: 716-285-6303
Web: http://www.flamecontrol.com
Email: flamec@flamecontrol.com

Annual Sales: $1 - 4.9 Million
Number of Employees: 10-49
President: John Marshall

Fire-retardant paints, coatings, and varnishes

Flamemaster

11120 Sherman Way
PO Box 1458
Sun Valley CA 91352
Phone: 818-982-1650
Fax: 818-765-5603
Web: http://www.flamemaster.com

Annual Sales: $1 - 4.9 Million
Number of Employees: 30
President: Joseph Mazin
CEO: Joseph Mazin

Flame retardant coatings for the aerospace and marine industries. Also produces adhesives and sealants. Total sales $4.8 million (9/03).

Flexabar

1969 Rutgers University Blvd
Lakewood NJ 08701
Phone: 732-901-6500
Fax: 732-901-6504
Web: http://www.flexabar-corporation.com
Email: Andy@Flexabar.com

Number of Employees: 10-49
Sales Manager: Andy Guglielmo

Vinyl and specialty coatings for marine industry.Sales about $2 million.

Flood Company

The Flood Company
PO Box 2535
Hudson OH 44236
Phone: 330-650-4070
Toll Free: 800-321-3444
Fax: 330-650-1453
Web: http://www.floodco.com
Email: askus@flood.com

Annual Sales: $14.7 Million
President: Anthony M. Ciepiel

Flood produces clear wood finishes and cleaners, paint removers and paint additives.

Fluorolast Coatings

2228 Reiser Avenue Southeast
New Philadelphia OH 44663
Phone: 330-339-3373
Toll Free: 800-785-3601
Fax: 330-339-1515
Web: http://www.laurencc.com/

Number of Employees: 200+
CEO: Dale Lauren
President: Dale Lauren
Marketing Manager: Peter G. Schessler
Sales Manager: Paul Hoffman

Industrial protective coatings

Forrest Paint

1011 McKinley Street
Eugene OR 97402
Phone: 541-342-1821
Fax: 541-344-5137
Web: http://www.forrestpaint.com

Annual Sales: $25 Million
Number of Employees: 150
Sales Manager: Ed Fender

Forrest manufactures industrial coatings, including UV-cured, water-reducible, low-VOC, low-HAPS, epoxy, ure-thane, and high-temperature coatings; primers; and alkyd enamel systems. It also produces polyester, epoxy, polyure-thane and hybrid powder coatings.

Four Seasons Paint Manufacturing

5700 Northwest 38th Street
Lincoln NE 68524
Phone: 402-470-3356
Toll Free: 800-435-6060
Fax: 402-470-6060
Web: http://www.fourseasonspaint.com

Annual Sales: $7.2 Million
President: Ron Barker
Marketing Manager: Al Williams
Manufacturing Operations Manager: Tom Laswell

OEM and aftermarket finishes.20 employees

Franklin Paint

Franklin Paint Company
259 Cottage Street
Franklin MA 02038
Phone: 508-528-0303
Toll Free: 800-486-0304
Fax: 508-528-8152
Web: http://www.franklinpaint.com

Annual Sales: $5 - 9.9 Million
Number of Employees: 10-49
Sales Manager: George Brophy, Jr

Paints and PU traffic paint and field markings.Sales $4 million.

Frazee Paint

Comex Group (Mexico)
6625 Miramar Road
San Diego CA 92121
Phone: 888-626-3527
Fax: 858-626-3449
Web: http://www.frazeepaint.com

Paints and coatings specifically formulated for the southwestern climate of the U.S. Frazee Paint operates 115 stores throughout California, Arizona, and Nevada. (Formerly Classic Paint)

Freecom

1800 Industrial Drive
PO Box 2119Big Spring TX 79721
Phone: 432-263-8497
Toll Free: 800-346-4299
Fax: 432-263-5269
Web: http://www.ceram-kote.com
Email: freecom@CeRam-kote.com

Number of Employees: 10-49
CEO: Gary Harrison

CeRam-Kote brand of industrial coatings.40,000 sq ft facility.

Futura Companies

795 Glendale Road
Scottdale GA 30079
Phone: 404-257-9251
Toll Free: 800-226-3006
Fax: 404-299-3420
Web: http://www.futura-companies.com

Annual Sales: $1 - 4.9 Million
Number of Employees: 20-49
Marketing Manager: Frank Pearson
Number of Employees: 10-49

Epoxy concrete coatings.

Fyn Paint & Lacquer

229 Kent Avenue
Brooklyn NY 11211
Phone: 718-388-4130
Fax: 718-388-4311

Industrial finishes: paints, varnishes, lacquers, and enamels.

G. J. Nikolas

2800 Washington Boulevard
Bellwood IL 60104
Phone: 708-544-0320
Toll Free: 800-346-4741
Fax: 708-544-9722
Web: http://www.finish1.com/
Email: info@finish1.com

Annual Sales: $7.2 Million
Number of Employees: 20-49
President: Dennis R. Hanlon
CEO: Dennis R. Hanlon
Sales Manager: Dennis Wacker

Coatings for metals, woods, glass and plastics.

Gaco Western

18700 South Center Parkway
Seattle WA 98188
Phone: 206-575-0450
Toll Free: 800-456-4226
Fax: 206-575-0587
Web: http://www.gaco.com
Email: info@gaco.com

Annual Sales: $4.2 Million
Number of Employees: 60
President: Peter Davis
CEO: Peter Davis
Marketing Manager: Kyle Sherk
Sales Manager: Chuck Skalski

Gaco Western manufactures coatings for waterproofing and insulation, including urethanes, acrylics, silicones, Hypalon, neoprene, polyurea, and polyurethane.

Gardner-Gibson

4161 East 7th Avenue
Tampa FL 33605
Phone: 813-248-2101
Toll Free: 800-237-1155
Fax: 813-248-6768
Web: http://www.gardnerasphalt.com/

Annual Sales: $98.5 Million
Number of Employees: 225
President: Raymond T. Hyer
CEO: Raymond T. Hyer
Marketing Manager: Raymond T. Hyer
Sales Manager: Raymond T. Hyer

A full line manufacturer of roof coatings, waterproofing coatings, pavement sealers, caulks, wall repair patching and wallpaper adhesives. The company operates 12 manufacturing and distribution facilities in the U.S. The company acquired Fields, Tacoma, WA in 2006.

Garland

3800 East 91st Street
Cleveland OH 44105
Phone: 216-641-7500
Toll Free: 800-321-9336
Fax: 216-641-0633
Web: http://www.garlandco.com

Number of Employees: 380
President: David M. Sokol
CEO: Dick DeBacco
Sales Manager: Bill Pancoast

The company manufactures primarily roofing and building maintenance systems, including adhesives for captive use. It also has a line of reflective coatings.

Garland Floor

4500 Willow Parkway
Cleveland OH 44125
Phone: 216-883-4100
Toll Free: 800-321-2395
Fax: 216-883-9076
Web: http://www.garlandfloor.com
Email: support@garlandfloor.com

Annual Sales: $13.7 Million
Number of Employees: 45
Marketing Manager: Nicole Koharik

The company produces polymer preparations and protective coatings for flooring, such as epoxies, polyurethanes, polyesters, and vinyl esters.

Gateway Paint & Chemical

2929 Smallman Street
Pittsburgh PA 15201
Phone: 412-261-6642
Toll Free: 800-381-4899
Fax: 412-261-0411

Annual Sales: $1 - 4.9 Mil
Number of Employees: 10-49
President: Harold Blumenfeld
Sales Manager: Harold Blumenfeld

Specialty and architectural paints.

Gavlon Industries

10531 Fisher Road
Houston TX 77041
Phone: 713-466-3866
Toll Free: 800-531-5411
Fax: 713-466-0733
Web: http://www.gavlon.com
Email: sales@gavlon.com

Annual Sales: $10 - 24.9 Million
Number of Employees: 10-49
Sales Manager: Mr. Heacock

Paints for iron and steel coating and preserving and chemical tank coatings.

Gemini Coatings

2300 Holloway Drive
PO Box 699El Reno OK 73036
Phone: 405-262-5710
Toll Free: 800-262-5710
Fax: 405-262-9310
Web: http://www.gemini-coatings.com
Email: info@gemini-coatings.com

Number of Employees: 125

Gemini produces stains and wood treatments, including aerosols and lacquers. Some lacquers are sold to paint companies for use in their products, and some directly to consumers. The company is 100% employee-owned.

General Coatings Technologies

24 Woodward Avenue
Ridgewood NY 11385
Phone: 718-821-1232
Fax: 718-381-6935
Web: http://www.generalcoatings.net

Annual Sales: $16.5 Million
President: Lee Walton

Roofing and other industrial coatings.

General Magnaplate

1331 Route One
Linden NJ 07036
Phone: 908- 862-6200
Toll Free: 800- 441-6173
Fax: 908- 862-6110
Web: http://www.magnaplate.com
Email: webmaster@magnaplate.com

Annual Sales: $10 Million (6/03)
Number of Employees: 130
President: Candida C. Aversenti
CEO: Candida C. Aversenti
Marketing Manager: Vince Meringolo
Sales Manager: Vince Meringolo

The company produces metal coatings for severe environments. Once publicly owned, it became a private company in 1999.

George Kirby Jr. Paint

163 Mt. Vernon Street
New Bedford MA 2740
Phone: 508-997-9008
Web: http://www.kirbypaint.com
Email: Info@KirbyPaint.com

Number of Employees: 24
President: George A. Kirby

Marine paints.

Gibraltar Chemical Works

114 East 168th Street
South Holland IL 60473
Phone: 708-333-0600
Fax: 708-333-0631
Web: http://www.gibraltarchemical.com
Email: sblack@gibraltarchemical.com

Annual Sales: $8 Million
Number of Employees: 50
Research & Development: Jan Hillis
Manufacturing Operations Manager: Rebecca Mason

Formulates and produces solvent-borne pigment dispersions for coatings and inks.

Gillespie Coatings

211 Gum Springs Road
Longview TX 75602
Phone: 903-753-0393
Fax: 903-757-7861

Annual Sales: $3.7 Million
Number of Employees: 27
President: Charles Kaplan
CEO: Charles Kaplan
Research & Development: Charles Kaplan
Marketing Manager: Charles Kaplan
Sales Manager: Charles Kaplan
Manufacturing Operations Manager: Charles Kaplan

Heavy-duty metal coatings; military specialty government supplier.

Glas Mesh

PO Box 1718
West Chester PA 19381
Phone: 610-696-9220
Fax: 610-344-7519
Web: http://www.glasmesh.com
Email: gbrock@glasmesh.com

Number of Employees: 10-49
President: Ms. Noelle Stevens

Corrosion control and anti-wear products for metal and plastic piping

Gloss-Flo

208 Dupont Street
Brooklyn NY 11222
Phone: 718-389-8800
Fax: 718-389-2819
Web: http://www.glossflo.com
Email: glossflo@nyc.rr.com

Annual Sales: $1 - 4.9 Million
Number of Employees: 10-49
Sales Manager: J Klein

Industrial finishesSales about $2 million.

Glyptal

305 Eastern Avenue
Chelsea MA 02150
Phone: 617-884-6918
Toll Free: 800-457-1201
Fax: 617-884-8376
Web: http://www.glyptal.com
Email: billhoag@comcast.net

Annual Sales: Under $1 Million
Number of Employees: 10-49
President: Bill Hoag

High-temperature electrical, non-corrosive coatings. Locomotive coatings.Also produces adhesives for severe environments. Total sales $5 million.

Govesan Manufacturing

D-Govesan SA
939 Monocacy Road
York PA 17404
Phone: 717-767-6996
Fax: 717-767-6993
Web: http://www.govesan.com
Email: govesan@govesan.com

Annual Sales: $10 Million
Number of Employees: 50
President: Darrell W. Auterson
CEO: Darrell W. Auterson
Marketing Manager: Barry Keating
Sales Manager: Eduardo Faz

The company produces powder coatings at a 50,000 sq ft plant. Applications include office furniture, computers, architectural components, automotive parts, household appliances.

Grythin

Richmond and Tioga Streets
3501 Richmond Street
Philadelphia PA 19134
Phone: 215-426-5976
Fax: 215-426-5920
Web: http://www.gryphin.com

Number of Employees: 50
Manufacturing Operations Manager: Michael E. Ludecker

Industrial coatings for metal and wood.

Gulf Coast Paint Manufacturing

30075 County Road 49
Loxley AL 36551
Phone: 251-964-7911
Fax: 251-964-7918
Web: http://www.gulfcoastpaint.com
Email: info@gulfcoastpaint.com

Number of Employees: 10-49
Sales Manager: Sherwin Williams

Steel and concrete maintenance.

H I S Paint Pant Manufacturing

1801 West Reno
Oklahoma City OK 73106
Phone: 405-232-2077
Toll Free: 800-553-2077
Fax: 405-232-2083
Web: http://www.hispaint.com
Email: hispaint@hispaint.com

Annual Sales: $7-8 Million
Number of Employees: 30
President: Joe Cox
CEO: Joe Cox
Marketing Manager: Chuck Northslett
Sales Manager: Greg Richardson
Manufacturing Operations Manager: Tony Cox

Paints.

H&C Concrete Care Products

101 Prospect Avenue
6 Guild Hall
Cleveland OH 44115
Phone: 800-867-8246
Web: http://www.hc-concrete.com
Email: HC-Concrete@sherwin.com

Annual Sales: $6.1 Billion
President: Christopher M. Connor
CEO: Christopher M. Connor

Concrete paints.

H.B. Fuller

1200 Willow Lake Boulevard
PO Box 64683
St. Paul MN 55164
Phone: 651-236-5900
Toll Free: 888-423-8553
Web: http://www.hbfuller.com
Email: inquiry@hbfuller.com

Annual Sales: $1.24 Billion
Number of Employees: 3,100
President: Michele Volpi

Fuller is primarily a producer of adhesives and sealants, but also manufactures coatings and paints through their Foster™ brand products: coating solutions for the industrial, commercial and residential construction and maintenance markets. H.B. Fuller's Grupo Kativo™ is the leader in Central America and Panama in the development, production and marketing of paints and coatings.

Hallman/Lindsay Paints

1717 North Bristol Street
PO Box 109
Sun Prairie WI 53590
Phone: 608-834-8844
Toll Free: 888-331-5330
Fax: 608-837-1064
Web: http://www.hallmanlindsay.com
Email: Paint@HallmanLindsay.com

Annual Sales: $15 Million
Number of Employees: 80
President: Tim Mielcarek
Sales Manager: John Heenan
Manufacturing Operations Manager: Steve Olson

The company produces a line of architectural coatings, stains and varnishes. It operates 20 retail stores in Wisconsin.

Hanley Paint

6050 Luckett Court
El Paso TX 79932
Phone: 915-533-7481

Number of Employees: 1-9
CEO: William M. Tunno

Paints and varnishes.

Harco Chemical Coatings

208 Dupont Street
Brooklyn NY 11222
Phone: 718-389-3777
Fax: 718-389-2032
Web: http://www.harcocoatings.com
Email: customer-service@harcocoatings.com

Annual Sales: $10 Million
Number of Employees: 40
President: Herb Wallenstein
CEO: Herb Wallenstein

Floor finishes

Harrison Paint

1329 Harrison Avenue SW
Canton OH 44706
Phone: 330-455-5125
Toll Free: 800-321-0680
Fax: 330-454-1750
Web: http://www.harrisonpaint.com
Email: sales@harrisonpaint.co

Annual Sales: $10 Million
Number of Employees: 100
Manufacturing Operations Manager: Tom Schmidt

The company produces consumer paints under the Dutch Standard name and consumer paints and light industrial coatings under the Midland brand.

Hartin Paint & Filler

219 Broad & 14th Street
Carlstadt NJ 07072
Phone: 201-438-3300
Fax: 201-438-7568

Annual Sales: $9 Million
Number of Employees: 10-49
CEO: John G. Hartin

Industrial finishes.

Hawthorne Paint

66 Fifth Avenue
Hawthorne NJ 07506
Phone: 973-423 2335
Fax: 973-423-9363

Annual Sales: $2 Million
Number of Employees: 8
President: Murray Green
CEO: Murray Green
Research & Development: Murray Green
Marketing Manager: Murray Green
Sales Manager: Murray Green
Manufacturing Operations Manager: Murray Green

Commercial, residential, and industrial, paints

Hempel Coatings (USA)

S- Hempel A/S (Denmark)-P
600 Conroe Park North Drive
Conroe TX 77303
Phone: 936-523-6000
Toll Free: 800-678-6641
Fax: 936-523-6073
Web: http://www.hempel.us
Email: hempel@us.hempel.com

Annual Sales: $1.3 Billion
Number of Employees: 85
President: Pierre-Yves Jullien
CEO: Pierre-Yves Jullien
Research & Development: Martin Wieses

In the United States Hempel produces a variety of industrial coatings, including marine paints (a leader) and heavy-duty paints for rail cars, containers, pipelines, and the petrochemical industry.

Hentzen Coatings

6937 West Mill Road
Milwaukee WI 53218
Phone: 414-353-4200

Fax: 414-353-0286
Web: http://www.hentzen.com
Email: coatings@hentzen.com

Annual Sales: $30 Million
Number of Employees: 100
President: Al Hentzen
CEO: Al Hentzen
Marketing Manager: James Koval

The company produces liquid coatings (urethane, epoxy, acrylics and waterborne) and powder coatings (polyesters, hybrids, epoxies, acrylics, textures, and bonded metallics). Markets include the military, OEM, aerospace, millwork, appliance and other industrial.

Heresite Protective Coatings

822 South 14th Street
Manitowoc WI 54221
Phone: 920-684-6646
Fax: 920-684-0110
Web: http://www.heresite.com
Email: sales@heresite.com

Number of Employees: 50
President: Tom Fritzke
CEO: Jeff Lidan
Research & Development: Steve Brunar
Marketing Manager: Tom Fritzke
Sales Manager: Tom Fritzke
Manufacturing Operations Manager: Jeff Lidan

Heresite manufactures and applies industrial coatings for customers. Products include heat-resistant epoxies and baked and air-dried phenolic coatings, urethanes and polyesters. Markets include HVAC, aircraft, aerospace, food and beverage, mining, petrochemical, steel container, transportation and other industries.

High-Performance Coatings

14788 South Heritagecrest Way
Bluffdale UT 84065
Phone: 801-501-8303
Toll Free: 800-456-4721
Fax: 801-501-8315
Web: http://www.hpcoatings.com
Email: hpcsales@hpcoatings.com

Number of Employees: 11-50
President: Jeff Holm

Coatings for motor sports and aircraft.

Hill Brothers Chemical

1675 North Main Street
Orange CA 92867
Phone: 714-998-8800
Toll Free: 800-821-7234
Fax: 714-998-6310
Web: http://www.hillbrothers.com

Annual Sales: $32 Million
Number of Employees: 10-49
Sales Manager: Matt Thorne

Hill produces a variety of products for the construction and industrial markets for distribution ion the western United States, including chemicals, concrete additives and such coatings as flooring sealers, tile/masonry sealers and finishes, deck coatings, related materials under the Desert bran. It has six manufacturing facilities.

Hillyard

302 North 4th Street
St. Joseph MO 64501
Phone: 816-233-1321
Toll Free: 800-360-5158
Fax: 800-360-5153
Web: http://www.hillyard.com

Annual Sales: $120 Million
Number of Employees: 600
President: Jim Caralous
CEO: Jim Caralous
Research & Development: Mark Algaier
Marketing Manager: Bruce Windsor
Sales Manager: Jack George
Manufacturing Operations Manager: Craig Snieder

Hillyard is primarily a manufacturer of cleaning and maintenance suppliers. Coatings are mostly floor maintenance products.

Hirshfield's

725 Second Avenue North
Minneapolis MN 55405
Phone: 612-377-3910
Toll Free: 800-358-6332
Fax: 612-436-3384
Web: http://www.hirshfields.com/
Email: mrh@hirshfields.com

Annual Sales: $93 Million
Number of Employees: 450
President: Hans Hirshfield
Marketing Manager: Jeff Oien
Sales Manager: Jeanne Genadek

Hirshfield's Paint Manufacturing, Minneapolis, a subsidiary, produces paints, stains and specialty finishes for residential, commercial and industrial markets. The company claims to be the largest paint manufacturer in Minnesota. The parent distributes its paints and also wall paper and paint sundries through about 23 stores in the region.

Hoffer Coatings

310-T South Bellis Street
Wausau WI 54403
Phone: 715-845-7221
Toll Free: 800-433-6331
Fax: 715-848-9230
Web: http://www.hciinfo.com

Number of Employees: 20-49
President: Erik Hoffer

Industrial and specialty coatings for wood, metal, masonry and other substrates.

Homax Products

P O BOX 5643
Bellingham WA 98227
Phone: 360-733-9029
Toll Free: 800-729-9029
Fax: 360-647-1071
Web: http://www.homaxproducts.com
Email: homax@homaxproducts.com

Annual Sales: $35 Million
Number of Employees: 270
President: Ross Clawson
CEO: Ross Clawson
Sales Manager: Ronnie Peterson

The company produces textures, wall patch and repair products, abrasives, tile products, spot removers, specialty coatings and paint removers for the DIY consumer and contractors. Paint products include aerosol and brush-on specialty coatings. Headquarters and manufacturing is at Bellingham, with distribution in Chicago, IL and other facilities in Hamel, MN and Woodstock, ON. The company was acquired by Olympus partners in 2004.

Hunting Industrial Coatings

S-Hunting Plc (England)
10448 Chester Road
Cincinnati OH 45215
Phone: 513-771-6870
Toll Free: 800-879-9451
Fax: 513-771-2308
Web: http://www.huntingindustrialcoatings.com
Email: sales@HuntingIndustrialCoatings.com

Annual Sales: $2 Billion
Number of Employees: 40
Sales Manager: David Sullivan

The company manufactures industrial coatings for the transportation, general industrial, aerosol, aerospace, polymer/plastic, pipe and tank lining, fiber cement industries.

Hydromer

35 Industrial Parkway
Branchburg NJ 08876
Phone: 908-526-2828
Toll Free: 877-493-7663
Fax: 908-526-3633
Web: http://www.hydromer.com

Annual Sales: $6.8 Million
President: Manfred F. Dyck
CEO: Manfred F. Dyck
Research & Development: Rainer Gruening

Specialty coatings, including marine coatings.

Hydrosol

8407 South 77th Avenue
Bridgeview IL 60455
Phone: 708-598-7100
Fax: 708-598-6572
Web: http://www.hydrosol.com
Email: info@hydrosol.com

Annual Sales: $46.4 Million
Number of Employees: 150
President: Al Howarth
CEO: Al Howarth

Hydrosol produces fills aerosols for others and preformulated aerosols. Products include coatings for protection against rust and corrosion on ferrous bare metal and previously galvanized surfaces and to reduce disk brake squeal.

Hyklas Paints

1401 South 12th Street
Louisville KY 40210
Phone: 502-634-9406
Toll Free: 800-458-2842
Fax: 502-637-8326
Web: http://www.kelleytech.com
Email: kelley@ntr.net

Annual Sales: $18 Million
Number of Employees: 40
President: John R. Kelley, Jr
CEO: John R. Kelley, Jr
Marketing Manager: Brink Spruill
Sales Manager: Brink Spruill

The company manufactures architectural paints, stains, primers, and also traffic paint. It sells products through home centers, paint stores and similar outlets in the southeast.

I. Pulloma Paint

1 Day Lane
Carpentersville IL 60110
Phone: 847-426-4140

Industrial finishes.

IBC Manufacturing

416 East Brooks Rd
Memphis TN 38109
Phone: 901-344-5350
Fax: 901-344-5320
Web: http://www.woodguard.com

Number of Employees: 20-49
Manufacturing Operations Manager: Susan Cooper

Produces Woodguard brand oil-based exterior wood preservative.

ICI Americas

S-Imperial Chemical Industries plc (England)-P
10 Finderne Avenue
Bridgewater NJ 08807-3300
Phone: 908-203-2800
Fax: 908-685-5005
Web: http://www.ici.com

Annual Sales: $1,600 Million
Number of Employees: 6,000
CEO: John McAdam

The parent is a leading producer of paints, adhesives, and starches, specialty synthetic polymers, and electronic and engineering materials, flavors and fragrances, surfactants, and oleochemicals.

Illinois Tool Works

3600 West Lake Avenue
Glenview IL 60025-1215
Phone: 847-724-7500
Fax: 847-657-4261
Web: http://www.itw.com

Annual Sales: $13.9 Billion
Number of Employees: 60,000
President: David B. Speer
CEO: David B. Speer
Sales Manager: Tom Gerringer

ITW has approximately 840 decentralized business units in 57 countries. Polymers & Fluids division: adhesives, sealants, lubrication and cutting fluids, epoxy and resin-based coating products for industrial applications. Transportation division: fluids and polymers for maintenance and appearance, fillers and putties for auto body repair, polyester coatings and patch and repair products for the marine industry. Other Businesses division: paint spray equipment.

Imperial Paint

2526 Northwest Yeon Avenue
Portland OR 97210
Phone: 503-228-0207
Toll Free: 800-228-0207
Fax: 503-228-9683
Web: http:www.imperialpaint.com
Email: info@imperialpaint.com

Annual Sales: $1 - 4.9 Million
Number of Employees: 10-49
President: Steve Rearden

Heavy duty industrial finishes, low VOC paints, commercial, industrial, residential, and automotive coatings.

INCA: Insulating Coatings of America

Synta
675 Park North Boulevard
Ste 120
Clarkston GA 30030
Phone:
Toll Free: 800-234-5001
Web: http://www.incacoatings.com
Email: Info@synta.com

Number of Employees: 26
President: Thomas Curtis

Innovative heat management coating products for roofs, walls, decks, and other surfaces.

Indmar Coatings

237 West Main Street
PO Box 468
Wakefield VA 23888
Phone: 800-400-2361
Fax: 800-400-2370
Web: http://www.indmarcoatings.com
Email: sales@indmarcoatings.com

Number of Employees: 20
President: Chuck Rowe

Polyurethane and epoxy industrial and marine coatings.

Induron Coatings

PO Box 2371
3333 Richard Arrington Jr. Boulevard North
Birmingham AL 35234
Phone: 205-324-9584
Toll Free: 800-324-9584
Fax: 205-324-6942
Web: http://www.induron.com/
Email: info@Induron.com

Annual Sales: $10 Million
Number of Employees: 70
President: David Hood
CEO: David Hood
Research & Development: John Anspach
Marketing Manager: Don Matthews
Sales Manager: Don Matthews
Manufacturing Operations Manager: Davies Hood

Induron produces industrial coatings, mostly for the water piping and equipment. It formerly produced architectural paints.

Industrial Finishing Products

465 Logan Street
Brooklyn NY 11208
Phone: 718-277-3333
Fax: 718-827-6321
Web: http://www.industrialfinishings.com
Email: info@industrialfinishings.com

Annual Sales: $5 Million
Number of Employees: 30
President: Dr. Robin Hoffman
CEO: Dr. Robin Hoffman
Marketing Manager: Mark Foster

The company manufactures such industrial finishes as appliance lacquers, two-component polyurethane coatings, and water-borne clear and colored stains.

Industrial Powder Coatings

S-Sudbury
202 Republic Street
Norwalk OH 44857
Phone: 419-668-4436
Fax: 419-660-2494
Web: http://www.ipcoatings.com
Email: sales@ipcoatings.com

Annual Sales: $55 Million
Number of Employees: 450
President: Toni Cooley

The company produces custom powder coatings for captive use. It has five facilities in the Midwest.

Industrial Protective Coatings

1855 Enterprise Drive
De Pere WI 54115
Phone: 920-336-0801
Toll Free: 800-236-1164
Fax: 920-336-6463
Web: http://www.anchorbond.com

Number of Employees: 10-49
President: Gerald Brosteau
Marketing Manager: Toby Brosteau
Sales Manager: Jerry Brosteau

Flooring coatings.

Ingels

PO Drawer 600
Jonesboro AR 72403
Phone: 870-935-9977
Toll Free: 888-263-1189
Fax: 870-931-3903
Email: ingels@ritternet.com

Number of Employees: 1-9
President: Marlin Thyer
Sales Manager: Julia J. Thyer

Coatings and dispersions.

Innotek Powder Coatings

S-Wagner & Brown, Ltd.
3400 West Seventh Street
Big Spring TX 79720
Phone: 432-263-5263
Toll Free: 800-753-5263
Fax: 432-267-1318
Web: http://www.innotekpowdercoatings.com/
Email: sales@innotekllc.com

Number of Employees: 100-150
President: Wes Wagner

Powder coatings. Company formerly known as PFS Thermoplastic Powder Coatings, Inc

INSL-X Products

Benjamin Moore
101 Paragon Drive
Montvale NJ 7645
Phone: 800-225-5554
Fax: 888-248-2143
Web: http://www.insl-x.com
Email: CustomerCare@insl-x.com

Annual Sales: $31.4 Million
Number of Employees: 195
President: James A. Weil

The company manufactures industrial and architectutal paints, such special purpose coatings as lead encapsulating coatings, epoxy floor coating, tennis and basketball court coatings, concrete coatings, traffic marking paints, and swimming pool paints. INSL-X acquired Bruning Paint Co., Lenmar, Inc. and Coranado Paint Co. in 2004. In 2006 it acquired Trinity Wood Coatings.

Integrated Polymer Industries

3029 South Harbor Boulevard
Santa Ana CA 92704-6448
Phone: 714-434-0800
Fax: 714-434-0888
Web: http://www.ergun.org
Email: IntegratedPolymerIndustries@msn.com

Annual Sales: $4-6 Million
Number of Employees: 40
President: Steevy Kelly

The company manufactures such specialty coatings as acid-resistant and water-resistant products.

Integrated Polymer Industries

3029 South Harbor Boulevard
Santa Ana CA 92701
Phone: 714-434-0800
Fax: 714-434-0888
Web: http://www.ergun.org
Email: IntegratedPolymerIndustries@msn.com

Annual Sales: $1 - 4.9 Million
Number of Employees: 10-49
Marketing Manager: John A. Doyle

Corrosion resistant coatings for power generation, pulp and paper, and marine; waterproofing compounds, primers, sealers.

Intercoastal Paint

14029 West Hardy
Houston TX 77060
Phone: 281-448-5258
Fax: 281-448-2664
Web: http://www.intercoastalpaint.com
Email: intercoastalpaint@hotmail.com

Annual Sales: $1 - 4.9 Million
Number of Employees: 10-49
President: Shaunte Angelo
CEO: Shaunte Angelo

Industrial and marine coatings.

International Coatings

13929 East 166th Street
Cerritos CA 90702-7666
Phone: 562-926-1010
Toll Free: 800-423-4103
Fax: 562-926-9486
Web: http://www.iccink.com
Email: icinfo@iccink.com

Annual Sales: $13.4 Million
Number of Employees: 10-49
President: Stephen Kahane

Waterborne primers to bond vinyl plastisols and other materials to metals.

IVC Industrial Coatings

2245 Valley Avenue
Indianapolis IN 46218
Phone: 317-636-4407
Fax: 317-636-4436
Web: http://www.teamivc.com

Annual Sales: $15 Million
Number of Employees: 125
President: Mike McCrackenn
CEO: Mike McCrackenn

The company manufactures powder coatings at Grand Haven, MI (60 employees). It also has U.S. facilities in Arizona (2), Minnesota, and Arizona.

J.C. Whitlam Manufacturing

200 West Walnut Street
PO Box 380
Wadsworth OH 44282
Phone: 330-334-2524
Toll Free: 800-321-8358
Fax: 800-537-0588
Web: http://www.whitlampaint.com

Annual Sales: $5 - 9.9 Million
Number of Employees: 50-99
President: Jack C. Whitlam IV
CEO: Douglas A. Whitlam

Marking paints.

Jamestown Powder Coatings

Jamestown Coating Technologies
710 Beaver Road
Girard PA 16417
Phone: 724-932-3101
Toll Free: 800-628-3565
Fax: 724-932-5147
Web: http://www.jamestownpowder.com
Email: jdwalton@jamestowncoatings.com

President: J. D. Walton
CEO: Michael P. Walton
Research & Development: Jan Smith
Sales Manager: J. D. Walton

Industrial paints and coatings. Formulates environmentally friendly and fully customized colors.

Jasco Chemical

1008 Fuller Street
PO Box 715Santa Ana CA 92701
Phone: 650-968-6005
Toll Free: 888-345-2726
Web: http://www.jasco-help.com
Email: homax@homaxproducts.com

Annual Sales: $1 - 4.9 Million
Number of Employees: 10-49
Marketing Manager: Shea Jones

Wood finishes coatings. Also concrete sealers, architectural paint, and adhesive removers.

Jellico Chemical

829 South 26th Street
Louisville KY 40251
Phone: 502-772-2547
Fax: 502-772-2552
Web: http://www.jellicocoatings.com/
Email: theresajellico@bellsouth.net

Annual Sales: $4.3 Million
Sales Manager: Gene Lanning

Industrial finishes.

Jema-American

824 South Avenue
Middlesex N.J. 08846
Phone: 732-968-5333
Fax: 732-968-1269
Web: http://www.jema-american.com
Email: info@Jema-American.com

Number of Employees: 26
Sales Manager: Dave S. Davis

Decorative and functional metalizing finishes.

John L. Armitage

545 National Drive
Gallatin TN 37066
Phone: 615-452-6556
Fax: 615-452-4147

Annual Sales: $15 Million
Number of Employees: 25
President: Norman Armitage
Research & Development: Steve Nichols
Sales Manager: Craig Hood

Armitage produces protective coatings for metal, wood and plastic substrates, including marine products. It also manufactures water- and solvent- based primers for metal buildings and for structural steel roof and floor deck.

John P. Nissen, Jr.

2544 Fairhill Avenue
PO Box 339
Glenside PA 19038
Phone: 215-886-2025
Fax: 215-886-0707
Web: http://www.nissenmarkers.com
Email: sales@nissenmarkers.com

Annual Sales: $10 million
Number of Employees: 25
President: John P. Nissen

Aerosol paints and paint markers.

Jones-Blair

PO Box 35286
2728 Empire Central
Dallas TX 75235
Phone: 214-353-1600
Toll Free: 800-492-9400
Fax: 800-325-6321
Web: http://www.jones-blair.com
Email: sales@jones-blair.com

Annual Sales: $85 Million
Number of Employees: 575
President: Jeff Powell
Marketing Manager: Bob Coleman
Sales Manager: Will Dryden

The company operates two divisions: (1) Jones-Blair Industrial Coatings: industrial OEM, maintenance applications and corporate re-imaging; (2) Neogard Construction Coatings: elastomeric coatings (waterproofing and roof, floor, and wall coating systems). Products are based on urethanes, acrylics and alkyds. Markets include general mainte-nance, oil-field service, automotive parts, off-road equipment, transportation, coil coating, service station imaging, storefronts and signs, wood/millwork and recreation. The company also produces resins for captive use.

Jotun Paints USA

Jotun Group
9203 Highway 23
Belle Chasse LA 70037
Phone: 504-394-3538
Toll Free: 800-229-3538
Fax: 504-394-3726
Web: http://www.jotun.com/us
Email: mailusa@jotun.com

Number of Employees: 51
President: Emile Oustalet
CEO: Emile Oustalet
Research & Development: Dr Stan Turnbull
Marketing Manager: Tim LaBorde
Sales Manager: Tim LaBorde

In the US the company produces marine, offshore and protective coatings at Belle Chasse. It imports powder coatings from other company locations and operates a warehouse in LaPorte, TX. It also produces decorative coatings for sale outside the USA.

K.A Dutcher Paint & Varnish

607 South Thomas
California MO 65018
Phone: 573-796-4721

Number of Employees: 1-9

Paints and varnishes.

Kalcor Coatings

37721 Stevens Boulevard
Willoughby OH 44094
Phone: 440-946-4700
Toll Free: 800-422-8484
Fax: 440-946-4704
Web: http://www.kalcor.com
Email: kalkor@kalcor.com

Annual Sales: $8 Million
Number of Employees: 40
President: Newton Zucker
CEO: Newton Zucker
Research & Development: Tim Hlabse
Marketing Manager: Don Mihalik
Sales Manager: Don Mihalik
Manufacturing Operations Manager: Cory Zucker

Kalcor produces OEM and specialty coatings for the transportation, construction, rubber/tire, graphic arts and fabricated metal markets.

Kansas Correctional Industries

PO Box 2
4th & Kansas
Lansing KS 66043
Phone: 913-727-3249
Fax: 913-727-2331
Web: http://www.kancorind.com
Email: KCI_Sales@doc.ks.gov

Annual Sales: $9 Million
Number of Employees: 54
President: Rodney Crawford
Manufacturing Operations Manager: Rodney Crawford

Kansas Correctional, a part of the Kansas Prison System, produces latex wall paint, polyurethane floor enamels, pain thinners and sealers, machinery and industrial paint, traffic paint, polyester shower paint, special purpose paints, and colorants. Products are sold primarily to state of Kansas, state agencies, non-profit organizations, and also to the merchant market.

Karnak

330 Central Avenue
Clark NJ 07066
Phone: 732-388-0300
Toll Free: 800-526-4236
Fax: 732-388-9422
Web: http://www.karnakcorp.com
Email: info@karnakcorp.com

Annual Sales: $23.1 Million
Number of Employees: 75
President: James D. Hannah
Sales Manager: John McDermott

Karnak produces cold-applied coatings and cements for the roofing and waterproofing industry.

Kel-Glo

54 Northeast 73rd Street
Miami FL 33138
Phone: 305-751-5641
Toll Free: 800-451-5641
Fax: 305-756-6481
Web: http://www.kelglo.com

Annual Sales: $1 - 4.9 Million
Number of Employees: 20-49
President: Borja Isidro

Industrial finishes.

Kelley Technical Coatings

1445 South 15th Street
Louisville KY 40210-3726
Phone: 502-636-2561
Toll Free: 800-458-2842
Fax: 502-635-5170
Web: http://www.kelleytech.com

Annual Sales: $18 Million
President: John R. Kelley
CEO: John R. Kelley
Manufacturing Operations Manager: Gary Beard

The Convoy division manufactures non-skid coatings; the Olympic divison produces pool coatings, deck coatings and allied pool products; and the KelTech division manufactures architectural and industrial maintenance coatings.

Kelly-Moore Paint

987 Commercial Street
San Carlos CA 94070
Phone: 650-592-8337
Toll Free: 800-874-4436
Fax: 650-592-1215
Web: http://www.kellymoore.com

Number of Employees: 1,800
President: Steven DeVoe

Kelly-Moore produces architectural paints, industrial-maintenance coatings and related products under the Kelly-Moore name. Products are sold through approximately 163 stores in 10 western United States. It operates plants at San Carlos, CA; Hurst, TX; and Seattle, WA.

Kelsey Coatings

800 Coronis Way
PO Box 11364
Green Bay WI 54307
Phone: 920-336-4455
Fax: 920-336-3115
Web: http://www.kelseycoatings.com

Annual Sales: $14.9 Million
Number of Employees: 8
President: Thomas Kelsey
CEO: Thomas Kelsey
Marketing Manager: Michael Kelsey
Sales Manager: Michael Kelsey

Paints and coatings.

Kemco Industries

1374 East Main Street
Lehi UT 84043
Phone: 801-768-4408
Toll Free: 877-450-5877
Fax: 801-768-9150
Web: http://www.kemcooil.com
Email: info@kemcooil.com

Concrete coatings.

Kempen Paint

2500 State Street
East Carondelet IL 62240
Phone: 618-286-5292
Fax: 618-286-3121
Web: http://www.kempenpaint.com
Email: salesandinfo@kempenpaint.com

Number of Employees: 20-49
President: Ed Kempen

Industrial finishes, maintenance coatings.

Ken-Lac

47 Slade Street
Fall River MA 02906
Phone: 508-676-1969

Number of Employees: 10-49

Industrial coatings.

Kentucky Paint Manufacturing

S- Color and Supply
909 National Avenue
Lexington KY 40502
Phone: 859-254-3836
Fax: 859-254-7752
Web: http://www.colorandsupply.com
Email: info@colorandsupply.com

Annual Sales: $8 Million
Number of Employees: 40
President: Joseph Deifel
CEO: Joseph Deifel
Research & Development: Gary Reynolds
Manufacturing Operations Manager: Louis Love

The company produces architectural paints and related supplies.

Kirker Automotive Finishes

Coventry Coatings
89 Taft Avenue
Newburgh NY 12550
Phone: 845-562-5666
Toll Free: 800-307-7951
Fax: 845-562-8986
Web: http://www.kirkerautomotive.com
Email: info@kirkerautomotive.com

Number of Employees: 15
President: Bruce Sklak
Sales Manager: Gerald Elsing

High quality automotive refinishes, paints and related products including primers, clear coats, and additives.

Klinger Paint

5555 Willow Creek Drive Southwest
Cedar Rapids IA 52404
Phone: 319-366-7735
Fax: 319-366-1534
Web: http://www.klingerpaint.com
Email: rklinger@klingerpaint.com

Number of Employees: 10-49
President: Bob Klinger

Industrial coatings, traffic paints.

Kool Seal Coatings

S- Perfection Industries.
1499 Enterprise Parkway
Twinsburg OH 44087-2241
Phone: 330-425-4717
Toll Free: 888-321-5665
Fax: 888-296-5665
Web: http://www.koolseal.com
Email: customerservice@kstcoatings.com

Annual Sales: $8 Million
President: Stephen R. Hudak

The Industrial Division manufactures reflective roofing coatings and patching materials and the Thoro Consumer Products Division manufactures waterproofing coatings and deck and concrete repair products. In 2001 the company acquired ORD Products, a producer roofing coatings, from SWK-MBT Management, in turn a subsidiary of SKW Trostberg, Germany.

Kwal Paint

Comex Group (Mexico)
5575 DTC Parkway
Greenwood Village CO 80111
Phone: 303-371-5600
Toll Free: 800-383-8406
Fax: 303-373-5688
Web: http://www.kwalpaint.com
Email: info@kwalpaint.com

Number of Employees: 800
CEO: Marcos Achar Levy

A leading manufacturer and retailer of paints and coatings serving customers located in the Rocky Mountains, Midwestern and Southwest regions of the United States. It operates over 100 service centers in 13 states from Idaho to Alabama and has the capacity to produce over 15 million gallons of paint per year.

L & L Coatings

5102 Santa Fe Road
Tampa FL 33594
Phone: 813-248-3704
Toll Free: 800-437-8119
Fax: 813-247-4319
Web: http://www.landlcoatings.com
Email: llcoating@aol.com

Annual Sales: $1 - 4.9 Million
Number of Employees: 10-40
Sales Manager: Bill Buckman

Elastomeric coatings for metal, masonry, fiberglass, and other materials.

L H B Industries

10440 Trenton Avenue
St. Louis MO 63132
Phone: 314-423-7955
Toll Free: 800-542-3697
Fax: 314-423-6918
Web: http://www.lhbindustries.com

Number of Employees: 10-49
Research & Development: Kevin Kempen

Aerosols paints

LA-CO Industries

1201 Pratt Boulevard
Elk Grove Village IL 60007
Phone: 847-956-7600
Toll Free: 800-621-4025
Fax: 800-448-5436
Web: http://www.laco.com

Annual Sales: $15 Million
Number of Employees: 142
President: Jeffrey Kessler
CEO: Dan Kleiman
Marketing Manager: Michael Madej
Sales Manager: Bill Migirditch

Under Markal brand the company produces paint-in-sticks for marking identification on metal, wood, ceramics, plastics and other materials and also fluorescent crayons for computerized scanning equipment to help identify wood grades in lumber processing mills. Other products include thread sealants, soldering fluxes, repair sealants and specialty chemicals. End uses include the plumbing, HVAC, industrial, agricultural, and lumber.

Lauren International

2228 Reiser Avenue
New Philadelphia OH 44663
Phone: 330-339-3373
Toll Free: 800-683-0676
Fax: 330-339-1515
Web: http://www.lauren.com

Number of Employees: 500
President: Kevin E. Gray

Molded and extruded polymers, coatings and caulks.

Lawrence-McFadden

7430 State Road
Philadelphia PA 19136
Phone: 215-624-6333
Toll Free: 800-877-7430
Fax: 215-624-2270
Web: http://www.lawrence-mcfadden.com
Email: carol@lawrence-mcfadden.com

Number of Employees: 60
President: Lawrence McFadden

The company produces wood coatings and related products, including water- and solvent-based stains, fillers, sealers, lacquers, urethanes, polyesters, UV and coatings.

Lazon Paint & Wallpaper

17-12 River Road
Fair Lawn NJ 07410
Phone: 201-796-3500
Fax: 201-797-5973
Web: http://www.lazon.8m.com
Email: lazon.paints@verizon.net

Annual Sales: $2-5 Million
Number of Employees: 20
President: Robert Landzettel
CEO: Robert Landzettel
Marketing Manager: Donald Landzettel
Sales Manager: Donald Landzettel
Manufacturing Operations Manager: Walter Landzettel

Lazon brand consumer paints

Lenawee Industrial Paint Supply

5645 Cogswell Road
Wayne MI 48184
Phone: 734-729-8080
Fax: 734-729-8101
Web: http://www.lenaweepaint.com
Email: paintman@lenaweepaint.com

Annual Sales: $1.8 Million
Number of Employees: 10-49
President: Craig Morrison
CEO: Craig Morrison
Marketing Manager: Ron Quail

Solvent quick dry coatings, high solid coatings, latex emulsions and water based paints , cleaning solvents and thinning agents, 2 part epoxy coatings, machine enamels, material handling equipment coatings, wood stains and preservatives.

Lenmar

INSL-X Products
4701 O'Donnell Street
Baltimore MD 21224
Phone: 410-534-3300
Toll Free: 800-883-4193
Fax: 410-534-3326
Web: http://www.coronadopaint.com

Annual Sales: $28.5 Million
Number of Employees: 90

Manufacturing Operations Manager: Paul Kearney

Lenmar manufacturers aerosol concentrates and coatings for wood floors, cabinets, and furniture at a 142,000 sq ft facility in Baltimore. In July 2004 both Lenmar and Coronado Paint were sold to INSUL-X Products of Berkshire Hathaway's Benjamin Moore.

Life Paint

PO Box 2488
12927 Sunshine Avenue
Santa Fe Springs CA 90670
Phone: 562-944-6391
Toll Free: 800-400-0516
Fax: 562-946-5921
Web: http://www.lifepaint.com
Email: lifepaint@verizon.net

Annual Sales: Under $1 Million
Number of Employees: 40

Architectural coatings and house paints.

Liquid Ceramic International

PO Box 473262
Charlotte NC 28247
Phone: 704-889-5222
Toll Free: 800-466-2691
Fax: 704-889-4607
Web: http://www.liquidceramic.com
Email: info@liquidceramic.com

Annual Sales: Under $1 Million

Exterior and interior architectural paints and roofing coatings blended with acrylic for longevity and protection.

Liquid Plastics

Sika AG
79 Bradley Street
Middletown CT 06457
Phone: 860-613-2688
Toll Free: 888-635-5228
Fax: 860-613-2689
Web: http://www.liquidplasticsinc.com
Email: info@liquidplasticsinc.com

Annual Sales: $3.2 Million
Number of Employees: 23
President: Robert Gorick
CEO: Chuck Fitzgerald

Cold, fluid applied waterproofing coatings and repair materials for such building surfaces as floors, walls and floors in 25,000 sq ft facility.

Loes Enterprises

1457 Iglehart Avenue
St. Paul MN 55104
Phone: 651-646-1385
Toll Free: 800-869-1088
Fax: 651-646-3067
Web: http://www.loesent.com
Email: Loes@LoesEnt.Com

Number of Employees: 10-49
CEO: Virginia Loes
Marketing Manager: Dan Loes
Sales Manager: Dan Loes

Plastisol coatings. Adhesives and other plastisols.

LORD Corp.

111 Lord Drive
Cary, NC 27511-7923
Toll Free: 877-275-5673
Web: http://www.lord.com

Annual Sales: $610 Million
Number of Employees: 2,600
President: Richard L. McNeel
COO: Jack DeLeon

Founded in 1924, Lord Corp. provides adhesives coatings and motion management solutions for aerospace defense, automotive, and industrial companies. There are 17 manufacturing facilities in 9 countries.

LPS Laboratories

4647 Hugh Howell Road
PO Box 105052
Tucker GA 30085
Phone: 770-243-8800
Toll Free: 800-241-8334
Fax: 770-243-8899
Web: http://www.lpslabs.com

Annual Sales: $33 Million
Number of Employees: 100
Sales Manager: Al Spare

LPS primarily manufactures lubricating oils and greases and also corrosion-inhibiting paints and primers and epoxy coatings.

M&R Performance Coatings

3845 Hickman Road
Kodak TN 37764
Phone: 865-933-1478
Toll Free: 877-321-9929
Fax: 865-933-7881
Web: http://www.amr-coatings.com
Email: info@amr-coatings.com

Number of Employees: 400
President: Stephen Kahane

High-temperature performance coatings for automotive and motorcycle applications.

M.A.B. Paints

Web: http://www.mabpaints.com

A business unit of Sherwin-Williams.

Magnet Paint & Shellac

336 Bayview Avenue
Amityville NY 11701
Phone: 631-842-7700
Toll Free: 800-922-9981
Fax: 631-842-8222
Web: http://www.magnetpaints.com
Email: info@magnetpaints.com

Annual Sales: $10.5 Million
President: Eric Rosenthal

Polyurethane floor coating.Industrial paints.

Magni Group

390 Park Street
Suite 300 Birmingham MI 48009
Phone: 248-647-4500
Fax: 248-647-7506
Web: http://www.themagnigroup.com
Email: dpaul@themagnigroup.com

Annual Sales: $40 Million
Number of Employees: 175
Marketing Manager: Douglas Paul
Sales Manager: Bob Keagy

Flood produces clear wood finishes and cleaners, paint removers and paint additives.

Mahoning Paint

PO Box 1282
Youngstown OH 44501
Phone: 330-744-2139
Fax: 330-744-5826
Web: http://www.mahoningpaintcorp.com
Email: mail@mahoningpaintcorp.com

Annual Sales: $5 - 9.9 Million
Number of Employees: 25
President: Charles C. Rumberg
CEO: Charles C. Rumberg
Research & Development: Ray Morain
Manufacturing Operations Manager: Andy Audley

Produces annually 800,000 gal of Industrial finishes at 18,000 sq ft facility.

Mainline Paint Manufacturing

768 Main Street
Pawtucket RI 2860
Phone: 401-726-3650
Fax: 401-725-6850

Number of Employees: 5
CEO: Richard Main

Industrial maintenance paints.

Majic Paints

Yenkin-Majestic
1920 Leonard Avenue
Columbus OH 43219
Phone: 614-253-8511
Toll Free: 800-848-1898
Fax: 614-258-3062
Web: http://www.majicpaints.com
Email: info@majicpaints.com

Annual Sales: $85 Million
Number of Employees: 500
President: Jonathan Petuchowski
CEO: Andrew Smith
Marketing Manager: Cathy Strang
Sales Manager: Gary Dinnell
Manufacturing Operations Manager: Paul Ulrey

Yenkin-Majestic produces architectural paints and industrial coatings at a 400,000 sq ft facility. The Architectural Paint Division manufactures paints under the Majic name through four divisions: chain stores, automotive stores, private label, and export. Chain stores products include oil-base and acrylic enamels, spray paints, basement paints, interior and exterior wood stains and clears, pool paints, waterproofing sealers, and traffic paint. The Automotive Division produces tractor and implement enamels, rust kill enamels, catalyst hardeners, and engine enamel sprays. The Dealer Division and Export Division manufacture similar products.The Industrial Coatings Division produces primers, alkyds, acrylics, epoxies, urethanes, coil coatings, and powder coatings. OPC Polymers, part of the Industrial Coatings Division, produces water-soluble and high-solids resins.

Manion Paint & Hardware

640 North Seneca Street
Oil City PA 16301
Phone: 814-676-8944
Fax: 814-677-6934
Web: http://www.manionpaintandhardware.com
Email: sales@manionpaintandhardware.com

Stains and Muralo paints.

Manus Products-Florida

3706 Mercantile Avenue
Naples FL 34104
Phone: 813-643-3070
Fax: 813-643-3064

Number of Employees: 1-9
Sales Manager: Joel Bump

Specialty paints,Sister companies produce adhesives and tapes.

Mapei

C- Mapei SpA (Italy)
530 Industrial Drive
West Chicago IL 60185
Phone: 630-293-5800
Toll Free: 800-426-2734
Fax: 630-293-5079
Web: http://www.mapei.com

Annual Sales: $299.4 Million
Number of Employees: 70
President: Nicholas Di Tempora
CEO: Giorgio Squinzi

Mapei manufactures materials for installation and restoration of concrete, ceramic tile and stone, floor coverings, and pools, including carpet and vinyl adhesives, mortars, grouts, self levelers, and concrete repair products. It also has a line of pool finishes, deck stains, sealers, and cleaners. The parent company has 11 manufacturing facilities and about 600 employees worldwide.

Marcus Paint

235 East Market Street
Louisville KY 40202
Phone: 502-584-0303
Fax: 502-587-0922
Web: http://www.marcuspaint.com

Annual Sales: $8 Million
Number of Employees: 45
Manufacturing Operations Manager: Steve Marcus

The company produces a line of industrial finishes. It manufactures liquid and powder coatings here and liquid coatings in Nashville, TN.

Marine Industrial Paint

4590 60th Avenue North
St. Petersburg FL 33714
Phone: 727-527-3382
Toll Free: 800-459-3382
Fax: 727-521-1405
Web: http://www.tuf-top.com
Email: stevec@tuf-top.com

Number of Employees: 12
Marketing Manager: Steve Cook

Marine paints, industrial finishes

Martin F. Weber

2727 Southhampton Road
Philadelphia PA 19154
Phone: 215-677-5600
Fax: 215-677-3336
Web: http://www.weberart.com
Email: info@weberart.com

Annual Sales: $10 Million
Number of Employees: 50
President: Michael Gorak
CEO: Dennis Kate
Marketing Manager: Michael Gorak
Sales Manager: Michael Gorak
Manufacturing Operations Manager: Mary Cohen

The company manufactures artist's paints and related materials.

Masco

21001 Van Born Road
Taylor MI 48180
Phone: 313-274-7400
Fax: 313-792-6135
Web: http://www.masco.com

Annual Sales: $7.7 Billion
Number of Employees: 35,400
CEO: Timothy Wadhams

Paints and stains are included in the Decorative Architectural Products segment (sales $1,714 million). The segment also includes mechanical and electronic lock sets; and door, window and other hardware. Major paint brands are Behr, Behr Premium Plus, Kilz and Hammerite. Domestic paint sales are estimated at $750 million in 2003.

Mayco Colors

S-DecoArt
4077 Weaver Court, South
Hillard OH 43026
Phone: 614-876-1171
Fax: 614-876-9904
Web: http://www.maycocolors.com
Email: info@maycocolors.com

Annual Sales: $9 Million
Number of Employees: 60
CEO: James S. Twerdahl

The company manufactures acrylic paints, glazes, and stains for arts, crafts, and ceramics.

McCormick Paints

2355 Lewis Avenue
Rockville MD 20851
Phone: 301-770-3235
Toll Free: 877-724-6855
Fax: 301-770-9814
Web: http://www.mccormickpaints.com
Email: info@mccormickpaints.com

Annual Sales: $27 Million
Number of Employees: 165
President: Richard M. Patterson
Sales Manager: Bill Ackerman
Manufacturing Operations Manager: Kim Master

McCormick manufactures architectural paints, primers and clear finishes which it sells through independent dealers and also 20 company-controlled retail outlets in Maryland, Virginia, and Washington, DC. It also produces traffic paints and maintenance coatings. The company has plants in Rockville and Frederick, MD.

Mercury Paint

4804 Farragut Road
Brooklyn NY 11203
Phone: 718-469-8787
Toll Free: 800-858-8787
Fax: 718-941-8133
Web: http://www.mercurypaintcorp.com
Email: JRBerman@aol.com

Number of Employees: 75
Sales Manager: Fred Tichner

Mercury Paint manufactures architectural and industrial finishes for DIY and the government. Products are sold along the East Coast through dealers and two company-owned stores. It has a warehouse in Hollywood, FL.

Metal Coatings International

S- NOF Industries (Japan)
275 Industrial Pkwy.
Chardon OH 44024
Phone: 440-285-2231
Toll Free:
Fax: 440-285-5009
Web: http://www.metal-coatings.com
Email: sales@metal-coatings.co

Annual Sales: $11 Million
Number of Employees: 45
President: Kenneth Penske
Marketing Manager: Cecilia Hijuelos
Sales Manager: Jack Poe

MCII manufactures corrosion-protective coatings for ferrous, aluminum, and zinc substrates. Michigan Metal Coatings, Rochester Hills, MI, applies the company's coatings.

Metalcrete Industries

10330 Brecksville Road
Cleveland OH 44141
Phone: 440-526-5600
Toll Free: 800-526-5602
Fax: 440-526-5601
Web: http://www.metalcreteindustries.com
Email: sales@metalcreteindustries.com

Number of Employees: 30
President: Ben R. Earl

Epoxy and urethane coatings; floor resurfacing materials.Adhesives.

Metalflake

28 Artemis Road
Salem NH 03079
Phone: 800-227-2683
Fax: 603-890-0247
Web: http://www.metalflakecorp.com
Email: info@metalflakecorp.com

Automotive repair paints.Metal foil and leaf, metallic and plastic flake.

Michigan Industrial Finishes

9045 Vincent Street
Detroit MI 48211-1560
Phone: 313-925-0030
Toll Free: 800-280-8615
Fax: 313-925-2110
Web: http://www.michiganindustrialfinishes.com

Annual Sales: $8.6 Million
Number of Employees: 10-45
President: Norman Solomon

Industrial finishes

Mid-America Protective Coatings

1395 Louis Avenue
Elk Grove Village IL 60007
Phone: 847-593-3239
Fax: 847-593-3391
Web: http://www.midamcoat.com
Email: info@midamcoat.com

Annual Sales: $5 - 9.9 Mil
Number of Employees: 10-49
Sales Manager: Jeff Jackson

Industrial paints and lacquers.

Mid-States Paint & Chemical

9315 Watson Industrial Park
St. Louis MO 63126
Phone: 314-961-6464
Fax: 314-961-6243
Web: http://www.midstatepaints.com
Email: info@midstatespaint.com

Annual Sales: $3.7 Million
Number of Employees: 50-99
President: James Barry

Industrial and technical powder coatings, paints, and bulk correction fluid. Aquawood stains, finishes for plastic, primer stains.

Miller Paint

317 Southeast Grand
Portland OR 97214
Phone: 503-233-4491
Toll Free: 800-852-3254
Fax: 503-233-7463
Web: http://www.millerpaint.com/
Email: support@millerpaint.com

Annual Sales: $35 Million
Number of Employees: 100-200
President: Steve Dearborn
CEO: Steve Dearborn
Marketing Manager: Brian Sethness
Sales Manager: Tim Doolittle

Miller Paint manufactures architectural paints and industrial coatings, which are sold through 18 retail outlets in Oregon and Washington and through other retail outlets.

Miller Purcell

244 West Third Avenue
New Lenox IL 60451
Phone: 815-485-2142
Fax: 815-485-2143

Number of Employees: 3
President: Jim Miller

Exterior aluminum paints

Molecular Coating Specialists

1001 Mt. Lebanon Rd
PO Box 2439
Cedar Hill TX 75106
Phone: 972-291-7474
Fax: 972-291-6224
Web: http://www.mcsworldwide.com

Number of Employees: 10-49
Research & Development: Sheldon Broedel

Industrial coatings for steel, iron, aluminum, wood, or concrete.

Morwear Paints / MGuard Coatings Technology

Diversified Coatings Commerce, CA 90040
620 Lamar Street
Los Angeles CA 90031
Toll Free: 800-605-2627
Web: http//www.morwear.com

Morwear brand paint was acquired by Diversified Coatings- paints, enamels, and primers.

Multi-Color Specialties

S- Oak Partners
1532 South 50th Court
Cicero IL 60650
Phone: 708-656-4990
Fax: 708-656-4989
Web: http://www.multicolorpaint.com

Annual Sales: $25 Million
Number of Employees: 50
President: Harry Cody
Sales Manager: Tim Kearney

The company produces decorative paint as aerosols or sprays that consist of individual flecks of different colors so as to give the natural appearance of such materials as granite, cork, leather and stone. Products are manufactured at two locations and distributed through independent paint dealers and paint store chains.

Murco Wall Products

2032 North Commerce
Fort Worth TX 76106
Phone: 817-626-1987
Toll Free: 800-446-7124
Fax: 817-626-0821
Web: http://www.murcowall.com/
Email: sales@murcowall.com

Annual Sales: $4.4 Million
Number of Employees: 5-9
President: Joan Benton
CEO: Joan Benton
Manufacturing Operations Manager: Jeff Cauwels

Wall paint and texture products.

Murmac Paint Manufacturing

1300 Harvey Street
Beloit WI 53511
Phone: 608-362-1900
Fax: 608-362-2057

Annual Sales: $5 Million
Number of Employees: 12
President: Charles Rydberg
CEO: Charles Rydberg
Research & Development: Charles Rydberg
Marketing Manager: Charles Rydberg
Sales Manager: Charles Rydberg
Manufacturing Operations Manager: Charles Rydberg

Architectural interior and exterior paints and finishes, drywall finishes.

N. Siperstein

415 Montgomery Street
Jersey City NJ 07302
Phone: 201-333-2215
Fax: 201-333-2299
Web: http://www.siperstein.com

Annual Sales: $67 Million
President: Steve Siterstein
CEO: Steve Siperstein

Siperstein manufactures architectural, marine, and industrial coatings and sells wallpaper and paint sundries. It has 15 stores in New Jersey, three in Connecticut and one in Massachusetts.

National Bronze Powder

9945 Franklin Avenue
Franklin Park IL 60131
Phone: 847-678-3160
Fax: 847-678-3161
Web: http://www.neyra.com

Annual Sales: Under $1 Million
Number of Employees: 1-9
Sales Manager: Sam Ford

Paint, specialties

National Paint Products

500 Chancellor Avenue
Irvington NJ 7111
Phone: 973-375-3559

Number of Employees: 10-49
President: J. Andrew Doyle

Industrial finishes.

National Polymers

9 Guttman Avenue
Charleroi PA 15022
Phone: 724-483-9300
Toll Free: 800-831-5600
Fax: 724-483-9306
Web: http://www.nationalpolymers.com
Email: questions@nationalpolymers.com

Annual Sales: $14.75 Million
Number of Employees: 30
President: Darry Budkin

The company produces concrete restoration and protective flooring products for industrial and commercial applications. Products are sold only under private label.

Nationwide Chemical Coatings

6067 17th Street East
Bradenton FL 34203
Phone: 941-753-7500
Toll Free: 800-423-7264
Fax: 941-753-1773
Web: http://www.nationwidecoatings.com
Email: info@natcoat.net

Annual Sales: $1 - 4.9 Million
Number of Employees: 40
CEO: Bob Warner
Marketing Manager: Steve Ellis
Sales Manager: Jim Manco

Paint.

NCP Coatings

225 Fort Street
Niles MI 49120
Phone: 269-683-3377
Toll Free: 800-627-1948
Fax: 269-683-3305
Web: http://www.ncpcoatings.com

Annual Sales: $72.3 Million
Number of Employees: 135
President: C.M. Hannewyk III

The company is also known as Niles Chemical Paint, Inc. It produces asphalt, electrostatic, industrial, and ship coatings and tree marking paints. Products are manufactured under Government Specifications.

Nelson Paint

One Nelson Drive
PO Box 2040
Kingsford MI 49802
Phone: 906-774-5566
Toll Free: 800-236-9278
Fax: 906-774-4264
Web: http://www.nelsonpaint.com
Email: paintball@nelsonpaint.com

Annual Sales: $6 Million
Number of Employees: 45
President: Richard C. Louys
Marketing Manager: Bert Miikkulainen
Sales Manager: Laurie Marcotte

Nelson produces such specialties as tree marking paints, paintballs, and associated equipment. Production is at Birmingham, AL, McMinnville, OR, and Sault St. Marie, ON.

New England Paint Manufacturing

51 Higginson Avenue
Central Falls RI 2863
Phone: 401-722-4606
Fax: 401-722-4672

Annual Sales: Under $1 Million
Number of Employees: 5

Tennis court, basketball court, playground, running track, walkway, and traffic paints.

New Nautical Coatings

14805 49th Street North
Clearwater FL 33762
Phone: 727-523-8053
Toll Free: 800-528-0997
Fax: 727-523-7325
Web: http://www.seahawkpaints.com
Email: contactus@seahawkpaints.com

Number of Employees: 5-9
President: Erik Norrie
CEO: Erik Norrie

Marine paints under Seahawk brand.

Neyra Industries

10700 Evendale Drive
Cincinnati OH 45241
Phone: 513-733-1000
Toll Free: 800-543-7077
Fax: 513-733-3989
Web: http://www.neyraindustries.com/
Email: info@neyra.com

Number of Employees: 10-49
Research & Development: Greg Houser
Sales Manager: Joe Conwell
Manufacturing Operations Manager: Jerry Reed

Ceramic coatings, roofing coatings, and wood, metal and concrete coatings.

NIC Industries

7050 6th Street
White City OR 97503
Phone: 541-826-1922
Toll Free: 866-774-7628
Fax: 541-826-6372
Web: http://www.nicindustries.com
Email: info@nicindustries.com

Number of Employees: 15-45
President: Chris Fish
Sales Manager: Doug Thomas

NIC Industries manufactures ceramic, elastomeric, and powder coatings for the aerospace, automotive, general manufacturing, marine, military, firearms, construction, and other businesses. It operates four divisions. The Micro Dyne division produces liquid ceramic coatings under the Cerakote brand; the Thermo Dyne division provides training in the application of Micro Dyne materials; the Poly Tech division manufactures elastomeric coatings for roofing, decks, and patios, weather protection, insulation, and waterproofing; and the Prismatic Powders division produces powder coatings.

NoFire Technologies

21 Industrial Avenue
Upper Saddle River NJ 7458
Phone: 201-818-1616
Toll Free: 800-603-4730
Fax: 201-818-8775
Web: http://www.nofiretechnologies.com
Email: (nofirenj@aol.com

Annual Sales: $62 Million
President: Sam Benn
CEO: Sam Benn
Marketing Manager: Gary Moore

Fire retardant coatings.

North American Paint

3504 Rose Avenue
Asbury Park NJ 7712
Phone: 732-713-0200

Paints.

North American Powder Coatings

4680 Iroquois Avenue
Erie PA 16510
Phone: 814-899-0621
Fax:
Web: http://www.northamericanpowdercoatings.com
Email: paint@erieonline.com

Annual Sales: $1.646 Billion
Sales Manager: Leon Akerly

Powder coatings

Northern Coatings & Chemical

705 6th Avenue
Menominee MI 49858
Phone: 906-863-2641
Toll Free:
Fax: 906-863-6671
Web: http://www.finishing.com/

Number of Employees: 30
President: Larry MelGary
CEO: Larry MelGary
Marketing Manager: Larry MelGary
Sales Manager: Larry MelGary

Industrial finishes, coil coating

Northwest Coatings

7221 South Tenth Street
Oak Creek WI 53154-1903
Phone: 414-762-3330
Fax: 414-762-9132
Web: http://www.northwestcoatings.com
Email: nwc@northwestcoatings.com

Annual Sales: $24 Million
President: Jeffrey Holdsberg
CEO: Jeffrey Holdsberg

Northwest Coatings produces UV/EB and water-based adhesives and coatings for the tag and label and other printing and converting markets, and industrial applications. It operates two plants in Oak Creek. In 2002 the company was acquired by managers and Caltius Capital Management, American Capital Strategies, and Antares Capital Corp.

Norton & Son

148 East 5th Street
Bayonne NJ 07002
Phone: 201-437-0770
Toll Free: 800-631-3440
Fax: 201-437-2316
Web: http://www.muralo.com
Email: snorton.devine@muralocompany.co

Annual Sales: $35 Million
Number of Employees: 300
President: Jim Norton
Marketing Manager: Daniele Martin
Sales Manager: Peter Seaborg

Over half of sales come from consumer paints, with the balance in such related products as repair compounds and brushes and rollers. Paints are manufactured by the Muralo Co., Bayonne and Synkoloid Co., Los Angeles, CA and sold through independent retailers.

NPA Coatings

Nippon Paint
11110 Beara Road
Street 2Cleveland OH 44102
Phone: 216-631-2002
Toll Free: 800-231-2002
Fax: 216-634-2450

Annual Sales: $70.4 Million
Number of Employees: 215

The company produces powder and liquid coatings, mostly for the automotive industry, and also under private label for such industries as industrial, lawn and garden, architectural and steel office furniture. Nippon Paint, Tokyo, Japan is the largest paint company in Asia. It produces paints and coatings for the automotive industry, the major end use, and also for industrial products, and ships. The company also manufactures paints for residential and commercial buildings and the do-it-yourself market. (Formerly Seibert Powder Coatings)

Nycote Laboratories

12750 Raymer St # A3
North Hollywood CA 91605
Phone: 818-764-9498
Fax: 818-764-0195
Web: http://www.nycote.com
Email: sales@nycote.com

Annual Sales: Under $1 Million
Number of Employees: 1-9
President: Bob Washburn
Sales Manager: Sergio Rosas

Modified liquid nylon protective coatings.

O'Leary Paint

300 East Oakland
Lansing MI 48901
Phone: 517-487-2066
Toll Free: 800-477-2066
Fax: 517-487-1680
Web: http://www.olearypaint.com
Email: info@olearypaint.com

Number of Employees: 120
President: John O'Leary

The company manufactures architectural and industrial paints. Products are sold in 12 company stores in Michigan and Indiana.

Old Village Paint

PO Box 1030
Fort Washington PA 19034
Toll Free: 800-498-7687
Fax: 610-238-9002
Web: http://www.old-village.com
Email: info@old-village.com

Number of Employees: 5
President: Lamey Landis
CEO: Lamey Landis
Marketing Manager: Lamey Landis
Sales Manager: Lamey Landis

Restoration paints.

Old Western Paint

2001 West Barberry Place
Denver CO 80204
Phone: 303-825-5147
Toll Free: 888-765-9827
Fax: 303-825-2437
Web: http://www.oldwesternpaint.com
Email: paint@oldWesternPaint.com

Annual Sales: $5 - 9.9 Million
Number of Employees: 10-49
President: Adeline M. Smith
CEO: Paul Delmonico
Sales Manager: John Zerebeckyj

Architectural coatings and floor finishes.

Oliver Paint Manufacturing

3357 Torrey Road
Flint MI 48507
Phone: 810-233-7204
Toll Free:
Fax: 810-233-5381

Number of Employees: 5-9
Marketing Manager: John F. Proud
Sales Manager: John F. Proud

Architectural and industrial finishes.

ORB Industries

PO Box 1067
Brookhaven PA 19015
Phone: 610-874-2537
Fax: 610-277-4390

Number of Employees: 30
President: Ram Banin

Corrosion-resistant, marking paints, aerosol touch-up paints

Osmose Holdings

980 Ellicott Street
Buffalo NY 14209
Phone: 716-882-5905
Fax: 716-882-5139
Web: http://www.osmose.com
Email: info@osmose.com

Annual Sales: $300 Million
Number of Employees: 1,900
President: James Spengler
CEO: James Spengler
Sales Manager: Nelson Bingel

The company offers primarily wood preservatives and related services for the utility, railroad and other industries. Osmose, Inc., Griffin, GA, an affiliate, sells wood preservatives and treating plant equipment to wood treating plants. It operates a number of groups and subsidiaries, including the Consumer Products Group, which markets brush-on water repellents, stains, and specialty fasteners through retail lumber dealers. Osmose, Inc. also produces color additives, mold inhibitors, and water repellents for use with wood preservatives.

P&D Paints

2511 Highland Avenue
Cincinnati OH 45212
Phone: 513-351-5800
Fax: 513-351-3299
Web: http://www.pdpaints.com
Email: med@pdpaints.co

Annual Sales: $15 Million
Number of Employees: 85
President: Sally H. Derrick
Sales Manager: Mark E. Derrick

Perry & Derrick paints. Brands include Master Piece, Dutch Brand, Pro-Type Premium, Pro-Type Premium HD, and Dubl-Life. Products are sold through independent dealers.

Pace Products

4510 W. 89th Street
Ste 110
Shawnee Mission KS 66207
Phone: 913-469-5588
Toll Free: 888-389-8203
Fax: 913-469-4067
Web: http://www.Pceproducts.com
Email: sales@paceproducts.com

Annual Sales: Under $1 Million
Number of Employees: 8
President: Michael M. Intosh
Marketing Manager: Karen Parnell

Protective coatings, maintenance coatings.

Palmer Paint Products

1291 Rochester Road
Troy MI 48083
Phone: 248-588-4500
Toll Free: 800-521-1383
Fax: 248-588-3878
Web: http://www.palmerpaint.com
Email: info@palmerpaint.com

Annual Sales: $9 Million
Number of Employees: 120
Research & Development: Chris Bailey
Sales Manager: Garrett Hess

Palmer produces paint products for the craft, school and hobby market.

Pandalai Coatings

PO Box 100
837 6th Avenue
Brackenridge PA 15014
Phone: 724-224-5600
Fax: 724-224-4825
Web: http://www.pandalaicoatings.org
Email: pacifichighlands@aol

Annual Sales: Under $1 Million
Number of Employees: 5
President: Bhanu Pandalai

VOC compliant coatings, 100% solids coatings, UV cure baking enamels, and powder coatings.

Paris Paint & Varnish

506 Wortman Avenue
Brooklyn NY 11208
Phone: 718-272-7550
Fax: 718-257-0633

Annual Sales: Under $1 Million
Number of Employees: 10-49

Architectural paints.

Parker Coatings

2451 West Mason Street
Green Bay WI 54307
Phone: 920-494-9676
Toll Free: 800-236-9676
Fax: 920-494-6162
Web: http://www.parkercoatings.com/
Email: parkercoatings@aol.com

Annual Sales: Under $1 Million
Number of Employees: 10-49
President: Nick Napp
CEO: Nick Napp

Industrial coatings for pulp and paper, chemical, food, pharmaceutical, containment areas, and other.

Passonno Paints

500 Broadway
Watervliet NY 12189
Phone: 518-273-3822
Fax: 518-273-1566
Web: http://www.passonnopaints.com
Email: passonno@passonnopaints.com

Number of Employees: 50
President: Richard B. Cunningham
CEO: Richard B. Cunningham

Passono manufactures consumer paints, which are sold through seven retail stores within a 50-mile radius of Albany, NY.

Patriot Paint

304 Blaine Pike
PO Box 1051Portland IN 47371
Phone: 260-726-6633
Fax: 260-726-6344
Web: http://www.patriotpaint.com
Email: skaderly@patriotpaint.com

Annual Sales: $2.1 Million
Number of Employees: 10-49

Sales Manager: Susan Kaderly

Metal finishing coatings.

Pearl Paint

308 Canal Street
New York NY 10013
Phone: 212-431-7932
Toll Free: 800- 451-7327
Fax: 212-274-8290
Web: http://www.pearlpaint.com
Email: Pearlsite@aol.com

Annual Sales: $40 Million
Number of Employees: 250
CEO: Bob Buchsbaum

The company produces artist paints and also sells adhesives, brushes, frames, and stationery.

Peerless Chemical Coatings

1611 22nd Street Southeast
Cullman AL 35055
Phone: 256-734-5000
Fax: 256-734-0059
Web: http://www.peerlesscoatings.com

Number of Employees: 20-49

Industrial finishes

Penn Jersey Paint & Varnish

1255 McCarther Highway
Newark NJ 07104
Phone: 973-482-5430

Paints and varnishes.

Penn Valley Paint

8000 Bristol Pike
Levittown PA 19057
Phone: 215-949-0800
Toll Free: 800-6429505
Fax: 215-949-9422
Web: http://www.pennvalleypaint.com/http://www.
Email: jim@pennvalleypaint.com

Annual Sales: $1-5 Million
Number of Employees: 12
Sales Manager: Jim Villie

Architectural paints, tin roof paints, lacquers, enamels, and stains.

Perfection-Letz Paint

1617 South Washington Avenue
Kennewick WA 99337
Phone: 509-586-1195
Fax: 509-586-0750

Industrial finishes.

Performance Coatings

PO Box 1569
360 Lake Mendocino Drive
Ukiah CA 95482
Phone: 707-462-3023
Fax: 707-462-6139
Web: http://www.penofin.com
Email: info@penofin.com

Annual Sales: $20 Million
Number of Employees: 30
President: Castle Skip Newell III
CEO: Dr. Barbara Newell
Manufacturing Operations Manager: Melissa Quinlan

The company produces the Penofin brand of exterior and interior wood finishes. It also manufactures wood restorers. It is not related to the company with the same name in Auburn, WA.

Performance Industries

51 Tucker Street
Trenton NJ 08618
Phone: 609-392-1450

Number of Employees: 10-49

Paints, finishes

Performance Polymers

6601 Rockbrook Avenue
St. Louis MO 63133
Phone: 314-382-1810
Fax: 314-382-2611
Email: ppolymers@aol.com

Annual Sales: $1 Million
Number of Employees: Less than 100
President: Gary R. Zimmerman
CEO: Gary R. Zimmerman
Research & Development: Gary Burton

Industrial paints

Performance Powders

2699 Grassland Drive
Louisville KY 40299
Phone: 502-499-0244
Fax: 502-499-0457
Web: http://www.performancepowders.com

Annual Sales: $3.5 Billion
Number of Employees: 13,300
President: Mick Fahinger

Powder coatings

Perma

605 Spring Road
Bedford IA 01730
Phone: 978-667-5161
Fax: 978-670-5797
Web: http://www.perma.com
Email: info@perma.com

Number of Employees: 10-49
Sales Manager: Michael Gwinn

Floor coatings and cleaners andwater-based concrete and wood coatings

Perma Tech

2009 Commercial Street
Waterloo IA 50700
Phone: 319-433-3000

President: Allen Warner
Annual Sales: $10 - 24.9 Million

Protective coatings.

Permalite Plastics

1131 Baker Street
Costa Mesa CA 92626
Phone: 714-241-3865
Toll Free: 800-633-0302
Fax: 714-241-8926
Web: http://www.permaliteplastics.com

Number of Employees: 10-49
President: Rick Van Bergh
Manufacturing Operations Manager: Dick Van Bergh

Epoxy and other coatings. Adhesives and color concentrates

Permatite Manufacturing

4551 Judicial Road, Suite 115
Burnsville MN 55306
Phone: 952-898-3200
Toll Free: 800-817-1827
Fax: 952-898-3232
Web: http://www.permatite.com
Email: info@permatite.com

Number of Employees: 20-49
Manufacturing Operations Manager: Leon Yeager

Aerosol roofing coatings, adhesives and sealants.

Permite Paint

PO Box 33127
Decatur GA 30033
Phone: 404-292-4842
Fax: 404-296-4825
Email: scott@pareto.net

Annual Sales: $1 Million
President: Samuel R. Emmerson

Industrial coatings.

Pervo Paint

6624 Stanford Avenue
Los Angeles CA 90001
Phone: 323-758-1147
Toll Free: 800-892-3647
Fax: 323-778-9719
Web: http://www.pervo.com
Email: sales@pervo.com

Annual Sales: $17 Million
Number of Employees: 100
President: John Haupenthal

The company makes traffic coatings; acrylic waterproofing coatings for walls, floors, and decks; thermoplastic marking materials; interior and exterior finishes; and industrial enamels. Products are sold primarily in the western states.

PFI

9215 Santa Fe Springs Road
Santa Fe Springs CA 90670
Phone: 562-946-6666
Fax: 562-946-4000
Web: http://www.pfiinc.net
Email: info@pfiinc.net

Number of Employees: 20-49
President: Steve Holst
Sales Manager: Tom Dern
Manufacturing Operations Manager: Ralph Guerrero

Industrial finishes, primers, and enamels.

Pioneer Manufacturing

4529 Industrial Parkway
Cleveland OH 44135
Phone: 216-671-5500
Toll Free: 800-877-1500
Fax: 800-877-1511
Web: http://www.pioneerathletics.com
Email: generalinquiry@pioneerathletics.com

Annual Sales: $40 Million
Number of Employees: 200
President: Doug Schattinger

Pioneer produces athletic field marking paint for natural grass and synthetic turf and field striping machines.

Pioneer Metal Finishing

PO Box 387
Franklinville NJ 8322
Phone: 856-694-0400
Fax: 856-694-4597
Web: http://www.pioneerpowdercoating.com
Email: Fred@pioneerpowdercoating.com

Number of Employees: 132
President: Delbert W. Johnson
CEO: Delbert W. Johnson
Research & Development: Pinakin Patel

Thermoset powder coatings.

Pittcon Architectural Metals

6409 Rhode Island Avenue
Riverdale MD 20737
Phone: 301-927-1000
Fax: 301-699-8690
Web: http://www.pittconindustries.com
Email: support@pittconindustries.com

Number of Employees: 10-49

Manufacturing Operations Manager: Robert Dean

Architectural finishes, branches in Arizona and Maryland.

PJH Brands

8747 East Via de Commercio
Scottsdale AZ 85258
Phone: 480-991-3137
Toll Free: 800-628-7596
Fax: 480-607-1550
Web: http://www.pjhbrands.com
Email: info@pj1.com

Number of Employees: 10-49
CEO: P.J. Harvey

Specialty lubricants, paints and maintenance products.

Plascoat Systems

4115 Sherbrooke St. West
Suite 610
Montreal QU
Phone: 514-931-7278
Toll Free: 800-489 7236
Fax: 514-931-7200
Web: http://www.plascoat.com
Email: sales@plascoat.com

Number of Employees: 9
President: Lawrence Moquett
CEO: Lawrence Moquett
Marketing Manager: Lawrence Moquett
Sales Manager: Lawrence Moquett

Thermoplastic powder coatings.

Plastic Coatings

PO Box 1068
St. Albans WV 25177
Phone: 304-755-9151
Fax: 304-755-0229
Web: http://www.plasticoating.com

Annual Sales: $1 Million
Number of Employees: 7
President: Larry Widdecombe
CEO: Larry Widdecombe
Manufacturing Operations Manager: Larry Widdecombe

Thermal and waterproofing coatings.

Pleko Southwest

222 South date Street
Mesa AZ 85210
Phone: 480- 968-0113
Web: http://www.pleko.com

Number of Employees: 20
President: Larry C Fischer

Stucco paints.

Polibrid Coatings

6700 FM 802
Brownsville TX 78526
Phone: 956-831-7818
Fax: 956-831-7810
Web: http://www.polibrid.com
Email: marketing@polibrid.com

Annual Sales: $1-4.5 Million
Number of Employees: 10-49
President: Robert Harrison

Elastomeric polyurethanes coatings for heavy-duty protective coatings and linings.

Polymorphic Polymers

1755 Broadway # 527
New York NY 10019
Phone: 212-262-9220
Toll Free:
Fax: 212-262-9223
Web: http://www.ppccoatings.com
Email: ppc@ppccoatings.com

Annual Sales: $ 9.3 Million
Number of Employees: 10
President: Dr. Bugay
Marketing Manager: Judith Peter
Manufacturing Operations Manager: Richard H. Estes

Products to coat, protect and renovate concrete, metal and fiberglass.

PolySpec

6614 Grant Road
Houston TX 77066
Phone: 281-397-0033
Toll Free: 888-797-0033
Fax: 281-397-6512
Web: http://www.polyspec.com
Email: info@polyspec.com

Annual Sales: $9 Million
Number of Employees: 42
President: Milton Ellisor Jr.

PolySpec manufactures chemical-resistant coatings and linings and floor and polymer products for construction and corrosion protection in industrial, institutional, commercial and marine markets.

Polytech Coating Labs

951 Morgantown Rd.
Reading PA 19607
Phone: 610-375-1175
Toll Free:
Fax: 610-375-8115
Web:
Email: info@polytechcoatingslab.com

Number of Employees: 8
President: James Simpson
CEO: James Simpson
Marketing Manager: James Simpson
Sales Manager: James Simpson
Manufacturing Operations Manager: Nick Nowatarski

Powder coatings

Polyvine USA

S- Polyvine Ltd. (England)
500 Palm Street #22
West Palm Beach FL 33401
Phone: 561-820-1500
Fax: 561-820-1575
Web: http://www.polyvine.com
Email: info@polyvineusa.com

Number of Employees: 30
President: John G. Gleacher
CEO: Eric R. Hanson
Sales Manager: Barry Steinhorn

Varnishes and stains.

Port City Paints

RepcoLite Paints
1250 9th St
Muskegon MI 49440
Phone: 231-726-5911
Fax: 231-722-4081

Annual Sales: $1 - 4.9 Million
Number of Employees: 15-49
Sales Manager: Leigh Strong Jr

Industrial finishes and other.

Potter Paint

21 Crawford Street
PO Box 150Cortland NY 13045
Phone: 607-753-6754
Fax: 607-753-6757

Number of Employees: 20-49
Sales Manager: Peter A. Potter

Industrial coatings.

Powder Technology

551 Alderson Street
Schofield WI 54476
Phone: 715-359-4999
Fax: 715-359-4126
Web: http://www.powdertechnology.com
Email: sales@powdertechnology.com

Annual Sales: $8 Million
Number of Employees: 50
President: Al Towle
CEO: Al Towle
Manufacturing Operations Manager: Louie Stark

The company produces thermosetting powder coatings.

PPG Industries

One PPG Place
Pittsburgh PA 15272
Phone: 412-434-3131
Web: http://www.ppg.com
Email: jmaurer@ppg.com

Annual Sales: $12.2 Billion
Number of Employees: 39,900
CEO: Charles E. Bunch
Research & Development: Charles Kahle II
Marketing Manager: Patrick J. Kenny

PPG is a leading paints, coatings and specialty products company. In 2008 it made one of its largest acquisitions to date- that of SigmaKalon Group bringing a strong architectural paint, protective, marine, and industrial coatings presence into Western and Eastern Europe, Asia, and Africa. Of the $12.2 Billion in annual sales, 34% comes from the Performance Coatings segment, 25% from the Industrial Coatings segment, and 16% from the Architectural Coatings segment. Major end uses are automotive, aircraft, maintenance, packaging and consumer/contractor.

Premier Coating

2250 Arthur Avenue
Elk Grove Village IL 60007
Phone: 847-439-4200
Toll Free: 800-323-0633
Fax: 847-439-4211

Paints, varnishes, stains.

Premier Performance Coatings

D- P&L Plastics
West Plains MO 65775
Phone: 417-255-0552
Web: http://www.pvdfpowders.com/

Number of Employees: 45

Powder coatings for aluminum.

Prime Coatings

PO Box 1223
Amelia LA 70340
Phone: 985-385-5600
Fax: 985-384-1879
Web: http://www.petronet.net
Email: support@petronet.net

Annual Sales: Under $1 Million
Number of Employees: 10-49
President: Richard E Capolupo

Paint for industrial maintenance in Southern Louisiana.

Prism Powder Coatings

2890 Carquest Drive
Brunswick OH 44212
Phone: 330-225-5626
Toll Free: 877-774-7664
Fax: 330-225-5688
Web: http://www.prismpowder.com
Email: sales@prismpowder.com

Annual Sales: $ 25 Million
Number of Employees: 70
President: Raj Patel
Marketing Manager: Barry Keating
Sales Manager: Eduardo Faz
Manufacturing Operations Manager: Rod Graham

Powder coatings

Products/Techniques

PO Box 760
3271 South Riverside Avenue
Bloomington CA 92316
Phone: 909-877-3951
Fax: 909-877-6078
Web: http://www.ptipaint.com
Email: info@ptipaint.com

Annual Sales: $2 Million
Number of Employees: 10
President: Steven D. Andrews
CEO: Steven D. Andrews
Sales Manager: Shirley Turner

Top coats, primers, dry film lubricants and specialty coatings. Applications include wood, concrete, and metal.

Professional Coatings

1807 3rd Avenue Southeast
Cullman AL 35055
Phone: 256-739-1611

Number of Employees: 10
President: Terri Hardien
CEO: Terri Hardien

Paints.

Progress Paint Manufacturing

201 East Market
Louisville KY 40202
Phone: 502-587-8685
Toll Free: 800-626-6407
Web: http://www.progresspaint.com
Email: JimHeil@ProgressPaint.com

Annual Sales: $15 Million
Number of Employees: 200-499
Sales Manager: Jim Heil

Progress produces architectural paints under the Gray Seal and Kurfees names. a small volume of industrial paints in the east, south, and Midwest. It sells through independent paint stores and one company-owned store in Louisville. The company purchased the non-Servistar assets of KCI Kurfees Coatings) from Service Star Coast to Coast Hardware Co. in 1997. The purchase included a plant in Louisville.

217

Progressive Epoxy Polymers

Frog Pond Hollow
48 Wildwood Drive
Pittsfield NH 03263
Phone: 603-435-7199
Fax: 603-435-7182
Web: http://www.epoxyproducts.com
Email: info@epoxyproducts.com

Annual Sales: $1 million
President: Oman Paul

Epoxy coatings for marine and industrial markets.

Protech Powder Coatings

Protech/Oxyplast Group (Canada)
21 Audrey Place
Fairfield NJ 7004
Phone: 973-257-0505
Fax: 973-257-0114
Web: http://www.protechpowder.com
Email: sales@protechpowder.com

Annual Sales: $11.8 Million
Number of Employees: 54
President: James Hardie

The company produces thermoset and other types of powder coatings. It has facilities in New Jersey, Pennsylvania, Canada, South America, Europe, and Africa.

Pruett-Schaffer Chemical

3327 Stafford Street
Pittsburgh PA 15204
Phone: 412-771-2000
Fax: 412-771-2205
Web: http://www.pruett-schaffer.com
Email: info@pruett-schaffer.com

Annual Sales: $14.9 Million
Number of Employees: 10
President: William Coyle
CEO: William Coyle
Research & Development: William Coyle
Marketing Manager: William Coyle
Sales Manager: William Coyle
Manufacturing Operations Manager: William Coyle

Industrial finishes.

Quality Coatings

972 South Green Street
Tupelo MS 38801
Phone: 662-844-2777
Toll Free: 800-816-1065
Fax: 662-680-3251

Annual Sales: $1 - 4.9 Million
Number of Employees: 10-49
President: Dean Keener

Industrial finishes.

Quiet Solution

1250 Elko Drive
Sunnyvale CA 94089
Phone: 408-541-8000
Toll Free: 800-797-8438
Fax: 408-715-2560
Web: http://www.quietsolution.com
Email: info@QuietSolution.com

Acoustical coatings.

Number of Employees: 90-100
President: Kevin Surace
CEO: Kevin Surace
Sales Manager: Pam Preston
Manufacturing Operations Manager: Dale Huber

Quikrete Companies

3490 Piedmont Road
Atlanta GA 30305
Phone: 404-634-9100
Toll Free: 800-282-5828
Fax: 404-841-0289
Web: http://www.quikrete.com

Masonry coatings.

Annual Sales: $111 Million
President: James E. Winchester Jr.

R. J. McGlennon

198 Utah Street
San Francisco CA 94103
Phone: 415-552-0311
Fax: 412-552-8055
Web: http://www.maclac.com
Email: INFO@MACLAC.COM

Wood finishes, also known as Maclac. Branch in Fresno, CA. About 25 employees

Number of Employees: 10-49
CEO: Pat McGlennon

R.C. Shaheen Paint

1400 Street Paul Street
Rochester NY 14621
Phone: 585-266-1500
Web: http://rcshaheen.com/
Email: info@rcshaheen.com

Industrial and house paints.

Number of Employees: 48-50
President: David Shaheen
CEO: Rick Shaheen

RV Tech

801 Magnolia Avenue
Elizabeth NJ 7201
Phone: 908-469-8701
Fax: 908-469-8707

Waterproofing coatings.

Number of Employees: 10
President: Mayur Shah

Raabe

PO Box 1090
Menomonee Falls WI 53052
Phone: 262-255-9500
Toll Free: 800-966-7580
Fax: 262-255-0684
Web: http://www.raabecorp.com

Annual Sales: $12 Million
Number of Employees: 90
President: K J Quinn
CEO: Fred Quinn
Marketing Manager: Kimberly Hein
Manufacturing Operations Manager: Joey Golliver

Raabe produces touch up paints, including aerosols (about 80% of sales), brush-in-cap bottles, and other consumer specialties. About half of sales are from custom color touch-up paints for such end uses as architectural metals, including windows and doors, appliances, lawn mowers, lawn and garden furniture and agriculture equipment. The remainder is derived from custom packaging for paint marketers and manufacturers.

Raffi and Swanson

S- High Street Associates
100 Eames Street
Wilmington MA 01887-3389
Phone: 978-988-0880
Fax: 978-658-3366
Web: http://www.raffiandswanson.com
Email: info@raffiandswanson.com

Annual Sales: $30 Million
Number of Employees: 200
President: William J. Kotek
CEO: William J. Kotek

Raffi and Swanson produces paints and coatings for both rigid and flexible substrates. It also manufactures printing inks and emulsion polymers and performs contract manufacturing.

Ralrube

36977 Fox Glen
Auburn Hills MI 48331
Phone: 248-661-0260
Toll Free: 800-663-4057
Fax: 248-661-3941
Web: http://www.chemsol.com
Email: sales@chemsol.com

Number of Employees: 6
President: Steven Fine

Industrial paints under private label for the automotive aftermarket, boating industry, industrial and government markets. Operates a 10,000 sq ft plant in Bridgewater, MI.

Ranbar Technology

PO Box 607
Route 993Manor PA 15665
Phone: 412-486-1111
Toll Free: 800-486-1113
Fax: 724-864-8232
Web: http://www.ranbar.com
Email: glenshawsales@ranbar.com

Annual Sales: $10 - 24.9 Million
Number of Employees: 10-49
CEO: Randy Russell

UV, alkyd, polyester and other specialty coatings for the steel tube industry.

Randolph Products

33 Haynes Circle
Chicopee MA 01020
Phone: 413-592-4191
Fax: 413-594-7321
Web: http://www.randolphproducts.com/
Email: sales@randolphproducts.com

Annual Sales: $12 Million
Number of Employees: 80
President: Randolph H. Levine
Marketing Manager: Jeff Randolph
Sales Manager: John Smoragiewicz

The company produces aircraft, general industrial, and aerospace coatings under military specifications.

Raven Lining Systems

S- Cohesant Technologies -P
1024 North Lansing Avenue
Tulsa OK 74106
Phone: 918-584-2810
Toll Free: 800-324-2810
Fax: 918-582-4311
Web: http://www.ravenlining.com

Number of Employees: 13
President: Stewart Nance
CEO: Morris Wheeler

Protective coatings and grouts for infrastructure rehabilitation and protection. Applications include concrete or steel pipelines, vaults, tanks, and brick manholes

RBC Industries

80 Cypress Street
PO Box 8340
Warwick RI 02888-2119
Phone: 401-941-3000
Toll Free: 888-722-3769
Fax: 401-941-0150
Web: http://www.rbcepoxy.com/
Email: support@rbcepoxy.com

Annual Sales: $5-15 Million
Number of Employees: 85
President: Kay H. Duckworth, Jr
CEO: Kay H. Duckworth, Jr
Sales Manager: Karlene Kelly

Epoxy, polyester, silicone, adhesive, and UV decorative coatings; flooring coatings.

RCB Elite Coatings

120 Tremon Street
Gordon Georgia 31031
Phone: 478-628-2111
Toll Free: 800-633-5318
Fax: 314-644-3353
Web: http://www.rcbcoatings.com
Email: sales@rcbcoatings.com

Number of Employees: 20-49
President: Andrew Jackson

Railcar, marine, industrial and D.O.T. coatings.

Ready Seal

1440 South Highway 121 Suite 3
Lewisville TX 75067
Phone: 972-434-2028
Toll Free: 888-782-4648
Web: http://www.readyseal.com
Email: webmaster@readyseal.com

Number of Employees: 20
CEO: Mr. Vosburg

Oil based semi-transparent sealer and stain.

Red Spot Paint and Varnish

1107 East Louisiana Street
Evansville IN 47711
Phone: 812-428-9100
Toll Free: 800-457-3544
Fax: 812-428-9167
Email: customerservice@redspot.com

Annual Sales: $11.1 Million
Number of Employees: 480
President: Charles Storms
CEO: Charles Storms
Research & Development: Mark Lutterbach
Sales Manager: David Vranesich
Manufacturing Operations Manager: George P. Lord

Red Spot produces plastics coatings and other industrial finishes. The automotive industry accounts for about 90% of corporate sales, with sales to nearly all automobile manufacturers. Major formulations are two-component polyurethanes and UV-curable coatings. It operates plants in Evansville (351,000 sq ft, 381 employees) and Westland, MI (87,000 sq ft, 101 employees). In 2000 the company acquired Seibert Oxidermo, Inc., Romulus, MI, a producer of coatings for automotive, trucks and off-road equipment, from Detrex Corp. Products are now manufactured in both Red Spot plants.

Reilly Industries

PO Box 42912
Indianapolis IN 46242
Phone: 317-248-6411
Fax: 317-248-6402
Web: http://www.reillypcg.com

Annual Sales: $329.6 Million
Number of Employees: 900
President: Robert D. McNeeley
CEO: Robert D. McNeeley

The Pipeline Coatings Group produces coatings for pipelines.

RepcoLite Paints

473 West 17th Street
Holland MI 49423
Phone: 616-396-1275
Fax: 616-396-9654
Web: http://www.repcolite.com
Email: info@repcolite.com

Annual Sales: $8.2 Million
Number of Employees: 50
President: Dave Altena

The company produces a line of architectural and industrial paints. It acquired Port City Paints.

Rexcel Coatings

4600 Ripley Drive
El Paso TX 79922-1648
Phone: 915-584-9491
Fax: 915-581-9120
Web: http://www.rexcelcoatings.com/

Industrial finishes.

Number of Employees: 20-49
President: Clay Smith

Rich Paint Manufacturing

14 Morton Drive
S. Hutchinson KS 67505
Phone: 316-669-0487
Toll Free: 800-722-4634
Fax: 316-669-0233

Industrial finishes.

Annual Sales: $1-4.9 Million
Number of Employees: 10-49
President: Richard B. Cunningham
CEO: Richard B. Cunningham

Richard's Paint Manufacturing

200 Paint Street
Rockledge FL 32955
Phone: 321-636-6200
Toll Free: 800-432-0983
Fax: 321-633-0866
Web: http://www.richardspaint.com
Email: info@richardspaint.com

Annual Sales: $20 Million
Number of Employees: 120
President: Eric Richard
Sales Manager: Chuck Gantz
Manufacturing Operations Manager: Edward Richard Jr.

The company manufactures architectural and industrial coatings at a 62,000 sq ft facility. Products include acrylic and PVA interior and exterior house paints and construction coatings and urethane and acrylic industrial enamels, epoxies, and aliphatic urethane industrial coatings. Annual capacity is over 2 million gallons.

Richardson Paint

4821 Garden Street
Philadelphia PA 19137
Phone: 215-535-4500
Fax: 215-535-7884

Maintenance coatings, roofing coatings

Riley Paint

106 Washington Street
Burlington IA 52601
Phone: 319-753-0309
Toll Free: 800-635-2663
Fax: 319- 753-1038
Web: http://www.rileypaint.com
Email: contactus@rileypaint.com

Annual Sales: $5 - $10 Million
Number of Employees: 9-29
President: James S. Jennison
Marketing Manager: Jim Jennison
Manufacturing Operations Manager: Bob Crawford

Industrial and roof coatings

Rinchem

4115 East Jackson Street
Phoenix AZ 85019
Phone: 602-233-2000
Web: http://www.rinchem.com
Email: sales@rinchem.com

Number of Employees: 10-49
President: Jim Moore

Paints.

River Valley Coatings

800 North Highland Avenue
Aurora IL 60506
Phone: 630-896-8333
Fax: 630-896-4683

Industrial finishes.

Rock-Tred

3415 Howard Street
Skokie IL 60076
Phone: 847-673-8200
Toll Free: 800-762-8733
Fax: 847-679-6665
Web: http://www.rocktred.com
Email: sales@rocktred.com

Number of Employees: 20
President: Paul L. Matson
Marketing Manager: Kathy Zellermayer
Sales Manager: Bryan Miller
Manufacturing Operations Manager: Lori Goucher

Polymer flooring coatings, such as epoxies, urethanes, and acrylics

Rodda Paint

6107 N. Marine Drive
Portland OR 97203
Phone: 503-521-4300
Toll Free: 800-242-3713
Fax: 503-521-4400
Web: http://www.roddapaint.com/

Annual Sales: $74.5 Million
Number of Employees: 200-300
President: Al Mordy
CEO: Al Mordy
Research & Development: Mark Holcomb
Marketing Manager: Todd Braden
Sales Manager: Bill Boone
Manufacturing Operations Manager: Mark Holcomb

Rodda produces a line of consumer paints and some industrial finishes, which are sold principally in 44 retail outlets in Oregon, Washington Idaho and Alaska. In 2004 Rodda and Cloverdale Paint agreed to merge. Business will be conducted under the Rodda name in the United States and under the Cloverdale name in Canada.

Rohm and Haas Chemicals

Dow Chemical100 Independence Mall West
Philadelphia PA 19106
Phone: 215-592-3000
Fax: 215-592-3377
Web: http://www.rohmhaas.com; www.dow.com

Rohm and Haas' 8 locations were acquired by Dow Chemical in 2009.

Royal Chemical

8679 Freeway Drive
Macedonia OH 44056
Phone: 330-467-1300
Toll Free:
Fax: 330-468-1289
Web: http://www.royalchemical.com
Email: info@royalchemical.com

Number of Employees: 25-49
Research & Development: Alexander Beveridge
Marketing Manager: Marilyn Radu
Sales Manager: Marilyn Radu

Custom chemical compounder, contract manufacturer and toll blender of cleaning compounds, coatings, soaps and detergents for the metal finishing, janitorial, laundry, food and dairy industries.

Royston Laboratories

D- Chase Corp.
128 First Street
Pittsburgh PA 15238
Phone: 412-828-1500
Toll Free: 800-245-3209
Fax: 412-828-4826
Web: http://www.roystonlab.com
Email: Royston@chasecorp.com

Annual Sales: $5.3 Million
Number of Employees: 40
Sales Manager: Joan Greygor
Manufacturing Operations Manager: Doug Zuberer

Royston produces insulating and protective mastics, coatings, and tapes for pipelines, bridges, and highways, and also waterproof membranes for highways and commercial and residential construction.

RPM

2628 Pearl Road
PO Box 777
Medina OH 44258
Phone: 330-273-5090
Fax: 330-225-8743
Web: http://www.rpminc.com
Email: Info@rpminc.com

Annual Sales: $3.4 Billion
Number of Employees: 9,700
President: Frank Sullivan
CEO: Frank Sullivan
Manufacturing Operations Manager: Paul G. Hoogenboom

A multinational holding company with subsidiaries that manufacture and market high-performance coatings, sealants and specialty chemicals, primarily for maintenance and improvement. In 2009, sales were $3.4 billion, with 67 percent to industry worldwide and the remaining 33 percent to consumers mainly in North America. It operates 92 manufacturing facilities in 22 countries. Its products are sold in approximately 150 countries and territories.

Rudd

1141 Northwest 50th Street
Seattle WA 98107
Phone: 206-789-1000
Toll Free: 800-444-7833
Fax: 206-789-1001
Web: http://www.ruddcompany.com
Email: info@ruddcompany.com

Annual Sales: $18 Million
Number of Employees: 60
CEO: Alan Park

Four units are involved in paints and coatings. The OEM Wood Coatings division manufactures stains and coatings for the wood industry; The Forest Products division produces marking paints for the forest industry and other end uses; The Aerosol & Specialty Products division performs custom and contract aerosol packaging; and Preferred Products, Inc. produces floor finishes. Most sales are in 11 western states and British Columbia.

Rutland Fire Clay

PO Box 340
38 Merchants Row
Rutland VT 05702-0340
Phone: 802-775-5519
Toll Free: 800-544-1307
Fax: 802-775-5262
Web: http://www.rutland.com
Email: sales@rutland.com

Number of Employees: 26
President: Thomas Martin

Stove paints. Manufacturing at Jacksonville, ILAlso produces sealants for fire places and stoves.

Safety Coatings

PO Box 399
Foley AL 36536
Phone: 251-943-1638
Toll Free: 800-557-8810
Fax: 251-943-3689
Web: http://www.safetycoatings.com
Email: info@safetycoatings.com

Number of Employees: 15
President: Charles D.Carneal
CEO: Charles D.Carneal
Research & Development: Charles D.Carneal
Sales Manager: Janay Stuckey
Manufacturing Operations Manager: Michael Morris

Traffic and parking lot marking paints.

Sampson Coatings

1900 Ellen Road
Richmond VA 23230
Phone: 804-359-5011
Toll Free: 800-368-2677
Fax: 804-359-2945
Web: http://www.sampsoncoatings.com
Email: mclarke@sampsoncoatings.com

Annual Sales: $125 Million
Marketing Manager: Bill Nicol
Sales Manager: Dan Corrieri
Manufacturing Operations Manager: Mike Clarke

Sampson produces paints, lacquers, roof coatings, and industrial coatings for wood, metal, concrete and other surfaces.

Sanchem

1600 South Canal Street
Chicago IL 60616
Phone: 312-733-6100
Toll Free: 800-621-1603
Fax: 312-733-7432
Web: http://www.sanchem.com

Annual Sales: $3 Million
Number of Employees: 22
President: Estelle Flicher

Rust and corrosion preventive coatings.

Sandstrom Products

224 Main Street
Port Byron IL 61275
Phone: 309-523-2121
Toll Free: 800-747-1084
Fax: 309-523-3912
Web: http://www.sandstromproducts.com
Email: mark@sandstromproducts.co

Annual Sales: $6 Million
Number of Employees: 40
President: Brian Suhl
Research & Development: Russ Burt
Sales Manager: Mark Lousberg
Manufacturing Operations Manager: Dave Steele

Sandstrom manufactures marine paints, flooring coatings, tennis court coatings, weapons coatings, dry film lubricants, sign paints, EMI/RFI shield coatings, driveway coatings and sealers, waterproofing paints, adhesives, repair and patching products and similar items, both solvent and waterborne.

Schafco Packaging

PO Box 893
730 Georgetown Road
Lancaster PA 17608-0893
Phone: 717-687-7017
Fax: 717-687-0812
Web: http://www.schafco.com
Email: sales@schafco.com

President: Brian Schaefer

Industrial finishes, aerosols, and related packaging. (Formerly Schaefer Paint.)

Schilling Enamels

12532 Triskett Road
Cleveland OH 44111
Phone: 216-252-6242
Fax: 216-252-6248

Number of Employees: 10-49
President: Alfred Schilling Sr.

Paints, coatings, and wallpaper.

SDC Technologies

45 Parker
Ste 100
Irvine CA 92618
Phone: 714-939-8300
Toll Free:
Fax: 714-939-8330
Web: http://www.sdctech.com
Email: customercare@sdctech.com

Annual Sales: $20 Million
Number of Employees: 50-99
President: William A. Gregg
CEO: William A. Gregg
Marketing Manager: Tony Grigoriou
Sales Manager: Sapna Blackburn

The company manufactures abrasion-resistant coatings for metals, plastics and glass.

Seaboard Asphalt Products

3601 Fairfield Road
Baltimore MD 21226
Phone: 410-355-0330
Toll Free: 800-536-0332
Fax: 410-355-5864
Web: http://www.seaboardasphalt.com
Email: sales@seaboardasphalt.com

Annual Sales: $4.2 Million
Sales Manager: Shawn R. Campbell

Roofing and foundation coatings.

Seagrave Coatings

209 N. Michigan Avenue
Kenilworth NJ 7033
Phone: 201-933-1000
Toll Free: 800-426-0496
Fax: 201-933-3646
Web: http://www.seagravecoatings.com
Email: lab@seagravecoatings.com

Number of Employees: 50
CEO: Peter Tepperman

Seagrave produces such industrial finishes as wood coatings, glass and maintenance paints, special effect paints, varnishes and shellacs for aerospace, industrial, defense, maintenance and home furnishing markets. Sherwin-Williams purchased Seagrave Coatings, Portsmouth, VA, a sister company, in 1996. The company produced products for the marine industry under the Seaguard name.

Seal Master

2520 South Campbell Street
Sandusky OH 44870
Phone: 419-626-4375
Toll Free: 800-395-7325
Fax: 419-626-5477
Web: http://www.sealmaster.net
Email: info@sealmaster.net

Annual Sales: $3 Million
Number of Employees: 200
President: Edward L. Bittle

Sealers, additives, paints and crack fillers for surfaces.

Seal Peel

Calmar
PO Box 250
Troy MI 48099
Phone: 248-540-8393
Web: http://sealpeel.com
Email: sales@sealpeel.com

Number of Employees: 5-9

Hot melt wax protective coatings; strippable coating products.

Seal-Krete

Convenience Products
306 Gandy Road
Auburndale FL 33823
Phone: 863-967-1535
Toll Free: 800-323-7357
Fax: 863-965-2326
Web: http://www.seal-krete.com
Email: sales@seal-krete.com

Number of Employees: 10-49
President: David Shumate

Concrete, waterproofing, skid-proof, luminescent, graffiti-barrier coatings.

Sea-Master Marine Coatings

Mar Max Supply
993 Sheldon Road
Channelview TX 77530
Phone: 281-452-6200

Marine coatings-paints and varnishes.

SEM Products

651 Michael Wylie Drive
Charlotte NC 28217
Phone: 704-522-1006
Toll Free: 800-831-1122
Fax: 714-522-7008
Web: http://www.semproducts.com/
Email: cservice@sem.ws

Annual Sales: $1 Billion
Number of Employees: 1,000
President: Richard Menze
Marketing Manager: Brian Joyner
Sales Manager: Patrick McAvoy

Automotive repair and refinishing adhesives and coatings.

Sentinel Paint & Varnish

2301 North Pulaski Road
Chicago IL 60639
Phone: 773-342-1272
Toll Free: 800-373-0633
Web: http://www.senpro.com
Email: getinfo@senpro.com

Annual Sales: Under $1 Million
Number of Employees: 5-9
Sales Manager: Maureen Mann

Architectural paints.

Sermatech International

Praxair Surface Technologies
159 S. Limerick Road
Royersford PA 19458
Phone: 610-474-1200
Fax: 610-474-1191
Web: http://www.sermatech.com
Email: info@sermatech.com

Annual Sales: $85 Million
Number of Employees: 500
President: Mark F. Gruninger

Engineered protective coatings for the aerospace, chemical processing, industrial, oil & gas, and semiconductor markets.

Seymour of Sycamore

917 Crosby Avenue
Sycamore IL 60178
Phone: 815-895-9101
Toll Free: 800-435-4482
Fax: 815-895-8475
Web: http://www.seymourpaint.com

Annual Sales: $37 Million
Number of Employees: 130
President: Nancy Heatley
CEO: Nancy Heatley
Marketing Manager: John Wilson

Seymour manufactures aerosol and bulk paint coatings and chemicals for automotive, industrial, marine and hardware markets.

Shakertown

PO Box 400
Winlock WA 98596
Phone: 360-785-3501
Toll Free: 800-426-8970
Fax: 360-785-3076
Web: http://www.shakertown.com

Annual Sales: $10 Million
Number of Employees: 50
Sales Manager: Jeff Coffey

Shakertown manufactures stains for captive use to stain cedar shakes and panels and also for sale to distributors, modular home builders, manufacturers and paint stores.

Shannon Luminous Materials

304A North Townsend Street
Santa Ana CA 92703
Phone: 714-550-9931
Toll Free: 800.543.4485
Fax: 714.550.9938
Web: http://www.blacklite.com

Annual Sales: Under $1 Million
Number of Employees: 10-49
President: Richard F Cruce

Luminous coatings.

Sheboygan Paint

1439 North 25th Street
Sheboygan WI 53082
Phone: 920-458-2157
Toll Free: 800-773-7801
Fax: 920-458-5620
Web: http://www.shebpaint.com
Email: info@shebpaint.com

Annual Sales: $20 Million
Number of Employees: 90
President: Charlie Malingowski

Sheboygan Paint manufactures a wide line of maintenance and powder coatings. End uses include agricultural equipment; container refinishing; electric motors, generators, and transformers; gasoline engines; molded wood flour toilet seats; fabricated plastics; transportation; warehouse racking; and wood finishing. Technologies are alkyds, urethanes, high solids, water reducible, and epoxies. It operates plants in Sheboygan, MI and in Cedartown, GA. Sheboygan acquired Sentry Paint in 2003, a producer of military spec paints, primers, enamels, primers, and undercoats.

Sheffield Bronze Paint

17814 South Waterloo Road
Cleveland OH 44119
Phone: 216-481-8330
Fax: 216-481-6606

Annual Sales: $7.2 Million

Specialty coatings.

Sherwin-Williams

101 W. Prospect Avenue
Cleveland OH 44115
Phone: 216-566-2000
Fax: 216-566-2559
Web: http://www.sherwin-williams.com

Annual Sales: $7.1 Billion
Number of Employees: 29,220
President: John G. Morikis
CEO: Christopher M. Connor

For more than 140 years it has been a leader in coatings technology. Global capabilities include aerospace coatings, automotive finishes, protective and marine coatings, and product finishes. The Cosumer Group sales ($1.23 billion) made up 17% of total sales, Global Finishes Group ($1.65 billion) made up 23% of sales, and Paint Stores Group ($4.21 Billion) made up 59% of sales.

Shubert Paints

2157 Mountain Industrial Boulevard
Tucker GA 30084
Phone: 770-938-3600
Fax: 770-938-9508
Web: http://shubertpaintsinc.com
Email: shubertpaintsinc@bellsouth.net

Annual Sales: $1.4 Million
Number of Employees: 10-15
President: Jeff Shubert

Environmentally safe (no mercury, lead, or ethylene glycol) specialty coatings for consumers.

Sico

Akzo Nobel Canada
2505 de la Metropole
Longueuil QB J4G 1E5
Phone: 514-527-5111
Toll Free: 800-463-7426
Fax: 450-651-1257
Web: http://www.sico.com
Email: info@sico.ca

Annual Sales: $243 million
Number of Employees: 950
President: Pierre Dufresne
CEO: Pierre Dufresne

Sico is the largest Canadian manufacturer of architectural paint and a supplier of metal coatings to the transportation industry. It operates 6 plants in Quebec and Ontario. The company manufactures architectural paints, stains, varnishes, caulking compounds and related products (sales C$234 million). It holds 24% of the Canadian market for architectural coatings.

Sigma Coatings USA

PPG
1401 Destrehan
Harvey LA 70058
Phone: 504-347-4321
Fax: 504-341-9120
Web: http://www.sigmacoatings.com
Email: sigma@sigmacoatingsusa.com

Annual Sales: $35 Million
Number of Employees: 170
President: Marcel de Wolf
CEO: Marcel de Wolf
Marketing Manager: Azucena R. Overman

Sigma Coatings is a brand of PPG--a strong brand in the architectural, shipping, protective and industrial application of paint and coatings worldwide. These can be used for decorating, marine, protective and industrial purposes. Major end uses are oil and gas refineries, pipelines, storage tanks and off-shore platforms and drilling rigs; power generation plants and equipment; petrochemicals; pulp and paper; bridges; water and waste treatment facilities; food and beverage; and transportation equipment.

Sika

S - Sika AG-P (Switzerland)
201 Polito Avenue
Lyndhurst NJ 07071
Phone: 201-933-8800
Fax: 201-933-6225
Web: http://www.sikausa.com
Email: info@sika-corp.com

Annual Sales: $130 Million
Number of Employees: 900
President: William L. Pringle
Marketing Manager: Russ Livermore
Sales Manager: Stephen L. Hall

Sika produces a limited volume of coatings and primers, primarily for concrete and masonry. Major products are sealants, adhesives, concrete mixes, specialty mortars, epoxies, structural strengthening systems, industrial flooring, and specialty acoustic reinforcing materials.

Silpro

2 New England Way
Ayer MA 01432-1514
Phone: 978-772-4444
Toll Free: 800-343-1501
Fax: 978-772-7456
Web: http://www.silpro.com
Email: info@silpro.com

Annual Sales: $75 Million
President: Ray Andrews
CEO: Heydon Hall

Masonry coatings.

Silversword

1320 Centre Street
Newton Center MA 02459
Phone: 617-965-9696
Toll Free: 800-225-4444
Fax: 617-965-9690
Web: http://www.sclsterling.com
Email: info@sclsterling.com

Annual Sales: $5 - 9.9 Million
Number of Employees: 10-49

Specialty coatings.

Simpson CoatingsGroup

111 South Maple Avenue
S. San Francisco CA 94080
Phone: 650-873-5990
Toll Free: 800-877-5997
Fax: 650-873-7441
Web: http://www.simpsoncoatings.com

President: T. Simpson

Traffic/curb marking paints, wood coatings, urethane/epoxy coatings, industrial/enamel coatings, lacquers, and specialty products.

Soc-Co Plastic Coating

11251 Jersey Boulevard
Rancho Cucamonga CA 91730
Phone: 909-987-4753
Fax: 909-987-6335
Web: http://www.soccoplastics.com
Email: jgrace999@msn.com

Number of Employees: 10-49
Sales Manager: Peter Michael Smits

Plastic coatings for petro-chemical, chemical, power, aerospace, water, wastewater, food and drug industries.

Somay Products

4301 Northwest 35th Avenue
Miami FL 33142-4382
Phone: 305-633-6333
Toll Free: 888-247-6629
Fax: 305-638-5524
Web: http://www.somay.com
Email: paint@somay.com

Number of Employees: 2,300
President: Garth R. Parker
CEO: Garth R. Parker

Architectural paints, traffic marking, concrete and floor coatings, roof paints.

Sound Specialty Coatings

PO Box 13160
Burton WA 98013
Phone: 206-517-2611
Toll Free: 800-261-4207
Fax: 206-517-2783
Web: http://www.soundspecialtycoatings.com
Email: sales@soundspecialtycoatings.com

Epoxies and coatings for acoustical flooring, clean rooms, rebars, fisheries, the lining of brewery tanks, and marine vessels.

Southern Aerosols

325 Clear View Drive
Cleveland NC 27013
Phone: 704-278-9800

Annual Sales: $4.9 Million
Number of Employees: 18172

Aerosol paints.

Southern Diversified Products

2714 Hardy Street
Hattiesburg MS 39400
Phone: 601-271-2588
Toll Free: 888-714-9422
Fax: 601-296-7351
Web: http://www.southerndiversifiedproucts.com

Annual Sales: Under $ 1 Million

Develops and markets American Pride ® Interior Paints in cooperation with the University of Southern Mississippi. American Pride® paints are Green Wise certified, are always solvent-free (zero VOC), and never contain chemicals that are suspected carcinogens.

Southwestern Paint & Supplies

5036 E. Broadway Boulevard
Tucson AZ 85711
Phone: 520-795-0545

Number of Employees: 5-9
President: Robert Torres

Since 1952, paints at 2 store locations.

Specialty Coating

1012 Commercial Boulevard, North
Arlington TX 76001
Phone: 817-467-1111
Toll Free: 800-344-4250
Fax: 817-465-1304
Web: http://www.fluid-aire.com/
Email: jsawyer@fluid-aire.com

Annual Sales: $9 Million
President: Paul Sawyer
CEO: Paul Sawyer
Sales Manager: Ernie Divin

Industrial finishes.

Specialty Coatings

2500 Delta Lane
Elk Grove Village IL 60007
Phone: 847-766-3555
Toll Free: 800-782-2400
Fax: 847-766-3595
Web: http://www.specialty-coatings.com
Email: salesinfo@specialty-coatings.com

Annual Sales: $23 Million
Number of Employees: 85
President: Jack Leens

The company is reportedly the leading supplier of coatings for aluminum and steel coil coaters. Applications include commercial and residential construction, automotive parts, office furniture, computer parts, house ware products, blinds, drapery accessories, appliances and suspended ceiling systems.

Specialty Coatings & Chemicals

7360 Varna Avenue
North Hollywood CA 91605
Phone: 323-875-0233
Fax: 818-764-8669
Web: http://www.specialtycoatingsnchem.com/

Annual Sales: $10 - 24.9 Million
Number of Employees: 20-49
President: Alastair MacDonald

Industrial finishes, UV cured coatings

Specialty Polymer Coatings

1500 West Esplanade Avenue
Kenner LA 70062
Phone: 504-469-0661
Web: http://www.spc-net.com/

Annual Sales: $2346 Million
Number of Employees: 3,632
President: Bob Alliston
CEO: Bob Alliston
Sales Manager: Darryl Hanks

Liquid epoxy and polyurethane coatings for marine, industrial and pipeline markets.

Spectra-Tone Paint

PPG-Pittsburgh Paint Architectural Finishes
1595 East San Bernardino Avenue
San Bernardino CA 92408-2946
Phone: 909-478-3485
Toll Free: 800-272-4687
Fax: 909-478-3499
Web: http://www.ppgaf.com

Annual Sales: $13 Million
Number of Employees: 60
Sales Manager: Rodney Jones

Spectra-Tone manufactures primarily architectural coatings at a 60,800 sq ft facility.

Spectrum Coatings Laboratories

217 Chapman Street
Providence RI 02905
Phone: 401-781-4847
Fax: 401-781-1075
Web: http://www.spectrumcoatings.us/

Annual Sales: $1 - 4.9 Million
Number of Employees: 10-49
Manufacturing Operations Manager: Earl Faria

Military spec. coatings, other

Spectrum Paints

3859 Covington Highway
Decatur GA 30032
Phone: 770-981-3349
Fax: 770-442-1093
Web: http://www.spectrumpaintsinc.com/

Annual Sales: $10 Million
Number of Employees: 50
President: Bipin Merchant

Spectrum produces branded and private label architectural paints at a 60,000-sq ft facility. It operates seven stores in the Atlanta area. The company claims to be the largest locally owned manufacturer of architectural paints in Atlanta and North Georgia.

Spray Products

1323 Conshohocken Rd
Plymouth Meeting PA 19462
Phone: 610-277-1010
Toll Free: 800-543-7710
Fax: 610-277-4390
Web: http://www.orbindustries.com
Email: info@sprayproducts.com

Annual Sales: $25 Million
President: Andrew Bastian

Automotive and industrial aerosol products and spray paints.

Spraylat

143 Sparks Avenue
Pelham NY 10803
Phone: 914-738-1600
Toll Free: 800-867-7729
Fax: 914-712-2838
Web: http://www.spraylat.com
Email: macrem@spraylat.com

Annual Sales: $114 Million
Number of Employees: 350
President: Raymond T. Chlodney
CEO: Michael Borner
Marketing Manager: Frank Manning
Sales Manager: Mike Macrae
Manufacturing Operations Manager: Lyle Schott

Spraylat manufactures over 100 coatings is organized into four business units: Liquid Coatings, Powder Coatings, Conductive Coatings, and Mirror Coatings. It has facilities in the United States (4), Germany (2), Turkey (1), Korea (1), Japan (1), Taiwan (1), the Philippines (1), Singapore (1), and China (2). US sales are estimated at $70 million.

Stabler Paint Manufacturing

2700 25th Street
North Birmingham AL 35207
Phone: 205-328-6331
Fax: 205-252-0750

Number of Employees: 5
Manufacturing Operations Manager: J. P. Jones

Industrial coatings.

Stahl USA

Stahl International BV (Netherlands)
13 Corwin Street
Peabody MA 1960
Phone: 978-531-0371
Fax: 978-532-9062
Web: http://www.stahl.com

Annual Sales: $35 Million
Number of Employees: 100

The Permuthane business under the Performance Coatings sector of Stahl produces coatings and finishes for the synthetic leather, automotive interior, textiles and floor coverings.

Standard Coating

461 South Broad Avenue
Ridgefield NJ 07657
Phone: 201-945-5058
Toll Free: 800-772-3675
Fax: 201-945-5483
Web: http://www.nitrostan.com/

Number of Employees: 5
Manufacturing Operations Manager: David Rooth

Automotive coatings.

Standard Tar Products

2456 West Cornell Street
Milwaukee WI 53209
Phone: 414-873-7650
Toll Free: 800-825-7650
Fax: 414-873-7737
Web: http://www.icemelters.com
Email: standtar@aol.com

Annual Sales: $24.9 Million
Number of Employees: 10-49
President: Edward Chouinard
CEO: Edward Chouinard
Marketing Manager: Rick May

The company produces log home and wood coatings, stains, finishes and sealers and also ice melters and deicers.

Star Bronze

803 South Mahoning Avenue
PO Box 2206
Alliance OH 44601-0206
Phone: 330-823-1550
Toll Free: 800-321-9870
Web: http://www.starbronze.com
Email: email@starbronze.com

Number of Employees: 5,000
President: James Raber

Paint, clear wood finishes and stains.

Starlite Paint & Varnish

724 East 140th Street
Bronx NY 10454
Phone: 718-292-6420
Web: http://www.steelcotemfg.com

Architectural and industrial coatings.

Steelcote Manufacturing

5147 Natural Bridge
St. Louis MO 63115
Phone: 314-771-8053
Toll Free: 800-737-0282
Fax: 314-771-7581
Web: http://www.steelcotemfg.com
Email: info@steelcotemfg.com

Annual Sales: $1 Million
Number of Employees: 5
President: John Milner
CEO: John Milner
Marketing Manager: Tim Mauzy
Sales Manager: Tim Mauzy
Manufacturing Operations Manager: Sally Acey

Coatings for plant maintenance.

Sterling Lacquer Manufacturing

S- *Sunbrite Manufacturing*
3150 Brannon Avenue
St. Louis MO 63139
Phone: 314-776-4450
Fax: 314-771-1858
Web: http://www.detcomarine.com

Annual Sales: $5 Million
Number of Employees: 40
President: Leo V Mitchell
CEO: Leo V Mitchell
Marketing Manager: Debra Bartooa
Sales Manager: Debra Bartooa

The company manufactures coatings and caulks for yachts, including Sterling brand two-component aliphatic linear polyurethane primers and lacquers and varnish under the Detco Marine Crystal brand. Detco also produces two-component deck and hull caulks.

Sto Corporation

3800 Camp Creek Parkway
Building 1400, Suite 120
Atlanta GA 30331
Phone: 404-346-3666
Toll Free: 800-221-2397
Fax: 404-346-3119
Web: http://www.stocorp.com
Email: marketingsupport@stocorp.com

Annual Sales: $25 Million
Number of Employees: 150
President: David Boivin
CEO: David Boivin
Research & Development: Tom Remmele
Marketing Manager: Alec Minne
Sales Manager: Larry Kushner

Sto manufactures specialty coatings, exterior claddings, including EIFS (synthetic stucco) and hard coat stucco and also concrete repair and air and moisture barrier products. Plants are located in Atlanta, Rutland, VT, and Glendale, AZ and Albuquerque , NM.

Strathmore Products

1970 West Fayette Street
PO Box 151
Syracuse NY 13201
Phone: 315-488-5401
Fax: 315-488-2715
Web: http://www.strathmoreproducts.com
Email: info@strathmoreproducts.com

Annual Sales: $9 Million
Number of Employees: 30
President: William M. Udovich
CEO: Eric T. Burr

Strathmore produces chemical coatings, lacquers, and water-reducible finishes, and paints.

Stuart Industrial Coatings

11740 South Front Avenue
Chicago IL 60628
Phone: 773-928-0202
Fax: 773-928-4616
Email: stuartindcoat@sbcglobal.net

Number of Employees: 10
President: M. Kowalsai
CEO: M. Kowalsai

Industrial finishes, lacquers.

Sumter Coatings

2410 Highway 15 South
Sumter SC 29154
Phone: 803-481-3400
Toll Free: 888-471-3400
Fax: 803-481-3776
Web: http://www.sumtercoatings.com
Email: kharkins@sumtercoatings.com

Annual Sales: $15 Million
Number of Employees: 60
President: Ross McKenzie
Research & Development: Randy White
Sales Manager: Jimmy Reynolds
Manufacturing Operations Manager: Brad Wooten

Coatings, primers, and sealers for industrial applications

Sun Paints & Coatings

4701 E. 7th Avenue
Tampa FL 33605
Phone: 813-367-4444
Fax: 813-367-0263
Web: http://www.suncoatings.com

Annual Sales: $7.4 Million
President: Barton J. Malina

Low VOC coatings and adhesives, clear and white latex coatings. Private label partners and chain of SunKote stores. 90,000 sq. ft. production facility.

Sundur Powder Coatings

824 South Vandeventer Avenue
St Louis MO 63110
Phone: 314-531-4950
Fax: 314-531-5002
Web: http://www.sundur.com

Number of Employees: 30
President: Leo Mitchell
CEO: Leo Mitchell
Research & Development: Leo Mitchell
Marketing Manager: Leo Mitchell
Sales Manager: Leo Mitchell
Manufacturing Operations Manager: Leo Mitchell

Powder coatings.

Super Stone

1251 Burlington Street
Opa-Locka FL 33054
Phone: 305-681-3561
Toll Free: 800-456-3561
Fax: 305-681-5106
Web: http://www.superstone.com
Email: superstone@superstone.com

Number of Employees: 40
Sales Manager: Germania Hernandez
Manufacturing Operations Manager: Gerry Sadleir

Coatings.

Superior Coatings

S-Gemini Industries.
550 Fort William Road
Dallas TX 75217
Phone: 807-345-4511
Fax: 807-345-3656
Web: http://www.superiorcoatings.com
Email: info@superiorcoatings.ca

Wood finishes.

Number of Employees: 60
President: Hector Arrellano

Superior Environmental Products

4101 Lindbergh Drive
Addison TX 75001
Phone: 972-490-0566
Fax: 972-490-0567
Web: http://www.novocoat.com/
Email: info@novocoat.com

100% solids industrial coatings.

Number of Employees: 1-10
President: Roger Shafen
CEO: Roger Shafen

Surface Protection Industries

3411 East 15th Street
Los Angeles CA 90023
Phone: 323-269-9231
Toll Free: 800-360-7744
Fax: 323-307-4111
Web: http://www.zolatoneaim.com
Email: customersupport@zolatoneaim.com

The company makes OEM produces refinishes, clear coats and primers under the Zolatone name.

Annual Sales: $10 - 24.9 Million
Number of Employees: 200-499
Sales Manager: Cindy Berger

Surface Research

S- Franklin Steel
1333 Research Road, Gahanna Industrial Park
Reynoldsburg OH 43068
Phone: 614-861-4524

Paint for steel drums, industrial finishes

Surplus Coatings

2900 Wilson Avenue Southwest
Suite 700
Grandville MI 49418
Phone: 616-538-4050
Toll Free: 800-804-8003
Fax: 616-538-9260
Web: http://www.surpluscoatings.com
Email: sales@surpluscoatings.com

Recycled and virgin powder coatings.

Number of Employees: 10-25
President: Dwayne Behrens
Sales Manager: Bill MacKechnie

Synta

675 Park North Boulevard
Ste 120
Clarkston GA 30030
Phone: 404-508-9194
Fax: 404-508-9905
Web: http://www.synta.com
Email: Info@synta.com

Number of Employees: 26
President: Thomas Curtis

Specialty architectural coatings, Americolor ™ latex paints, craft paints, and industrial coatings.

T.J. Ronan Paint

749 East 135th Street
Bronx NY 10454
Phone: 718-292-1100
Toll Free: 800-247-6626
Fax: 718-292-0406
Web: http://ronanpaints.com/
Email: info@ronanpaints.com

Annual Sales: $9 Million
Sales Manager: Bob Chlupsa

Decorative paints.

Tamms Industries

3835 State Route 72
Kirkland IL 60146
Phone: 815-522-3394
Toll Free: 800-862-2667
Fax: 815-522-2323
Web: http://www.tamms.com
Email: info@tamms.com

Annual Sales: $8.8 Million
President: M. Thomas McCall
Marketing Manager: Stephen Scarpinato

Concrete restoration, curing, coating, grouting, traffic deck systems, and waterproofing products.

Tanglefoot

314 Straight Avenue Southwest
Grand Rapids MI 49504-6485
Phone: 616-459-4139
Fax: 616-459-4140
Web: http://www.tanglefoot.com
Email: info@tanglefoot.com

Annual Sales: $1 Million
President: Joe Skendzel

Tree sealing paints.

TCI Coatings

220 Industrial Boulevard
Austin TX 78745
Phone: 512-442-1488
Fax: 512-442-6759
Email: susan@tci-coatings.co

Annual Sales: $2 Million
Number of Employees: 20
President: Kathleen Tims
CEO: Kathleen Tims

Protective coatings distributed in Southwest

Technical Coatings

56 Clarendon Avenue
Kingston NY 12401
Phone: 845-331-7777
Fax: 845-339-0434
Web: http://www.techcoatings.com
Email: tccoatings@hvc.rr.com

Number of Employees: 14
President: Gerard Duffy

Powder coatings and industrial finishing done at a 12,000 sq. ft. facility for short and production-sized runs.

Technical Coatings Laboratory

205 Old Farms Road
PO Box 205
Avon CT 06001
Phone: 860-673-3245
Toll Free: 800-782-8704
Fax: 860-673-3688
Web: http://www.e-tcl.com
Email: info@e-tcl.com

Annual Sales: $16.8 Million
President: David W. Jaffin
Research & Development: Alphonso J. Foddrell
Sales Manager: Michael J. Campbell

The company produces hot-stamping foils and specialty coatings and paints

Technical Urethanes

S- Seaward International.
3470 Martinsburg Pike, PO Box 61
Clear Brook VA 22624
Phone: 540-667-1770
Toll Free: 888-832-4842
Fax: 540-667-7987
Web: http://www.polyurethane.com
Email: mail@polyurethane.com

Annual Sales: $9 Million
Number of Employees: 60
Research & Development: John Phillips
Sales Manager: Robert Taylor

Technical Urethanes manufactures polyurea spray elastomer linings

TechStar Industries

740 South Prairie Lane
TSI Industries
Marshfield MO 65706
Phone: 417-859-2275
Fax: 417-468-2195

Number of Employees: 15
President: Adam Donahue
CEO: Adam Donahue

Industrial finishes and maintenance coatings.

Tek-Rap

13835 Old Beaumont Highway
Houston TX 77049
Phone: 281-459-2491
Fax: 281-458-5114
Web: http://www.tek-rap.com

Annual Sales: $28.9 Million
Number of Employees: 50-99
Sales Manager: Cindy Smith

The company produces industrial coatings and adhesives.

Tempil

D-Air Liquide America
2901 Hamilton Boulevard
South Plainfield NJ 07080
Phone: 908-757-8300
Toll Free: 800-757-8301
Web: http://www.tempil.com
Email: tempil@tempil.com

Number of Employees: 50
President: Michael E. Gerkin Sr.
CEO: Michael E. Gerkin Sr.

High-temperature coatings.

Tennant

701 North Lilac Drive
Minneapolis MN 55440
Phone: 763-540-1200
Toll Free: 800-553-8033
Fax: 763-513-2142
Web: http://www.tennantcompany.com
Email: Info@tennantco.com

Annual Sales: $507.8 Million
Number of Employees: 500-999
President: Janet M. Dolan
CEO: JanetM. Dolan

Tenant primarily manufactures floor and driveway equipment. The Protective Coatings Division manufactures property maintenance products and specialty coatings for industrial

Tennessee Technical Coatings

1421 Higgs Road
Lewisburg TN 37091
Phone: 931-359-6666
Fax: 931-359-6680
Web: http://www.tntechcoatings.com/
Email: custsvc@tntechcoatings.com

Annual Sales: $10.8 Million
Number of Employees: 10-49
President: D. Brooks Hodges, Jr.
Marketing Manager: Gerald M. Stoltz
Sales Manager: Gerald M. Stoltz
Manufacturing Operations Manager: Make Tatum

Industrial finishes.

Texas Refinery

840 North Main Street
PO Box 711
Fort Worth TX 76106
Phone: 817-332-1161
Toll Free: 800-827-0711
Fax: 817-336-8441
Web: http://www.texasrefinery.com
Email: trc711@texasrefinery.com

Annual Sales: $28 Million
Number of Employees: 240
President: Warren Gamaliel Harding

Sales Manager: Kirk Walker
Manufacturing Operations Manager: Gary Hosack

The company principally produces specialty lubricants, cleaners, fuel additives. It also manufactures coatings for the waterproofing of roofing systems, repair and sealing of asphalt parking lots and driveways, and concrete floor maintenance

Textured Coatings of America

2422 East 15th Street
Panama City FL 32405
Phone: 850-769-0347
Toll Free: 800-454-0340
Fax: 850-769-8339
Web: http://www.texcote.com
Email: info@texcote.com

Annual Sales: $13 Million
Number of Employees: 65
President: J Haines
CEO: J Haines
Marketing Manager: Chris Sherman

The company produces architectural protective coatings, sealers and primers for commercial, industrial, transportation and residential applications. It claims to be the largest producer of textured paints worldwide. The company has a branch plant in Los Angeles, CA and a sales office in Fort Lauderdale, FL

Thermoclad

361 West 11th Street
Erie PA 16501
Phone: 814-456-1243
Fax: 814-459-2853
Web: http://www.thermoclad.com
Email: info@thermoclad.com

Annual Sales: $30 Million
Number of Employees: 70
President: Mick Gashgarian
CEO: Alan I. Renkis
Research & Development: Das Gujrati
Marketing Manager: Robert Clark
Sales Manager: Robert Clark
Manufacturing Operations Manager: Tom Dietsch

Thermoclad produces plastic powder coatings for protective and decorative uses, principally thermoplastic vinyls. It operates two plants in Erie

Thermo-Shield

RR 2
Box 208A
Custer SD 57730-0208
Phone: 605-673-3201
Fax: 605-673-3200
Web: http://www.thermoshield.com
Email: spm@thermoshield.com

Number of Employees: 6
President: Joe Raver

Protective coatings for decks and homes

Thortex America

12 Iron Bridge Drive
Collegeville PA 19426
Phone: 610-831-0222
Toll Free: 800-578-2772
Fax: 610-831-1910
Web: http://www.thortex.com
Email: info@thortex.com

Annual Sales: $4 Million
Number of Employees: 10,000
President: James S. Marlen
CEO: James S. Marlen
Sales Manager: Jeff Wage

Metal and other industrial coatings.

Thybony Wall Coverings

3720 North Kedzie Avenue
Chicago IL 60618
Phone: 773-463-3005
Fax: 248-649-4281
Web: http://www.thybony.com
Email: info@thybony.com

Number of Employees: 70-99
President: Jim Thybony
CEO: Jim Thybony

Linseed oil primer, other specialty paints

Tiger Drylac USA

S- Tiger Drylac Japan KK
1251 East Belmont Street
Ontario CA 91761
Phone: 909-930-9100
Fax: 909-930-9111
Web: http://www.tigerdrylac.com
Email: tiger@tigerdrylac.com

Annual Sales: $19 Million
Number of Employees: 500-999
President: Karl Rijkse
CEO: Kurt Berghofer
Marketing Manager: Ute Wallner

The company produces powder coatings. Manufacturing facilities are in Ontario, St. Charles, IL, and Reading, PA, with sales offices in Arlington, TX and Kennesaw, GA

Titan Coatings

2025 Exchange Place
Bessemer AL 35022
Phone: 205-426-8149
Fax: 205-426-8152
Web: http://www.titancoatings.com

Annual Sales: $10.1 million
President: Robert P. Hanna
Sales Manager: Colby Hanna
Manufacturing Operations Manager: Bob Hanna

Coil, container, and industrial coatings.

Titan Paint

1425 Blondell Avenue
Bronx NY 10461
Phone: 718-892-1334

Paints.

TK Products

D-Sierra Corp.
11400 West 47th Street
Hopkins MN 55343
Phone: 952-938-7223
Toll Free: 800-441-2129
Fax: 952-938-8084
Web: http://www.tkproduct.com
Email: tkproduct@AOL.com

Number of Employees: 50-99
Sales Manager: Mike Boulka

Concrete and masonry coatings.

Tnemec

6800 Corporate Drive
Kansas City MO 64120-1372
Phone: 816-483-3400
Fax: 816-483-3969
Web: http://www.tnemec.com/
Email: marketing@tnemec.com

Annual Sales: $81 Million
Number of Employees: 300
President: Pete Cortelyou
CEO: Tom Osborne
Marketing Manager: Mark Thomas

Tnemec primary products are corrosion-resistant and protective products for maintenance of concrete

Toledo Floor Resurfacing

5221 Tractor Road
Toledo OH 43612
Phone: 419-476-6446
Toll Free: 800-839-6446
Fax: 419-476-8876
Web: http://www.toledofloor.com

Number of Employees: 50-99
President: Richard A. Coleman

Epoxy floor coatings.

Toledo Paint & Chemical

33 Blucher Street
PO Box 324
Toledo OH 43697
Phone: 419-244-3726
Fax: 419-244-4561

Annual Sales: $1 Million
Number of Employees: 5
President: David Peter
CEO: David Peter
Research & Development: Thomas Cadwallader
Sales Manager: Thomas Cadwallader

Specialty paints.

Torginol

710 Forest Avenue
PO Box 102
Sheboygan Falls WI 53085
Phone: 920-467-2471
Toll Free: 800-558-7596
Fax: 920-467-8674
Web: http://www.torginol.com
Email: sales@torginol.com

Annual Sales: $14.9 Million
Number of Employees: 10-49
President: Patricia Hilliard
Sales Manager: Gene Kiela
Manufacturing Operations Manager: Lisa D. Schefsky

Specialty epoxy and polyurethane coatings for wood and flooring.

Trail Chemical

9904 Gidley Street
El Monte CA 91731
Phone: 626-442-4140
Fax: 626-350-1364

Annual Sales: $7.9 Million
President: Andrew Goldfarb

Industrial finishes.

Transstar Autobody Technologies

2040 Heiserman Drive
Brighton MI 48114
Phone: 810-220-3000
Toll Free: 800-824-2843
Fax: 800-477-7923
Web: http://www.tat-co.com
Email: info@tat-co.com

Annual Sales: $37.4 million
President: Charles Fuqua Jr.
Sales Manager: Charles Fuqua Jr.

Automotive aftermarket coatings.

Triangle Coatings

1930 Fairway Drive
San Leandro CA 94577
Phone: 510-895-8000
Toll Free: 800-895-8000
Fax: 510-895-8800
Web: http://www.tricoat.com
Email: info@tricoat.com

Number of Employees: 10-49
President: Ned Kisner

Triangle manufactures architectural paints, industrial maintenance coatings, OEM product finishes, graphic arts coatings, and powder coatings, and also coatings under government specifications. It also performs custom formulation and toll manufacturing

Tri-Chem

681 Main Street
Builing No. 24
Belleville NJ 07109
Phone: 973-751-9200
Toll Free: 800-874-2273
Fax: 973-450-1260
Web: http://www.trichem.com
Email: TrichemSS@aol.com

Number of Employees: 200-499
CEO: David Chernow

Artists' paint.

TriCom Coatings

2639 N. 31st Avenue
Phoenix AZ 85009
Phone: 602-243-3293
Toll Free: 888-947-4447
Fax: 602-268-6801
Web: http://www.tricomcoatings.com
Email: info@tricomcoatings.com

Annual Sales: $2.5 Million
Number of Employees: 15
President: Robert D. Commissio
CEO: Lisa Commisso
Sales Manager: Ruben Segoviano
Manufacturing Operations Manager: Bob Commisso

Aviation coatings, industrial enamels, architectural coatings, floor coatings, industrial coatings, primers, and thinners. (Formerly Griggs Paint) Customers are Garrett Turbine Engine (military and commercial aircraft), local municipalities, the State of Arizona, Maricopa County, the General Services Administration, Honeywell and Arizona Dept. of Corrections.

Trimite Powders

S- Trimite plc (England)
PO Box 2785
Spartanburg SC 29304
Phone: 864-574-7000
Toll Free: 800-866-8666
Fax: 864-584-6152
Web: http://www.trimiteusa.com
Email: info@trimite.com

Annual Sales: $45 Million
Number of Employees: 50
President: Dean Edwards
CEO: Dean Edwards
Research & Development: Dean Edwards
Manufacturing Operations Manager: Pete Marston

Powder coatings.

Trinity Coatings

G&W Enterprises
1800 Park Place
Fort Worth TX 76110
Phone: 817-926-6811
Toll Free: 800-777-5683
Fax: 817-926-9346
Web: http://www.trinitycoatings.com

Annual Sales: $25.3 Million
Number of Employees: 50-100
President: Jim Gardner

Trinity produces coatings for wood and metal, including rail cars and trailers.

Truco

4301 Train Avenue
Cleveland OH 44113
Phone: 216-631-1000
Toll Free: 800-227-4569
Fax: 216-281-0034
Web: http://www.truco-inc.com
Email: mail@truco-inc.com

Annual Sales: $7 Million
President: Christopher Hoskins

Roofing coatings

Truserv

8600 West Bryn Mawr Avenue
Chicago IL 60631-3505
Phone: 773-695-5000
Fax: 773-695-6558
Web: http://www.truevalue.com

Annual Sales: $2,024 Million
Number of Employees: 600
President: Lyle Heidemann
CEO: Lyle Heidemann
Marketing Manager: Carol Wentworth
Sales Manager: Steve Mahurin

Truserv resulted from the merger of Cotter & Co. and ServiStar Coast to Coast Corp. in 1997.

Trylaner International

Coventry Coatings89 Taft Avenue
Newburgh NY 12550
Phone: 800-307-7951
Fax: 800-914-2981
Web: http://www.trylaner.com
Email: info@trylaner.com

Strippable protective coatings for various media and scientific applications.

Tucker Industrial Liquid Coatings

407 North Avenue
East Berlin PA 17316
Phone: 717-259-8339
Toll Free: 800-753-5171
Fax: 717-259-8733
Email: btucker854@aol.com

Annual Sales: $7 Million
Number of Employees: 20
President: Bernie Tucker
CEO: Bernie Tucker
Marketing Manager: Bernie Tucker
Sales Manager: Bernie Tucker
Manufacturing Operations Manager: Bernie Tucker

Paints.

Tuff-Kote

427 East Judd Street
Woodstock IL 60098
Phone: 815-338-2006
Toll Free: 800-827-2056
Fax: 815-338-9105
Web: http://www.tuffkoteco.com
Email: info@tkcoatings.com

Number of Employees: 10-49
Sales Manager: Susan M. Geye

Interior and exterior patching and coating products for waterproofing.

UCI Paints

1320-T Northwest 23rd Avenue
Fort Lauderdale FL 33311
Phone: 954-581-6060
Toll Free: 800-273-1683
Fax: 954-581-6085
Web: http://www.ucipaints.com

Number of Employees: 20-49
Manufacturing Operations Manager: David Cary

Union Chemical Industries

1320 Northwest 23rd Avenue
Ft. Lauderdale FL 33311
Phone: 954-581-6060
Toll Free: 800-273-1683
Fax: 954-581-6085
Web: http://www.ucipaints.com

Annual Sales: $6.5 Million
Number of Employees: 30
President: Richard Devick

Union Chemical produces architectural paints, including waterproofing coatings

Union Tank Car

175 West Jackson Boulevard
Chicago IL 60604
Phone: 312-431-3111
Fax: 312-431-5020
Web: http://www.utlx.com

Annual Sales: $5.37 Billion
Number of Employees: 6,140
President: Kenneth P. Fischl
CEO: Kenneth P. Fischl

Union Tank produces coatings for captive use in manufacturing of rail cars. It entered the paint business subsequent to the acquisition of the Plas-Chem line of protective coatings for interiors of rail tank cars and plastic hopper cars from East Texas Coatings Co., Nash, TX, in 2000. Products include epoxies, zincs, urethanes, vinyl esters, and alkyds

United Coatings

19011 East Cataldo
Greenacres WA 99016
Phone: 509-926-7143
Toll Free: 800-541-4383
Fax: 509-928-1116
Web: http://www.unitedcoatings.com

Annual Sales: $20 Million
Number of Employees: 125
Marketing Manager: Bill Mann
Sales Manager: Joy Warden

The company produces water-repellent coatings at a 90,000 sq ft plant. Products are targeted at DIY consumers and contractors for architectural, roofing and industrial uses. It operates branches at Tempe, AZ and Indianapolis, IN.

United Gilsonite Laboratories

Jefferson Avenue & New York Street
PO BOX 70
Scranton PA 18501
Phone: 570-344-1202
Toll Free: 800-272-3235
Fax: 570-969-7634
Web: http://www.ugl.com
Email: sales@ugl.com

Annual Sales: $40 Million
Number of Employees: 210
President: Thomas White
CEO: Thomas White
Manufacturing Operations Manager: A Anderson

United Gilsonite produces maintenance coatings, stains, water-proofing coatings, and clear wood finishes and also caulks and sealants. Products are sold through jobbers and dealers to retail outlets throughout the United States. Brand names include UGL, Cerfex, Mex, Gilsalume, Plaster Patch, Dylok and Zar.

United Paint & Chemical

24671 Telegraph Road
Southfield MI 48033
Phone: 248-353-3035
Toll Free:
Fax: 248-353-4865
Web: http://www.unitedpaintonline.com
Email: info@unitedpaint.com

Annual Sales: $15 Million
Number of Employees: 45
CEO: John Piceu
Marketing Manager: Robert Racz

The company produces automotive paints and coatings and industrial finishes. In February 2004 United Paint entered into partnership with C.F. Jameson Co., Bradford, MA, a producer of flexible material coatings to pursue coating opportunities in the flexible vinyl and urethane plastic market for vehicles in North America

Universal Chemicals & Coatings

1975 Fox Lane
Elgin IL 60123
Phone: 847-931-1700
Fax: 847-931-1799
Web: http://www.unicheminc.com
Email: solutions@unicheminc.com

Annual Sales: $12 Million
Number of Employees: 60
President: Leonard H. Berenfield
CEO: Leonard H. Berenfield
Marketing Manager: Paul B. Leinbach

Unichem produces industrial finishes, powder coatings, and coil coatings for steel containers, industrial and automotive uses. It has a branch plant in Elk Grove Village, IL.

US Chemical and Plastics

S-Alco Industries
600 Nova Drive Southeast
Massillon OH 44648
Phone: 330-830-6000
Toll Free: 800-615-5503
Fax: 330-830-6005
Web: http://www.uschem.com
Email: csr@uschem.com

Annual Sales: $20 Million
Sales Manager: Chevron Phillips

The company produces professional autobody, construction, industrial, aviation, and marine repair and appearance products, including polyester and epoxy fillers, epoxy adhesives, and other repair compounds.Morton Paint Co. manufactures specialty coatings for the automotive repair and refinishing market. Major products are coatings for truck bed liners, surface cleaners, and specialty refinish products for repairing and painting plastic parts

US Paint

831 South 21st Street
St. Louis MO 63103
Phone: 314-621-0525
Fax: 314-621-0722
Web: http://www.uspaint.com
Email: info@uspaint.com

Annual Sales: $16.9 Million
Number of Employees: 100
President: John Duchardt
CEO: John Duchardt
Marketing Manager: Nancy Duchardt
Sales Manager: Nancy Duchardt
Manufacturing Operations Manager: Mike Smock

The company produces urethane, epoxy, high-solids, and anti-fouling finishes, thinners, reducers, and additives primarily for the automotive industry. In 2002, the company sold the worldwide marine and aerospace coatings business (sales $30 million) to Akzo-Nobel AG. The acquisition excluded the St. Louis manufacturing facility. The company, once controlled by NOF Corp. (Japan), is now owned by managers

US Polychemical

584 Chestnut Ridge Road
10977
Chestnut Ridge NY 10977
Phone: 845-356-5530
Toll Free: 800-431-2072
Fax: 845-356-6656
Web: http://www.uspoly.com/
Email: richk@uspoly.com

Number of Employees: 10-49
President: Mr. Dave Naylor

Bowling lane coatings and related products

V. J. Dolan

1830 North Laramie Avenue
Chicago IL 60639
Phone: 773-237-0100
Fax: 773-237-2855

Annual Sales: $5 Million
Number of Employees: 25

Dolan produces lacquers, stains, sealers, and other industrial coatings.

Valley Paint Manufacturing

727 South 950 West
Woods Cross UT 84087
Phone: 801-298-4581
Fax: 801-298-7921

Industrial finishes.

Valspar

1101 Third Street South
PO Box 1461
Minneapolis MN 55415
Phone: 612-332-7371
Fax: 612-375-7723
Web: http://www.valspar.com
Email: webmaster@valspar.com

Annual Sales: $2.9 Billion
Number of Employees: 9,500
President: William L. Mansfield
CEO: Gary E. Hendrickson

Valspar Corporation is the fifth largest North American manufacturer of paints and coatings. It manufactures industrial coatings; architectural paints; basecoats and interior protective coatings; varnishes and stains; packaging coatings and inks for rigid containers; automotive refinish and other specialty coatings; and specialty polymers and dispersions, composites and colorants. In 2006, Valspar announced the acquisition of H.B. Fuller's powder coatings business, providing Valspar its first powder manufacturing capacity in Europe. In the same year, an agreement was made to enter into a joint venture with Tekno S.A. to supply coil coatings in Brazil. These two transactions extended Valspar's global reach of their industrial product line.

Vanex Color

PPG Industries
1700 South Shawnee Street
PO Box 987
Mt. Vernon IL 62864
Phone: 618-244-1414
Toll Free: 800-851-7390
Fax: 618-244-1461
Email: vanex@compuserve.com

Number of Employees: 25
President: Jim Montgomery

Latex and oil-based paints for architectural and industrial use.

Vanguard Paints & Finishes

1409 Greene Street
PO Box 654
Marietta OH 45750
Phone: 740-373-5261
Toll Free: 800-447-1939
Fax: 740-373-7165
Web: http://www.vanguardpaints.com
Email: email@vanguardpaints.com

Number of Employees: 50
President: Jeffrey L. Hollister

Vanguard produces architectural, institutional, and industrial paints, primers, wood finishes, and specialty paints for sale in 16 outlets in Ohio, West Virginia, and Pennsylvania, and OEM maintenance for such applications as hardwood handles, structural steel, truck wheel hubs, display shelving, electrical components, light fixtures, fine furniture, file cabinets, fork lifts, lawn and garden tools, steel drums, and kitchen cabinets.

Viking Paints

100 West 78th Street
Richfield MN 55423
Phone: 612-866-1212
Fax: 612-866-5821
Web: http://www.vikingpaints.com
Email: vikingpaints@earthlink.net

Annual Sales: $1.5 Million
Number of Employees: 8
President: John Eriksen
Manufacturing Operations Manager: Jason Cantwell

Architectural and industrial protective coatings.

Vimasco

PO Box 516
Nitro WV 25143
Phone: 304-755-3328
Toll Free: 800-624-8288
Fax: 304-755-7153
Web: http://www.vimasco.com
Email: vimasco@vimasco.com

Annual Sales: $3-5 Million
Number of Employees: 15
President: Reid Pugh
CEO: Reid Pugh
Research & Development: John Tidquist
Marketing Manager: Cathy Brown
Sales Manager: Cathy Brown
Manufacturing Operations Manager: John Tidquist

Protective coatings

Vinyl Industrial Paint

1401 Sycamore
Wyandotte MI 48192
Phone: 734-284-3536

Industrial paints

Vista Paint

2020 Orangethorpe Avenue
Suite 210
Fullerton CA 92631
Phone: 714-680-3800
Fax: 714-680-3809
Web: http://www.vistapaint.com
Email: rhartwig@vistapaint.com

Annual Sales: $108 Million
Number of Employees: 475
President: Eddie Fischer
CEO: Walt Jacobson

Vista manufactures architectural paints for sale through 48 retail stores in California and Nevada. Sales are primarily to contractors. It operates a 135,000 sq ft facility.

Vitricon

901 Motor Parkway
Hauppauge NY 11788
Phone: 631-231-1300
Toll Free: 800-777-6596
Fax: 631-231-1329
Web: http://www.vitriturf.com
Email: vturf@aol.com

Number of Employees: 2
President: Dr. Stuart Shapiro

Interior and exterior wall and flooring coatings for maintenance and construction

W. J. Ruscoe

PO Box 3858
Akron OH 44314
Phone: 330-253-8148
Fax: 330-253-2933
Web: http://www.ruscoe.com

Annual Sales: $15.4 Million
President: Paul Michalec

Plastic and rubber coatings for roofing applications. Adhesives and sealants are major product line. Total sales about $6 million

W.C. Richards

3555 West 123rd Street
Alsip IL 60803
Phone: 708-385-6633
Fax: 708-388-4491
Web: http://www.wcrichards.com
Email: info@wcrichards.com

Annual Sales: $9 Million
Number of Employees: 45
President: Sanders N. Stirman
Marketing Manager: K. Merrikh
Sales Manager: T. France
Manufacturing Operations Manager: Andy Hannan

Principal products are OEM liquid and powder coatings for heavy maintenance equipment, including coil coatings and other specialties. Plants are located here and in Aberdeen, NC.

Wall-Firma

733 East Main Street
Monongahela PA 15063
Phone: 724-258-6873
Toll Free: 800-333-4333
Fax: 724-258-3188
Web: http://www.wallfirma.com
Email: info@damtitewaterproofing.com

Number of Employees: 946
President: Robert J Revera

Coatings to waterproof, seal, protect and repair concrete, masonry, brick and stucco.

Warfield

Alocit Group
500 Abbott Dr # D
Broomall PA 19008
Phone: 610-328-9440
Fax: 610-328-6507
Web: http://www.alocit.us

Number of Employees: 30
Sales Manager: John Eoe

Protective coatings.

Warlick Paint

PO Box 1508
Statesville NC 28687
Phone: 704-873-2244
Fax: 704-873-4508

Number of Employees: 10-49
President: Bob Lodgek

Industrial maintenance coatings and OEM finishes

Warren Paint & Color

700 Wedgewood Avenue
Nashville TN 37203
Phone: 615-292-6655
Toll Free: 800-251-2625
Fax: 615-292-6654
Web: http://www.warrenpaint.com
Email: askus@warrenpaint.com

Annual Sales: $1 - 4.9 Million
Number of Employees: 10-49
President: Jeff Smythe

Industrial finishes and architectural paints.

Wasser High-Tech Coatings

4118 B Place NW
Suite BAuburn WA 98001
Phone: 253-850-2967
Toll Free: 800.627.2968
Fax: 253-850-3098
Web: http://www.wassercoatings.com

Annual Sales: $8 Million
Number of Employees: 50
Sales Manager: Joe Werner
Manufacturing Operations Manager: Bobby Carney

Wasser manufactures alkyds and epoxies, enamels and urethanes industrial coatings for such uses as oil and gas production, marine and offshore, pulp and paper, rail cars, bridges, hydropower, municipal water and wastewater treatment, infrastructure maintenance, and general manufacturing.

Waterlox Chemical and Coatings

9808 Meech Avenue
Cleveland OH 44105
Phone: 216-641-4877
Fax: 216-641-7213
Web: http://www.waterlox.com
Email: info@waterlox.com

Annual Sales: $2 Million
President: Jay Hawkins

Wood coatings, marine paints, other.

Watson Coatings Group

325 Paul Avenue
St. Louis MO 63135
Phone: 314-521-2000
Toll Free: 800-844-4212
Web: http://www.watsoncoatings.com
Email: watson@watsoncoatings.com

Number of Employees: 150
President: Gary Watson
CEO: Gary Watson

Industrial coatings.

Watson-Rhenania Coatings

S- Altana Chemie-P (50.1%)
PO Box 111411
Pittsburgh PA 15238
Phone: 724-275-1000
Fax: 724- 275-2000
Web: http://www.altana.com
Email: PR@altana.de.

Annual Sales: $10 Million
Number of Employees: 65
President: Tom George

The company produces end sealants coatings for cans and sealants for crowns and closures. Total sales of the Coating and Sealants business of Watson-Rhenania were 222 million euros in 2003, primarily in Europe. Most of its products are closure compounds and can sealants.

Whitford

33 Sproul Road
Frazer PA 19355
Phone: 610-296-3200
Toll Free: 888-240-3673
Fax: 610-647-4849
Web: http://www.superglide.com
Email: sales@whitfordww.com

Annual Sales: $10 - 24.9 Million
Number of Employees: 50-99
Sales Manager: Andrew Melville

Whitford produces fluoropolymer coatings, including stick-free coatings for consumer products, flexible finishes for the automotive industry, industrial finishes, and textile coatings.

Whitman Polymers

D- Alvin Products.
350 Merrimack Street
Lawrence MA 01843-1748
Phone: 978-975-9924
Fax: 978-975-2621
Web: http://www.whitmanpolymers.com
Email: sales@WhitmanPolymers.com

Annual Sales: $1.5 Million
President: Philip Dubois

100% solvent free protective coatings.

Wilko Paint

2727-T Ohio
Wichita KS 67204
Phone: 316-838-4288
Fax: 316-838-6328
Web: http://www.wilkopaintinc.com

Number of Employees: 20
President: Robert Martinez

Industrial finishes, powder coatings.

Willamette Valley

1075 Arrowsmith Street
PO Box 2280
Eugene OR 97402
Phone: 541-484-9621
Fax: 541-484-1987
Web: http://www.wilvaco.com
Email: info@wilvaco.com

Annual Sales: $79.2 Million
Number of Employees: 300
President: John R. Harrison
CEO: John R. Harrison

The company produces coatings, fillers, adhesive products, and customized robotic equipment. Coatings include stencil paint, a water based product that is used for painting company logos and identifying marks on beams, decks of plywood, and lumber and primers for use on siding, molding, and architectural woods. It also produces polyurea, a product used in such applications as coating for concrete, geotextiles, wood and metal for secondary containment, truck bed liners, parking garages, industrial floors and walls, and a roofing material. Polyurea is also used as a roll-on floor coating and a caulking material for concrete joints. Eclectic Products, Inc. Eugene, OR, a subsidiary produces water-based wood finishes and adhesives for a variety of industries at a plant in Pineville, LA.

Williams Hayward Protective Coatings

7425 West 59th Street
Summit IL 60501
Phone: 708-458-0015
Fax: 708-563-6266
Web: http://www.williams-hayward.com
Email: eddiekurcz@whpc.net

Annual Sales: $6 Million
Number of Employees: 50
President: John Irwin
CEO: Paul Murphy
Marketing Manager: Barry Keating
Sales Manager: Eduardo Faz

Proective coatings and industrial finishes for all sectors, such as appliance, automotive, lawn, garden, display, furniture, sports and recreation, medical, architectural, lighting and other general metal finishing industries.

Winfield Brooks

70 Conn Street
Woburn MA 01801
Phone: 781-933-5300
Toll Free: 800-343-4341
Web: http://www.winbro.com
Email: info@winbro.com

Annual Sales: $1 - 4.9 Million
Number of Employees: 10-49
Sales Manager: Jeff Huffman

Topcoats, barrier coats, slip coats, scratch-resistant coatings, impact-resistant coatings, and epoxy coatings.

Wohl Coatings

6161 Maple Avenue
St. Louis MO 63130
Phone: 314-725-3400
Fax: 314-725-6569
Web: http://www.wohlcoatings.com/
Email: david@@sbcglobal.net

Number of Employees: 1-9

Pipe coatings, epoxies, finishes, primers, and metal building coatings.

Wolke Paint

723 Quarry Road Northwest
Corydon IN 47112
Phone: 812-738-4141
Toll Free: 800-634-9390
Fax: 812-738-0775
Email: chris@wolkepaint.com

Annual Sales: $4 Million
Number of Employees: 10
President: Paul Burns
CEO: Paul Burns
Research & Development: Chris Williams
Marketing Manager: Paul Burns
Sales Manager: Paul Burns
Manufacturing Operations Manager: Paul Burns

Industrial paints.

Wood Kote Products

8000 Northeast 14th Place
Portland OR 97211
Phone: 503-285-8371
Toll Free: 800-843-7666
Fax: 503-285-8374
Web: http://www.woodkote.com
Email: info@woodkote.com

Annual Sales: $1.5 Million
Number of Employees: 10-49
Sales Manager: Harry Dangler

Wood and floor coatings--sealers, stains, lacquers, and polyurethanes.

Wurdack

4977 Fyler Avenue
St. Louis MO 63139
Phone: 314-351-6600
Fax: 314-351-5617
Web: http://www.wurdack.com
Email: info@wurdack.com

Number of Employees: 30
President: William Wurdack Jr

Industrial paints for the music, sport, aircraft, cosmetic, and leisure industries.

XIM Products

1169 Bassett Road
Westlake OH 44145
Phone: 440-871-4737
Toll Free: 800-262-8469
Fax: 440-871-3027
Web: http://www.ximbonder.com

Annual Sales: $1 Million
Number of Employees: 149
President: Richard D. Hardy
CEO: Oleg Mazu
Marketing Manager: Monte Goble
Sales Manager: Sophie LeMieux
Manufacturing Operations Manager: James Kirkland

Specialty coatings, primers, sealers and additives.

Xymax Coatings

Polyval (Canada)
1130 Republic Drive, Suite C
Addison IL 60101
Phone: 800-276-8582
Toll Free: 800-332-3136
Fax: 630-628-9365
Web: http://www.polyvalcoatings.com
Email: info@polyvalcoatings.com

Number of Employees: 225
CEO: Hans Wijers

Industrial protective coatings.

Z Technologies

26500 Capitol Avenue
Redford MI 48239
Phone: 313-937-0710
Toll Free: 800-653-6116
Fax: 313-937-1470
Web: http://www.ztechprotection.com
Email: louis@ztechprotection.com

Annual Sales: $18 Million
Number of Employees: 10-49
President: Ellis Breskman
CEO: Ellis Breskman
Research & Development: Roosevelt White
Sales Manager: Louis Breskman

Produces corrosion-preventative coatings used on trucks, trailers, heavy-duty machinery and rail cars. (Formerly a division of Ziebart International Corp.)

ZRC Worldwide

145 Enterprise Drive
Marshfield MA 02050
Phone: 781-319-0400
Toll Free: 800-831-3275
Fax: 781-319-0404
Web: http://www.zrcworldwide.com
Email: info@zrcworldwide.com

Annual Sales: $10 - 24.9 Million
Number of Employees: 50
President: Matthew Steele
CEO: Matthew Steele
Research & Development: Steven Collins
Marketing Manager: Steven Collins
Sales Manager: Lorraine Dewald
Manufacturing Operations Manager: Matthew Steele

Zinc coatings for iron and steel.

ZYP Coatings

120 Valley Court
Oak Ridge TN 37830
Phone: 865-482-5717
Fax: 865-482-1281
Web: http://www.zypcoatings.com
Email: info@zypcoatings.com

Annual Sales: $14.9 Million
Number of Employees: 10-49
President: Kathy Porter
CEO: Frank Sanders Barnes
Marketing Manager: Holcombe

High-temperature boron nitride coatings for ceramics, metals, or graphite substrates.

A

B

C

G

H

M

R

S

T

General Reference

American Environmental Leaders: From Colonial Times to the Present
An African Biographical Dictionary
Encyclopedia of African-American Writing
Encyclopedia of American Industries
Encyclopedia of Emerging Industries
Encyclopedia of Global Industries
Encyclopedia of Gun Control & Gun Rights
Encyclopedia of Invasions & Conquests
Encyclopedia of Prisoners of War & Internment
Encyclopedia of Religion & Law in America
Encyclopedia of Rural America
Encyclopedia of the United States Cabinet, 1789-2010
Encyclopedia of Warrior Peoples & Fighting Groups
Environmental Resource Handbook
From Suffrage to the Senate: America's Political Women
Global Terror & Political Risk Assessment
Historical Dictionary of War Journalism
Human Rights in the United States
Nations of the World
Political Corruption in America
Speakers of the House of Representatives, 1789-2009
The Environmental Debate: A Documentary History
The Evolution Wars: A Guide to the Debates
The Religious Right: A Reference Handbook
The Value of a Dollar: 1860-2009
The Value of a Dollar: Colonial Era
University & College Museums, Galleries & Related Facilities
Weather America
World Cultural Leaders of the 20th & 21st Centuries
Working Americans 1880-1999 Vol. I: The Working Class
Working Americans 1880-1999 Vol. II: The Middle Class
Working Americans 1880-1999 Vol. III: The Upper Class
Working Americans 1880-1999 Vol. IV: Their Children
Working Americans 1880-2003 Vol. V: At War
Working Americans 1880-2005 Vol. VI: Women at Work
Working Americans 1880-2006 Vol. VII: Social Movements
Working Americans 1880-2007 Vol. VIII: Immigrants
Working Americans 1770-1869 Vol. IX: Revol. War to the Civil War
Working Americans 1880-2009 Vol. X: Sports & Recreation
Working Americans 1880-2010 Vol. XI: Entrepreneurs & Inventors

Bowker's Books In Print®Titles

Books In Print®
Books In Print® Supplement
American Book Publishing Record® Annual
American Book Publishing Record® Monthly
Books Out Loud™
Bowker's Complete Video Directory™
Children's Books In Print®
El-Hi Textbooks & Serials In Print®
Forthcoming Books®
Large Print Books & Serials™
Law Books & Serials In Print™
Medical & Health Care Books In Print™
Publishers, Distributors & Wholesalers of the US™
Subject Guide to Books In Print®
Subject Guide to Children's Books In Print®

Business Information

Directory of Business Information Resources
Directory of Mail Order Catalogs
Directory of Venture Capital & Private Equity Firms
Food & Beverage Market Place
Grey House Homeland Security Directory
Grey House Performing Arts Directory
Hudson's Washington News Media Contacts Directory
New York State Directory
Sports Market Place Directory
The Rauch Guides – Industry Market Research Reports

Statistics & Demographics

America's Top-Rated Cities
America's Top-Rated Small Towns & Cities
America's Top-Rated Smaller Cities
Comparative Guide to American Suburbs
Comparative Guide to Health in America
Profiles of... Series – State Handbooks

Health Information

Comparative Guide to American Hospitals
Comparative Guide to Health in America
Complete Directory for Pediatric Disorders
Complete Directory for People with Chronic Illness
Complete Directory for People with Disabilities
Complete Mental Health Directory
Directory of Health Care Group Purchasing Organizations
Directory of Hospital Personnel
HMO/PPO Directory
Medical Device Register
Older Americans Information Directory

Education Information

Charter School Movement
Comparative Guide to American Elementary & Secondary Schools
Complete Learning Disabilities Directory
Educators Resource Directory
Special Education

TheStreet.com Ratings Guides

TheStreet.com Ratings Consumer Box Set
TheStreet.com Ratings Guide to Bank Fees & Service Charges
TheStreet.com Ratings Guide to Banks & Thrifts
TheStreet.com Ratings Guide to Bond & Money Market Mutual Funds
TheStreet.com Ratings Guide to Common Stocks
TheStreet.com Ratings Guide to Credit Unions
TheStreet.com Ratings Guide to Exchange-Traded Funds
TheStreet.com Ratings Guide to Health Insurers
TheStreet.com Ratings Guide to Life & Annuity Insurers
TheStreet.com Ratings Guide to Property & Casualty Insurers
TheStreet.com Ratings Guide to Stock Mutual Funds
TheStreet.com Ratings Ultimate Guided Tour of Stock Investing

Canadian General Reference

Associations Canada
Canadian Almanac & Directory
Canadian Environmental Resource Guide
Canadian Parliamentary Guide
Financial Services Canada
History of Canada
Libraries Canada

Grey House Publishing
4919 Route 22, PO Box 56, Amenia NY 12501-0056 | (800) 562-2139 | www.greyhouse.com | books@greyhouse.com